THE
CONFIDENCE MAN
IN AMERICAN
LITERATURE

THE
CONFIDENCE MAN
IN AMERICAN
LITERATURE

Gary Lindberg

New York   Oxford
OXFORD UNIVERSITY PRESS
1982

1/1982
am. lit.

For Judy
who makes skepticism
intimate and convivial

ACKNOWLEDGMENTS

It would suit the manner of my title character if I were to claim all the credit myself, but nothing actually gets done that way, and I am grateful to the many students and colleagues who have, with an appropriate blending of irony and enthusiasm, kept me confident that I had a subject worth pursuing. Once again David Levin has served as my trusted reader, both in his actual suggestions after a careful reading of the manuscript and in his presence in my imagination as a bearer of standards I cannot ignore. This book still preserves some of the spirit of the many conversations about American literature I had ten years ago with Alan Howard. At Oxford University Press Elaine Koss has been both tactful and vigilant in helping me polish the manuscript. Parts of the book were written on a Sesquicentennial Research Associateship from the University of Virginia and on a Faculty Summer Research Fellowship from the University of New Hampshire. I gratefully acknowledge permission to quote as follows:

To Random House, Inc. Alfred A. Knopf, Inc. for:

William Faulkner, *The Hamlet*, copyright 1940 by Random House, Inc.

William Faulkner, *The Town*, copyright 1957 by William Faulkner and Curtis Publishing Company.

Ralph Ellison, *Invisible Man*, copyright 1952 by Ralph Ellison, published by Random House, Inc.

Joseph Heller, *Something Happened*, copyright 1974 by Scapegoat Productions, Inc., published by Alfred A. Knopf, Inc.

Eric Berne, M.D., *Games People Play*, copyright 1964, published by Grove Press, Inc.

Eric Berne, M.D., *Beyond Games and Scripts*, edited by Claude M. Steiner and Carmen Kerr, copyright 1976, published by Grove Press, Inc.

To Simon and Schuster, Inc. for:

Joan Samson, *The Auctioneer*, copyright 1975.

Joseph Heller, *Catch-22*, copyright 1961 by Joseph Heller, published by Simon and Schuster, Inc.

To Viking Penguin Inc. for:

Saul Bellow, *The Adventures of Augie March*, copyright 1953 by Saul Bellow, published by The Viking Press, Inc.

Jack Kerouac, *On the Road*, copyright 1957 by Jack Kerouac, published by The Viking Press, Inc.

Ken Kesey, *One Flew Over the Cuckoo's Nest*, copyright 1962 by Ken Kesey, published by The Viking Press, Inc.

To Farrar, Straus & Giroux, Inc. for:

Tom Wolfe, *The Electric Kool-Aid Acid Test*, copyright 1968 by Tom Wolfe.

To Doubleday Publishing Company for:

John Barth, *The Sot-Weed Factor*, Revised Edition, copyright 1967 by John Barth.

Erving Goffman, *The Presentation of Self in Everyday Life*, copyright 1959, published by Anchor Books.

CONTENTS

We'll survive . . . despite all the polls and all the rest, I think there's still a hell of a lot of people out there, and from what I've seen they're—you know, they, they want to believe, that's the point, isn't it?

Nixon to Haldeman, April 1973

The abdication of Belief
Makes the Behavior small—
Better an ignis fatuus
Than no illume at all—

Emily Dickinson

THE
CONFIDENCE MAN
IN AMERICAN
LITERATURE

INTRODUCTION

When one says that the confidence man is a representative American, perhaps even our covert hero, one draws two characteristic responses. First there is the thoughtful, cautious, skeptical questioning: Haven't all cultures had their share of frauds, mountebanks, rogues, and tricksters? Haven't we had enough generalizing about the distinctly "American" character? Doesn't this hypothesis single out a few flashy examples, like Clifford Irving, and then distort the complex character of other figures, like Benjamin Franklin? The other response, which often occurs to the same mind that reacted skeptically, involves a curious act of faith; as Emerson puts it, "the ear instantly hears and the spirit leaps to the trope." Yes, we say, that must be it—there has to be some reason we produced P. T. Barnum and Madison Avenue, making it and credibility gap, Hollywood and the balloon house, Christian Science and Pragmatism. The puzzling thing about this response is that it is not primarily sardonic. We are, like Faulkner's Anse Bundren, kind of hangdog and kind of proud too. This mixed response itself shows that the confidence man, his game, and our attitudes toward him deserve scrutiny.

My hypothesis is in fact that the confidence man is a covert cultural hero for Americans. He occupies a central place in our popular mythology; yet not many of us would want to acknowledge this fact when stated so bluntly, and that is why we don't notice his centrality. What the con man represents about us can only be seen obliquely, in the discrepancies between our ideals and our conduct. When we denounce someone publicly and then privately laugh up our sleeves at his exploits, we celebrate the cult of the con man. It is not our official pieties that he represents but our unofficial reward systems, the strategies that we have for over two centuries

3

allowed to succeed. He clarifies the uneasy relations between our stated ethics and our tolerated practices. When I propose that the confidence man is an American culture hero, what I mean, then, is that he provides a model by means of which we can understand some important things about our history and our values.

We must begin with his name, for our attitudes are suggested by our labels. To look up "confidence man" in a dictionary is to enter the murky doubleness of his world. The definition will be some variant of "a swindler who practises on the confidence or trust of a credulous person," the emphasis being on criminality and on the exchange of valuables. But when examples of usage accompany the definition, as in the *Oxford English Dictionary*, especially when the verb "con" is taken into account, the definition ceases to define: "Intellectual theoreticians of pop culture have pulled a con," "Mansfield conned the critics," "Some crackpot had conned the newsroom." The relationship of definition to usage is like that of ethics to practice, and both are reflected in the differences between our official and our unofficial judgments of the con man himself. For "con" in everyday American usage applies to far more than a certain kind of swindle. Furthermore, it has a different value attached to it, a compound of admiration, amusement, and connivance.[1] Confidence men of the narrow sort officially defined (and disowned) by the dictionaries have themselves appeared with unusual frequency in the backgrounds of works of American literature, from Bradford's and Mather's histories to Mark Twain's and Bellow's fictions, and one could begin by speculating why they turn up so often.[2] But to ignore the ambivalence between definition and usage is to miss the complex appeal of the confidence man and thus to overlook his infiltration of the very centers of American values and of works of literature.[3] It is one thing to speculate on the social significance of the King and the Duke; it is another to see how the model of the confidence man accounts for Huck Finn as well.

If we want to understand the geniality with which Americans refer to "conning," we must recognize how the confidence man carries out some of our central aspirations. He is radically entangled with the myth of the "New World." But our traditional understanding of that phrase prevents our perception of the confidence man's role. What does "New World" most readily call to mind? Wilderness, frontier, the natural environment. And by implication the move to the New World has familiarly been taken as a metaphor for discarding the past, regaining youth and innocence, encountering a fresh countryside. When we associate a representative character with this notion of the New World, it is thus likely to be a pioneer, a frontiersman, or more imaginatively, an American Adam in the wilderness.[4] But what about the social situation implied by the concept of the New World? European settlers did not literally begin again when they arrived in the Western Hemisphere. Only rarely could they cast aside their habitual ways of seeing in order to encounter a truly fresh world. They brought with them artifacts, books, designs, tools, manners—all the models of the social world they had left behind. And their descendants continued to import such models. Instead of reinventing "civilization," they imitated, burlesqued, adapted, and jury-rigged it. And instead of renegotiating the entire social contract, they simply introduced more fluidity into social relations, so that even though people were still born into unequal positions, there were surprising possibilities for the individual to move about. Thus, when we examine "New World" as social concept rather than natural image, one of the major propositions characterizing it is that class background is not fate. What this means for the stereotypical pioneer is that one can leave society and start a new life in an unspoiled landscape. What the same proposition means to the confidence man is that one looks at society itself with a freshened sense of opportunity, recognizing that while the majority of people are still predictably shaped by inherited institutions and manners, some people are not.

How well the confidence man fit into the New World will be apparent if we turn from the emotionally charged phrase "New World" to the more objective concept of migration. What has demographically characterized the United States throughout its history has been an unusually extensive pattern of migration. Not only have immigrants continued to arrive from other countries but later generations born in this country have themselves tended to move about within the larger society. This repeated movement has had some obvious consequences. It has made many Americans restless, unstable, thirsty for novelty. It has loosened family and community bonds and has encouraged people to dwell imaginatively in the future. Institutions that depend on stable residence, like primogeniture and apprenticeship, have lost their power, and personal facility has been given a correspondingly wider field. In social relations this ceaseless movement has weakened the familiar patterns of identification. Instead of relying on family background, class habits, inherited manners, many Americans have had to confront each other as mere claimants, who can at best try to persuade each other who they in fact are. It is easy to see how a con man can slip into such a situation and exploit it. Simon Suggs's famous motto sums up the issue—"It is good to be shifty in a new country."

But this formula applies to more than swindlers. If the confidence man is representative, it is not simply because American demographic patterns created the perfect milieu for him. We must now return to the honorific phrase "New World." In the popular mythology all the restless activities of continuing migration were interpreted as gestures of creation: making a new nation, making new villages and towns, making new selves. If the immediate premium was placed on technical skill and contrivance, the larger enterprise was sanctified by a dazzling sense of promise. What counted was not who one was but who one could become. Why notice the uncleared stumps in the roadway or the half-finished portico and empty rooms when one could already almost see the promised boulevard lined with mansions? Self, town, and nation were matters of faith, and the act of faith—the acceptance of promise—came to be the definitive New World transaction. It is also, of course, the central transaction in a confidence game. Thus the confidence man not only revealed and acted upon the opportunities created by migration in the emergent American society; he also played to its prevailing promissory tone.

Consider the case of William Thompson, an enterprising man who was arrested in New York City on July 7, 1849. He had for two months been practicing a game of stopping a stranger on the street, engaging him in conversation, and then asking if the stranger had enough confidence in him to leave a watch with him until the next day. The game shows that Thompson understood the sacramental value attached by his countrymen to the act of faith, but it has a larger importance. It earned him the nickname "Confidence Man," which was then publicized in the *New York Herald*. What is interesting about this coinage is not only how quickly it took hold but how quickly it assumed a broader and more ambivalent significance. A week after Thompson's arrest the *New York Herald* ran an editorial generalizing his exploits and referring to the stock market as "The Confidence Man on a Large Scale."

A month later Evert Duyckinck in *The Literary World* rose to the defense of American suckers by arguing, "It is not the worst thing that can be said of a country that it gives birth to a confidence man. . . . It is a good thing, and speaks well for human nature, that . . . men *can be swindled*." [5] Clearly, in the period F. O. Matthiessen dubbed the "American Renaissance," confidence was in full tide. But the coinage of the term "confidence man" can also be dated by referring back six years to Poe's brilliant sketch "Diddling Considered as One of the Exact Sciences" and ahead six years to the first publication of Barnum's autobiography, events that remind us how confidence and humbug were entwined from the beginning. With such origins and such implications, the con man should not surprise us by slipping about from scoundrel to prophet. He is at once the celebrant of shared faith and the agent most capable of exploiting it.

We can best understand the confidence man, then, through the characteristic situation in which he appears, a highly fluid situation with two special qualities. First, the continued movement of people has severed the connections between their appearances and their social positions. Their everyday practices no longer indicate their larger identities or their underlying values. All one can be sure of in such a situation is the immediate gesture, the technique itself. Thus the confidence man is surrounded by people who look hard and carefully at how one does something, who come to admire technical facility for its own sake. They have a how-to-do-it mentality. But there is another essential quality in the confidence man's situation: everyone around him believes in some larger promise. This collective attitude assures the manipulator that if he manages his immediate operations skillfully, the larger ends will take care of themselves. And of course this same promissory atmosphere makes people susceptible to transactions of faith. With this twofold situation in mind, we can begin to understand the confidence game as the practical making and manipulating of belief without substance for it. The confidence man is a manipulator or contriver who creates an inner effect, an impression, an experience of confidence, that surpasses the grounds for it. In short, a confidence man *makes belief.*

The advantage of this looser definition is that it more clearly reflects the range and ambivalence of popular American usage and it relates a character-type to a particular kind of situation. It allows us to see "a swindler who practises on the confidence or trust of a credulous person" as a special instance of the more general model of the confidence man, who is thus an amalgam of possibilities. If his motive for making belief is illicit gain, we recognize the professional criminal, the official version of the con man. If the motive is to spread the air of belief itself, we are dealing with the booster. If the motive is to experience the pleasures of control and self-conscious dexterity, we are up against the gamesman. When the motive is self-creation, the agent is the familiar self-made man. There are even some who make belief deliberately because belief will enhance other people's lives—prophets, healers, political idealists, Thomas Jefferson and William James.

There are two more variants that deserve mention here although they are so little concerned with the impressions they make on others that they seem marginally related to belief-makers. The shape-shifter or jack-of-all-trades is the manipulator so caught up in personal facility with roles that self-transformation becomes an end in itself. And the gadgeteer is the manipulator whose technical dexterity is such a joy that the means *are* the ends. When we recognize, however, that both these figures are simply alternative ways of emphasizing the possibilities in the twofold situation I described, we see their fundamental connection to the others. The point is that it is the larger configuration, not the individual variants, that allows us to understand the centrality of the confidence man in America. The general model of the confidence man helps us perceive the essential connections between such apparently diverse American icons as booster, gadgeteer, and self-made man. And it begins to explain the fact that, at least in literary embodiments, we rarely meet one of these figures without some of the qualities of the others—booster *and* gadgeteer, jack-of-all-trades *and* gamesman, or more extremely, prophet *and* scoundrel.

For all the apparent open-endedness of the model I am proposing, there are many things it is not. The essential analogue of the confidence man is the primitive and universal trickster of folklore and mythology, and I will refer later, especially with Poe and with contemporary con men, to the specific ways in which the trickster figure can illuminate the confidence man. But they are far from equivalent. The trickster appears in virtually all literatures. His universality suggests that he has something to do with the human condition itself. Paul Radin and Carl Jung theorize that he represents an undifferentiated consciousness, an archetypal psychic structure of extreme antiquity, and that his progress takes him from a primordial, amorphous, instinctual past into the lineaments and psychic traits of human beings.[6] Clearly, the confidence man, who inhabits a modern, highly differentiated, literate society is a much more particularized being than the trickster. He tells us less about the universal human condition than he does about the peculiar qualities of American society that gave rise to him, like the theme of confidence itself. There is another, more telling difference. The trickster breaks boundaries and disrupts taboos. He is what Victor Turner calls a marginal figure who allows his celebrants a surrogate release from the rigidities of social structure[7] (a comparable function is served by fools and clowns in more developed social orders). The confidence man, on the other hand, does not provide an outlet for unruliness, nor does he disrupt the social bounds. He is a culturally representative figure, not a marginal one, and his message is that the boundaries are already fluid, that there is ample space between his society's official rules and its actual tolerances.

In the context of particularized, modern social conditions, the con man bears a much closer resemblance to the picaro of European fiction. Indeed certain versions of the American confidence man—Huck Finn, Augie March, the rogues of Southwestern Humor—are very close to the picaro: socially marginal, pragmatic, unprincipled, protean, resilient, peripatetic. But those American figures who are closest to the picaro are in fact trying to survive in a world dominated by confidence men, and they take on certain hues of their background. The more central confidence men differ from the picaro in several ways. The picaro lives for the present; the con man, trading on promise, lives for the future and tends to sustain more illusions. The picaro remains a partial outsider in his social order; often the confidence man gradually aligns himself with social powers and takes them over. Finally, the picaro usually has a good heart; the confidence man at his purest seems to have nothing inside.[8]

So much for the nature of my hypothesis. Now what is it good for? I do not wish to argue that the con man is a unique American institution. Aside from the universal trickster figure, there are many more modern analogues of the con man in other literatures, the picaro, the vice, the mountebank, the rogue. Odysseus, Volpone, and Felix Krull are enough to remind us that Americans have not patented tricksters. And some of the giants of professional criminal con artistry are truly international—Ivar Kreuger, Serge Alexandre Stavisky, Victor "The Count" Lustig. What I am suggesting is that the confidence man appears with surprising frequency and emphasis in American literature and popular culture, that this American trickster is peculiarly identified with the themes of promise and confidence, and that he reveals certain popular ambivalences of judgment, most immediately apparent in our everyday usage of "con."

I do not intend to prove that the confidence man is a representative figure by enumerating his appearances in American history and literature. Instead I use the image of the confidence man and the paradigm of the confidence game as models to help us think about American culture. Their potential value is in making things visible that would otherwise remain inconspicuous, or in showing the relations between situations, characters, and values that would otherwise seem isolated from each other. The strongest case I wish to make is that they are *good* models. In William James's pragmatic sense, they are good *for* a great deal in our understanding of American literature. They help us find broad hallways and well-lit corridors so that we can wander with a new facility among familiar books, asking new questions and tracing new implications. My strategy is to look at a range of American writings—literary, political, philosophical, sociological—*as if* they were the expression of a culture drawn to acts of faith and gestures of self-creation, a culture whose presiding genius is the confidence man.

One other warning is needed to prepare the Gentle Reader for what follows. When I was initially exploring the idea of the con man in America, the hypothesis seemed a cynical one—probably true but certainly dispiriting. And I read with a suspicious eye, trying not to be taken in by the frequent tricks of the writers I was reading. But there in the midst of the darkest Nixon years, something of the spirit of P. T. Barnum came over me, and I realized that celebration has as much to do with my subject as condemnation. The subject is manipulation of belief, and one can't comprehend belief from a posture of distrust. What the confidence man celebrates in American life is the delight of entering a series of roles and making them work. When I realized that by studying his successive incarnations in various books I was re-enacting his roles, I entered into the spirit of his plasticity and mimickry. Analysis kept turning into play, and I found the writing of the book more fun than I had dreamed. For this I make no apology. Thus my tone is alternately brassy, delighted, indignant, skeptical, extravagant, perverse. Yet this utter inconsistency of attitude is central to my subject, for the con man's infectious power depends precisely on his capacity to evoke such a multiplicity of responses. To see him as a cynic or a nihilist is almost inevitable philosophically, but it is wrong experientially.[9] Insofar as transactions of confidence are a game, as American usage suggests, the attitude of nihilism can hardly suit the spirit of the master at the game. As Roger Caillois argues, "the cheat's dishonesty does not destroy the game. The game is ruined by the nihilist who denounces the rules as absurd and conventional, who refuses to play because the game is meaningless. His arguments are irrefutable."[10]

For the role player and the believer, on the other hand, things open up in surprising ways. Near the end of *The Confidence-Man* Melville describes an "original character": "everything is lit by it, everything starts up to it . . . so that, in certain minds, there follows upon the adequate conception of such a character, an effect, in its way, akin to that which in Genesis attends upon the beginning of things." That was precisely the effect of Melville's Confidence-Man on me. It was not easy to become Melville's reader, but once

I did, his conception insinuated itself into my whole sense of American culture. By beginning here with my reading of his novel, I try to re-create this experience so as to define a reader for the rest of my own book, which can in turn be imagined as a reading of American literature through the eyes of Melville's Confidence-Man. Nearly as central to my understanding of what I was about were my gropings over several years with the oddities of Edgar Allan Poe. It was the hypothesis of the culturally central con man that allowed me to see the separated peculiarities in his work as connected to each other and as predicated on his self-conscious effort to be an artist in a society given over to con games. Poe gives me the occasion to discuss the situation of the artist and of the artisan in a "new country" characterized by the separation of technique and purpose, the loss of traditional authority, the imitation and burlesque of foreign models, the impersonation of identity.[11]

The commentaries on Melville and Poe in Part I disclose the meaning of the confidence man as a representative figure. Poe and Melville were assessing America at a special time. On the one hand, American confidence was at its peak and the possibilities of self-creation seemed especially promising. Their work just brackets the date of the coinage of "Confidence Man." On the other hand, the earlier feeling of opportunity was gradually slipping into something else, and the conventions of puffery, humbug, and promise were becoming so blatant that shrewd critics could both lampoon them and suggest their serious consequences.

Conceptually, the point at which Melville and Poe are poised marks the division between Parts II and III of this book. Part II, "How To Do It," traces the development of the central aspirations, beliefs, and habits that got muddled together in the confidence man. I begin with the model self projected in Franklin's *Autobiography*, a figure as historically central to the image of the con man as Melville's protagonist is conceptually central. Then I follow the careers of three more specialized descendants of Franklin's model self—the self-made man, the booster, and the self-reliant jack-of-all-trades. That section ends with an analysis of how the "hermit" of *Walden* draws on the social traditions of the confidence man.

Part III, "Tricking Tricksters," represents the underside of the preceding one, the things that Poe and Melville foretold as souring the confidence enterprise. Instead of offering opportunities for imaginative individuals, the con game now appears as the socially normal pattern of behavior, and the question is how one can hold onto one's inner being in a field of competitive and soul-less con men. The soured public world is reflected in P. T. Barnum, Tom Sawyer, the Robber Barons, and the Snopeses. In Huck Finn and V. K. Ratliff, Mark Twain and William Faulkner fashion the rogue-as-survivor, a special version of the con man.

Part IV deals with American culture since 1945. The con man and his game are not merely characteristics of the American past; the paradigms I use in the earlier chapters prove every bit as illuminating when employed with contemporary literature, and in one form or another most of the habits and values I analyze elsewhere are still in evidence. What the con man lights up in the social world around him is apparently going to be with us for some time to come, and it might pay us to see what he's up to and why we have honored him for getting away with it.

I

"It Is Good To Be Shifty in a New Country": Assessments of America

1

MELVILLE'S *THE CONFIDENCE-MAN:*
Duplicity and Identity in a New Country

Society is a masked ball, where everyone hides his real character, and reveals it by hiding. . . . A man cannot utter two or three sentences without disclosing to intelligent ears precisely where he stands in life and thought.

—*Ralph Waldo Emerson*

Why was it that his charm revealed
Somehow the surface of a shield?
What was it that we never caught?
What was he, and what was he not?

—*Edwin Arlington Robinson*

Living things in contact with the air must acquire a cuticle, and it is not urged against cuticles that they are not hearts.

—*George Santayana*

Let us treat the men and women well; treat them as if they were real; perhaps they are.

—*Emerson once more*

A con man never meets a stranger.

—*David W. Maurer*

When I ask you to become a game-player to read Melville's strange novel, I do not mean that he is playing games with us, like Nabokov. I mean something more radical. We witness from the outset transactions that are like shell games. There may be a pea under one of the shells, but no one can be sure. The lamb-like man, apparently mute, writes "Charity" on his slate and adds one phrase after another—"thinketh no evil," "believeth all things"—erasing each successive predicate but preserving the word "Charity." As he drifts to sleep, the other passengers describe him variously—"Odd fish!" "Poor fellow!" "Humbug!" "Singular innocence"—erasing each other's comments but keeping as their subject the drowsing stranger. This is the way things happen in *The Confidence-Man*. The most elementary acts of thought and speech become complicated, tentative, perhaps spurious. Why should one predicate for the lamb-like man be any more authoritative than another? A predicate is merely what someone predicates. An attribute is what someone attributes. Predicates and attributes summon up identities (the lamb-like man *is* a humbug or *is* peculiarly innocent), but the whole process is at best hypothetical. The search for identity and the search for truth turn out to be shell games, with predicates and attributes as the shells. Since, as the Cosmopolitan says, "you can conclude nothing absolute from the human form," all we have are shifting predicates and accumulating attributes.

Actually, that is not true. We do have something else: the players of the game. If each predicate is provisional, the act of predication appears as someone's personal gambit. We may or may not wish to credit the characters' assertions, but we can still learn by watching how they play the game. And when they make suppositions, they compound their gambits, for now there are shells within the shells:

> ". . . suppose I say to you, 'Barber, my dear barber, unhappily I have no small change by me to-night, but shave me, and depend upon your money to-morrow'—suppose I should say that now, you would put trust in me, wouldn't you? You would have confidence?"
>
> "Seeing that it is you, sir," with complaisance replied the barber, now mixing the lather, "seeing that it is *you*, sir, I won't answer that question. No need to."
>
> "Of course, of course—in that view. But, as a supposition—you would have confidence in me, wouldn't you?"
>
> "Why—yes, yes."

Here a stranger frankly asks to be regarded hypothetically, but the barber, being a shrewd and wary man, will have no suppositions. True, it is nearly midnight and he has never before seen the man preparing to be shaved, but he "can conclude something from that sort of talk, with that sort of dress." He rejects the stranger's tentative mask of moneylessness, because he sees the real attributes of the man, or rather, he attributes to the extravagant dress and urbane talk of the stranger the supporting qualities of wealth and breeding. And these qualities, for the highly practical barber, suffice to establish the stranger's identity; "seeing that it is *you*, sir," he won't be confounded in fast talk.

But "you" in this exchange is Melville's most devious and beguiling hero, the master of masks in a world of masks, and although we cannot be confident who he is, we are assured that the barber has foolishly underestimated him. This shell game of identity has run a fascinating course in American history and literature, and at the end of his major fictional career, Herman Melville wrote the most penetrating exposé in our literature of its methods, *The Confidence-Man: His Masquerade.* During his most intense writing of fiction, the period of *Moby-Dick* and *Pierre,* Melville was desperately concerned with "the great art of telling truth," and the problems of identity and knowledge seemed to him the stuff of metaphysical tragedy. By the time he wrote *The Confidence-Man,* however, he had redefined the dimensions of the case and accordingly shifted his attitude of investigation. *The Confidence-Man* is more devilish and less defiant than *Moby-Dick,* and Melville looks into its world with the cooler eye of comedy.

In the terminology of the shell game, the Melville of 1851 used all his energies to find the pea or to suggest its nature. He reveals his own method in describing Shakespeare's:

> Through the mouths of the dark characters . . . , he craftily says, or sometimes insinuates, the things which we feel to be so terrifically true that it were all but madness for any good man, in his own proper character, to utter, or even hint of them. Tormented into desperation, Lear the frantic king tears off the mask, and speaks the sane madness of vital truth.

Ahab is the mask by means of which Melville forces his narrative to probe beneath the world of appearance to its essential subject, and Ahab's own method is to pierce or strip away masks. But Ahab's procedure is dangerous, and not only for a whaler. In the game of predication, stripping away the mask means removing a false predicate to reveal the true one. But where do we stop? The very suspicion that impels us to remove one mask lingers to make us question the next, and as we strip away mask after mask, we come to doubt all predicates and all attributes. We are left, like Ahab, with an unidentifiable brute subject and a speculative world reduced to a white void, like the erased chalkboard of the lamb-like man.

The methods of the Confidence-Man are less dangerous and more disquieting. The Melville of 1857 was less concerned with the truth than with the telling; his interest had moved from the pea to the shells. His triumphant masquerader proceeds in a manner that would be incomprehensible to the more heroic but less devious Ahab. Instead of stripping away the mask, he covers it with another one to see how it wears; he deliberately, if tentatively, predicates something else. The fun is in watching what happens. For reality in this novel does not appear under the original mask; it appears in the discrepancies between the hypothetical mask and the observed conduct of its wearer. The characteristic revelation is, as Melville says in a chapter title, "a rupture of the hypothesis." Everyone may wear a mask, but no one wears it very well. The "great art of telling truth," Melville has discovered, may best be practiced by telling lies.

A man who utters plain truth reveals nothing of himself; he disappears in the truth he speaks. A man who lies has more possibilities. In creating his fiction he opens up the qualities of his own character, for he implies a purpose in the fiction, an audience for it, and a governing, if not always conscious, mode of invention. There are so few ways of being right and so many ways of being wrong. Throughout this novel Melville urges us to distinguish between the truth of a statement and the effects of it. Bypassing the problem of whether a given fabrication is true, we proceed *as if it is*. We must question why someone tells the story and what consequences it has. The dominant intellectual mode in *The Confidence-Man* is that of hypothesis or supposition, and the key question is, What *follows* from a given story? If we accept this narrative method, the meaning of the much-argued concluding sentence becomes clear—"Something further may follow of this Masquerade." Melville does not need to tell us that something will follow *after* the Masquerade, for it is obvious that the Masquerade, which is simply our social experience, will itself continue. But if we are more willing than the barber to play with suppositions, something more than Melville has directly stated may follow *from* the Masquerade.

To get at what follows from Melville's novel, we need to ask ourselves under what conditions this extensive masquerade could develop in the first place. Hypotheses are ruptured so often throughout *The Confidence-Man* that the discrepancy between belief and behavior comes to characterize a whole social world. What Melville is projecting in this book is a culture without authority. The absolute has been absolutely severed from the human. Melville's "ifness" constantly reminds us that without authority, one must be tentative, holding in mind the human source of each predicate, each assertion, each principle. This is hard to do. It is like saying that all human intercourse is a game of confidence. And that is precisely Melville's point about nineteenth-century America.

From this bold insight develops a strange and demanding novel. The problems of fiction making turn out to be the very problems of social experience. Thus it is not Melville's larger plot that reveals his point but rather the local transactions. In fact, as any reader quickly sees, there is little overall "action" in the book. The narrative consists of conversations and exchanges of stories aboard a steamer heading down the Mississippi on All Fool's Day, and in intervening passages a devious narrator describes the talkers and the scene. Yet the novel is not a philosophical dialogue or an allegory. It may not have the typical movement of fiction, but it has the texture. The characters and their verbal gestures, for instance, demand much more attention than the doctrines they espouse. What happens in the novel, however, happens *within* the conversations and exchanges of stories. Melville is dramatizing here the daily fictionalizing—the creating and erasing of characters—that makes up the game of identity in a new and protean society. And by baring his own literary devices, emphasizing the problems of fiction, he estranges us from that fiction-making world and allows us to see it and ourselves anew.

Discrediting the Interpreters

We have to begin with the difficulties of the novel, for they are severe. There is extensive critical disagreement not only about the larger value and meaning of the book but even about what is going on and how to make sense of the narrative. The problem begins with the source of information and judgment. This narrator is not trustworthy in the sense, say, of Jane Austen's tellers, but then again he isn't unreliable either. Like the world he presents to us, he simply lacks authority.

There is an exacting cautiousness in this narrator's voice which leads, very nearly, to pure circularity: "But, upon the whole, it could not fairly be said that his appearance was unprepossessing; indeed, to the congenial, it would have been doubtless not uncongenial . . ." His hesitant style abounds in double negatives and phrases of uncertainty, especially when it is "describing" immediate appearances. And in the longer paragraphs of "analysis" (see the third paragraph of Chapter 5) the narrator doubles back on himself, twisting through conjectures and appearances, gradually leading us toward what seem secure expectancies and generalizations, only to leave us with darker and more evasive fulfillments. If he rarely misinforms us, it is because he so rarely tells us anything definite. There is, then, some justice in Daniel Hoffman's remark about Melville's style in this novel: "What is given is taken away; what is removed, lingers."[1] With so little authority in the narrative itself, it is not surprising that readers find *The Confidence-Man* baffling. But for all its apparent self-negation, Melville's style here is functional, and his narrator tells us a great deal by implication. The doubling back, for instance, serves as a constant reminder that *no* interpretation is free of supposition, and this is one of Melville's points. To begin with, the style of *The Confidence-Man* makes us uncertain and self-conscious, as we must be to follow the "events."

Still more can be inferred from the ways in which the narrator speaks to us. Let me use the implications of a characteristic sentence as a way of getting into this strange novel. The sentence opens Chapter 12, the story of Goneril and the unfortunate man:

> It appeared that the unfortunate man had had for a wife one of those natures, anomalously vicious, which would almost tempt a metaphysical lover of our species to doubt whether the human form be, in all cases, conclusive evidence of humanity, whether, sometimes, it may not be a kind of unpledged and indifferent tabernacle, and whether, once for all to crush the saying of Thrasea, (an unaccountable one, considering that he himself was so good a man) that "he who hates vice, hates humanity," it should not, in self-defense, be held for a reasonable maxim, that none but the good are human.

Elizabeth Foster has noted Melville's syntactic habit, in this novel, of setting "main thoughts on relative grounds by tucking them into the terms of a comparison and then [putting] the whole upon even more minor and tentative grounds" by the clause of introduction.[2] Here every item pertinent to the "story" is subordinated to the characteristically evasive main clause "It appeared," and the familiar qualifiers, the hesitations, the labored tentativeness produce what Foster calls "the hinting and whispering which are the language of this novel" and what Warner Berthoff more bluntly labels "a kind of ponderous stuttering."[3] Yet in its elaborate and self-conscious arrangement of parts, this is a remarkably informative sentence, a small model of the narrative world. There are two obvious ways to misread it. One is to assume that it is *about* Goneril and the unfortunate man, in which case it takes us too far from its subject to advance the narrative. The other is to assume that it is advancing a principle, in which case the assertion is hopelessly confounded by the tentativeness and by the ironic pairing of Thrasea's statement with the final clause.

In fact, the sentence has to do with Goneril *and* with Thrasea, with characters *and* with principles. Looked at from one side, it is about the effort to derive from an observed human being some general ideas about humanity and conduct. Looked at from the other side, it is about the effort to relate general laws or principles to the uncertain appearances immediately around us. The distance between the human and the absolute is stylistically marked by the contrast between the overall indirection in most of the sentence and the epigrammatic purity of the pivotal principles—"he who hates vice, hates humanity" and "none but the good are human." Apparently, in the world of this novel, we cannot take such principles as "truths." Absolute in themselves, they are so deeply embedded in a non-absolute world that they appear as counters in a speculative game.

We are now in a position to recognize two curious and characteristic things about this sentence. There is a kind of dramatic action incorporated in the movement of the sentence, an assault. And the parts of the sentence involve a complex set of characters—Goneril, "a metaphysical lover of our species," Thrasea, and the hypothetical "qui" or "he who . . ." of classical rhetoric. The metaphysical lover of our species is the central character, for he mediates between Goneril and principle, incorporating the action of the sentence. The seeming circularity of many of the narrator's statements arises from this tendency to attribute any given observation or feeling to a specific kind of character. But why "a metaphysical lover of our species"? Because he is precisely the persona who will be threatened by the implications of Goneril's story. He is, to pick up one of the many puns in Melville's title, "a man of confidence," and his confidence derives less from habit and experience than from abstract principles; he loves our species metaphysically. Up against the hypothetical existence of such a being as Goneril, his "love" is unmasked. He loves "humanity," not human beings. Consider the desperate casuistry to which he is driven in separating the concept from the particular character. In "self-defense" he must finally announce, not a new principle, but the belief that sustained in the first place his metaphysical love of our species—"none but the good are human." His first "doubt" is the critical one, for the difficulty of inferring the absolute from the apparent—"humanity" from "the human form"—explains the discomfitures of most of the characters in this novel.

The chief actor in this sentence, then, is the "metaphysical lover," and the drama is an assault, by a hypothetical character, on his convictions, an assault that brings about a surprisingly thorough exposure of the character. The sentence is an episode, more or less complete in itself, which gains in clarity and implication by being compared with similar small episodes and by being enclosed in analogous larger ones. The "metaphysical lover of our species," having been unmasked, disappears almost as soon as he is introduced, and yet he is as much one of the novel's "characters" as Goneril or the herb-doctor.

This brings us to another difficulty in *The Confidence-Man:* there is little continuity in the characters and therefore little basis for a "story" in the familiar sense. Characters like the one in this sentence are created for the nonce; their existence is explicitly hypothetical—if such a man there be, here is what follows. Through such hypothetical figures, general principles are invested in human particularity, attributed to a certain speaker, uttered under pressing circumstances, and tested against the speaker's fuller character. Thus the narrator's apparent "stuttering" and evasiveness are his ways of clarifying the exact implications of the immediate hypothesis. The linguistic world of this novel is a brilliant refraction of the more general narrative world, and the "action" within a long sentence typifies the work of the passengers on the *Fidèle* and the readers of *The Confidence-Man.*

The world of the *Fidèle*—a floating labyrinth carrying a constantly changing body of passengers—is as disconcerting as the narrative voice that describes it. Perhaps by thinking about how we enter and leave this world we can locate Melville's reasons for projecting so strange a fiction. The opening and closing chapters edge off into pure mystery, not because their actions are opaque, but because things appear in an unwonted clarity, a stylization as alien to our human experience as the brilliant, disturbing world of Apocalypse. Melville's allusions to the founding of a new religion in Chapter 1 are mirrored by his allusions to Revelation in Chapter 45, and both chapters present extreme contrasts of fleecy innocence and diabolical guilt. The lamb-like mute and the snowy old man emerge from outside human experience; they bring celestial conceptions to a terrestrial scene. And their narrative episodes also partake of the extreme; with little mediation they present parables of the ultimate. The advent of the lamb-like man, who practices the impertinent doctrines from the thirteenth chapter of First Corinthians that he writes on his slate, illustrates what our world makes of and does to celestial innocence. Conversely, the progress of the comely old man from benign assurance to confused doubt shows what human innocence makes of its first real exposure to a fallen world.

These virtually allegorical figures and events are accompanied by eschatological signs and images, suggesting that the narrative can be interpreted along clear dialectical lines. In the opening chapter we confront, successively, the placard "offering a reward for the capture of a mysterious impostor," a slate bearing the mild words of Paul, and the barber's sign "NO TRUST." In the closing chapter Melville not only plays insinuatingly with the symbol of the "solar lamp," finally extinguished, but he painstakingly arranges the *Fidèle's* Bible into a cosmological figure:

> "Ah," cried the old man, brightening up, "now I know. Look," turning the leaves forward and back, till all the Old Testament lay flat on one side, and all the New Testament flat on the other, while in his fingers he supported vertically the portion between, "look, sir, all this to the right is certain truth, and all this to the left is certain truth, but all I hold in my hand here is apocrypha."

Surely all this is not without meaning.

But if the beginning and ending of *The Confidence-Man*, like the pages lying to the left and right in the Bible, edge off into apocalyptic "certain truth," they also point inward to the world between, the world we hold in our hands, the concealed and murky world of apocrypha. The ostensibly clear dialectic established by the placards and symbols darkens on examination. Paul's words about Charity and the barber's words "NO TRUST" appeal to distinct realms of experience; the logic of the verbal contrast disappears in the deeper absence of relation. The Cosmopolitan's blowing out of the solar lamp may be read, metaphysically, as a sign that he is Anti-Christ, the Deceiver clouding earthly comprehension, or as a sign that he is the "true sun" before which lesser suns dwindle; opposites tend to merge. And the image of the Bible loses its clarity of contrast when the Cosmopolitan points out that "apocrypha" and "certain truth" are, in the Bible of this world, bound together.

As in the sentence hypothesizing "a metaphysical lover of our species," Melville here seems less concerned with the clear interpretive modes offered by a discourse about last things than he is with the confusing discrepancies between final "truth" and human experience. Bound together are divine revelations—"Love thy neighbor" or "Blessed are the meek"—and experiential warnings—"If thou be for his profit he will use thee" or "Believe not his many words"; circulating together are genuine bills, counterfeit bills, counterfeit detectors, and spurious counterfeit detectors; side by side appear the signs "Charity believeth all things" and "NO TRUST."

The problem, then, is to establish a workable relationship between principle and experience, to square stated beliefs with immediate conduct. In a community informed by a vital religious belief, dogma can serve as a guide to conduct and as a means of understanding it. Even when religious fervor has decayed, communal habits, traditions, and manners may provide the authoritative ground on which the immediate situation is related to the larger principle. But on the *Fidèle* neither approach works. The captain never appears; indeed, no figure of recognized authority enters the narrative, and this is a manifestation of the more general and thorough absence of authority in the narrative world. Familiar hereditary patterns have been broken; class lines dissolve; "society" is not characterized by communal patterns but by the extreme fluidity of human encounters. In a typical scene mutual strangers confront each other or gather in a motley crowd. Eastern gentlemen mingle with western farmers, and no one automatically defers to anyone else. As the *Fidèle* accumulates and discharges a remarkable range of passengers, it provides a collective image of social life in "a new country."

Because the familiar bases of authority, class, and social position have been systematically uprooted in the culture Melville projects, each social gathering requires the *creation* of a credible authority. Black Guinea seems to be cajoling people into compassion, when the man with the wooden leg appears and bullies the crowd into distrust; his "authority" is in turn undermined by the militant Methodist minister: the pattern shiftingly repeats itself throughout the crowd scenes. In the more intimate scenes as well, the characters struggle self-consciously to find a ground upon which they can establish relations, each projecting an identity and asserting beliefs, each doubting and testing the other. Social relations appear as games of confidence. If the breakdown of communal patterns frees the characters to create and assume their own identities, it also removes their security in identifying others or knowing how to relate to them. The result is an air of suspicion, dissociated from the human understanding that could justly make use of it—"NO TRUST." The characters so fear they may be duped that they convert dialogue into a test of strength. If one does not *win*, one loses.

This overview of practical difficulties and their sources in *The Confidence-Man* should prepare us to explore directly and theoretically the situation of the reader. Many things that one conventionally seeks in a novel cannot be found here—authoritative interpretation by the narrator, reliable glimpses of the inner life, continuity of characters, development of story. Melville gives his readers no easier or more certain means of following and assessing the action than the characters themselves can find in a world without authority. The danger for both characters and readers is to leap too quickly into a comforting belief, to give unconditional confidence in a conditional world. The reader, however, has this advantage over the characters: the narrator posts constant warnings, and Melville's own art is designed to bring the reader into a new relation with fictive occurrences, a relation that acknowledges the essential gamesmanship of American culture. What he asks for is a willing suspension of *belief*, a self-consciousness about the credences that we all too easily and conventionally grant in reading fictions. Denied the authority of an overall story or a direct interpretation, we must look more closely at the local gambits and recognize the patterns underlying them. Like the narrator, we must consider predicates and principles as mere hypotheses and treat them accordingly.

Once we leave the conditional world of human encounters to predicate something absolute about one of the characters, we discover that logic fails. When the narrator guesses from outward appearance that the Cosmopolitan is a "mature man of the world, a character which, like its opposite, the sincere Christian's, is not always swift to take offense," he indicates one of the characteristic patterns in this novel: in outward appearance the representatives of two contrary predicates merge. We simply cannot derive an unconditional predicate from a conditional appearance. The many religious allusions in the novel may seem like hints at a subtext in which ambiguous appearances are clarified in fixed interpretations. But the very abundance of the allusions creates the effect of metaphysical punning, in which every appearance is, for allegorical purposes, multivalent.

The Confidence-Man presents a world of games, and we mistake it equally if we neglect the gamesmanship or if we refuse to take it seriously. In a game what counts is not the content or realistic detail but the gambit. The game-player is more interested in patterns than in meanings. As Melville transfers paradigms from one situation to another, he shows us how to read the actions in his novel. The "transfer-agent" of the Black Rapids Coal Company repeatedly shifts the application of any pattern he finds, thus enlarging the scope of "confidence games." His chief source of paradigms is, appropriately, the stock market. About "bears" he says: "these same destroyers of confidence, and gloomy philosophers of the stock-market, though false in themselves are yet true types of most destroyers of confidence and gloomy philosophers, the world over. Fellows who, whether in stocks, politics, bread-stuffs, morals, metaphysics, religion—be it what it may—trump up their black panics in the naturally-quiet brightness, solely with a view to some sort of covert advantage." Whatever we make of his opposition to "gloomy philosophers," we cannot ignore the value of his cast of thought. Rather than assess the local transaction on its explicit terms, he looks for the informing game pattern, for the manipulation of confidence. Characters in the novel who cannot make such transferences, who are fixed by the immediate reference, are repeatedly shown up as fools, especially by the Cosmopolitan. What Melville indicates by this emphasis on the paradigm is that a reader cannot follow this novel by having a personal stake in the characters, an intellectual stake in the metaphysics, or a moral stake in the principles. We follow the immediate action of *The Confidence-Man* as we follow the moves in a game.

How, then, do we find the "meaning" of the book? Usually this question is made into a telling metaphor—how do we get "beneath the surface"? Captain Ahab, with his concern for "the little lower layer," typifies a standard reading of nineteenth-century American fiction, especially Melville's. The events and appearances are "pasteboard masks," symbolizing or ironically concealing the "realities" beneath. Allen Hayman, writing about Chapter 33 of *The Confidence-Man,* states clearly the theoretical center of this approach:

> A writer concerned with this heightened reality is mainly interested not in the circumstantial events of daily experience, the surface of life, but rather in what lies beneath the surface, the meaning of the surface . . . [Hawthorne and Melville] probed deeper into experience than did the realistic novelist. They examined men's innermost beings—their souls, if you will—rather than their daily experiences . . .[4]

Despite its occasional usefulness, this method of reading has certain dangers. Practically, it requires an allegorical framework by means of which one can move with some certainty from surface to depth. Bunyan's *Pilgrim's Progress* and Hawthorne's "The Celestial Railroad" (in more complicated ways) provide such frameworks, but *The Confidence-Man,* despite one critic's reference to its "allegorical geometry," simply confounds such reading. Hayman's phrase "their souls, if you will" begs the very question about which Melville's art makes us self-conscious. More theoretically, the symbolic approach presupposes a segmentation of "daily experiences" and "men's innermost beings," assigning "reality" to the latter while showing impatience with the former. This amounts to an admission that moral character is severed from conduct. In *Moby-Dick* and the following fiction, Melville himself begins to reveal the ambivalence and open-endedness of symbolic reading, and in the stories of the 1850s he shows an increasing interest in the "surfaces" themselves, in voices, inflections, masks, and gestures. In *The Confidence-Man* he directly indicates how important "daily experience" is by systematically thwarting our efforts to get beneath it to "men's innermost beings." Although he often presents characters trying to leap from outward experience to its interior equivalents, he also shows up their efforts as not only futile but radically misguided.

The allegorist, with his impatience at "the surface of life," is in fact the anti-type of the game-player. The first wishes to displace subject or gesture with predicate or final attribute. The second considers attribution and predication as curious maneuvers of someone who probably ought to be watched. Thus to read the book in an allegorical state of mind is to confront the Confidence-Man with such uneasiness and distrust that he will naturally come to stand for the most dangerous of tricksters, Satan.[5] And conversely, the same allegorical temperament finds something not uncongenial in Colonel Moredock, the Indian-hater. Perhaps his particular sentiments and atrocities make one a bit squeamish, but at least he has the right impulses, hasn't he?—he commits himself absolutely to the hatred of evil. But that is precisely the problem. His absolute vow—"the hate of which is a vortex from whose suction scarce the remotest chip of the guilty race may reasonably feel secure"—extends itself naturally into the most bloodthirsty and reckless racism. For if the Confidence-Man is the novel's ultimate game-player, Colonel Moredock is its quintessential allegorist. He passes from misleading "surface" to "real" depth so facilely that he knows without hesitancy that an Indian is not a human being at all but simply another mask of evil. And he acts accordingly. If we need a final reason for turning from allegory to gamesmanship as an approach to the contingent world of this novel, we need only remember Colonel Moredock, who has "gone to his long home" before he is dead, transfixing his humanity, and thus that of others, on an unconditional predicate.

How the Game Is Played

Thus far I have emphasized the difficulties posed by *The Confidence-Man*, the conventions it defies, and the modes of interpretation it frustrates. The book is not a trick, however, nor an excursion into nihilism. If the overtly stated ideas or principles are consistently assigned to particular characters, made hypothetical and thus officially disowned, Melville does nonetheless develop important ideas. But we cannot perceive these unless we recognize the real issues at stake and learn how to relate to fictive events as game-players. The book does not turn on theological or moral questions but on the problems of identity and social relations. Melville is not speculating here primarily about the value of Christianity or of optimism and philanthropy, but about the means of making and recognizing identities in a fluid society. The contrived identity is literally a fiction, and the social activities of the novel's characters are fiction making and fiction reading. Thus the three chapters *about* fiction (14, 33, 44) are at once technical discussions of genre and epistemological comments on the narrative world itself. In stylizing his own fictive gestures and making us self-conscious about predication, belief, and interpretation, Melville is defining the mimetic mode of this novel. What he represents, directly and comprehensively, are the characteristic gambits in a cultural game of identities.

Predicates, suppositions, and principles belong among the counters in this game. They thus refer simultaneously to a subject and to a "player." The phrase, "Odd fish!," which opens Chapter 2, refers to its subject, the lamb-like man, but it tells us at least as much about the anonymous passenger who predicates it, especially when it is followed by many diverging predicates for the same subject, all of them substantiating the chapter title—"Showing that many men have many minds." When a player assigns a predicate or asserts a principle unconditionally, he gives himself away, for such a predicate or principle by its very fixity loses its reference to its subject (and even to its context) while clearly exposing the attitude of the player. In the chapter about Indian-hating, for instance, the overt subject of all the predication and supposition—the Indian—is scarcely illuminated at all: "as for what manner of man the Indian is, many know, either from history or experience." In contrast, the agents of predication—the backwoodsman, the Indian-hater, Judge James Hall (the historical source as well as the primary storyteller), and Charlie Noble (the character in the novel who retells the story)—reveal their own characters by their assumptions about the Indian and by their purposes in talking about him. Through such indirections, Melville analyzes the processes of character making. In game terms, character is not defined by the counter itself (predicate or supposition) but by the manipulation of it. This is why we must follow the actions like moves in a game. Let us now look at the kinds of ideas and implications that do emerge in this Masquerade.

The easiest way to begin is with the interior story telling, for here

Melville most openly stylizes the game. Throughout *The Confidence-Man* characters tell and retell, comment on and re-examine stories. And none of these stories remains innocent. Each comes to represent an attitude, and each sets off controversy. The first of these interior fictions, the story of Goneril, illustrates how Melville uses all of them as parts of games. The story is initially told in Chapter 4 to the country merchant as "my story" by the man with the weed, the third guise of Melville's hero:

> In a low, half-suppressed tone, he began it. Judging from his auditor's expression, it seemed to be a tale of singular interest, involving calamities against which no integrity, no forethought, no energy, no genius, no piety, could guard.
>
> At every disclosure, the hearer's commiseration increased. No sentimental pity. As the story went on, he drew from his wallet a bank note, but after a while, at some still more unhappy revelation, changed it for another, probably of a somewhat larger amount; which, when the story was concluded, with an air studiously disclamatory of alms-giving, he put into the stranger's hands; who, on his side, with an air studiously disclamatory of alms-taking, put it into his pocket.

And that's it—no "story" at all. To give us our first lesson in what stories mean, the narrator omits the content and presents instead the transaction for which the story serves as instrument. He fastens our attention on the reactions of the country merchant, not allowing our own "sentimental pity" to be stirred by the story itself. We are witnessing, of course, an elementary form of the confidence game, and we are forced to see it as a game because we observe nothing but the maneuvers, and even these only through shrewdly cynical guesses.

In the first instance, then, stories appear as the instruments by which the tellers effect their own ulterior purposes, and this emphasis on function shifts our interest from the tale to the telling, from content to methods, from "truth" to implications. But Melville is far from finished with Goneril's story. In Chapter 11 we find that the country merchant has learned further particulars of the story from the man in the gray coat (another appearance of the protagonist) and that he is about to tell it to the Black Rapids Coal Agent (still another appearance) as an example of the world's hidden and undeserved suffering. "But as the good merchant could, perhaps, do better justice to the man than the story," says the narrator with characteristic ambiguity (better justice to the man than to the story, or better justice to the man than the story could do?), "we shall venture to tell it in other words than his, though not to any other effect."

What finally follows, in Chapter 12, is the story itself, but the "other words" of the outside narrator do change its effect, partially by focusing so intently *on* the effect. The story concerns a woman of "cactus-like" beauty with an "anomalously vicious" nature, whose perversities of behavior drive away her "unfortunate" husband and her daughter and then reduce the husband to poverty in a courtroom battle. But whereas the country merchant retells the story as "a third case" illustrating the unmerited suffering in the world, the narrator seems more interested in character and belief. His description of Goneril's appearance and behavior makes her more repugnant than even the biased yet soft-hearted merchant would allow, but instead of stressing the husband's misfortunes, he presents the character of Goneril as a threat to human understanding. Given the observed (or reported) details, what does one predicate of Goneril? To call her "human" would raise doubts "whether the human form be, in all cases, conclusive evidence of humanity," and to say that she is "sane" would be, as the husband's lawyer maintains in court, "constructively a libel upon womankind." In other words, if a character like Goneril is credible, the categories in which one places her for understanding are themselves maligned. In this view of story telling, the story is again a means, now not to effect an exchange of money but to test the conventional images by which we understand ourselves and our kind.

But there is yet a third kind of transaction for which Goneril's story is the instrument. It involves neither the immediate emotional response of giving alms nor the intellectual response of analyzing character, but a broad fusion of the two. The nature of this potential transaction is suggested by the seemingly desperate efforts of the Black Rapids Coal Agent to modify or interpret the story so as to make it compatible with a confident view of human existence. What is at stake is not simply one's temporary mood (and thus one's pocketbook) nor one's intellectual grasp of human nature, but one's whole posture toward life, a posture including both a philosophical stance and a prevailing faith. To the Black Rapids Coal Agent the story of Goneril, which shows the triumph in this world of pure and deliberate wickedness, must be recast with enough qualifications and ambiguities to allow him, in a brilliant gambit of pseudo-reasoning, to conclude of Goneril's husband: "Great good fortune had this unfortunate man. Lucky dog, he dared say, after all." If not susceptible to such reinterpretation, the story would tend to undermine "confidence." It is in this view of story telling that it makes apparent sense to assert, as the Confidence-Man so often does, that certain stories, whether true or false, should simply not be told.

The point is not that stories are dangerously influential, but that the Confidence-Man's own favorite commodity is utterly precarious. "Confidence," as the Black Rapids Coal Agent readily admits, is not a posture to be maintained by reason, nor can it be subject to "such variabilities as everyday events"; rather it is essential to a "right conviction" of human and divine nature that, "based less on experience than intuition, it [rises] above the zones of weather." And it is confidence in this broader sense that is the ultimate subject of the confidence game.

The other stories told in *The Confidence-Man* also effect transactions like the three just described. Immediately, they help their tellers accomplish ulterior purposes—to make money or to change an opinion. Secondarily, through the intimacies of character making— predication and attribution—the stories raise questions about how we understand and imagine human beings. Finally, the stories can have longer-range, indirect effects on the very personality of the auditor, loosening his "fixed" convictions and undermining his posture toward life. Only one of Melville's interior storytellers, the protagonist himself, is aware of these secondary implications of story telling. It is here that the confidence game "increases in seriousness," for the stakes have been raised twice, from money to beliefs to identities. The "confidence game" in the ordinary sense of the term thus turns out to be itself merely a maneuver in this ultimate game of confidence. And only the narrator and the protagonist know that the ultimate game is even in play.

If an identity can be undone by the effects of a mere story, it must be shaky to begin with. In fact the characters in this novel are utterly vulnerable. Their difficulties begin in the outward situation. All they can use to get at the true natures of others are bewilderingly fluid appearances. Even when the other person is not deliberately trying to disguise himself, there is a masquerade. *Every* appearance and gesture becomes a mask insofar as it constitutes only one section of the character (note Melville's emphasis on the use of stylized tags like auburn hair, wooden leg). And since these sections of character often depend on circumstances and mood, they alter suddenly. The relation between mask and self is thus thoroughly problematic—does the mask cover, extend, express, or disguise the self? Being a practical expert in penetrating "disguises," like the barber, may ironically limit one's awareness of the more general entanglement of appearances and identity. The barber distinguishes between a fine roof and a fine wig—both artificial covers of the head—by saying that no one pretends his roof is part of himself, whereas "the bald man palms off hair, not his, for his own." When the Cosmopolitan points out that the bald man's fair purchase of the hair does make it *his*, he not only reduces all personal appearances to masquerade but hints at the general habit of taking *ownership* of things as an index of identity.

Aside from these difficulties in reading others, the characters have problems acting out *themselves*. As they manipulate their own masks, they have to keep in mind their real intentions, their circumstances, and their presumed audience. What is more, they must tacitly relate their temporary masks to their more durable sense of who they are. If they could depend on a stable community or on authoritative institutions for this larger sense of identity, perhaps they could play the temporary games more sportively and more deliberately. But they are *themselves* at stake. The very fluidity that opens the way for self-advancement weakens their self-assurance. Instead of identifying with a class, a party, a family, an occupation, even a persistent cluster of feelings or memories, these characters posit their sense of who they are on what they believe. Faced repeatedly with claimants, confronted with nothing but a series of masks, these characters come to regard the act of belief itself as the central human experience, the ultimate issue in any transaction. And the daily strain of probing every assertion brings about a yearning for the unconditional, the belief that passes for truth: thus Colonel Moredock reaches his resting point in Indian-hating and he will never again have to test an Indian. The more committed a character is to a set of principles in this novel, the more desperate his situation must be. It is in this sense that identities can be wagered and lost in the ultimate game of confidence.

The characters in *The Confidence-Man* are thus doubly vulnerable, confused in their reading of others and insecure about acting out themselves. If the characters have a hard time penetrating the nature of their new acquaintances, so do we. The narrator may give us exact accounts of the local transaction and he may hint about the larger stakes, but he refuses to define the inward nature of the characters. When he makes shrewd guesses based on their appearances, he goes on to "unauthorize" his readings by reminding us that they are only hypotheses. In other words, he forces us into the position of game-players ourselves, alert to gambits but hesitant about final identifications. He repeatedly emphasizes the inconsistencies of the characters, as when the man in gray drops his gravity to become enthusiastic. But such changes reveal less about the characters observed than about the difficulties of interpretation itself. The narrator's attitude may thus encourage us to be tolerant and tentative, but it also immerses us in the same immediate difficulties that make the characters themselves vulnerable in reading masks.

The other kind of vulnerability—the problem of performing and thus ratifying oneself—emerges as we follow the extended development of the game. It is in fact what the game is about. The issue can be summarized abstractly as follows: *if* one's identity is a posture toward life and a set of supporting beliefs or principles, one ought to be able to sustain these through the shifting masks that one assumes merely for the occasion. On the other hand, if in the course of the local gambits, one abandons the central faiths, the hypothesis is ruptured and the "identity" is undone.

Most characters in the novel are so superficial that they are undone or revealed quite quickly, but four are drawn into extended games before their proffered identities are erased—the country merchant Mr. Roberts, Pitch, Charlie Noble, and Mark Winsome-Egbert (these are two phases of the same "character"). Pitch stakes his identity on being shrewd, skeptical, experienced, hard; he believes that machines are dependable and boys are not. By dint of several masks and complicated transactions, the Confidence-Man reveals him to be softhearted, full of hope, ready once again to depend on a hired boy (whom he has not even seen). Mr. Roberts, on the other hand, is by prevalent posture a good and trusting man. In his encounters with four versions of the Confidence-Man, he gives charity or buys stocks in every instance. But the issue is not monetary for him or for Pitch; Pitch may *suspect* he has been duped, but we can't be absolutely sure that he has, and Roberts doesn't even *feel* he has been diddled. Instead his kindly nature and his confidence in ultimate goodness are being tested against stories of human misery. And when he retells the story of Goneril to the Black Rapids Coal Agent, he is himself victimized by it. He blurts out that charity and hope are mere dreams that burst in one's hand. Within a few minutes he sees that his passionate assertion was "out of character," and he more or less becomes himself again, but he has found himself questioning his "most important persuasions," and his identity will be harder to refurbish than his wallet.

The abrupt transformation of Mr. Roberts provides the occasion for Chapter 14, the theoretical discussion of inconsistency in characterization. Coming at the close of the first extended game in the novel, this chapter helps clarify what the games are about. Melville's point—to justify apparent contradictions in the drawing of character—has directly to do with fiction, but he argues from "nature," where character is neither easy to know nor consistent. A consistent fictional character thus either misrepresents reality or substitutes one section (one mask) for the complex whole. But since this novel is *about* character making, Melville's argument has another bearing. It suggests that to demand consistency of character is to assume that in life itself personal identity is stable and knowable. What *The Confidence-Man* demonstrates, on the other hand, and what the undoing of Mr. Roberts has just illustrated, is that identities are hard to know and easy to unsettle. When Melville argues in this chapter that no system has been found that can authoritatively explain human nature, he thus underscores the value of the gamesman's approach to social relations. And he hints at the proposition that he will in Chapter 33 make explicit—that the games of identity in his novel may actually reveal *more* reality about the characters, that Mr. Roberts in effect is *more* himself for experiencing the disruption of his premise that he and his "most important persuasions" are identical.

The theoretical problems raised in Chapter 14 are whether identity is stable and whether any system of analysis can account for it. These issues receive their fullest development in the extended game between the Cosmopolitan and Mark Winsome-Egbert, for Winsome purports to offer both a stable inner being and a fixed system of explanation. The essential feature of this system is the splitting of "celestial" and "terrestrial." The needs and affiliations of the soul (the higher, truer being) are distinct from those of the body (the mundane and unimportant outward self). According to this theory, the innermost self remains untouched by the exigencies of everyday life: "Tut! Frank. Man is no such poor devil as that comes to—no poor drifting sea-weed of the universe. Man has a soul; which, if he will, puts him beyond fortune's finger and the future's spite." In other words, Winsome's system holds that identity is invulnerable. This issue is at the base of the game between the Cosmopolitan and Winsome-Egbert. As with the other ideas and principles in the book, however, Winsome's system is attached to a person and invested in circumstances, so that in the first instance what is tested is not the system but the player's ability to manipulate it in a game of identities.

Winsome himself is not much of a game-player. He prefers to leave human experience, as he leaves wine, "in the lasting condition of an untried abstraction." Cold and aloof with others, he is unwilling to try his ideas in the mundane world. He does not even care to articulate them clearly or to sustain an argument. He speaks irresponsibly, and of all those in the novel who offer readings of the protagonist's inner nature, Winsome's is the most outlandish: "yours, sir, if I mistake not, must be a beautiful soul—one full of all love and truth; for where beauty is, there must those be." The Cosmopolitan's reply is characteristic: "A pleasing belief." Winsome's facile reading of the absolute from the apparent sets off the game, for the Cosmopolitan, playing out the premise of Winsome's statement, voices his own "confidence in the latent benignity of that beautiful creature, the rattle-snake," and Winsome outdoes the conceit by wishing to change personalities with the snake as "a perfectly instinctive, unscrupulous, and irresponsible creature." This transaction shows that Winsome will not defend or even clarify his ideas to another person. Indeed, he entirely neglects the human world, quite as he celebrates the irresponsibility of the snake.

As a game transaction, the encounter reveals still more. Clearly the Cosmopolitan has challenged the "pleasing belief." But Winsome declines the gambit and thus ignores the relation of persons. He is deaf to irony and obtuse about hypothetical thought. He cannot or will not play the game. This implies, in turn, that he refuses to take seriously the surfaces of human experience. In one sense, his behavior follows from his system, for Mark Winsome does remain more or less invulnerable. By disregarding others entirely, he avoids being duped by appearances. He can risk an erroneous reading of the other player's inner nature because he has absolutely nothing at stake, not even curiosity. If Melville has been more generally successful in educating his readers to the game-playing terms of the Masquerade, he will not even need to comment by this point on the naïveté of Mark Winsome's own theory about masks. Winsome calls them "labels" and argues that there is a symbolic correspondence between the apparent and the inward. Through the Cosmopolitan's immediate gambits and through the larger game patterns that provide an interpretive context, Melville thus reveals Mark Winsome's system for what it is—a philosophical account of inhuman experience.

If this were all there were to it, we could simply laugh off Winsome's system. But it has, like Winsome himself, "certain rear parts, very important parts, and these, like the rear of one's head, are best seen by reflection." Egbert is the rear part by which Winsome does his worldly business. He translates the theory into mundane practice and thus tries to make it intelligible. The theoretical split between celestial and terrestrial extends itself, as Elizabeth Foster has noted, into a split character. As Winsome's practical disciple, Egbert is significantly not an independent semi-ascetic, like Thoreau in *Walden*, but a "thriving young merchant," and in introducing him, Winsome not only endorses his life as an expression of the philosophic system but stresses the convergence between that system and "the ways of the world"—"still the plain truth remains, that mouth and purse must be filled." A philosophy stressing the purity of the soul's relations coexists with the most hardheaded business practice. But this is implicitly justified in Winsome's system, for if the soul is invulnerable to the contingencies of mundane life, the outward self may do as it pleases without accountability to the soul. Thus the larger game continues when Egbert replaces Winsome, but with this important change: both players are now in the game and both use masks. As a worldly man, Egbert knows how to manipulate masks, at least by habit, and he can both explain the operation of Winsome's philosophy and sustain an argument with some attention to his opponent. But by relating to the Cosmopolitan on such terms, the exponent of Winsome's philosophy becomes vulnerable, as the philosophy itself becomes vulnerable when finally tested against human experience.

If Winsome's theories are correct, Egbert should be able to play a series of conversational roles without identifying with them; he should remain deeply disengaged as he superficially wears masks and assumes hypotheses. But while Egbert is presented as an outward expression, a worldly mask, of Winsome's philosophy, this philosophy is in turn a counter to be manipulated in the game between the Cosmopolitan and Egbert, a mask for Egbert himself. The Cosmopolitan sees at once the circularity of the situation and makes it the basis of his first gambit. He proposes a test case and two roles: he is to be "Frank," a friend in need; Egbert is to be "Charlie," "the disciple of the philosophy in question." That is, he asks Egbert to *pretend* he is what he already claims to be. As the two characters play out these roles in Chapter 39, Egbert in his coldheartedness exposes the basic cruelty of Winsome's ideas, among them the hypothesis that a *true* friend will never be in need in the first place. The Cosmopolitan concludes this stage of the game by bluntly restating the masked situation itself: "Oh, this, all along, is not you, Charlie, but some ventriloquist who usurps your larynx. It is Mark Winsome that speaks, not Charlie."

If the first stage of the game traces out the worldly consequences of Winsome's system, the second stage reveals its misreading of human character. This stage begins when the Cosmopolitan reverses the original hypothesis—"Frank" would lend "Charlie" money if he were in need. The new hypothesis prompts Egbert to tell the story of China Aster, the candlemaker who accepts, against his own judgment, a loan from a friend to expand his business. The enterprise fails, the friend's character changes entirely into that of demanding creditor, and China Aster and his family are driven to madness and death. Egbert's point in recounting this bleak narrative is simply to enforce his argument by applying the moral—a loan between friends is dangerous to both parties. But in the larger transaction, he cannot control his own gambit. He approves the moral but disowns the "maudlin" style in which the tale was first told to him. Yet, as he confesses, the original storyteller has tyrannized over him. It is clear why Egbert objects to this narrative voice, for the teller repeatedly emphasizes just what Winsome's system denies, the power of circumstances to influence personality: "the poor candle-maker's scrupulous morality succumbed to his unscrupulous necessity, as is now and then apt to be the case." And it is precisely such narrative commentary that makes the story so powerful. Like many other stories told in this novel, it tends to undermine "confidence."

In fact, the voice is so powerful that the intended transaction is reversed, and Egbert's own "fixed convictions" are damaged by the telling. Egbert is supposedly using this voice in the deliberate sportiveness of a game maneuver, but it becomes another ventriloquist usurping his larynx. Although "Frank" is "still in character" for the ensuing discussion, "Charlie," who "seemed with his whole heart to enter into the spirit of the thing," cannot break out of the mood of the story. Despite what must have been his intentions, yet more forcefully than anyone else in the novel, he argues directly against Winsome's beliefs:

> the best man, as the worst, is subject to all mortal contingencies. . . . not to speak of other things that more or less tend to new-cast the character.
> . . . For there is no bent of heart or turn of thought which any man holds by virtue of an unalterable nature or will. Even those feelings and opinions deemed most identical with eternal right and truth, it is not impossible but that, as personal persuasions, they may in reality be but the result of some chance tip of Fate's elbow in throwing her dice. . . . and tell me, if you change this man's experiences or that man's books, will wisdom go surety for his unchanged convictions?

What happened in the story has happened in the game as well—"character" has succumbed to circumstances. Egbert loses control of the China Aster mask, disrupts his role as "Charlie," and even forgets the voice of Mark Winsome; his supposed identity has been "new-cast." Not only has Winsome's system been proved wrong in the game but Winsome himself is undone by proxy, for in introducing Egbert, he says: "Indeed, it is by you that I myself best understand myself."

More is at stake in this game, of course, than the ideas of "Mark Winsome." Melville is directly revealing here what he indirectly suggests throughout the novel—a cultural split between beliefs and practices. It is the segmentation Tocqueville observed between the American's exacting attention to technical details and his grandly vague affirmations in politics and philosophy. But the split also represents an assumption about the self that is widespread in American literature and thought: outward attributes and gestures do not provide an index of the inner self. Melville's immediate target is the most influential exponent of this idea, Ralph Waldo Emerson.[6] The basic idea appears in "Self-Reliance," where Emerson distinguishes between "primary" and "secondary" evidence of the self. Dismissing all public forms—dress, profession, family, appearance, manners, religious or political affiliations—as "screens" to the "proper self," he also refuses "this appeal from the man to his actions." What one *is* does not necessarily appear in what one *does*, and conversely, the realm of *doing* need not affect the realm of *being*. One can have certain relations mediated by manners, circumstances, and outward attributes, but these are essentially insignificant, for one can also have "immediate" relations, virtually intuitive approaches of soul to soul.

Melville shows how this presumed segmentation can damage both the inner and the outer selves. Severed from the circumstantial world of human relations, the inward self becomes blandly vague and uncertain, like the utterances of Mark Winsome, or it may fall into dangerous obsessions, unchecked by an acknowledgment of human limitations and frailty—Ahab and Colonel Moredock. On the other hand, the outward life, implicitly regarded as inconsequential, takes place without attention, understanding, or judgment. It becomes a game, and Melville presents it as such in *The Confidence-Man*. But since the characters refuse to take their outward gestures seriously, they cannot even play the game well. They get caught in their own masks. As their central beliefs become enmeshed in contingencies, they show that the self is not radically severed. Thus the game matters not only because so many people are playing it but because they all have more at stake than they wager.

A Representative Hero

I have been deliberately underemphasizing the "winner" in all these games, for Melville's protagonist has, in some fundamental ways, a secondary role. From his appearance as a lamb-like mute onwards, the Confidence-Man serves rather to bring out the qualities of surrounding characters than to interest us in his own inward nature or his development. He is an "original" character in the full sense of that term developed in Chapter 44:

> the original character, essentially such, is like a revolving Drummond light, raying away from itself all round it—everything is lit by it, everything starts up to it (mark how it is with Hamlet), so that, in certain minds, there follows upon the adequate conception of such a character, an effect, in its way, akin to that which in Genesis attends upon the beginning of things.

Like Melville's examples—Hamlet, Don Quixote, Milton's Satan— he casts a brilliant and disconcerting light on the characters around him. Melville compares an "original character" in fiction to "a new law-giver, a revolutionizing philosopher, or the founder of a new religion" in history. The allusion is to one of Emerson's primary theses, particulary evident in *Representative Men*, "Circles," and "The Poet": that a new idea (or the man acting on it) has the power to remake the world, to loosen old bonds and gather all people and things around itself as a center. So the presence of the Confidence-Man acts as a new center around which characters spring into startling clarity. And "the adequate conception" of this figure creates a new world, stylized and unfettered from the proprieties of ordinary life, but strangely familiar as all transactions are seen again from the center he occupies.

In his activity the Confidence-Man is our primary source of knowledge in the novel, for it is through his agency that the characters finally act out *themselves*. He is, in the Cosmopolitan's words, "a taster of races; in all his vintages, smacking my lips over this racy creature, man, continually." The unmistakable allusion to Satan is helpful if properly qualified.[7] Satan is the prototype of confidence men, and like Melville's protagonist he both tests men and relishes them. But Satan's delight in wiliness is tainted by malice; in his envy and contempt, he not only tastes men but devours them. We never *know* why the Confidence-Man tastes men, for he has no inwardness, no psychological or strictly personal character. Thus his apparent joy in the deft gambit is unmitigated; he seems to delight purely and simply in out-playing others. There is no evidence that he dislikes the game or the players.

What the Confidence-Man does work for—and this is all we can infer from his activities—is the unmasking of other characters. When Melville argues in Chapter 33 that the proprieties of real life prevent people from acting out themselves, he is suggesting that the harlequinade of his protagonist may produce more reality than ordinary experience allows. All these people who are masked by their own pretences and masked as well by unexamined beliefs, must be duped to become themselves.[8] As the agent of this revelation, the Confidence-Man uses two basic strategies. The first is a matter of overall posture—in all his appearances he is confident. He supposes that men are good, that nature is trustworthy, that fellowship is sincere; and outwardly he presents himself as one acting on such suppositions. As an experimental and tentative gambit, this posture encourages other people and their masks to emerge for what they are. One learns about others by measuring their divergence from the suppositions of trust, whereas outward distrust, the self-fulfilling prophecy, blocks the manifestation of all varieties of trustworthiness. The Confidence-Man's second strategy is more flexibly adapted to each opponent. With good-natured tolerance, he accepts *as hypotheses* the roles that the other players have set for themselves, and he tests their abilities to play out these very roles. In the ensuing games, he tricks his opponents into being *more* themselves.

As the master fictioneer in this world of fictions, the Confidence-Man differs from his opponents by never forgetting that a mask is a mask, that an hypothesis is only an hypothesis. Duplicity cannot fool him, for he treats *all* roles and *all* predicates—including his own—as hypothetical. His victims, in turn, are undone by their ways of losing their hold on the role as fiction: "You played your part better than I did mine; you played it, Charlie, to the life." Their roles are made more demanding by the Confidence-Man's compounding of masks. He knows, as his opponents do not, that within the masquerade of social relations, "character" is the creation of the moment, not the sustained personality of a lifetime. Thus, granting the opposing player's self-definition, the Confidence-Man asks him to play that role with certain complications— principles to discuss, fables from which to draw morals, fictional beings to analyze, conjectures to assess. Each of these hypotheses is a new mask to be superimposed on the given one, and when the player goes "out of character" in sporting the new hypothesis, his original mask is ruptured, and certain other, unacknowledged features of the self emerge. If Winsome claims to be a trusting man, believing that beauty is the sign of love and truth, let him *in that character* discuss the rattlesnake. What the Confidence-Man does, then, is perpetually to create and re-create the momentary characters of each of his opponents.

He further complicates this play of masks by his own guises. He knows that his appearance, manner, and temporary role will help define the role of the other player. His guise as wealthy and trusting Cosmopolitan *creates* Charlie Noble as would-be sharpster. This is another feature of the Confidence-Man's secondary position in the narrative: rather than express himself, he constantly adapts his mask to his immediate opponent. The most striking instance is the advent of "the man from the Philosophical Intelligence Office." Unlike the other major guises of the protagonist, this one appears only to one character, the toughest opponent, Pitch. The P.I.O. man is a role created for the nonce, the man who could officially provide another servant for Pitch but also the wheedling, fawning reminder of the thirty-five boys he has already hired as servants and blusteringly domineered and patronized to his own unacknowledged pleasure. This special personage, however, simply stylizes the protagonist's incessant adaptation, his shifting of roles to match the contingencies of the game.

It is in relation to this deliberate changing of role that we must regard the eight major appearances of the Confidence-Man: the lamb-like man, Black Guinea, the man with the weed, the man in gray (agent of the Seminole Widow and Orphan Asylum), the Black Rapids Coal Agent, the herb-doctor, the man from the Philosophical Intelligence Office, and the Cosmopolitan. We must be careful not to separate these guises too much from each other in our minds nor to stress the internal consistency of each one. The narrator himself seems uneasy with names for his protagonist, like Ringman, Truman, or Goodman. He prefers to indicate him by changeable tags of appearance—the weed, the gray coat, the brass plate. This strategy brings out the protagonist's flexibility *within* the given guise; the Cosmopolitan's manner varies as much in an hour as any earlier appearance does from another. The obvious changes of "person" simply stylize what happens from paragraph to paragraph.

How, then, are we to identify this protagonist? That question reveals the very basis of Melville's experiment with "character" in this book. The issue involves two interrelated acts of faith. First, as fiction readers, we expect a persistent protagonist and thus read a series of "characters" as the same man in disguise. This expectation is related to the habit Melville warns against in Chapter 14—taking one section of a character for the whole. The second act of faith is the widespread American assumption that the outward guises and gestures are severed from the "innermost man," whose integrity is not affected by their mutations. Melville's hypothesis, posed as a question, simultaneously reveals both acts of faith for what they are and demonstrates their problematic nature: What if the protagonist in a fiction were only a succession of shells with no narrative assurance that there even was an innermost man? On the one hand, Melville redirects our attention from underlying identity to momentary gambit. We learn to see how "character" is created and modified for the occasion.

On the other hand, we still ask who this strange and unnerving agent finally *is*. Melville refuses to let us answer that question in terms of personality. Instead he asks us—explicitly in Chapters 14 and 44—to think about the "conception" of a character. And indeed in conception this protagonist is more consistent than any of the other characters is in personality or sense of identity. As Melville forces us to consider paradigms and strategies instead of fixing on the immediate terms of each con game in the book, he abstracts "the Confidence-Man" from all the particular guises in which confidence men have appeared and been historically identified. And when Melville further frees this figure from the limits of particular personality, he produces the Confidence-Man par excellence, a model potent enough to redefine the very nature of social relations.

But there is even more to this protagonist. If he lacks personality and identity in the ordinary senses, if he appears secondary in each immmediate encounter, he gradually comes into the foreground and not merely as an abstract conception or function. His energy and animation come not from personal feelings or impulses or charismatic powers but from the very game he plays. What we come to see in him is not a troubled inner nature or a demonic power but an awesome mastery of his game, often concealed or clouded by our immediate feelings of pity, or at least uneasiness, for one of his "victims." But as he emerges from game after game ever the more aware and less foolish of the contestants, his gamesmanship gradually detaches itself from our moral responses. And in the contest with Charlie Noble, its full brilliance is openly revealed. Charlie is obviously what the other characters turn out to be only when we look a second or third time—a confidence man. He tries to fuddle his victim with wine, cigars, and fast talk, to create an air of confidence by discussing it, and to unsettle his victim's self-possession by story telling. In fact, the entire subject of Indian-hating comes up in the first place merely as a gambit: Charlie wants to gain the Cosmopolitan's confidence by "exposing" Pitch through analogy with Colonel Moredock.

But the Cosmopolitan holds a mirror up to Charlie Noble. He poses hypothetical cases involving each of Charlie's ploys. To reveal Charlie's own nature is, of course, not terribly challenging, especially as he cannot celebrate confidence without maliciously attacking agents of distrust and thus dropping his mask. In this contest of tricksters, however, the real gamesmanship is not only in revealing character but in making it. When the Cosmopolitan states that a man capable of a good loud laugh can hardly be heartless, Charlie explodes into laughter like an automaton. By asking him for money, the Cosmopolitan recasts Charlie as a fair-weather friend. Then he reverses the whole process by ritualistically encircling Charlie with gold coins and providing the first words by which his puppet will be restored to "himself." In the subtler game of making and undoing identities, the Cosmopolitan is exhibiting absolute mastery in the encounter. And because the game here is openly revealed as a game—two con men, both adept at the gambits, neither sympathetic in the usual sense—our fascination with the Confidence-Man's skill is unchecked. We find ourselves, perhaps uneasily, on his "side."

The protagonist is, then, our primary source of knowledge in another sense than as taster of men. He is the representative hero of the narrative world.[9] In the simplest sense, he always wins in a world that turns on contests. He cannot be caught by his own roles or by those of others, because his inward nature, if he has one, is so thoroughly disengaged from the Masquerade as to remain invisible. While tricking each opponent into becoming himself, and thus more generally demonstrating, against the assumptions of Winsome and Emerson, that all inner men get caught in outward shells, the Confidence-Man ironically enacts the public side of Emerson's system. He *does* without *being*. If Emerson's theoretical self, split between "primary" and "secondary" manifestations, actually existed, he would, *to all social appearances*, be like the Confidence-Man. Of course, Emerson's emphasis, and that of the cultural predisposition he reflects, rest officially on the innermost man, and in this sense Melville's hero seems inhuman. But the novel shows how much humanity can be brought into play when the outward masquerade is taken seriously. Emerson postulates a being who can exist quite independent of social relations; Melville counters with an agent who exists only in the mutability of those relations. If the Confidence-Man is only half a creature, he is the half too often officially disregarded, and this is precisely what allows social relations to remain con games. The philosophical cult of the innermost man coexists with its complement, a practical cult that celebrates pure, disengaged outward manipulation, and the Confidence-Man is its unacknowledged hero. He is the Drummond light raying about himself the ideal to which his victims, and perhaps his readers as well, unknowingly aspire.

Something That Follows

The extent to which *The Confidence-Man* offers a broad assessment of nineteenth-century America is suggested by the density and variety of its historical allusions. The figures of Colonel Moredock and Judge James Hall belong to the history of the American West, and many serious issues of this history are reflected in Melville's treatment of Indian-hating.[10] In the Missouri bachelor, Pitch, Melville refracts and recasts some of the qualities associated with the most famous fictional exemplar of frontier existence, Leatherstocking, and also some of the social attitudes of his creator, Cooper.[11] Emerson, Thoreau, Poe, and even Fanny Kemble have been cited as sources for four of the novel's characters,[12] and Melville's very title as well as some of his incidents grow out of the development that enjoyed notoriety in the New York newspapers in 1849—the adventures and arrest of William Thompson, whose exploits gained for him and for the language the sobriquet, "Confidence Man."[13] The recent war with Mexico and the operation of American justice and prisons lie behind the appearance of "the Soldier of Fortune," and various popular bogeys of the mid-nineteenth century are reflected in the comments and suspicions of the passengers—Mormons, Jesuit emissaries, Masons, bandits of the Ohio and Mississippi Valleys.

Finally, aside from the publicly familiar guises of the con man sported by the protagonist and by Charlie Noble, Melville often makes incidental reference to nineteenth-century American phenomena involving the wholesale manipulation of public credulity or distrust: financial panics; wildcat banking; the popular trade in counterfeit detectors; the colony of tuberculars in Mammoth Cave; the anti-Masonic campaign of 1826–27 during which Thurlow Weed coined that exacting name for a counter in the con game, "a good-enough-Morgan"; and some of the famous believe-it-or-not exhibits at P. T. Barnum's American Museum, on top of which, incidentally, was one of Barnum's triumphs of advertising, the first Drummond light seen in New York.[14]

Individually, each of these allusions conveys a satiric comment, but taken together, they suggest a broader purpose. Melville's references to actual persons and events are gradually stripped of their comforting historicity, their unique and local character, as he reveals the patterns that unite them. Such patterns begin to define a culture, for they show the ways in which a group of people in some proximity have tacitly agreed to get along with each other and to discover common values. Ordinarily, such cultural patterns are closely entwined with specific social manners and customs, but Melville was dealing with a new country, compounded out of many varying older societies. Thus the social activities of his characters are not governed by a "society" in the usual sense. Yet despite the extreme fluidity of social forms in the novel, the *Fidèle* is not a scene of anarchy nor are the characters utterly isolated from each other. If the crowds and conversations involve persons unknown to each other, they are not reluctant to talk with strangers.

In fact, their shared problems form the beginnings of a common world. Time after time we find characters trying to establish between themselves some acceptable common beliefs and some credible images of identity. It is as if, despite their civility, they existed prior to law, society, and authority and were trying to create these among themselves, a conjecture made more plausible by the turbulent crowd scenes, which partake equally of town meeting and lynch mob. Overtly they do not succeed in manufacturing a social order; quite the opposite. During the flow of talk, characters are being made and unmade; identities are forged, tested, and eradicated. Strangers to each other, the characters are also strangers to themselves. They must project and make credible not what they know but what they believe themselves to be. Yet covertly this behavior has its own rules and values, virtually a common culture, and *The Confidence-Man* reveals the patterns that make up this covert culture.

Melville's hypothesis, then, is that American social activity is a confidence game. Cut off from mutually accepted authority, his characters play upon each other's credulity to find what can be made credible. Melville's game patterns in the novel serve to stylize and clarify their manipulations. In one sense, the characters seem accustomed to this game playing, for they are shrewd and cautious in watching each other's maneuvers. But again and again their suspicions collapse dramatically in ill-founded and unrecognized acts of faith. As the Confidence-Man, with his dazzling verbal obfuscations, erases the predicates that order his victims' worlds, they find their very identities slipping. The problem is that they cannot see any relations between their outward skeptical game playing and their inward faiths. They act as if their inwardness were not engaged in their social relations. And they find, to their surprise, that it is. The act of faith is what brings the two worlds together. It represents one of the binding values of the covert culture. The characters are literally and figuratively riding the ship of faith.

Their inward faiths, of course, seem to rise above daily life, to make the leap beyond mundane experience that is so characteristic of American religious movements—Puritanism, Evangelical Protestantism, Transcendentalism. But Melville will not rest in such splitting of the self. His repeated religious allusions in the book are entangled with his game patterns to hint that the two ostensibly incongruous realms of experience may cross. And when Melville gathers his opening crowd around the placard offering a reward for the capture of a mysterious imposter, he insinuates even more about the relations of religious and mundane acts of faith:

> As if it had been a theatre-bill, crowds were gathered about the announcement, and among them certain chevaliers, whose eyes, it was plain, were on the capitals, or, at least, earnestly seeking sight of them from behind intervening coats; but as for their fingers, they were enveloped in some myth; though, during a chance interval, one of these chevaliers somewhat showed his hand in purchasing from another chevalier, ex-officio a peddler of money-belts, one of his popular safe-guards, while another peddler, who was still another versatile chevalier, hawked, in the thick of the throng, the lives of Measan, the bandit of Ohio, Murrel, the pirate of the Mississippi, and the brothers Harpe, the Thugs of the Green River country, in Kentucky—creatures, with others of the sort, one and all exterminated at the time, and for the most part, like the hunted generations of wolves in the same regions, leaving comparatively few successors; which would seem cause for unalloyed gratulation, and is such to all except those who think that in new countries, where the wolves are killed off, the foxes increase.

Following upon the opening allusions to Manco Capac and Christ, each "a founder of a new religion," this gathering seems both ironically worldly and appropriately sacramental. The religion celebrated, however, is not for innermost men but for outward selves; if the passengers' souls are presumably engrossed in myths of salvation, their fingers are enveloped in quite another myth. The "original genius" of this myth appears in the icon which has drawn them together and which consecrates their activity, while relics and the lives of the saints are peddled. This extended formal analogue to the advent of a new religion is not a satire on the practice of Christianity but a means of conveying the unofficial regard in which the confidence man and his game are held. And the sacramental is freely mixed with the diverting; in their willingness to be entertained by bold and skillful manipulations, the assembled characters reveal both their susceptibility to con men and their tendency to disengage moral judgment from social activity. Melville quickly associates this gathering with its historical circumstances, typically summing up a culture in one extraordinary sentence. The work of settling a new country has advanced far enough so that the characters are not only smug about their comparative safety from wolves and bandits, but nostalgically titillated by stories of earlier violence and audacity. If they have little to fear, they also have little to bind them together. This gathering is significantly not a community but a "public," and its underlying malaise is apparent in its yearning for even that minimal authority proclaimed by a wanted poster. Into this unnervingly fluid world, its uncertainties suggested in the multivalence of the very prose, comes the Confidence-Man to celebrate its open-endedness and to reaffirm its energies. Many implications of American social history follow upon the adequate conception of this Masquerade.

2

POE'S CREDENTIALS:
The Confidence Man as New World Artist

If we define democracy as the effort to give everything to everybody then you have to put the best light on things in order to sell them, you become preoccupied with appearances, with what looks good or sounds good. You put a premium on the believable rather than the true.

—Daniel Boorstin

[Quality of Birth] is a Commodity that cannot be carried to a worse Market than that of America, where people do not inquire concerning a Stranger, *What is he?* but, *What can he do?*

—Benjamin Franklin

The new individual must work out the whole problem of science, letters and theology for himself; can owe his fathers nothing. There is no history; only biography.

—Ralph Waldo Emerson

It is difficult to begin without borrowing.

—Henry David Thoreau

Poe is a writer who urgently raises the question of credentials. His reputation has not, like Longfellow's, varied with certain broad shifts in public taste. From the first he has been the subject of repeated, strident controversy, drawing on one side surprisingly nasty dismissals, and on the other unmeasured praise and fantastical exegesis. Is he a tragic exemplar of the artist chewed up in a bourgeois society, or is he a jingle man exploiting the banality of his world? How much of him is genius and how much sheer fudge? Does he reveal and explore our night-time impulses, or does he pander to pubescent tastes? Is he an artist or a mechanician? Two things should be noted about this controversy. Despite changes in immediate terminology and techniques of criticism (such as those introduced by Freudianism), the broad bases of disagreement have remained more or less the same, as can be seen in the overlapping of the illustrative questions. And Poe himself seems to have anticipated and indeed encouraged exactly this kind of controversy, writing both the haunting return of Madeline Usher and the Mad Trist of Sir Launcelot Canning, providing a spoof or a dissection for each of his Ravens.

It may be appropriate, then, not to take sides in the dispute and thus play down or disregard the other aspect of Poe but rather to try characterizing his work by the very dialogue it generates. Poe does so many things skillfully when he sets his mind to them that one cannot help suspecting him of being *deliberate* as he moves from horror to claptrap. Perhaps the reason his merits are so often argued is that he was himself exploring the nature of artistic credentials and forcing his readers to inspect the enginery of literary effect. Poe was acutely conscious of being a New World artist, subject at once to thoughtless hostility and ignorant puffery, and he made every effort to establish serious art in America. This is the aspect of Poe that William Carlos Williams seizes on in *In the American Grain*, the impulse to clear the ground, to fight free of a formless mass and begin again. Williams recognizes in Poe's cultural situation both the opportunity to erect literary art and criticism on clear first principles and the preliminary need to lift one's head through a triumphantly successful banality. Thus Poe's buffoonery appears as a savage burlesque of tawdriness, a means of laying bare the things that need the artist's attention.

But Poe's apparent attitudes were not consistently so highminded. He saw the New World not only as a place where artists should begin again but as a milieu in which *all* credentials were being tested. In such circumstances the hoax is more than a means of indirect subversion, it is a representative gesture. Poe's playfulness shows that he relished as much as he disdained the practices of his world. He utilized and then dissected the uncertainties of belief that accompanied the ongoing attempt to sever New World activities from Old World conventions. Rightly understood, the figure of the confidence man provides useful insights into Poe's artistry.

My subject is Poe's fundamental ambivalence. First I discuss nine seemingly separate tendencies in his work, several of them being sources of the impression that he is a banal, mechanical writer.

After establishing these specific components of Poe's ambivalence, I turn to the cultural habits that gave rise to them. And in showing how the apparently diverse tendencies in Poe's work relate to each other and to a broader cultural context, I propose the confidence man as a model through which one can clarify the ambivalence of the artist in a new world.[1]

1. *Literalizing*
"And now I found these fancies creating their own realities, and all imagined horrors crowding upon me in fact." (*The Narrative of Arthur Gordon Pym*)

In Poe's world it is best never to "bet the devil your head," for in pigeon winging your way over a turnstile in order to accept a challenge, you may discover, concealed in the dark archway, an iron bar at neck level. Trite phrases and long-dead metaphors spring into garish actuality, as in "Loss of Breath," and no decorum restrains "the scythe of time" from appearing first as a clock hand cutting slowly through Psyche Zenobia's neck and then as a razor-edged pendulum swinging over a prisoner's breast. When Fortunato will not believe, without a sign, that Montresor is a "mason," Montresor produces a trowel and walls him up. Apparently the thorough banality of one's words or thoughts cannot protect one from their significance, for some terrible yet comic force literalizes the idle phrase. Poe's game is serious; he plays as if one's commonplace habits *mattered.* His simple, shocking assumption is that his characters mean what they say and intend what their gestures imply.

A man contrives a mechanism. He borrows parts that have worked in other contrivances and labels them by function. When he shows his contraption, he tells how each part is to work, why it is there, which gimmicks are makeshift or defective. The machine, he explains, will say "Boo!" It might be Ligeia's husband and his bridal chamber, Roderick Usher and his house, Prince Prospero and his masquerade, or Edgar Poe and his Tale of Terror. The doors creak open, the draperies stir, strange shrieks are heard, a figure pops up and does say "Boo!" And WE JUMP. That is what interested Poe. Banal, jerry-built, shabbily imitative, its moving parts open to view, the contrivance somehow works. Poe's characters hasten to assure themselves that it's only a gaseous exhalation or a fan behind the curtains, that the fiction is hackneyed, that it is only a masquerade, only a formula, only a joke—that, in whatever way, the phenomenon is bounded, improbable, isolated from actual significance. And in assuring themselves, they also assure the reader that there is little reason to believe what they say. But these boundaries—between imagined and actual, between incredible and compelling—break down. Into the paltriest contrivance or the most ludicrous fantasy enters an imp of consummation to perfect the inmost idea, to execute the merely suggested. This imp is the informing spirit of Poe's best tales and many of the poems; he will not be restrained by taste, common sense, reason, or habit.

To say that Poe is a cold-blooded mechanician is not so much false as incomplete. He sets about to demonstrate that the most ludicrous incidents, the tritest details can produce effects that override common sense and skepticism. His subject is the formula that works too well. "The Fall of the House of Usher," for instance, reads as if it had been written to recipe from Burke's *Enquiry into . . . the Sublime and the Beautiful.* Burke's list of causes of the sublime foretells Poe's detail: general privations, depth and height for the idea of vastness, rough and vertical surfaces, minuteness repeated, buildings dark in daytime and light at night, intermittent light and sound, intolerable stench. Burke assigns the sublime a medical function—too continually relaxed a state for muscles and nerves produces melancholy and dejection, and these incumbrances can be cleared by non-noxious terror, which causes the same violent motions of the nerves as pain. Poe's narrator needs exactly this prescription: "There was an iciness, a sinking, a sickening of the heart—an unredeemed dreariness of thought which no goading of the imagination could torture into aught of the sublime." And his experience goads him from torpor back into sensation.

If Burke, following post-Lockean psychology, seems a bit mechanical in explaining how to induce effects on the emotions, Poe extends the impression by his narrator's self-conscious "explanations" along Burkean lines. By making the formula appear explicitly as formulaic, Poe virtually parodies it, as he spoofs the accompanying claptrap with "The Mad Trist" of Sir Launcelot Canning. But no inflation of banality will explode the effect; or rather, the more patently ludicrous the causes, the more purely alarming are the effects. Roderick Usher perishes "a victim to the terrors he had anticipated." After the narrator rationally accounts for the influence of outward objects on his own feelings, "there sat upon my very heart an incubus of utterly causeless alarm." No matter how tawdry or formulary its means, the mind can scare itself to spasms.

Something, then, is missing in Poe's world, the restraints that keep imagination imaginary and that protect us from what we agree not to believe in. More accurately, the boundaries of the actual or the credible have become disarmingly fluid. If the character finds that play has real consequences, readers find themselves drawn in despite their self-conscious incredulity. It is as if Poe were testing some compact about what is credible, and showing personal credulity to be far more erratic than our social and literary conventions would imply. This is why we have more or less agreed to admire Poe and to be embarrassed by our admiration.

2. *Dissection*
"Should you ever be drowned or hung, be sure and make a note of your sensations . . ." ("How to Write a Blackwood Article")

When Poe sends his characters on voyages, he never lets them discover much about new places. Rather than lead somewhere, even into the soul, the journeys provide unusual sensory experience. If the fictional occasions are absurd—a balloon voyage to the moon, the end of the world, mesmerism through death, descent into whirlpools—the sensations have, under the circumstances, some plausibility. Poe cares less about the moon or the bottom of the sea than about the sensory mechanism, and as he invents the sensation appropriate to the singular occurrence, he seems to be reinventing sensation itself. He not only deals with the conventional extremes of terror, anticipation, and pain; he dislocates sensation from sentiment and judgment, isolates the sensory organs from each other, dissects the body, and inflates the most bizarre feelings. Poe contrives extraordinary situations so as to tear experience free from hackneyed responses. He treats the modes of sensation as if no one had ever felt before.

One of Poe's more outrageous burlesques, "A Predicament," provides the key to his concern with sensation. The title seems to refer, with preposterous understatement, to Psyche Zenobia's plight in finding her neck caught in a giant clock face by the descending minute hand. But the "predicament" that interests Poe develops after she starts to come apart. One is surprised at her sensations and then surprised at the surprise. When her first eye falls into the gutter, it winks and blinks at her, which is "inconvenient" as it causes the other eye to wink in sympathy! After both eyes have fallen, her neck is severed, and she is not sorry *"to see"* the head leave the body. And then the perfected idea—"My senses were here and there at one and the same moment." The sillier Poe gets, the more engaging, precisely because of his concern with sensory predicament. When one's common sense dismisses Signora Zenobia's continued feelings, one is still caught up momentarily in minor problems—how could the eye wink without its socket? How could she see the head fall? And these problems refer back to "common sense" in its original signification as the power to unite the evidence of separate sensory organs. How does this work? How does the body "hear" the head? How is intelligible sensation possible at all?

Psyche Zenobia is only one of many figures in Poe-land who go to pieces under the pressure of strange circumstances. Often the image is grotesquely physical: Pym's companion Augustus cannot be conveniently thrown overboard when he dies, for his leg comes off at the grasp; M. Valdemar, seven months dead, but preserved intact by mesmerism, is finally allowed to depart from his flesh, which immediately becomes a liquid mass of putrescence; the narrator who suffers "Loss of Breath" can no longer prove on the glass that he is alive and thus loses his ears, his nose, and several of his viscera before being hanged and buried alive.

This garish motif involves more than an obsessive loathing of the flesh. Hans Pfaall's semi-comic reasoning about the new environments to which the body *ought* to be capable of adjusting suggests the experimentalism of Poe's attitude. Even when his writing is highly serious, he dismembers the sensory mechanism and rearranges the faculties. He places his characters in predicaments that break up the habitual clusters of sensation and judgment, thus forcing them to explore the unimproved frontier of sensation, where the senses are individually too acute, like Roderick Usher's, and where no proprieties have been established to attach certain sensations, like those of sliding down a whirlpool, to the inevitable sentiment, like horror. Poe's characters nonchalantly continue to have sensations when they should be dead, and their responses are often ludicrously inappropriate. What they test is propriety itself.

Poe's sensory experimentalism begins in analysis, but it has a synthetic impulse as well, like the culture it reflects. If tales like "A Predicament" and "Loss of Breath" take the self apart to see how it works, others like "The Man That Was Used Up" and "The Spectacles" project selves rebuilt from artificial components. Brevet Brigadier-General John A. B. C. Smith is a thorough tribute to "a wonderfully inventive age!" Not only has the "odd-looking bundle of something" that was used up after the Bugaboo and Kickapoo battles been refurbished with the best in manufactured legs, arms, shoulders, bosoms, wigs, teeth, eyes, and palates; it has also been built up out of set phrases in churches, theaters, card games, and newspapers as one of the "remarkable" heroes of the age. He is in every sense a "made" man, thrust forward as Poe's playful hypothesis about the relation between personal identity and public life following the era of Jackson. The appeal of Poe's sensational characterization is to an inventive, analytic, technological, puzzle-solving people, for whom the self is a clever mechanism but one that could be refitted.

3. *Analysis of Sensibility*

"Of the innumerable effects, or impressions, of which the heart, the intellect, or (more generally) the soul is susceptible, what one shall I, on the present occasion, select?" ("The Philosophy of Composition")

Poe takes his characters apart to see how they work. His readers, too, he finds it necessary to dismember. Concerned more about the effectiveness than the intrinsic qualities of a tale or a poem, Poe divides the reader's sensibility into components, each subject to its own excitation, and he analyzes the literary work in turn by its "modes of inculcation," its operations on specific fragments of the psyche. Whether as receptor of sensation or reader of literature, the human being appears to Poe as a set of fragments, some of which are isolated by the concerns or stimuli of the moment, the rest temporarily disregarded.

Each of the various organs or faculties has its own office, and the overall implication of Poe's criticism is that these offices are mutually exclusive, that the engagement of one virtually rules out the engagement of another. The precision with which Truth appeals to the intellect, for example, is antagonistic to the power of Beauty to elevate the soul; and Passion, in exciting the heart, degrades the soul. Apparently the self can use only one faculty at a time. In many of the tales passion or temporary hope excludes thought, whereas the coolness of despair restores curiosity and analysis.

One can account for the apparent discrepancy between Poe's mechanistic treatment of technique and his exalted sense of the poet by noting that his emphasis on "supernal beauty" signals a certain irreverence for human experience. Since the ideal, the organic, the unitary belong to another world, it may seem less than blasphemous to analyze inhabitants of *this* world as mechanisms. The ideal poet Israfel can surrender to the authenticity of his passions, for he inhabits that other realm where "the ecstasies above" suit his "burning measure." But whatever Poe may say of Israfel, "Whose heart-strings are a lute," he often treats the earthly artist as a psychologist-technician, who analyzes the reader's soul in order to contrive a mechanism which will produce the desired effects on that soul. Not what the poet says but what the poem does to the reader—this is the immediate locus of Poe's criticism. The dropping of the water on the rock, the pressing steadily down of the stamp upon the wax, the esthetic value in ratio of the elevating excitement—in such metaphors Poe represents the power of art. The corollary questions "How did he do that?" and "How does that work?" apply simultaneously to reader and to literary artifact; they represent the essence of Poe's critical method. There is unintentional appropriateness, then, in his elegant defense of American potentiality in the arts against commonplace slander: "Having been forced to make railroads, it has been deemed impossible that we should make verse. Because it suited us to construct an engine in the first instance, it has been denied that we could compose an epic in the second."

4. *Testing Credibility*
"Tellmenow Isitsöornot" ("The Thousand-and-Second Tale of Scheherazade")

Poe's stress on "effect" in analyzing literature reorients the artist's primary concern from the demands of his subject to the disposition of his audience. Not only must the writer study the psychic faculties he wishes to excite; he must also investigate credence and credibility, conviction and the means of manipulating it. Poe's own interest in these matters is emphatic and persistent. "The Thousand-and-Second Tale of Scheherezade" sets the credible fictions of the Arabian Tales against the unbelievable "facts" of recent technology and discovery. In scornfully commenting on the European reception of "Mesmeric Revelation" and "The Facts in the Case of M. Valdemar," Poe is equally amused by the credulity with which the tales were generally accepted and by the inadequate grounds on which the few skeptics argued their disbelief. And such characteristic assessments of belief are merely the overt manifestations of Poe's thorough engagement with the machinery of conviction.

Ironically, it is neither Poe's imaginative literature nor his critical analyses but his "Book of Truths" about "the Material and Spiritual Universe" that most fully develops the implications of his interest in manipulating belief. *Eureka* does not read like the record of a mind's search for truth, nor does it have the bardic authority of inspiration or the scientific authority of clear demonstration. Its "cosmology" indeed often seems an excuse for a series of observations and experiments regarding the bases of human conviction. "In the conduct of this Discourse," Poe argues, with a comment pertaining also to the rhetoric of the tales, "I am aiming less at physical than at metaphysical order. The clearness with which even material phaenomena are presented to the understanding, depends very little, I have long since learned to perceive, upon a merely natural, and almost altogether upon a moral, arrangement." He seems to mean that he adjusts his language and movement of thought not to the nature of his subject but to the capacities and predispositions of his audience. What but a "moral arrangement" could account for the language of Poe's astrophysics—"that the appetite for Unity among the atoms is doomed to be satisfied *never*"; "Rëaction is the return from the condition of *as it is and ought not to be* into the condition of *as it was, originally, and therefore ought to be*"; "the majestic remnants of the tribe of Stars flash, at length, into a common embrace"?

In contrast with his earlier systematic separation of Poetry and Truth, Poe here argues that the two are one, for the "truths" of *Eureka* have more to do with the capacities of the soul to be moved and convinced than with the properties of the observable universe. The criteria of truth are esthetic—symmetry, consistency, simplicity, reciprocity. It satisfies the soul. The test of a "philosophic" explanation is its capacity to give pleasure by a simple accounting for complex phenomena, and the "force of conviction" is "proportional to the amount of *complexity* intervening between the hypothesis and the result." Poe scorns the limits, the rules, and the methods of scientific proof: "according to the schools, I *prove* nothing. So be it:—I design but to suggest—and to *convince* through the suggestion." He is not merely defending intuitive as against demonstrable truth, but shifting the locus of demonstration. Not what can be shown and verified—truth is what can be made compelling.

More is involved here than the rhetorician's efforts to persuade. *Eureka* is filled with methodological asides—explanations of local intent, descriptions of rhetorical procedure, summaries of the techniques and laws of persuasion. Rather than conceal itself, Poe's art revels in open display of its means. Poe is not only concerned himself with problems of credence and conviction; he assumes that his readers have a lively interest in such issues, that they enjoy being told exactly how they are being convinced or moved. Poe dismantles his own machinery of persuasion as avidly as he disassembles the logic, the scientific hypotheses, the experiments and argumentation of others. For an audience initially interested in how the universe works, he guesses an analogous interest in how philosophical or scientific transactions work. In another context, also an analysis of credibility, he suggests the function of all this explicitness about methodology: "Pleased at comprehending, we often are so excited as to take it for granted that we assent."

5. *Suggestiveness*

"We do not hesitate to say that a man highly endowed with the powers of Causality . . . will, even with a very deficient share of Ideality, compose a finer poem . . . than one who, without such metaphysical acumen, shall be gifted, in the most extraordinary degree, with the faculty of Ideality. For a poem is not the poetic faculty, but the *means* of exciting it in mankind." (Review of Drake's *Culprit Fay* and Halleck's *Alnwick-Castle*)

Poe has a poetics of deliberate suggestiveness. The "poetic sentiment" appertains to experience that we cannot have as human beings; we thirst for "supernal beauty," which is not afforded "by any existing collocation of earth's forms," and poesy tries to satisfy this thirst "by *novel* combinations." What Poe all but says is that the poet's business is pure illusion; he contrives "multiform combinations among the things and thoughts of Time" to give an indeterminate glimpse of what cannot, by its nature, be grasped now. For Poe the poem is a deliberate assemblage of components which can, in combination, produce an effect beyond the power of the constituents and not entirely within the grasp or determination of the poet himself. If the faculty of Ideality, which intuits the supernal, is related to the ends of poetry, the poet himself needs rather the organ of Causality to analyze psychic effects, "without even conceiving the nature of these effects," and thus to simulate the ethereal by practicable means. He creates, exactingly and in full deliberation, an instrument to evoke the indeterminate, as with Tennyson, who seems to have proposed to himself "a suggestive indefinitiveness of meaning, with the view of bringing about a definitiveness of vague and therefore of spiritual *effect*." The mystic is the technician's implied alter ego.

The status of "meaning" in a literary work is related for Poe to this deliberate suggestiveness. If an intellectual or moral purpose is uppermost, the work commits "the heresy of the didactic." If a secondary meaning accompanies the overt concerns and becomes excessive, so as to interfere with them, the work involves "allegory," for which Poe can find no serious defense. But if a suggested meaning "runs through the obvious one in a *very* profound undercurrent," it can provide a richness "which we are too fond of confounding with *the ideal*." "Meaning," then, is simply a device that brings about a desired effect; if it has a decided, determinate character (that is, if it is comprehensible), it mars the ethereal quality of the work. Although Poe presumably did not compose "The Raven" so methodically as his reconstruction suggests, it is significant that he chooses to analyze the last two stanzas as an addition of "complexity" and "suggestiveness" calculated to impart ideality to the whole. Although supernal beauty is for Poe the ground of Poesy and of the poetic sentiment, it can be neither incorporated within a poem nor grasped by a human being. The poem is not a bridge between mundane and supernal, but a contrivance designed to simulate the effects of such a bridge.

6. *Boundaries and Clear Steps*

"It is the curse of a certain order of mind, that it can never rest satisfied with the consciousness of its ability to do a thing. Still less is it content with doing it. It must both know and show how it was done." (*Marginalia*)

Despite his esthetic aspiration to "suggestive indefinitiveness," Poe's imagination fixes on the determinate. Even when he extols the supernal, he is concerned to mark off precisely those aspects of the self to which it appeals; he refers to the realm of the poet's authority as "the circumscribed Eden of his dreams." When he admits that "Poesy" cannot be defined, he immediately turns his attention to the poetic sentiment, which *can* be described distinctly enough for practical analysis. The buried metaphors of Poe's critical language characteristically indicate limits and boundaries, as his critical habits emphasize distinction and definition, the marking off of areas within which analysis can be exact. His faith in the power of words, precisely used, approaches arrogance: "I have never had a thought which I could not set down in words."

More is involved here than a demand for clarity of expression. To Poe the finest quality of a thinking mind is to comprehend its own operations as it performs them. Dupin is the fictional exponent of this self-cognizance, as the speaker of "The Philosophy of Composition" is the critical one. Not only does Poe attempt to seize the very processes of creation and choice, but he dramatizes the analytic mind solving a puzzle and discovering the means of solution in the analysis of its own procedures and barriers. Rather than imply a superhuman penetration in the minds of his great analysts—Dupin and the speakers of *Eureka* and of the critical treatises—Poe points to the inadequacies of their supposed peers—the Parisian police, the Baconian and Aristotelian philosophers of science, the dominant literary critics—who apply their methods rigidly because they do not examine their own mental processes or intentions. Better the ungraceful explicitness of a mind puzzled at itself than the smooth conventionality of one who takes for granted that he knows how to think.

Of Poe's method William Carlos Williams says the perfect thing: "Constantly he labored to detach SOMETHING from the inchoate mass." Whether it be the vagueness of unformed thought or the blurring of issues through habitual usage, the amorphous makes Poe uneasy until he can wrest from it a clear statement, a rule, a definition. Not only hints and intuitions but shadowy processes as well Poe wants to formulate. Throughout the tales one finds emotive developments and rapid mental operations broken down into clear sequences of steps, certain of which, like those accompanying burial alive, can be transposed from one context to another as if the process had been systematically defined for all occasions. Poe's interest in mechanistic rules for thought and feeling is the most striking expression of his concern for the determinate. Rather than share experience, he wants to simulate it, to reduce habit to formula. In criticism this means beginning as if there were no customary procedures. Poe's minute analyses of grammar, prosody, plot show his urge to determine the sources of pleasure, to establish the rules by which art is effective.

If it merely appeared in his critical practice, Poe's determinateness could be ascribed to a desire for clarity, system, a firmly based esthetic. But it is more extreme, a radical penchant for finitude, delimitation. If something must be complex or extensive, Poe wants to demonstrate that it is composed of simple elements clustered by simple rules—spirit is refined matter; morality extends the principle of reaction; metaphysics is physics made subtle. What cannot be accommodated to such a scheme must be broken up, so that certain parts can be considered in isolation.

The worlds of the best tales and poems are tightly hemmed in, and Poe's comment on the fact is revealing: "it has always appeared to me that a close *circumscription of space* is absolutely necessary to the effect of insulated incident." Insulated from what? From complexity, distraction, inappropriate habits or sentiments, from the full personality and from the shared human world. Poe dislikes the novel and the long poem, the multiplication of characters and the elaboration of poetic feet, the unexplainable insight and the complex personality. Whatever suggests the absence of bounds he rejects, as he rejects the idea of an infinite universe. Only in a finite universe can those self-contained, reflexive, symmetric, consistent "truths" be true at all.

7. Puzzle Solving

"Now, I have elsewhere observed that it is by just such difficulties as the one now in question—such roughnesses—such peculiarities—such protuberances above the plane of the ordinary—that Reason feels her way, if at all, in her search for the True." (*Eureka*)

Poe's emphasis on containment and formula makes him peculiarly vulnerable to whatever thwarts or intrudes, to angels of the odd and imps of the perverse. In his fiction and his commentaries he does allow for contingency and entanglement, but threatening as these experiences appear, they turn out to be illusory. The defining movement is the emergence of design, and the whimsical elements that conceal the design only make the effort to discover it more engaging and artful. Torn between his wish for simple laws and his fear of chance and confusion, Poe becomes a contriver of puzzles.

The very processes of comprehension appear in Poe's work as a mode of puzzle solving. He splits perception into distinct elements—sensation and analysis. The period of sensation is dominated by chance and oddity: "We had seen and felt, but we could neither think nor act, until, alas, too late." In contrast, the work of reflection and analysis proceeds with an exaggerated disengagement from feeling. Thus protagonists in such tales as *Pym*, "A Descent into the Maelstrom," and "The Pit and the Pendulum" appear alternately in fragmented guises—a passive self swept along by sensation, and an active self coolly discerning useful patterns. Rather than show the understanding in complex immediate interaction with the senses and the feelings, Poe reserves it for the assessment of mysterious data, the solution of puzzles posed by experience. The alternation of terror and rational analysis is a familiar sequence in gothic fiction, but Poe's interest is less in the supernatural elements legitimized by such a procedure than in the protagonist's discernment of pattern in the confusion. Instead of contriving an explanation so as to exploit magical beliefs or to reveal their psychic sources, he contrives the predicament so as to exploit the pleasure of resolution. The Sphinx, apparently a horrible beast crawling down a distant slope, is reduced, after the narrator's intense description and compulsory swoon, to an acceptable pattern—a small insect crawling down a spider's filament a sixteenth of an inch from the narrator's eye.

From Pym's strenuous sufferings and their later rationalizations, it is a short step to the fright contrived in "The Sphinx" so that calm intellection can make its final showing. The same pattern, projected and generalized, reappears as the core of the detective story. C. Auguste Dupin is the representative hero of Poe's world, and disentangling is the supreme achievement. Not actions or voyages or conflicts, but puzzles to solve—these are the accomplishments Poe sets for his characters. In "Maelzel's Chess Player" he solves the problem of the automaton, and in *Eureka* he solves the problem of the universe. Each of the Dupin stories has a puzzle as its very impetus, as do such other stories as "The Gold-Bug" and "Thou Art the Man!," but even the less ratiocinative tales are filled with smaller problems and their ingenious solutions—Pfaall's water-dripping alarm clock, Pym's phosphor rubbings to read a letter in the dark. Whenever possible, Poe turns from narrative as a mode of development to mystery and resolution.

Poe appeals to a special cast of imagination, one that does not regard human experience as a development of complications and consequences but seizes rather on enigmas to be resolved by the intellect as detective. In its elementary form, this is the imagination that delights in conundrums, secret codes, cryptography—the disentangling of what someone else has entangled. It involves a faith that oddness, accident, indeterminacy are merely screens; that what appears peculiar actually provides a clue; that mechanical problems have more actuality than moral or social ones. Such are the illusions that Dupin quickens and that Poe's art sustains. By constructing artificially isolated arenas, virtual game spaces, Poe converts the protuberance to the means of explication—the bizarreness of the violence in the Rue Morgue isolates the agent as playful Ourang-Outang, and a cloud appearing in *Eureka* is sure to conceal *the* answer needed at the moment, for it is assumed that the universe is bounded and artfully contrived.

8. *Diddling*

"Diddling—or the abstract idea conveyed by the verb to diddle—is sufficiently well understood. Yet the fact, the deed, the thing, *diddling*, is somewhat difficult to define. We may get, however, at a tolerably distinct conception of the matter in hand, by defining—not the thing, diddling, in itself—but man, as an animal that diddles." ("Diddling")

Although his commonly anthologized tales and poems make one think of Poe as a haunted man, an explorer of forbidden and disturbing inner ground, the bulk of his work yields as easily to the inference that he cannot pass up a good hoax. Not merely a playful means to insinuate officially disowned matters, diddling is itself serious for Poe, as is the public susceptibility to it. He delights in exposing a hoax, like that of "Maelzel's Chess Player," and he delights in perpetrating one, as in "The Balloon-Hoax," "The Facts in the Case of M. Valdemar," and "Mesmeric Revelation." In fact, his very gambits for publicity—the ones just cited, the challenge that he could solve any cryptogram sent in, the exploitation of "The Raven" by "The Philosophy of Composition"—repeatedly take shape in his grasp of the correlation between notoriety and hoaxes: one may make money by tricking the public, but one is certain to find a larger market for showing how it was done. Poe seems willing not only to burlesque his own serious themes but to capitalize on the suspicion that he is a trickster.

Poe's practical criticism—his minute analysis of how the literary apparatus works to create effects—converges with his habit of suspecting and exposing imposture. That he compulsively charges other writers with plagiarism is only a superficial aspect of his methodical revelation of tricks of the trade. From Dickens's machinations with plot in *Barnaby Rudge* to Elizabeth Barrett's "quaint" phrasing for indefinite effects, he seizes on the particular means by which an artist manipulates the reader's response. Often the exposure is part of a savage attack on sham artistry, but even when Poe admires a work, he delights in showing how it was done. When he turns from the individual artist to the literary establishment, however, there is little ambiguity in his denunciation of humbug. Again his emphasis is on how the literary con game works, how critic and publisher relate by blackmail, how coteries manipulate reputations by puffery, how machination triumphs over merit.

Yet denunciation is not the primary spirit in which Poe assesses diddlers. His title "Diddling: Considered as One of the Exact Sciences" expresses the combination of play and bland curiosity with which he confronts hoaxes, and the essay itself shows his delight at recounting good diddles. In this it resembles several other minor tales and parodies that turn on dramatized tricks: "The Business Man," "A Tale of Jerusalem," "Thou Art the Man!," "The Duc de L'Omelette," "Bon Bon," "X-ing a Paragrab." Poe seems to be drawing on and appealing to a popular tradition of diddling lore. But he is not content to swap tales. Diddling, like other human activities, must have a formulable theory, and Poe breaks the "compound" down into its "ingredients": "minuteness, interest, perseverance, ingenuity, audacity, *nonchalance,* originality, impertinence, and *grin.*" The entire analysis is shrewd and instructive. Poe knows the delicate balance of feelings appropriate to the diddler, the absence of nerves in public and the capacity for private enjoyment of the day's work.

When Poe argues that the diddler is guided by self-interest, however, he broaches a difficult issue and contradicts himself. Although diddling clearly involves a spirited regard for "the main chance"

("He looks to Number One. You are Number Two, and must look to yourself"), Poe's own practice belies his assertion that the diddler "scorns to diddle for the mere *sake* of the diddle." In fact, several of Poe's "modern instances" involve effort entirely out of proportion to the monetary gain. And his analysis of the diddler's art, like his analysis of the allied science of "Mystification," shows a concern more joyous and systematic than would be appropriate to what Poe could actually regard as a scramble for booty. He is not entirely joking when he asserts of man, "To diddle is his destiny." This exact science offers an intrinsic satisfaction which Poe exploits in three of his finest tales, each the story of a very good diddle indeed, "The Purloined Letter," "The Cask of Amontillado," and "Hop-Frog."

9. Reflexive Worlds
"Nemo me impune lacessit." ("The Cask of Amontillado")

Montresor's motto and his arms—a foot crushing a serpent whose fangs are embedded in the heel—describe perfectly the essential reflexiveness of Poe's imagined world. It is a world of vengeance and retribution. The force that has been walled up or seemingly destroyed (red death, conscience, madman, rival, lover, sister, cat) somehow gets back. The oppressor is thwarted; wrongs are redressed; the disturbance is corrected. "Justice," even "poetic justice," will not quite describe this model, for there is no agency, divine or political, responsible for its operation, and one's pleasure at the spectacle is not primarily moral. Rather than delight at the appropriate punishment decreed by an adequate judge, one watches the inevitable and exacting reflex. Poe's aggressors are not brought to trial; like William Wilson, they act against a mirror. Moreover, the image of a balance has less to do with Poe's tales than the image of a circuit. As response circles back on provocation, "wrong" and "retribution" become counterparts, and the language of moral discrimination folds in on itself: "I must not only punish," says Montresor, "but punish with impunity. A wrong is unredressed when retribution overtakes the redresser." What power Poe can give his characters arises as a response, not an initiative. It is expressed in analysis, diddles, and revenge. William Wilson and his double gather their force by thwarting each other, and Hop-Frog borrows his power from the tyrants he destroys. Rather than assert mastery over others, Poe's figures pair off in mutual and measured opposition.

It is not action but reaction that characterizes Poe's tales. The voyages do not trace the progress of the protagonist's will but rather catalogue his sensations and analytical responses to bizarre phenomena. The tales of vengeance and the disentanglements both involve secondary actions, as does Poe's more general fascination with puzzle solving. If his characters do not assert themselves in plans or initiatives, neither do they properly express themselves in their conduct. Instead, they analyze the maneuvers of others, resolve the predicaments in which they find themselves, and impersonate or burlesque their opponents.

More abstractly regarded, Poe's world is a closed system of action and reaction. This formulation will account for the cosmology in *Eureka* as well as vengeance and puzzle solving in the tales. In place of an endlessly elaborating sequence of causes and effects, he projects a system of reciprocity. The closure of the system allows all parts to interrelate, making cause and effect interchangeable. In plot analyses as well, Poe is less interested in narrative sequence than in cross-reference and mutual adaptation of parts. Like the Universe, a proper plot is "that in which no part can be displaced without ruin to the whole." He frequently describes the process of composition—other authors' as well as his own—as a working backwards from denouement to initial complication, final effects literally causing the earlier causes. Although the fragments of action derived from the predetermined reaction may simulate an open-ended, complex actuality (consider simply the first half of "Murders in the Rue Morgue"), the procedure itself and the systemic enclosure convert reality to a game. If there is crude brutality in the actions of ourang-outangs, kings, and counsellors, the reactions of Dupin and Hop-Frog convert it to art.

These closed systems are, of course, stylized and sealed off from the ongoing entanglement of human experience. More is involved in the transmutation than the familiar principle that art orders life, for here the order is a peculiarly simplified game of puzzle solving, and one can see some reason for T. S. Eliot's referring Poe's imagination to our pubescence. But there is another way of looking at these closed systems. With the reflexive response looping back on the disturbance, the systems are self-corrective. Like a steam engine and an ecosystem, they are cybernetic models, and the concept of identity is subtly altered within such systems. The similarity of the House of Usher to an ecosystem is obvious. But more generally, Poe's characters find that they cannot act on or against something else without personal consequence; their "selves" are not sealed within their own skins. In acting on the system, they affect themselves, and the reaction shares the nature of the action. It is not so much Dupin's power matched against the ourang-outang's, but a power in the system that contains Dupin and ourang-outang, with the former taking his "character" from the latter. In a time when it is urgent that we more humbly conceive our place in a larger system, Poe's tales may help us in imagining ourselves.

The Winnebago Indians had a culture hero, Wakdjunkaga, a trickster who is the subject of an elaborate cycle of stories. He begins his career by violating the tribal rituals of the warpath, breaking the sacred and practical implements of warfare and hunting, arguing that his *bow* cannot fight, only *he* can. He reverts from a tribally familiar world to an existence with neither human nor animal adaptations, clumsy, erratically cunning, and disintegrated. During his adventures his right arm gets into a quarrel with his left and wounds it, and when his anus fails to keep its appointed watch over a dinner while he sleeps, Wakdjunkaga deliberately burns it in anger. Something like this is going on in Poe's world. What I have been describing in his work are separate manifestations of a cultural phenomenon, a cast of mind and feeling that Poe both exemplifies and portrays. It is peculiarly adapted to the New World, not as primitive frontier, but as the Old World dismembered, a new country in which inherited habits come apart, in which virtually nothing is taken for granted. Having been freed of certain social and political forms of the European past, the representative inhabitant of this New World finds himself questioning more radically the order and integration of daily life. If Melville in *The Confidence-Man* projects the masquerade of social relations in a country without a shared order, Poe projects the masquerade of technology. In this world of technicians, analysis is the essential act. Everything is taken apart, the sensory-nervous system, the body, the reader's psyche, the mechanism of persuasion, the rhythm of poems, the chess-playing automaton. The world is recast by two simple questions: How did he do it? How does it work?

The subtler complexes of feeling and assumption—manners, sentiments, moral responses—seem to have come undone in Poe's world, as if civilization had failed to transmit its tacit effects. This is what Allen Tate is responding to in the work of "Our Cousin, Mr. Poe," when he argues that the characters have sensations without "sensibility," that their naked sensitivities are not "regulated to the forms of the human situation."[2] If they seem to Tate to be "machines of sensation and will," operating without moral consciousness or a shared human world, it is because all the settled habits and beliefs that made the world shareable have been unsettled again. Although the social, moral, and esthetic know-how of the European past has not been left entirely behind, it no longer tacitly guides the conduct and feelings of the characters. The old implicit bonds between individual and humanity have been made explicit, open to question, and even the interior habits that integrate sensation with feeling and action have broken down.

There is another way as well in which convention has lost its authority in Poe's work. In our daily experience we ordinarily could reach reasonable agreement about what to believe and what to doubt, what to take seriously and what to regard as fanciful. Although the situation is obviously more complicated in imaginative literature, here too conventions have developed, especially within literary types or genres, to help us know how to "take" a given incident, what to expect. But in Poe's work figures of speech materialize and games turn serious. No common sense or taste interferes with the most bizarre extension of an imagined experience. If the characters are not protected from their own idle fancies, the reader is not protected by consistency of literary convention. At his most serious, Poe can suddenly turn buffoon. He seems to be searching for the point at which a literary convention will explode into burlesque or the point at which an absurd situation will command serious response. He tests a reader's capacity to believe and to resist belief, and he shows that neither act is dependable enough to be taken for granted.

On the one hand, then, Poe represents a world in which taste, common sense, convention, sensibility—the integrating assumptions and habits—have either broken down or lost credit. On the other hand, he shows a radical propensity to analyze. The loss of authority in the old models of conduct encourages, even forces, the habit of analysis, and this habit further dismembers the inherited world. Poe's situation as artist, in other words, is closely related to the conditions he projects in his tales, poems, and criticism. That he takes the "New World" seriously is apparent in his constant demands for originality.[3] Yet he cannot literally start again; there are too many models. "Originality" and "invention" come to mean, not a pristine relationship to raw experience, but a new attitude toward traditional forms, especially esthetic ones. Instead of mastering and adapting the conventions of his medium, the artist disassembles them, scrutinizes their workings, and rigs a new contrivance from the fragments. This seems to be Poe's meaning when he argues that the second element of Poesy is the attempt to satisfy the thirst for supernal beauty by *"novel combinations, of those combinations which our predecessors, toiling in chase of the same phantom, have already set*

in order.'' His constant effort to establish art and criticism on clear
first principles expresses both his habit of dissecting conventions
and his uneasiness about the public status of art. In analyzing and
reinventing his trade, he is also trying to re-establish on explicit
grounds the credentials of art in America and of his own role as
artist.

Poe's response to his situation as New World artist may be
quirky and extreme, but it also illuminates the more general situation of the New World technician and artisan, the provincial who
has not lost the European past, only its habitual familiarity, who
knows the social forms by etiquette books and architectural forms
by burlesque. In place of inherited assumption, patient apprenticeship, tacit agreement, this technician demands explicit laws of procedure. The secret of both his comic crudities and his technological
power is that he analyzes all accepted methods, reduces habitual
process to painstaking formula, translates *savoir faire* to how-to-do-
it. Thus Poe composes a "Rationale of Verse" to establish prosody
on clear numerical grounds, codifying the measures of verse and
syllable so that one could write or read by rule and not "by ear,"
reinventing the ear itself, not as organ but as mechanism.

The impulse is the same behind the etiquette book, the rationale
of verse, and the analysis of sensation—to convert natural, integral,
habitual, or more generally, complex and undifferentiated processes
into distinct, clear steps. It is the expression of machine technology,
replacing organic wholeness with duplicable parts. The cyborg was
not born yesterday. The strengths of the New World technician are
ingenuity, contrivance, and analysis. He is uneasy with moral, social, and organic complexity. For open-ended difficulties he substitutes game spaces, limited and determinate models, puzzles to be
solved by technical facility. Poe's concerns for boundedness, for design, for reflexive and closed systems all show his affiliation with
the New World technician, a figure also projected in the characters
themselves, with their love of masquerades and enclosures, crypts
and cryptograms.

The representative figure I have called the New World technician
is not to be equated with the confidence man; he is a preliminary
phase of this interesting agent, inhabiting the same world, responding to the same shifty conditions, preparing the ground. Both
arise in a world that has inherited models without the customary
feelings, a world in which common sense, established boundaries,
old integrations have to be renegotiated, in which habit must be
replaced by technique. The New World technician steps into this
fluid world and tastelessly asks how things work and how people

act, as if such matters had not been settled. As old pieties disappear, so do traditional place and patient apprenticeship, leaving a new opportunity for personal facility, reinvestigation of procedure, improvisation. When the New World technician reduces complex process to duplicable parts, he provides the model by which the con man reduces another's gestures to imitable steps and dissects habits of belief so as to manipulate them. The tendency to isolate game spaces is also common to technician and con man. By tinkering with immediate processes and local gambits, they sever means from ends, obscuring questions about purpose by the dazzling manipulation itself.

But the con man goes beyond the New World technician, and Poe goes with him. The confidence man sees more opportunities in New World fluidity, not merely to improve his lot by cleverness and technical proficiency but actually to recast the self through cunning imitation. He becomes the specialist in secondary, reproducible identities. Similarly, he goes beyond technical improvisation to burlesque. The severance of inherited models from inherited certainties provides him with the chance not merely to improvise freely in method but to exploit the new subjective uneasiness, to experiment both with technique and with its overtones. When the technician detaches a manipulable segment from complex experience, he ignores the rest, blandly taking the larger effects for granted while he looks skeptically at the immediate instrument. The con man is the New World technician with an added interest in effects.

What, in essence, is the confidence game? It is the creation of an inner effect, an impression, a belief that surpasses the grounds for it. The model appears repeatedly in Poe's work. Tawdry formulas work too well. Mechanical contrivances are overpowered by a spirit that perfects their secret implications. Gloom, superstition, and fear transcend their causes, and sentiments are dissociated from sensations. Poe's theoretical interests have the same pattern: technical exactitude serving the indefinite; reversibility of cause and effect; unmotivated or inadequately explained occurrences. The effects within the worlds of the tales converge with the operation of the story on the reader, for the literalization of phrases within the fiction is the equivalent of a shifting attitude toward the tale, a change in belief, and this is the locus of Poe's experimentation.

The con man differs from the New World technician, then, by operating within the closed game space in such a way as to suggest something—confidence—outside the container. He not only analyzes technical means but dissects the process by which these maneuvers indirectly influence people's attitudes. The confidence man is the technologist of belief. He analyzes credibility and credulity, diddlers and their effects. His experiments with technique are less involved with how to do his task better, than with how to make his operations more effective. His art, par excellence, is to manipulate effects, to burlesque human activities, to contrive beliefs. If Poe is a stylized exemplar of all these qualities, he is not isolated from other American artists. Such varying writers as Emerson and Melville, Mark Twain and James, Dickinson, Stevens, and Faulkner share Poe's skeptical attitude toward his medium, his effort to see how it can have any effects at all. Many curious features of American prose and poetry emerge from this scrutiny, irreverent, deliberate, even crude, into the very elements of literary belief.

II

How To Do It:
Making a Self
for Fun and Profit

3

BENJAMIN FRANKLIN AND
THE MODEL SELF

Anybody could have done it.

—*Mark Twain's comment on Franklin's
famous entrance to Philadelphia*

I did not care what it was all about. All I wanted to know was how to
live in it. Maybe if you found out how to live in it you learned from
that what it was all about.

—*Hemingway's Jake Barnes*

My present trade is the only one that requires no apprenticeship.

—*Jeremy Diddler*

Those who have the time and talent to perform a task well may not,
because of this, have the time or talent to make it apparent that they
are performing well.

—*Erving Goffman*

Many a small thing has been made large by the right kind of advertising.

—*The Connecticut Yankee*

I didn't want you to think I was just some nobody.

—*Jay Gatsby*

How did a country that prided itself on innocence and exemplary
rectitude ever develop as a culture hero—even a covert one—so ambiguous a being as the confidence man? To understand the powerful attraction of this figure, one must begin with the set of popular
aspirations, habits, and beliefs that seemed for generations to be
positively associated with the idea of America. These include the

success ethic with its icon of the self-made man; the promissory tradition with its hero, the booster; and the cult of practical ingenuity, as celebrated by the jack-of-all-trades. These figures often overlap in practice, and that is in part because they arise from similar conditions and embody common attitudes. It is in giving us access to those similarities that the confidence man is so valuable a model, for he is the complex figure who gathers the gestures, habits, and values of several specialized popular icons and shows their hidden significance.

The root of the matter is a peculiar sense of the self, at once buoyant and practical, visionary and manipulative. To *make a self*—such is the audacious undertaking that brings one into a world of masks and roles and shape-shifters, that requires one to manipulate beliefs and impressions, that elevates technical facility and gives one the heady sense of playing a game. The central document of such self making is Franklin's *Autobiography*. My purpose in this section is to clarify the significance of the model self projected there and to trace its development in more specialized forms in the nineteenth century.

Benjamin Franklin assembled the most influential model in American history—the do-it-yourself Self. For two centuries he has been the exemplary self-made man. Yet to approach Franklin through this motif is to be initially misled by a popular stereotype that equates self making with the rise from rags to riches. That stereotype developed in the nineteenth century and considerably narrowed the overt basis of Franklin's popular appeal. He himself was less interested in the larger goals and shapings of a life than he was in the contributing means and techniques. As the fun of a do-it-yourself plumbing book involves far more than a wish for a dripless faucet, so the appeal of Franklin's *Autobiography* goes beyond its promise of eventual success. When he summoned up a self out of the pressures and possibilities of his situation, Franklin developed a model so adapted to the conditions of the emerging country that it became his chief legacy to future Americans. His clear instructions, his comic enjoyment, his flexibility, his distance from and curiosity about his own activities are more important components of this model than its eventual wealth and prestige. To recover what is most appealing in Franklin's sense of the self is also to recognize what such diverse descendants as booster and gadgeteer, self-made man and jack-of-all-trades, have in common with each other and with the larger cultural model of the confidence man.

Fascinating and exemplary as it was, however, Franklin's own life is not the issue. His influence arose from a special version of himself transmitted in his two most popular works, *The Way to Wealth* and the *Autobiography*. And it is in the latter work that he assembled the do-it-yourself Self. He acknowledges at the outset that he does not expect readers to be interested in his unique, personal experience. Instead, he projects the general image of one risen from poverty and obscurity to affluence and reputation and notes that "the conducing Means I made use of . . . my Posterity may like to know, as they may find some of them suitable to their own Situations, and therefore fit to be imitated." He deliberately creates a model self, emphasizing those actions and pursuits that can be imitated. One of the most memorable qualities of the *Autobiography* is Franklin's capacity to break down success and development into clear, repeatable steps. Claiming neither genius nor luck nor grace, he converts life to technique, and the very accessibility of his model makes up part of its charm.

To a certain extent the nature of the model self is determined by the effort to project one. For instance, by selecting what is applicable to others, Franklin necessarily understates or omits much of his experience, especially in its emotional or psychological dimensions. And by stressing what can be imitated, he avoids those complexities of situation to which practical methods do not apply. Yet this model of the self also purports to *be* Benjamin Franklin. Emotional disengagement and technical mastery thus emerge not as conditions of the writing but as attractive qualities of the model self. To understand such qualities more fully and to recognize how Franklin's sense of the self would invite generations of followers, we must begin with the social conditions projected in the *Autobiography*.

What kind of a world does the model self move in? First, it is thoroughly urban. In radical contrast with the popular image of an American hero alone in the natural frontier, Franklin presents a model self making his way among throngs of human beings, so that the juggling and discerning of appearances counts for more than self-discovery or sanctification in the natural world. The imagined city is not, however, simply a given condition. The self *comes* to it or discovers in it a change of values, and in this sense it anticipates much more modern cities.

Although Franklin was born and raised in Boston, his childhood is described within a tradition-bound community. His father's family has always worked hard both in England and in the colonies simply to maintain itself; there is a firm apprenticeship system; and people seem to know each other well enough to exercise sound judgment. Franklin's journey to Philadelphia takes him imaginatively to circumstances so different that one is reminded of later country-born youths migrating to the city. Not only does he escape his own apprenticeship and the limitations of opportunity in his father's world but he also moves away from the solidity (and skepticism) of his father's judgment. In what he refers to as "my new Country" people do not seem to know each other as well as they did in Boston. The situation is more fluid and judgments far more uncertain. Soon the governor himself encourages the young Franklin and sends a letter recommending him to his own father for a loan to start a business. It is characteristic of the tradition-based world that Josiah Franklin views this letter primarily as ground to doubt Governor Keith's discretion; it is equally characteristic of the fluid milieu of Philadelphia that Keith's promise to assist Franklin should later prove a gross deception. The point is that the model self is going to make his way in a shifty world where appearances are extremely important but also deceptive, where opportunity expands as judgment becomes less stable.

In such a world people have to keep their eyes on each other. The model self operates in a field of competitors. Occasionally the competition appears directly, as when Franklin tells how he rose over the two other printers in Philadelphia. But the competitors are not simply rivals in trade. Franklin projects his story against a background of timid, imprudent, or stodgy figures who cannot get ahead: the Oxford scholar who turned up in Philadelphia as an indentured servant, the croaker who refused to buy a house in a city on the verge of destruction and finally had to pay five times as much because of his delay, Franklin's friend John Collins who forfeited his intellectual promise and his industry by drinking and gambling. In one sense such figures function like Christian's foils in *Pilgrim's Progress;* they illustrate specific errors and dangers while the protagonist shows exemplary behavior.[1] But such an approach does not explain the smug delight with which these stories are told. It seems as if the model self needs the surrounding failures in order to savor his own skills and self-control. He experiences his identity in comparing himself with others. Although Franklin offers great promise to his would-be imitators, the world he projects is largely peopled with incompetents.

When Franklin measures his own economic success in London against the relative failure of his friend James Ralph, who vainly chases the Muses, there is a tacit suggestion that he has beaten Ralph. Perhaps it is the latent sense of a game in play that makes the model self experience victory when he recounts another's inadequacy. In any case, the game does not remain latent. Franklin delights in recounting diddles, tricks, and impostures. He observes the "crafty old Sophister" Bradford drawing out the secret plans of his son's naïve competitor, Keimer. He explains how he and Ralph tricked Osborne into acknowledging that he liked Ralph's poetry, a trick made more effective by Franklin's canny role playing. And he matches wits with the Quakers in their equivocations to give money for war while holding to their pacific principles (they appropriate funds for "wheat *or other grain*"; Franklin requests the purchase of a "Fire Engine"). While such instances are primarily amusing, the tendency of people to take advantage of each other can be more serious. When Franklin tells of Governor Keith's "trick" of promising him a letter of credit in London and giving him nothing but the assurance that made him go there, or of Keimer's plan to exploit Franklin as a teacher of his apprentices, he indicates that the world of the model self is a risky place where people will impose on others if they can. Thus the sense of comparison with a vast field of competitors is often focused in a contest of wits.

Keeping one's eye on others can mean more than measuring oneself against them or watching out for their cunning maneuvers. One can also enter the game, study the motives of the other players, and try to take advantage oneself of these motives. This, in fact, is the pattern of the classical confidence game, the exploitation of people's wishes to get something for nothing or to profit by extralegal means, as summed up in the cliché "You can't cheat an honest man." The celebrated twentieth-century con man Joseph "Yellow Kid" Weil focuses his memoirs not simply on his own techniques but on his thorough analysis of the illicit motives of his victims; he notes that a con man differs from his marks by his interest in and studied mastery of human nature.[2] Like such later figures as Sam Slick, Sut Lovingood, Huck Finn, and "Yellow Kid" Weil, Franklin projects in the *Autobiography* a detached curiosity, sometimes amounting to wonder, at elements of human nature, from the devotion that keeps an ascetic woman alive on mere water gruel to the weakness for rhetoric that makes him contribute against his own will all the cash in his pockets after one of George Whitefield's sermons. The world of the model self yields easily to mechanical manipulation, and this is most apparent in Franklin's many references to the predictability of human response. The protagonist of the *Autobiography* plays on people's motives as confidently and effectively as Franklin himself had performed his electrical experiments.

Ordinarily, of course, these motives are not dishonest like those of the Yellow Kid's victims; as an effective eighteenth-century politician, Franklin sees merely that people can be manipulated by what they regard as their own interests. But on two important occasions Franklin shows the model self entering the murky world of other people's unscrupulous motives and playing the classical confidence game. About one of them Franklin gives his own emphasis: "I do not remember any of my political Manoeuvres, the Success of which gave me at the time more Pleasure. Or that in after-thinking of it, I more easily excus'd my-self for having made some Use of Cunning." The issue was how to get the country members of the Pennsylvania Assembly to agree to fund a public hospital in the city. Franklin proposed a matching grant, contingent on a large voluntary contribution, thus playing on the duplicity of the legislators who believed they could get public credit for charitable intentions without actually having to pay. The people of Philadelphia in turn contributed generously because they saw it as a way to get extra funds from the Assembly.

Even more significant, because of its place in the career of the model self, is Franklin's maneuver to escape his apprenticeship to his brother. Having offended the Assembly of Massachusetts by some pieces in the *New England Courant*, James Franklin was forbidden in 1723 to print the paper. He tried to slip through this ruling by making Benjamin the nominal publisher, but to make this transference appear legal he had to cancel the articles of indenture that bound Benjamin to four more years of service. Although new secret articles of indenture were drawn up, Benjamin guessed that James would not dare to produce them and thereby acknowledge his duplicity, so the young apprentice struck out for himself. Franklin does acknowledge that his gambit was unfair, that it was "one of the first Errata of my life," but his narrative shows it to have been cleverly managed, and he encloses it in a complex pattern of justification. His brother's motives were themselves at best dubious, and he was a harsh master, frequently beating Benjamin. Furthermore, the apprenticeship system appears, with historical hindsight, unfairly limiting, especially for a young man of such skill, industry, cleverness, and enterprise as the seventeen-year-old Benjamin Franklin.

Symbolically even more is suggested. The apprenticeship system is an inherited institution, supported by law. To resist indenture and to support enterprise and self-determination is thus to be, at least covertly, indignant at inherited institutions themselves and at laws that appear stiff and confining. If one is restrained by seemingly outmoded laws from healthy enterprise, especially when it will later benefit the public as well, one may be justified in using extralegal dexterity in evading those laws, and the dexterity itself may serve as evidence of the very enterprise that has been stifled. No wonder the Robber Barons admired Franklin's *Autobiography!*

As Franklin deviously works his way out of the limits of inherited institutions, he indicates a major change in the role of such traditions. The world of the model self is neither the Old World nor the New World but an intermixture of the two. Old institutions, manners, and rewards surround one, but they need not be binding. New opportunities are not lying about like fruit in the Garden of Eden; they are available only if one works to create them. For the opportunist, there are opportunities. In contrast with the tradition analyzed in R. W. B. Lewis's *The American Adam*, Franklin's *Autobiography* does not project a new man in a new world. It shows instead that the old systems and values are porous, that if one is adroit and alert one can open up new avenues to success and renown. It is important to note that the first part of the *Autobiography* was written before the Revolution while Franklin still had visions of the British Empire expanding across the American continent. The social equivalent of this political image is his presentation of his own achievement—he has *English* leisure and *English* fame. In one sense his story shows new ways of getting old rewards.

In this mixture of old and new, it is appropriate that Franklin emphasizes the signs of transition. Whatever is routine and stable in a stage of his life—apprenticeship, general learning, work in Philadelphia—Franklin treats in quick summary. He spends much more time explaining those techniques that allow for actual or potential advancement—his learning to write, his composition of the Dogood letters, his acquirement of a modest manner. And he reserves his fullest detail and dramatization for his transition from Boston apprentice to Philadelphia beginner—the break with his brother, the hardships of the voyage (during which he appropriately digresses on *Pilgrim's Progress*), his unprepossessing appearance on Sunday morning, his first impressions of Governor Keith. Similarly Franklin stresses the incipient nature of colonial society at large, especially in regard to publication. His interest in books and his ability to write recommend the seventeen-year-old to two governors. The small circulation of books gives special value to a popular manual of instruction like *Poor Richard's Almanack*. Because there are few newspapers in the colonies, each assumes great power, and single innovations of any kind have wide effect within the context of the still formative society. It is a world with room for new publication, and at the same time there are well-established models such as London's *Spectator*. The cue given by such a world is not to originate and invent but to copy, adapt, and publicize.

Given its fluid appearances, its unstable judgments, and its competitive gamesmanship, the urban world of the *Autobiography* seems to admonish one to be cautious, watchful, perhaps even cynically exploitative. But the transitional nature of this world offsets such effects. Where others are not settled in their judgments of a person, he has opportunities to become something that traditional institutions would deny him. Furthermore, for all the characters in the *Autobiography* who appear ready to deceive or take advantage of a young man, there are also figures like the Quaker merchant Denham and the older Franklin himself who look out to help youths of industry and promise. Governor Keith, who belongs in both camps, exemplifies the ambivalence of Franklin's world. He shows the hasty and indiscreet assurance characteristic of a fluid situation, and he provides the major instance of false promises and imposition on an innocent youth. Yet Franklin's narrative of being duped into a trip to London not only shows no rancor toward Keith but presents him with a certain charm and affection. Instead of letting the later disillusionment color the early narrative, Franklin reinvests himself in his own innocence so that the flattering notice of the Governor can resume its full value as a first impression: "He said I appear'd a young Man of promising Parts, and therefore should be encouraged."

What is the effect of Keith's imposition? Immediately it raises Franklin's self-esteem and even ratifies his identity in the eyes of his family. And although Franklin's trip to London involves grave risks with no backing, it serves him well in his own later rise as a printer. When Franklin apologizes for the governor's conduct by noting that with the best will and no real power he merely gave promises, it is already apparent that such promises will serve as currency in the world of the model self. Keith simultaneously conned the young Franklin and gave him confidence. In a growing world such dualities merge.

What are the ideal qualities of a self fitted to such a fluid, ambivalent, risky, and promising world? First of all, he exists among appearances. The model self lives for the public, always on stage or preparing for the performance. Although Franklin himself was a man of solid skill and accomplishment, the *Autobiography* concentrates more on public impressions than on the workman's merits. The good responsible printer emphasizes that he actually got his business because "this Industry visible to our Neighbours began to give us Character and Credit." Character and credit being currency, one earns them by keeping the shop lighted at night, by trundling one's own paper conspicuously through the streets in a wheelbarrow, by dressing plainly and avoiding public diversion. "In order to secure my Credit and Character as a Tradesman, I took care not only to be in *Reality* Industrious and frugal, but to avoid all *Ap-*

pearances of the Contrary." Such is the most famous piece of advice in the *Autobiography*. As will happen so often later in Horatio Alger's fables of success, the deserving young man gets his good breaks by having made the right impressions on the right people.

The fluid world of the strange city demands attention on appearances, and Franklin's model self is constantly alert to them. He treats in detail the contrasts in clothing he wore the first and second times Deborah Read saw him; he gloats over his new suit, his watch, the silver in his pockets when he returns to Boston to impress his former fellow apprentices and to offend his brother James. And his major quarrel with his employer Keimer occurs after Keimer makes a public spectacle of scolding him. The model self keeps his eye so fixed on the public that he even measures virtues by social performance. For his purposes it is sufficient that although he failed to develop genuine humility, he succeeded in acquiring the appearance of it.

Living among appearances, the model self does not characteristically engage in private activities or introspection. The scene of his life is the place of public exchange. Unlike John Adams, who deeply distrusted Franklin as a wily diplomat, he does not imagine himself as a debater whose fervid loyalty to certain principles determines his defense of them. Instead, he sees and projects himself as an arbitrator, a means to facilitate compromise. Warning repeatedly against disputation as a source of ill will, he stresses his own ability to remove prejudices. It is essential to the image of the model self that he is an intermediary figure. He presides over the phenomena of convergence and interchange, showing how people can join to promote their mutual interests. It is not a peripheral matter that the model self is a printer. In this quintessentially urban business, publicity and promotion are not merely useful adjuncts but the calling itself. As printer, the model self lives for and in publication. If the urban world at large demands care about public impressions, the work itself turns on them. Thus the model self frequently regards his whole life as a publication and his sins as "errata."

Instead of growing, making, or producing something, the printer gets his livelihood by being a publicist. The newspapers and almanacs of Franklin's time were in good part vehicles of exchange, compiled of borrowings from other works. Poor Richard comically acknowledges this in his Preface to the 1747 Almanack: "Why then should I give my Readers *bad Lines* of my own, when *good Ones* of other People's are so plenty?" The printer could regard himself as promulgating knowledge, promoting the useful exchange of ideas, inventions, inquiries. Rather than claim credit for particular suggestions or distinguish carefully between what is borrowed and what is original, the model self responds to the needs of a growing country by publishing for its own sake whatever is useful. Franklin's attitude toward his own inventions, his opposition to patents, his effort to pool freely information about scientific experiments all exemplify this spirit of open promotion.

Because promotion is useful to the public, the model self can take pride in his skills at it. Franklin notes that whenever he was about to solicit support for a public cause, he printed a pamphlet or wrote in his newspaper "to prepare the Minds of the People," and he gives extensive practical advice about how to influence others. Anticipating the spirit of P. T. Barnum and the Chautauqua movement, he explains how he helped an associate in his electrical work combine popular experiments, educative lectures, and public spectacle into a profit-making venture. And Franklin himself showed such mastery of the effects of printed material that he could play on them in several hoaxes, such as the letter to an English newspaper spoofing exaggerated reports about the colonies and noting that "the grand Leap of the Whale in that Chace up the Fall of Niagara is esteemed by all who have seen it, as one of the finest Spectacles in Nature! Really, Sir, the World is grown too incredulous." [3]

In all this promotion, the model self may seem to fade into the background, a mere agent of exchange, and so Franklin likes to pretend. After all, he freely acknowledges that Dr. Thomas Bond was the real projector of the Philadelphia hospital Franklin helped to promote, and that John Clifton originated the idea of the street lamps later credited to Franklin. But once the project or idea is dissociated from its inventor, the public credit is juggled, and the person most likely to end up with it is the juggler himself, the promoter. Quite apart from the specific items Franklin erroneously claims for himself in the *Autobiography*—that the public watch in Philadelphia was established at his suggestion instead of seventeen years later, that he proposed the Philosophical Society, that he never asked for public office or sought votes, that he offered the bill for paving the streets of Philadelphia—he obviously benefits by association with everything he has promoted. Even without false claims, promotion extends into self-promotion. And the model self, existing in that dazzling interchange of projects and public credit, becomes the very center of attention.

The second general quality of the model self is that he is buoyantly practical. As promoter and arbitrator, he needs to remove prejudice, and thus he should himself be as free of it as possible. Although he recognizes that people hold inherited beliefs, he disengages life from the mysterious and the sacred. Notions derived from beyond the world of the senses he regards either as obstacles to be removed in his dealings with others or as levers by which they can be manipulated. Human nature as pondered by humanists and theologians yields to another view wherein people's responses are mechanically predictable and to study human nature is simply to gain experimental knowledge of the springs of action so as to control them. Thus Franklin shows how effective it is to subordinate one's vanity by proposing one's own idea as the project of several others; he explains how to turn an enemy into a friend by having him do you a kindness; and he helps a chaplain get soldiers to attend worship by doling out their rum after prayers. Vanity in others he sees not as a sin but as a power through which they may be maneuvered to do good.

Whenever he can, Franklin turns away from subjects invested with awe and toward those responsive to method and control. Sometimes he is deliberately comic in converting the metaphysical or the sacred to the practical, as in describing the promise he made with John Osborne that the first of them to die would return and tell the other what the next world is like, or in disregarding George Whitefield's preaching in order to measure how far his voice could be heard and to compute how many people could hear him. This irreverence has two functions. The first is to weaken the force of fear and superstition by mocking it. The second is to build up a practical faith in experiment and method. Instead of merely admiring the writing of *The Spectator*, Franklin shows how to master it by coolly disassembling it, leaving the pieces a while, and then practicing at rebuilding something as good as or even better than the model. Similarly, rather than expect his readers to venerate the unique sage Benjamin Franklin, he dissects his own experience and offers step-by-step procedures in place of personal narrative. Those who view Franklin as a stuffy moralist or sermonizer have implicitly been asking the wrong question about his *Autobiography*. They ask what he is like, and expect certain personal and inward revelations. The question the *Autobiography* really responds to is, How did he do it? Franklin's prudential advice is not offered like the preacher's abstract injunctions to be good. Instead he shows what can be gained when one has mastered a certain technique and then presents instructions as clearly as the popular how-to-do-it manuals.

The most revealing and at the same time the most easily misconstrued of these procedures is Franklin's scheme to attain moral perfection by an Art of Virtue. Formerly commentators on the *Auto-*

biography took for granted that Franklin was quite serious about his charts of virtues and either applauded his advice or, like D. H. Lawrence, ridiculed his moral naïveté. More recently it has become fashionable to recognize the elements of satire in the proposal—the self-inflation, the surprise at the persistence of sin, the emphasis on tables and charts—and thus to regard the piece as one of Franklin's jokes for his urbane French audience of 1784. Franklin, however, is quite serious about the value of his proposal and at the same time quite amused at the self who "conceiv'd the bold and arduous Project of arriving at moral Perfection." Unless one can recognize a mode of being in which such apparently antithetical states of mind can coexist—in which one is both innocent and shrewd, spiritual and practical, compassionate and detached, serious and playful, or as Whitman put it, "both in and out of the game"—unless one accepts such poise in ambivalence, one cannot understand either Franklin's model self or the most characteristic version of the American confidence man.

The point about the Art of Virtue is that although Franklin discovered he could not be as good as he hoped he also got better. We must see the Art of Virtue in the context of the very doctrines that make it seem morally naïve in order to respond to its practical value. Centuries of painstaking study and speculation had made of moral character something mysterious, subtle, and complicated. One could not hope to change it without discipline and will, external guidance and prayer. And such an awesome undertaking was made all the more hopeless by the immediate context of Calvinism with its assurance that one's innately depraved inner being could be improved only by the arbitrary and improbable visitation of God's grace. As Franklin's cunning opportunism gave him a way out of the stifling conditions of apprenticeship, so his Art of Virtue offers a way out of this gloomy view of the self. He adapts the practical methods of a buoyant age of projects to an area of human experience previously left to moralists. His emphasis is on encouragement. As the letter from Benjamin Vaughan introducing this part of the *Autobiography* says, "your apparatus is simple." Franklin is perfectly serious in offering clear do-able techniques for self-improvement, in showing how they work, and in assuming that the method *will* make people better. His joking attitude toward himself has more complex bearings. Immediately, it makes the model self attractive rather than pompous and encourages would-be imitators by showing that even the model was not perfect. But its major implication has to do with the oppressive historical context of moral analysis. Franklin's easy mockery of his pretensions is a tacit recognition of that context. He lets his readers see that he is not such a fool as to assume this is all there is to the moral life. The ludicrousness of his simple advice to "imitate Jesus and Socrates" reminds us that Franklin knows what an awesome task that would actually be. But the playful humor about such matters also cancels out the awesomeness. To joke about all that Franklin has disregarded in the Art of Virtue is to show how easy it is after all to dismiss what is left out.

With his anxiety about the supernatural checked by the sprightly humor, the model self is free to revel in apparatus and technique. Like the authors of twentieth-century self-improvement books and instant development programs, he substitutes mechanical devices for discipline and will. Introspection gives way to charts and account books, and the interest in improving character turns into fascination with improving the techniques themselves. Thus Franklin replaces his paper tables with ivory leaves permanently ruled, the ultimate improvement in externalizing the soul for it allows past shortcomings to be, as Melville's master con man puts it, "quite erased from the slate." The whole procedure is highly encouraging, for the more practical the method, the more imitable seem the results. But in emphasizing practical methods, it suggests that whatever is do-able has more reality than what is complex or inward. For the model self, being is doing.

To know the self is to experiment with the instrument of that doing, to test how the body works on a vegetable diet, for instance, or to demonstrate that water gruel makes a sronger workman than strong beer. And to improve the self is to improve an instrument. It is not accidental that Franklin's famous anecdote about his shortcomings in self-improvement should close, "I think I like a speckled Ax best." Not only is the Art of Virtue a highly practical approach; the very precepts Franklin lists are instrumental:

> Eat not to *Dulness* . . .
> Speak not but *what may benefit* . . .
> Let all Things have *their Places* . . .
> Resolve to perform *what you ought* . . .
> Make no Expence *but to do good* . . .
> Be always employ'd in *something useful* . . .
> Use no *hurtful* Deceit.

Whatever one's final motives or goals—and these are left conspicuously open—to be virtuous is to make oneself into an efficient *tool* for performance. Franklin nearly attains the circularity of ends and means that marks the most efficient instrument of the American frontier, Cooper's Deerslayer, whose philosophical prudence "appeared to render him superior to all motives but those which were best calculated to effect his purpose." If one knew precisely what one's purpose was, what was useful or beneficial or hurtful, Franklin's method would help one attain the self-control and subordination of impulse to achieve that purpose. But in the *Autobiography* the means easily appear as the ends, and what is admirable is a self so functional and efficient that it creates the illusion of perfect mastery and containment.

One can perform *with* such a self or *upon* it—it is an instrument in both senses. What is the relation of performer to instrument? That question brings up the third and major quality of the model self—his detachment. Many observers have noted this aspect of Franklin. His biographer Carl Van Doren wrote: "He moved through his world in a humorous mastery of it. Kind as he was, there was perhaps a little contempt in his lack of exigency. He could not put so high a value as single-minded men put on the things they give their lives for."[4] And Herman Melville, developing the studied ambivalence through which he would soon present his own representative American, the Confidence-Man, made this famous portrait of Franklin:

> This philosophical levity of tranquillity, so to speak, is shown in his easy variety of pursuits. Printer, postmaster, almanac maker, essayist, chemist, orator, tinker, statesman, humorist, philosopher, parlor man, political economist, professor of housewifery, ambassador, projector, maxim-monger, herb-doctor, wit:—Jack of all trades, master of each and mastered by none—the type and genius of his land.[5]

Mastered by none—that is the key to Franklin's model self. Nothing matters so much—no pursuit or occupation, no feeling, no relationship—that it fixes the character. The performance does not implicate the performer. It is as if there *were* no inner self, no seat of passion and pain and urgency. Being a model for others and existing in the stir of appearances, the model self is free of inward complications.

Benjamin Franklin the human being was obviously not devoid of feeling. He could be petulant, bitter, grieved, kindly, anxious, and ardent. He even acknowledges in the *Autobiography* some strong personal impulses, his quarrelsomeness with his brother, his vanity, his "hard-to-be-govern'd" sexual desires, his urge to go to sea. But as the wise, dispassionate narrator looks on at a father desperately seeking a trade on land to prevent his son from running off to sea, he is simply recording another instance of the way people behave toward each other. The same untroubled curiosity about the springs of action that makes him wonder at the ardor of Whitefield's listeners also makes him observe the boy's "inclination" for the sea without in any way acknowledging that this was *his* feeling. When he reveals the personal feelings of the boy, he is actually amusing us with instances of foibles to be overcome. The *model* self emerges as such foibles are controlled. The early political struggles in Pennsylvania, in which Franklin was a bitter opponent of the proprietors, appear in the *Autobiography* through the calm, humorous disengagement of the aged diplomat. Partly by selecting and transmuting what he tells us, partly by playing so artfully on the contrast between early actor and urbane narrative observer, Franklin carefully shapes the image of a self detached from all complications of feeling and urgency.

An important source for this disengagement and for its popular appeal was the Puritan attitude toward worldliness. The concept of the two callings—a sacred one to devote oneself to God, and a secular one to work at a specific occupation—celebrated diligent attention to one's worldly business and ultimate detachment from it. One's affections were to be weaned from the world. The correlation between this ethic and the rise of capitalism is well known.[6] But the Puritan values also created a curious attitude toward the self. The habit of diligence combined with disengagement could survive pious devotion to God and become an attitude celebrated for its own sake. Franklin captures this spirit in discussing checkers on his way back from London at age twenty: "the persons playing, if they would play well, ought not much to regard the *consequence* of the game, for that diverts and withdraws the attention of the mind from the game itself. . . . if two persons *equal* in judgment play for a considerable sum, he that loves money most shall lose . . ."[7] It may sound as if such a program were merely a controlled way of getting rich, and as if the self had actually transferred its weaned affections from God to wealth. But that is not the bearing of Franklin's model self. He celebrates his ability to retire from business in his early forties as enthusiastically as he had celebrated his ability to succeed in it. Getting rich is simply one more role to play well without *becoming* it.

The jack-of-all-trades is not only mastered by none of them but is also master of each. The model self is highly skillful as a role-player.[8] He emphasizes his experiments and postures as things deliberately "put on" for a time: he came upon a book about avoiding meats and put on a vegetable diet; he learned about the Socratic method and "put on the humble Enquirer and Doubter." Rather than express himself, he tries out a series of identities and adapts himself to the situation and the audience.[9] Such role playing is not merely an exercise in far-sighted opportunism. It is a source of intrinsic satisfaction. One of the most engaging qualities of the *Autobiography* is Franklin's exhilaration in performance. What fun it must be to enter roles so skillfully and to drop them so easily!

He even rearranges material to emphasize different roles. The comic sequence about giving up his vegetable diet to eat cod is removed from the narrative of his journey to Philadelphia, where it would interrupt the role of pilgrim in a threatening world. It is introduced later, seemingly an afterthought, to head up one of the sprightliest performances in the *Autobiography*. As Franklin smells the fish and yearns for them but thinks they should not be killed as they've done him no harm, he remembers seeing smaller fish in their bellies and thus justifies his inclination: "So convenient a thing it is to be a *reasonable Creature*." Here he not only shows his ability to change roles but he sports with the notion of reason itself. Immediately after this "digression," he tells of his disputes with his employer Keimer, who is made foolish by Franklin's cleverness at Socratic dialogue. He then tells how he diverted himself by agreeing to join Keimer's "sect" if they can include a vegetable diet in the precepts, a procedure so painful to Keimer that he finally yearns for "the flesh pots of Egypt," orders a roast pig to share with Franklin and two women, and eats it up himself before they arrive. Again the sense of competition helps set off the model self, for Franklin's dexterity, poise, and self-effaced role playing stand out against Keimer's stodgy helplessness and his bondage to appetite. The narrator celebrates his earlier self-control through his zest in reperforming the incident for its full comedy, a demonstration that self-control is not mere asceticism.

For the model self, life is essentially a game. Although there may be substantial winnings at stake, to put one's attention on the goal is, as Franklin noted, not only to make oneself vulnerable as a player but to miss the joy of the game itself. The model self feels exhilarated less by final rewards than by the immediate sense of competition and play. His identity emerges in the relative skill of his gambits. He is a humorist both in seeming to keep a "real self" at some distance from the immediate situation and in living for and in the amusement of the present performance. But he is disengaged from more than the stakes of the game and his inward feelings. Life appears not as one long game but as many alternative ones. The skillful player can move easily from one game to another, say from business to politics, as he senses more invigorating play or more interesting and satisfying competition. Uncommitted to any final goals or absolute values, contented only for the moment in his immediate mastery of technique, he is restless and inquisitive. His flexibility contributes to his skill but it also shows that he cannot love any role or purpose so well as to identify with it.

In one of his many voices, Ralph Waldo Emerson said, "We live amid surfaces, and the true art of life is to skate well on them."[10] That, perhaps, is the image to unite the three major qualities of the model self—his existence among appearances and publicity, his practicalism, and his detachment, or to name these aspects by the roles he will later inhabit, the booster, the gadgeteer, and the gamesman. To *live* amid surfaces—where appearance is reality, where practice replaces metaphysics, where all is a game. Franklin disengages the sensory, practical, public world of surfaces from all suggestions of "depth," from religion and transcendence, from emotion and commitment, from ultimate purposes and absolute principles. His model self finds the ends of action hazy, evanescent, unsure, but he is wonderfully adept at the means, so adept that his technical prowess and his promotional flair become satisfying in themselves. As with the Carpenter aboard Melville's *Pequod,* his brains ooze out through his fingers. Franklin himself acted, on the whole, for praiseworthy ends, but this is not what he celebrates in his model self. In fashioning a being who lives in appearances and promotion, who finds practical experiments more substantial than moral values, who specializes in games and roles, he makes one of the most compelling cases in our literature for the confidence man as an image of the self.

4

MAKING IT:
From Enlightenment to Gilded Age

It is possible for all of us to become fleetingly for ourselves the worst person we can imagine that others might imagine us to be.

—*Erving Goffman*

Damn it, where's my *real* jacket?

—*Robert Altman's Buffalo Bill*

C: Why "stardom," Zed?
Z: Well, I'd be a completed personality. People would know who I was.
C: Yes?
Z: And they could tell me.

—*The Covet Interview*, New Times

Come up.

—*Flem Snopes*

Franklin's model self is one of the major products of the American imagination. It is significant not only because so many people actually did find it fit to be imitated, but because it brought together so many diverse cultural values and suggested their underlying unity. One can see it developing with equal propriety into the self-made man or the booster or the jack-of-all-trades, and it also seems naturally associated with the Yankee peddler and the gadgeteer. What happened to the model self in the nineteenth century, in fact, was that the composite being broke down. The various descendants of the model self were specialists who exaggerated certain of its qualities and thus became exemplars of contrasting popular traditions. The most influential of these traditions was the ethic of success, which transformed the model self into the self-made man and stereotyped Franklin as patron saint of the rise to fame and fortune. What qualities of the model self encouraged such a transformation? How did the aspirations of the self-made man change the habits and powers of the model self? What was it like for actual people, with their inward complexities, to try to become the model self?

To examine such issues, one must consider the model self not as a static figure projected in one particular book but as a historical convergence of qualities, as part of a continuing process of development. On one side of Franklin's model was the "Renaissance man" with his ideal mastery of all fields of endeavor. On the other side was the jack-of-all-trades. On one side was the worldly good sense and sociability of the Enlightenment; on the other was the glad-handing spirit of the booster. Preceding Franklin's model was the effort of scientists and philosophers to delimit terminology and to connect each word with a clear idea; following on the model self came the gadgeteer for whom obscure issues simply vanish as he concentrates on practicable method. Such transformations, of course, were not Franklin's doing. They emerged in larger processes of change. But the *Autobiography* condenses and dramatizes the changes, so that the model self seems at one moment simply a product of eighteenth-century attitudes and at the next a prophetic vision of the mid-nineteenth-century American. And some of the changes in cultural values evident in the model self were directly brought about by Franklin's imaginative artistry, which at once celebrated the Enlightenment and anticipated the Gilded Age.

Franklin did not invent the model self. He assembled it out of what was available.[1] First, there was the Enlightenment faith in reason, inquiry, experiment. Deists resisted enthusiasm. Neoclassicists urged imitation of the best models. And scientists in the wake of Newton sought to discover the general laws of the natural world. In such a context Franklin was encouraged to experiment with the self, find the general laws of effective social behavior, and create an impersonal model. Second, Locke's sensational psychology put new theoretical emphasis on appearances and thus underwrote the effort of Franklin's model self to adapt to the shifting reality presented by his senses. Third, there was a popular spirit of mutual improvement, represented by two of the books Franklin stresses as influential in his early reading, Defoe's *Essay upon Projects* and Mather's *Essays To Do Good (Bonifacius)*. Fourth, an extensive body of self-help literature had developed in seventeenth-century England and was widely read in the colonies. Homilies and pamphlets, such as the Reverend William Perkins's popular "Treatise of Vocations"

(1603), stressed the virtues of sobriety, diligence, thrift, and industry and often presented guidelines on how to accumulate wealth. Both the essays on projects and the self-help manuals demonstrated the power of individuals and groups to improve their circumstances by practical efforts. Indirectly and often inadvertantly they thus suggested that inherited communal roles were not binding, as Franklin so memorably showed in the first part of his *Autobiography*. Fifth, the Puritan tradition in New England demanded that one be both diligent in a worldly calling and yet detached from it, and that one examine one's life to trace the workings of God's will. Although Franklin played down the Puritan exercise of moral introspection, he used the *Autobiography* to scrutinize personal experience and find providential signs. More important, he boldly adapted to his own memoirs the Puritan habit of telling exemplary lives. (Many people have noted similarities between the *Autobiography* and Cotton Mather's Life of Sir William Phips in *Magnalia Christi Americana*.) Yet, sixth, a general transference of energy from religious to secular pursuits licensed Franklin's use of Puritan habits divested of reference to God.

When all these strands of influence met in Franklin's model self, of course, each complicated the effects of the others. One way in which Franklin imaginatively recast the traditions on which he drew was simply to combine them. By deriving his worldliness simultaneously from Newtonian science, from Enlightenment sociability, and from Puritan vocationalism, he compiled a model self that no longer resembles any of its sources. It is at once detached, confident, urbane, cautious, and methodical. Such eclectic fusion indicated the spirit of the model self that was most conspicuously lost in the nineteenth century—its rich variety.

But there were other ways as well in which Franklin transformed his sources, and they suggest more directly how the model self would be assimilated to popular American traditions. He minimized larger purposes and scorned metaphysics. Thus he severed techniques and habits from their supporting systems. When he adopted a Puritan posture toward worldly activity, he dismissed the theology that ratified it. He carried on the efforts of seventeenth-century philosophers to be precise about terminology and method, but he detached this habit from its base in scientific inquiry and made it a rubric for all human experience. Most important, as a man of the Enlightenment, he was confident that an orderly system underlay all observable phenomena. To become master of the universal law, to find out what works in the world, could be regarded as a way of worshiping the being who, in Franklin's phrase, is author and owner of this system. The more possibilities one acts out in the world, the fuller the worship. But Franklin did not transmit that larger faith, only the immediate sense of assurance and delight. Again and again the model self simply discovers that one activity happens to connect with another. By being flexible and omnivorous—the nineteenth-century term would be *shifty*—he turns out to be systematic.

Another way in which Franklin transformed the attitudes in the background of the model self was to incorporate them in an active figure who could live an imagined life independent of the supporting assumptions. Instead of describing the moral or scientific or social structure of the world, he showed what one can *do* in it, how one can create and recast a self, what fun it is to perform. By isolating techniques from larger systems and creating a vigorous, amusing agent for these techniques, Franklin at once made the model self marketable and broke its ties to its own origins. He freed it to enter the domain of popular lore. There it would keep reappearing over the next century in more specialized transformations. These variations become more comprehensible when considered as variations, for the model self (and covertly the confidence man) indicates how they are related to each other, and it provides a comprehensive character type against which we can more readily see what is given up and what is exaggerated in each of its descendants.

From Yankee Peddler to Self-Made Man

The first variant on the model self can hardly be described as a descendant, for by the time Franklin's memoirs were published it was already living an energetic life of its own in jokes, anecdotes, and popular drama. But as a figure of folklore, the Yankee peddler[2] can give us some useful insights into the development of the more significant stereotype of the self-made man. There is the very issue of popularity—what in fact was being celebrated in the folklore of the Yankee? Although stereotyped by his critics as an avaricious cheat, ready to profit by any means, the Yankee peddler, like Franklin's model self, was more gamesman than profiteer. He regarded both conversation and economic exchange as contests of wit, and the many anecdotes celebrating his enterprises presented him as a shrewd and often charming trickster whose pleasure is more in the transaction than in the gain. The circulation of these anecdotes and the persistence of the character type demonstrated a widespread fascination with the image of the peddler and revealed a set of covert cultural values far different from those on which Americans had begun to proclaim themselves a peculiarly moral people.[3]

These mixed values are indicated in the comments of two contemporary observers. Timothy Dwight, the president of Yale, was troubled by the stereotype of Yankee acuteness presented by foreign visitors. When Dwight wrote his *Travels in New England and New York* (published in 1821–22 but written near the turn of the century), he wanted among other purposes to defend the New England character. Yet the very qualities which he saw as happily distinguishing New Englanders—enterprise and activity, energy of mind and ingenuity, willingness to take risks and to avail themselves of "occurrences which are unregarded" by other men—were also characteristics of the problematic peddler. Clearly it was not easy to draw the line between one kind of commerce and another. Dwight wanted to demonstrate that the stereotype of the Yankee peddler was false; yet he also felt that peddling was dangerous and not to be equated with commerce. Thus the vehemence of his remarks on the peddler can probably be ascribed to the very entanglement of his own purposes:

> Men who begin life with bargaining for small wares will almost invariably become sharpers. . . . The tricks of fraud will assume in his mind the same place which commercial skill and an honorable system of dealing hold in the mind of a merchant. . . . I believe this unfortunate employment to have had an unhappy influence on both the morals and manners of the people, so far as it has extended. . . . Many of the young men employed in this business part at an early period with both modesty and principle. Their sobriety is exchanged for cunning, their honesty for imposition, and their decent behavior for coarse impudence.[4]

What Dwight reveals inadvertently about the mixture of American attitudes toward the Yankee peddler, Frances Trollope treats directly. This distinguished English visitor of the 1820s found the peddler interesting not for what he did but for what Americans said and felt about him:

> I never met a single individual in any part of the Union who did not paint these New Englanders as sly, grinding, selfish, and tricking. The Yankees (as the New Englanders are called) will avow these qualities themselves with a complacent smile, and boast that no people on the earth can match them at over-reaching a bargain. I have heard them unblushingly relate stories of their cronies and friends, which, if believed among us, would banish the heroes from the fellowship of honest men for ever. . . . It is by no means rare to meet elsewhere, in this working-day world of our's, people

who push acuteness to the verge of honesty, and sometimes, perhaps, a little bit beyond; but, I believe, the Yankee is the only one who will be found to boast of doing so. . . . if you listen to [his character] from himself, you might fancy him a god—though a tricky one; Mercury turned righteous and notable.[5]

This warning-celebration revealed that popular American values were fundamentally mixed, and in the development of the self-made man that same mixture is even more apparent.

The Yankee peddler can also help us understand the self-made man by the contrasts in the two stereotypes. Both share important qualities with Franklin's model self, but they emphasize quite different features of it. Like the model self, the legendary peddler is buoyant, cunning, and self-reliant. He operates in the same fluid, open-ended world, and he is more concerned with means than with ends. It is this feature of the model self that is exaggerated in the peddler, for finally this figure lives for the gambit and the anecdote. There is no development, no larger program of self-creation, no social rise for the peddler. If he seems more avaricious than the model self, he does not get rich or gain power; he simply plays more and more audacious variations on his own game. The self-made man, in contrast, lives for the larger story, as his very name indicates. Although he may, like the peddler, take immediate pleasure in a canny transaction, officially he tends to disregard the means of his rise. His concern—and here he distorts Franklin's model self in the opposite direction—is with the ends, the rise in the world, the transformation not only of self but of position.

The coexistence of these two variants on the model self reveals the doubleness of nineteenth-century American attitudes toward success. In his valuable study *Apostles of the Self-Made Man* John G. Cawelti analyzes two strains of popular fiction about social mobility in the decades before the Civil War.[6] In didactic and sentimental novels about rising in society, the authors did not imagine their subjects' careers in human terms; they relied on magical changes instead of cause-effect developments. In contrast, comic and satiric literature presented a detailed, amoral image of a mobile society in which shrewd, enterprising, roguish operators succeeded by cleverly seizing the main chance—Major Jack Downing with his Yankee brass, Davy Crockett with his vigorous self-promotion. The contrast is like the one I suggested between figures who live for the larger stories and those who revel in the local maneuvers. Cawelti sees in the contrasting fictional traditions an analogue of the split between the pieties and the practices of nineteenth-century business developers, such as Daniel Drew, expert in stock watering and pillar of the Methodist Church. The virtues celebrated in the success tracts—sobriety, thrift, industry, honesty—were not the means by which the great American fortunes were amassed. And the same public that overtly approved the Protestant ethic, covertly enjoyed the enterprises of a Sam Slick or a Commodore Vanderbilt. Looking at such discrepancies, Cawelti hypothesizes that the function of the self-help tracts was less to guide behavior than to rationalize it, to explain the confusing changes within an industrial society in terms of the shaken verities of the Protestant ethic.

Benjamin Franklin's model self was well adapted to such duplicity. The officially acceptable maxims of the *Autobiography* and *The Way to Wealth* could salve a reader's conscience while his imagination was engaged in the gamesmanship of the model self. In contrast with the success tracts of the Gilded Age with their stuffy platitudes and their earnestness about getting rich, Franklin's model self maintains a humorous poise, enjoying the Yankee peddler's cunning without risking his reputation, celebrating the prudential virtues without moralizing heavy-handedly or fawning on riches. More specifically, the model self's version of business enterprise could confuse imitators whose field would be industrial development or financial maneuvering. For if the printing shop is a simple place of work where diligence and sobriety actually pay off, it also forecasts some of the complexities of later capitalism by equating business with publication, work with advertisement, and production with publicity. The model self succeeds not only because of the virtues taught by Poor Richard but because of his shrewd grasp of promotion and human engineering. Then, too, for all Franklin's emphasis on his ability to *retire* from business after getting "a sufficient tho' moderate Fortune," he does begin his projection of the model self with the promising image of one who rose to affluence.

But if we think chiefly of the invitations to hypocrisy, we will miss the direct appeal of Franklin's model self in the nineteenth century, for the attractiveness of the model consists in its *not* being hypocritical or fragmented. Industriousness and cunning complement each other; they are not alternatives. What is good for the model self does turn out to be good for a larger community as well. The model self has both the peddler's zest in the gambit and the self-made man's pride in the accomplishment. The problem in the mid-nineteenth century was that this happy blending of qualities could no longer be sustained. And the irresistibly tempting aspect of the model self was the promise of mobility, the new start that had been all along in one form or other the romance of the European settlement of North America. When the model self was made into an icon of upward mobility, when change in self became less important than change in status, the sprightly disengagement of Franklin's memoirs turned into something closer to desperation.

External rewards figured more prominently in the life of the self-made man than in that of the model self. The model self's delight in the game yielded to the self-made man's concern with the stakes. By focusing on the possible change of status, the self-made man came to depend on the social structure that decreed what was of value. And by the middle of the nineteenth century, these values had narrowed considerably from Franklin's time. Political, agricultural, scientific, and technological pursuits had all become secondary. What one did to rise was to get money in business. Not only did this development make the self-made man narrower than the model self; it made him more earnest and vulnerable. Horatio Alger's heroes are pathetically mindful of the outward signs of respectability—suits and watches and clean faces and bankbooks. And the risen capitalists found their very identities at stake in the recurrence of financial panics. If the self-made man lost the detachment of the model self, he also lost the flexibility. Franklin's model self continually changed roles and frequently changed games as well. The self making of the self-made man was fixed in one game. For all the practicality, method, and canniness that he inherited from Franklin, the self-made man tended to become more rigid as he became more successful. In this sense the continuing appeal of Franklin's *Autobiography* in the Gilded Age may have resulted from the imaginative needs of "successful" men, who would clearly rather see in themselves the poise and variety of the model self than their own more desperate dependencies.

We can look at these contrasts in another way as well. The model self has virtually no inwardness. The self-made man's very desire for success and rewards indicates how his inward experience complicates his gambits and roles. To want is to have strong feelings. And that same inwardness can be subject to confusion. Both self-made man and model self inhabit a world in which appearances are all-important, but they handle these appearances differently. The model self masters them, whereas the self-made man is more often confused and victimized by them. Although the model self needs to be cautious amid fluid appearances, he also knows how to manipulate them for his own purposes. When he makes a self, he remembers that he is also making an impression, and part of the fun of his game is to test out the self he has become in someone else's eyes. The self-made man, in contrast, cares so much about what others seem to think of him that he cannot engineer impressions and read motives as coolly as his predecessor. If he takes over values and goals from his society, he also depends on other people's impressions for his sense of who he is. Like the confidence man and the model self, he lives in appearances and roles played out for the public, but he has far less initiative and control over the parts he plays.[7]

In practice, of course, such figures are not so clearly separated as in theory, and when we turn to imaginative literature for versions of self making, we find the stereotypes tangled with each other in complicated and illuminating ways. What was it like to try to live as the model self? How did the inwardness of real human experience complicate the gambits of self making? Virtually by genre the novel is adapted to explore such questions, for it characteritically tests fictive constructs against the density of actual experience. Many American novels have in fact probed the self-made man. I want to use three of them to reveal the inward consequences of self making—Charles Brockden Brown's *Arthur Mervyn* (1799–1800), William Dean Howells's *The Rise of Silas Lapham* (1885), and Theodore Dreiser's *An American Tragedy* (1925). These books are widely enough separated in time and issue to reveal indirectly part of the social history of the self-made man and quite a range of his problems. But they also have certain things in common that make them useful for my purpose. Arthur Mervyn, Silas Lapham, and Clyde Griffiths all discover new selves in the impressions others seem to have of them. Each is victimized and confused by the very opportunities arising from such impressions. They all live in appearances, sometimes manipulating them, more often being manipulated by them. And appropriately, all three novels blur the lines between model self, self-made man, and confidence man.

Arthur Mervyn as Fluid Self in a Fluid World

In spirit as well as time *Arthur Mervyn* is much closer than the other two novels to Franklin's memoirs. Properly speaking, the "self-made man" had not yet come into existence, at least not as a social stereotype that would compel imitators (Senator Henry Clay coined the term in 1832). Mervyn's experience, like Franklin's, is esentially open-ended, not hemmed in by a prevalent success ethic. But it has some significant complications not apparent in the *Autobiography*, and these develop as a consequence of that same fluidity of appearance that Franklin had found so promising.

Dubious impressions are, in fact, the basis of Charles Brockden Brown's fiction. Over and over his characters have to "solve" appearances. His narratives are contrived to emphasize ambiguities, and what is given seems always to admit of wrong constructions. To some degree his mysteries and sinister hints reveal Brown's roots in gothic fiction, but his interests are not in suspense or in supernatural events. He cares less about what happened than about how his characters can judge it. What can be deduced from present appearances? How many constructions are possible? How can one best act on the murky evidence now available? Such are the issues for Brown's characters. When the outside narrator of *Arthur Mervyn*, Dr. Stevens, wonders whether to believe the first half of the story Mervyn has told him, he reveals the difficulty all Brown's characters face in connecting motives to appearances: "Motives are endlessly varied, while actions continue the same; and an acute penetration may not find it hard to select and arrange motives, suited to exempt from censure any action that an human being can commit." Clara Wieland, the narrator of *Wieland*, puts the matter more desperately: "Let that man who shall purpose to assign motives to the actions of another blush at his folly and forbear."

Brown creates fictional worlds in which appearances are completely cut off from motives. Characters of great tact conceal selfish purposes; those with benevolent aims tend to blunder into ridiculous situations. Arthur Mervyn's actions are repeatedly open to damaging interpretations, and instead of correcting the errors of those who condemn him, he perversely praises them for judging soundly on the misleading evidence they had available. In the face of such discrepancies between impression and actuality, characters of good motive tend to be impatient with public opinion. In this sense Arthur Mervyn himself seems the inverse of a confidence man, for, content with his pure motives, he cares little about the impressions he makes. When his generous impulses come up against a complex, deceptive, suspicious world, he will not wait for clearer circumstances. He must act *now* and explain later. And Brown arranges the narrative so that the reader, like the surrounding characters, must wait some time for a reliable view of the protagonist. Midway through the novel, Wortley manages to cast suspicion on a great part of Mervyn's own story, and by raising the possibility that the young man is simply an apprentice to the swindler Welbeck, he reminds Dr. Stevens and readers as well how little we know for sure about Mervyn: "It was time . . . that your confidence in smooth features and fluent actions should have ended long ago."

The unreliability of appearances makes such suspicions appropriate, but as in the world of Melville's *The Confidence-Man* the suspicious characters are strangely gullible, perhaps because their suspicion is itself so generalized and erratic. Even the master fraud Welbeck is easily taken in by several people. One has, after all, to believe in something. One must assent to *some* construction of appearances. And this is where the confidence man comes in. When appearances drift so erratically, when characters of good heart disregard the impressions they make, when judgment is so dubious, there is an open field for someone who manipulates impressions and beliefs.

Brown seems to have invented his first major confidence man, Carwin, as a means of testing the shaky beliefs and assumptions of the characters in *Wieland*. Carwin is a ventriloquist, that is, a specialist in the feigning of sensation; he is an ideal agent to demonstrate the risks of credulity. For much of the narrative he appears to be a shadowy gothic villain with the stock traits of deep insight, mysterious powers, and penetrating eyes. But the European demon turns out to be merely an American technician after all. Unlike his prototype in gothic fiction who has intuitive knowledge and supernatural powers, Carwin hides in closets, reads people's diaries, and throws his voice. Where the gothic villain has a deep but perverted nature, Carwin is upright but shallow.

In Carwin, Brown projected a cluster of qualities that were to appear often in American fictional characters: an uncontrollable curiosity about others, a tendency to test others so as to gain knowledge and exercise his talent, a love of showy effects, a helpless addiction to his own skills, and a fundamental absence of depth or inwardness. Essentially he is a muddle-headed mechanic. His easy resourcefulness as ventriloquist and mimic encourages him to bumble further and further into difficulties, and despite his powers, he does not understand the springs of human action. Although he knows how to scatter wonder and fear, he cannot anticipate the inward consequences of his tricks. His playful casting of voices precipitates the central psychic crisis of the novel in which Wieland "hears" God commanding him to kill his wife and children, but in the end Carwin seems too superficial to be judged.

If Carwin demonstrates that the world of Brown's fiction is disturbingly open to imposture, Arthur Mervyn shows how one can rise in such a world. Less deceptive and more benevolent than Carwin, Mervyn seems a comparatively innocent young man. In fact, Carwin's qualities are split in the later book between Arthur Mervyn and his patron, Thomas Welbeck, the harmless intentions and ungovernable curiosity going to Mervyn and the duplicity and contrivance to Welbeck. But both of these figures have something Carwin lacks—far-sighted ambition. Each is prepared to take greater advantage of a fluid world than Carwin can imagine. The pairing of Mervyn and Welbeck is central to Brown's characterization—witness the continuing suspicions that they are in league—and in my circuitous approach to this shifty young man, I want to consider what it means that the career of a naïve youth on the make is counterpointed to the gambits of a known swindler.

Despite the mysteries he surrounds himself with, there can be little final doubt about Welbeck's nature. Shortly after they meet, Mervyn sees Welbeck assume a new self at a party so skillfully that the young man himself cannot tell which is the real Welbeck. His accomplishments as a deceiver have been the means by which he could carry out his youthful ambition—to gain opulence and respect without industry. For one who dissimulates so well, it is fitting that Welbeck's ruling passion should be for the regard of others. In short, Welbeck has become a rather straightforward confidence man, and some of his major frauds have been at the expense of scoundrels who deal in money as a commodity and whose motives in their own transactions with Welbeck were to cheat him: "Grown grey in studying the follies and the stratagems of men, these veterans were overreached. No one pities them."

What is a good-hearted youth from the country doing with a man like that? Of course they come together accidentally and Mervyn has already agreed to serve as Welbeck's live-in secretary well before he begins to discover the true nature of his patron. He is properly horrified by Welbeck's tactics and motives, and yet he maintains a puzzling loyalty to him. He finds himself excited by Welbeck's surroundings and even more so by his powers. Later Mervyn defends his association with the swindler by saying that it taught him many things and allowed him to meet people in the city. Welbeck has given the young man, who left the country impatient with drudgery, a five-day apprenticeship in urban possibilities. He has dressed him opulently, put him by chance in possession of a fortune, and introduced him to the dazzling world of transferable wealth. Although Mervyn constantly protests that his own motives are generous and Welbeck's selfish, he has learned from his patron that one needn't labor for wages and that in a world of floating capital surprising things can be gained by credit and reputation. He has entered the domain of the criminal confidence man and of Franklin's model self, and if he isn't so clearly a scoundrel as the former, he also isn't so clearly attractive as the latter. There is something finally dubious about Arthur Mervyn, some erosion of the line between opportunity and opportunism.

The problem with Mervyn is that although he has a generous, sound heart—far greater depth in this regard than Carwin—his outward nature is quite severed from his inner self. His ruling motives are benevolence and curiosity, the one proceeding from his inner nature or "real" self, the other relating to the surfaces of his experience. It is as if one self feels and another self experiments. Because he recognizes the gap between appearance and motive in his world at large, he glosses over the discrepancies in his own conduct, assuring himself that his benevolent aims make it unnecessary to scrutinize his behavior. His curiosity and its consequences thus draw him along unchecked. For both Carwin and Mervyn, what "curiosity" amounts to is an instinctive alertness to the outward possibilities of their worlds. They are drawn helplessly into what might be done in the given circumstances, and thus they both assume whatever shapes are currently available. As Mervyn says, "The stuff I was made of was at once damnably tough and devilishly pliant." He persists in his good intentions and at the same time sinuously adapts himself to take advantage of every opportunity. Like Carwin, he spends part of his first night in the city hiding in a closet, listening to a plot of fraud against a rich scalawag, and like a born confidence man he intuitively grasps the possibility: "By means as inscrutable as those which conducted me hither, I may hereafter be enabled to profit by this detection of a plot."

His entire introduction to Philadelphia shows how his outward self can drift from his inner nature. As he arrives in the city, despite his consciousness of his own benevolence, he somehow *knows* that the seeming generosity of others is not to be trusted. While continuing to celebrate inwardly the values and constraints of his rural upbringing, he drops them easily in his outward responses. He had been brought up to despise luxury and pomp, "but at the distance at which I now stood, the lofty edifices, the splendid furniture, and the copious accommodations of the rich, excited my admiration and my envy." And when Welbeck suddenly offers him a position and a change from country fustian to elegant silks and satins, Mervyn feels himself the creature of "some magic that disdains the cumbrousness of nature's progress": "I could scarcely recognize any lineaments as my own." Even when we come to know his feelings reliably, his "innocence" remains ambiguous, for his qualities conflict—good motives, high-minded disregard for the impressions he makes, readiness to seize on what's available. His immediate conduct is constrained neither by his own inspection nor by the opinions of others, and yet his innocence of bad intentions encourages good people in the long run to trust him.

The city that offers him such bedazzling new opportunities also changes his sense of who he is and blurs the concept of integrity. He comes to like the very feeling of change, the constant shifting of goals and promises. When circumstances make it possible for him to marry Eliza Hadwin, the rustic girl he has apparently loved from a distance, he discovers that there has been "a revolution" in his mind and that the agrarian virtues and aspirations of his past are now rather boring. "I had passed," he says, "from my cottage to the world," and he has enjoyed his "rapid progress" so much that he does not want to limit his choices now. Rather he commits himself for several years "to activity and change," recognizing as he does so that he wants to affirm the flexible self he has become: "Should I mix with the world, enrol myself in different classes of society; be a witness to new scenes; might not my modes of judging undergo essential variations?"

Indeed they do. Mervyn becomes more and more adaptable, both in manners and in judgment. He takes on new shapes—rearranges his very life—so easily that one wonders if he has any inward resistance at all or any control over his metamorphoses. His behavior seems as fluid as the appearances in his world, as if it were utterly disconnected from his feelings. In this sense he resembles Franklin's model self, for he can control others by keeping his feelings detached from his maneuvers. He sits through the passionate outbursts of Welbeck and Philip Hadwin in comical calmness, and he flirts with Betty Lawrence to learn about urban manners while remaining entirely unmoved by her seductions. Yet Brown's world has a psychological density that is not part of Franklin's memoirs, and it thus offers a perspective in which Mervyn's detachment is disturbing. It is not a sign of his self-control but of his discontinuity. Welbeck's aims—seamy as they are—emerge clearly and do guide his conduct. Mervyn remains murky, for no matter how commendable his motives, one can never be sure he will effectively act on them. As he rushes about from one plot to the next, ready at any new event to change his entire plan of conduct, he becomes quite unpredictable, even to himself. Perhaps his good heart will never be corrupted or even tempted by the blandishments of the fluid urban world; perhaps he can rise in this world without losing his balance. It doesn't really matter. With his peculiar kind of innocence, Brown's young man on the make might *do* anything.

Silas Lapham as Mimic of Manners

Like Arthur Mervyn, Silas Lapham mixes with the urban world, enrolls himself in different classes of society, and finds himself confused by the promises of his situation. But whereas Brown emphasizes the unreliability of appearances, Howells shows appearances to be only too firmly the index of personal differences. He tests the fiction of the model self by exposing it to a world in which manners are far more than imitable gestures to be adapted at will. And by giving his protagonist a well-developed substantial character, he reveals precisely how difficult and dangerous it is to try to become the model self. Interestingly enough, Howells picks up Lapham's story after he is already a self-made man, reputedly worth a million dollars, and his economic success has actually been the result of the virtues making up the popular ideal of success—diligence, enterprise, probity, and a product of high quality. The "rise" of the title is not his climb to fame and fortune but his drift into some of the consequences of his earlier accomplishment. For Howells the model self and the self-made man represent possibilities at different phases of a career, and the nature of self making changes fundamentally with these phases.

The book opens at precisely that point in Lapham's career when he has achieved in its simplest form the cultural goal of rising from meager means to affluence, and to mark his achievement he is being interviewed for the "Solid Men of Boston" series. When Bartley Hubbard, the journalist, refers to Lapham as "a fine type of the successful American," he immediately poses one of the basic problems of the novel, how to relate the personal to the typical. Lapham's early story so perfectly recapitulates the cultural stereotype—the "regulation thing," as Hubbard irreverently calls it—that despite his justifiable pride, Lapham is embarrassed by the familarity of his experiences. Hubbard tries to hurry him "past the period where risen Americans are all pathetically alike in their narrow circumstances, their sufferings, and their aspirations," and in writing the story, he transmutes Lapham's actual experiences back into the conventional commodity—the education by Poor Richard, the emphasis on opportunity and luck waiting for the observant man, the availability of Lapham's life for emulation by aspiring boys. Later Lapham's business friends imply that they have come up themselves and know that the standard terms of praise in the article are fraudulent. Yet neither Hubbard's cynicism nor the knowing smiles of these friends can offset the fact that Lapham has satisifed the simple, standard expectations of a self-made man. Although he has been highly practical and promotion oriented (he paints large rocks in conspicuous places to advertise his product), he has not become a gamesman. He believes in his paint and in hard, honest work.

The problem for Lapham is that his social self is lagging behind his business self. He had made his money without much effort to change his status or his habits. Unlike Arthur Mervyn and Clyde Griffiths, he has come to the city belatedly and for several years has regarded it only as the necessary scene of his business activities. His initiation to the possibilities of urban fluidity takes place when he is already in his fifties. It is thus complicated by his aging and his family. He cannot meet his new opportunities with the confident energy and resilience of his younger self, and his own motives for himself are entangled with his wife's desires and judgments and with his wish to provide opportunities for his daughters. Yet if his family is a source of many of the misunderstandings in the book, it is also an index of Lapham's complex solidity, and this in turn is what resists his adventures as the model self. At the outset of the novel, however, something is happening to Silas Lapham. In the past he has identified with his work, his making of money, his simple family life. Now he begins to identify with his own accomplishment, to see himself in the eyes of the public as a person of some interest for having made himself. With his "hopeful temperament and fondness for round numbers" he sets his figures beyond his actual worth, and he is ready to transfer to other pursuits the confidence inspired by his money making.

Like so many men on the make, Lapham discovers accidentally what there is to want and to be. At a summer watering place Mrs. Lapham helps nurse one of the Corey daughters, whose mother then returns a calling card; young Tom Corey develops a genuine interest in the paint business; Bromfield Corey visits Lapham's office. In these attentions Silas Lapham learns about a new and most attractive set of manners, and the apparent esteem in which he is held by these estimable people enlarges his sense of his own possibilities. The fact that the Coreys and the article in the *Events* have made something of Lapham, tempts him to start again in a new field of accomplishment. Taking his cue from a situation he did not create or anticipate, he begins to think he can "hobnob" on Beacon Hill. No sooner does he feel himself a self-*made* man than he finds he is still to be made. Thus through much of the novel Lapham falls into double-thinking, an unstable mixture of his pride in the past and his obsequiousness and insecurity about the future rise. He sums up his new, desperate assumptions in talking his wife into accepting the Coreys' dinner invitation: "If we're ever going to be anybody at all, we've got to go and see how it's done."

This statement marks Lapham's transition from the earlier and simpler phase of self-made man to the more open-ended possibilities of the model self. Most of the assumptions are there—the sense of promise and self-creation, the plasticity of character, the attention to appearances that can presumably be gotten up. The family needs to consult an etiquette book before the dinner, for Lapham assumes that "society" is simply a set of learned roles. But where the model self not only masters the play of appearances but skillfully takes his cue from them, Lapham finds that it is not so easy to "read" observable manners. He does not know that the "great man" whose manner of saying "What name?" he copies when meeting people, was being deliberately rude, nor does he know that James Bellingham's habit of tucking his napkin in his collar, which Lapham also imitates, is merely a tolerated eccentricity. After dinner he reads the gentlemen's grave concern over his own drunkenness as interest in himself and tribute to his social abilities. Such misreadings are at the base of Howells's realism. He shows that the presumed plasticity of the model self· fails to account for the actual entanglement of manners with inner qualities and class assumptions. Society, for Howells, is more complex and substantial—more real—than allowed for in the fiction of the model self, and human character itself is also more weighty. At the dinner Lapham is not only confused about the innuendoes but troubled by his own slowness. In contrast with the light, flexible model self, Lapham finds himself less and less able to perform because of the soddenness induced by the wine and by his own lack of social exercise. He is a drag on the game.

At the same time that the simple self-made man is introduced to a new phase of social self making, his business affairs reach a critical stage of complexity. And Lapham's problems in making this transition are curiously similar to those he has in society. The symbol and immediate agent of the change is his former partner, Milton K. Rogers. Rogers is a business con man. He masters the appearance of bland caution and good citizenship, preserves his gamesman's self-possession in business maneuvers, and manages to cast issues in such fluid and complex terms that one's moral judgment is stymied. He lives for speculation and appears quite ready to deceive investors and exploit their confidence or their desire to make an extralegal profit. In one sense he simply victimizes Lapham by drawing on him for bad loans. But when Lapham is himself gradually lured into speculation, against his own former principles, it is apparent that Rogers symbolizes a more general crisis. Lapham is at the transition between industrial and finance capitalism, between producing goods and trading paper. His confidence in his skills at the former tempts him to think he can also master the latter and outwit any rascal he comes up against. As the Coreys showed him his social possibilities, Rogers introduces him to new business modes, and in the moral murkiness surrounding Rogers's deals, Lapham feels adrift from his own principles. He needs to become the model self—expert at games and master of financial interchange—in order to carry on with Rogers or to bargain with the West Virginia company that has finally mounted serious competition against his own paint.

As Howells presents them, both high society and finance capitalism require a certain lightness and flexibility, and they both depend, as a guest at the Corey dinner puts it, on a person's willingness to say things he isn't sure of. Lapham is a drag on both. As the wine and his inexperience slowed him down at the dinner, his moral paralysis and financial hesitation keep him from taking advantage of Rogers's gambit to unload nearly worthless mill stock on unsuspecting English investors. And his inability to move into finance capitalism with its dependence on quick insight and exact timing, means more than a loss of new opportunity. It costs him much of his honestly gained fortune. Of course, Howells presents this defeat as a triumph. The separation between real self and model self, posed as a problem in the opening interview, is finally effected by Lapham's moral test and by his experience of adversity. But it is not simply that Silas Lapham has survived a moral crisis. The reason he fails to become the model self in society and business is that his substantial character drags behind the fictive image. His heaviness is his humanity. He has, finally, what a good confidence man cannot have, a "simple, rude soul."

Clyde Griffiths as Failed Con Man

Whereas Howells shows that in the end the actual self is better than the model, Dreiser hints that failure to become the model self may be due to basic defects of character. In the years between 1896 and 1929 the philosophy of success took on new themes, and Dreiser, who was highly sensitive to popular myths, absorbed some of these themes to complicate the earlier tradition of the self-made man. Popular writers and lecturers like Russell Conwell, George Lorimer, Roger Babson, and especially Orison Swett Marden (for whose magazine *Success* Dreiser wrote at the turn of the century) put new stress on the development of personality.[8] Instead of frugality, diligence, and sobriety, one needed power of will and personal magnetism in order to compete for what were now seen as a limited number of prizes. Doors would open almost magically for the person who could tap the inner energies of faith, confidence, and ambition, who could forcefully say I WILL. The new success philosophy explained failure by noting that some people with weak wills simply could not act independently or take initiative.

Dreiser assesses Clyde Griffiths against just this standard: "Clyde had a soul that was not destined to grow up. He lacked decidedly that mental clarity and inner directing application that in so many permits them to sort out from the facts and avenues of life the particular thing or things that make for their direct advancement." Such inner force, almost an emotional idealism, had already been basic to Dreiser's characterization of Sister Carrie and of Frank Cowperwood. And in *An American Tragedy*, where the drama of personal relations so often turns on characters' trying to take emotional advantage of each other, the characters are divided by their inner "force." Gilbert Griffiths, Sondra Finchley, and Hortense Briggs have it; Clyde Griffiths and Roberta Alden do not.

Yet if it is given that Clyde is much smaller and more pathetic than his dreams, the drama of his development turns on quite different issues. His failure, as it is actually built up for the reader in painstaking detail, is measured more directly against the old-fashioned images of the model self and the self-made man. To see how this is so, we must begin with the immediate consequences of his lack of "mental clarity and inner directing application." Like Dreiser's other protagonists, Clyde has a powerful yearning. He feels himself "more refined" than those around him, "a thing apart," innately superior and thus unsuited to manual labor and contemptuous of drudges. Yet because he cannot focus and express this yearning, Clyde depends on suggestions from his environment. Even more than Brown or Howells, Dreiser indicates how thoroughly and pathetically the self-made man takes on the collective dreams spun out in his surroundings. By the time he has been a few years away from his youth in Kansas City, Clyde has developed "the compulsion to make his own way." As he puts it in a letter to his mother, "I got to get on in this world." The images of getting ahead that he has absorbed from his experience, however, involve traditional self-creation, not development of magnetism. He believes, as Horatio Alger had promised in over 100 novels, that if he works steadily and behaves respectably, he will make the right connection. And his rich uncle in Lycurgus, New York, sees his encouragement of Clyde in the same terms; he will offer his nephew the chance "to do something and be somebody."

But Clyde absorbs more from his environment than a definition of success. He also picks up hints about the means of advancement. He has a "fluid temperament," alert to the promises of each situation. His introduction to the world of the Green-Davidson Hotel in

Kansas City is the equivalent of the model self's journey to the city. In "the moving panorama of the main lobby" he sees "what it meant to be rich." Although Dreiser sees it as a "materially affected or gaudy" realm, Clyde finds the frank display of appearances simply gorgeous. And the sudden transition from an impoverished, morally rigid background to this "grandeur" impresses him, as it did Arthur Mervyn, with the possibility that he can quickly transform himself in a magical world. The astonishing change in his own appearance when he puts on the bellboy's uniform confirms this suggestion, as does the easy flow of money in tips, so dissociated from the actual work he has to do. More generally, he is tempted by the absence of restraint, the sense that the world is more fluid and unstable than he had dreamed. It is not surprising that one of the educative stories in this world involves a confidence artist who rips off both the hotel and the woman he brought with him. Similarly, when Clyde arrives in Lycurgus, he has the heady experience of being taken for something he is not—a member of the most affluent and prestigious family—and this again not only opens possibilities for him but inwardly traps him in a set of delusive hopes.

Clyde not only senses the promise in a given place; he quickly notes the image of himself that others seem to see. In his first application for a job, "it occurred to him that if he wanted to get on he ought to insinuate himself into the good graces of people—do or say something that would make them like him." He is repeatedly excited about making impressions, and during his three-year apprenticeship in Chicago he conscientiously develops "smoothness of address" and a gentlemanly, reserved air. But in contrast with the model self, he does not control the impressions he makes as much as he is controlled by them. Like the self-made man, he depends on others' opinions, as does his uncle, who merely accepts himself "at the value that others placed upon him and all those who, like himself, were successful." But Clyde is even more abject. He shows what it is like to have one's whole sense of self turn on others' valuations. When he arrives in Lycurgus, his cousin Gilbert coldly condescends to him, whereas other employees defer to him as someone important, and his self-image undergoes corresponding variations. He assumes more bravado with Roberta Alden because she believes that he is part of the local aristocracy. And at the end of the book he even depends on his mother's faith for his own sense of innocence.

Furthermore, it is not simply a problem of who he is but who he is *to be*. Dreiser gets hold of something disregarded in much of the literature of the self-made man, the inability of a man on the make to relate to his present situation. Clyde cannot work properly "at the bottom" as a demonstration of his capacity to move up because he does not regard his beginning tasks as his real work. Similarly, he does not know who should be his friends. Not only does he feel above those working at his level; he fears that association with them will hamper his chances with the people whose class he aspires to. But he is not *yet* qualified for social relations with the Finchleys and Griffithses. Hence his loneliness and his secret affair with Roberta Alden.

At his most extreme, Clyde is a creature deliberately made up by the attitudes others assume. If his uncle Samuel Griffiths wants to make him "somebody," Sondra Finchley, partly as a joke on the stuffy Gilbert Griffiths, has the whim to make Clyde a socially eligible young man. And her feigned interest in him not only causes others of her class to think more of Clyde but convinces him of his own merits so that his conviction in his new role turns Sondra's pretense of regard into something like love. It is virtually a caricature of William James's description of a pragmatic justification for faith: "The desire for a certain kind of truth [in personal relations] brings about that special truth's existence." Like Lapham at the Corey dinner, Clyde feels himself full of new possibilities at the parties he attends with Sondra, and he even makes up a new past and a new self to support the image others apparently have of him. And at his trial, "Clyde Griffiths" is a fabrication of the defense lawyers, who engage in a "frank program of trickery and deception on his behalf," creating a story of his motives in the drowning of Roberta Alden and coaching him in how to play the role on the stand.

Dreiser's devotion to willpower, magnetism, and "inner directing application" was only one aspect of his relation to popular notions of success. Much more of his characterization of Clyde Griffiths draws on the earlier myth of the self-made man and the ideal of the model self. Like the self-made man Clyde is more victim than manipulator of appearances, and a gamesman in only a limited way, for he is simply desperate to get ahead. But he has another and larger failure, one that Benjamin Franklin and Horatio Alger would have analyzed as Dreiser did although without so sympathetic an account of it. Franklin confesses "that hard-to-be-govern'd Passion of Youth, had hurried me frequently into Intrigues with low Women that fell in my Way, which were attended with some Expence and great Inconvenience." Dreiser would call it "sex" and "chemisms," but the issue is the same. Franklin's model self emerges as such passions are put in separate compartments so that one can move lightly and at will from one pursuit to another. Clyde's problem is that he simply can't do it. His emotions are so strong and so hard to conceal that, despite his aspirations and plans and contrivances, he cannot play his own games. Although Dreiser overtly divides his characters between those with force and those without, he makes it plain that the actual struggle of Clyde's life is between sex and success.

Except for the explicitness and indulgence in detail, Book One of *An American Tragedy* sounds like Horatio Alger giving an exemplary tale about the temptations of urban life to be overcome by a boy who would rise in the world—the drinking, the expensive clothes, the extravagant dinners, the moral fluidity of reckless youths, and worst of all, the women. The long sequence of Clyde's infatuation with Hortense Briggs shows him losing his savings, his promise, and his reputation, just as Alger would have warned, and Dreiser is so effective at making us feel the degradation that he implicitly reinforces the ideal of the model self's detachment. Clyde's hopeful self making repeatedly gives way to passionate self-destruction. After he flees from Kansas City, he enters a period of self-control. He develops self-reliance and deliberateness. And most important, at the prestigious male club in Chicago where he works as a bell-boy, he sees a group of highly successful men who are unaware of or unaffected by "that element of passion, which, to his immature mind up to this time, had seemed to propel and disarrange so many things in those lesser worlds." He resolves to become indifferent to sex, "a disgraceful passion." Yet in Lycurgus his carefully planned social career is again disarranged when he cannot maintain indifference.

What thickens the model self for Dreiser is human emotion. Ungovernable sexual urges and helpless infatuations disrupt the program of self-creation, and Clyde's energy and imagination are withdrawn from the game he has been playing. Yet Dreiser's implications about the model self are vastly different from Howells's. Howells had shown that something was missing in the ideal of the model self—it disregarded too much about character and about social class. Dreiser, in contrast, shows what kind of pressures made the fiction of the model self so persistently attractive in American history. Novelistically, he immerses us in nagging worries. Slowly, in painstaking detail he builds up for us the ordinary quality of Clyde's emotional experience. Each twist in his feelings or in his circumstances is oppressively catalogued, and neither Clyde nor the reader can step back from the experience to abridge it, summarize it, put it in a controlling perspective. Dreiser forces us to share Clyde's yearning for detachment, lightness, and flexibility, for the summarizing and abstracting power that Faulkner will give to Thomas Sutpen—another descendant of Franklin—who can simply say, "So I went to the West Indies."

Such abridgments, such magical compressions and transformations of ordinary experience, represent one of the great powers of the model self. They are essential parts of the myth of self-creation. By detaching himself from the pressures of feeling and of circumstance, the model self maintains a puzzling innocence, which unites such diverse characters as Arthur Mervyn, Thomas Sutpen, and Jay Gatsby. But Clyde Griffiths cannot rise to such innocence, nor can he exercise the consequent power of abridgment; and for Dreiser the problem is not in the ideal of the model self but in Clyde's own character. Clyde comes to trial and execution not merely because he has been ruthless in pursuit of success, but because he lacks the poise, disengagement, and control of appearances to carry it off. He cannot become the confidence man he should be.

5

PROMISE LAND

Exhilaration is the Breeze
That lifts us from the Ground
And leaves us in another place
Whose statement is not found—

—Emily Dickinson

What would happen to us who live on the surface, if this fellow in some new transmigration should have acquired power to do what he now delights to say? He must be watched.

—Ralph Waldo Emerson

The confidence that we have always had as a people is not simply some romantic dream or a proverb in a dusty book that we read just on the Fourth of July. It is the idea which founded our nation and which has guided our development as a people. Confidence in the future has supported everything else—public institutions and private enterprise, our own families and the very Constitution of the United States. Confidence has defined our course and has served as a link between generations.

—Jimmy Carter

Mister, I ain't a boy, no I'm a man,
And I believe in a promised land.

—Bruce Springsteen

Boosters—Pep!

—George F. Babbitt's lapel button

When the complex qualities of Franklin's model self were broken up in separate figures in the nineteenth century, the one who gathered to himself the strongest affirmative energies was the booster, a being who lives in and on promise: not any specific promised reward, but promise itself, trust, confidence. Emily Dickinson spoke for many who "dwell in possibility, A fairer house than prose." From Captain John Smith's promotional assurances about the year-round abundance of game and fruit and fish on the delightful coast of New England to Del Webb's tracts describing miracle communities now about to be developed in Arizona's deserts, America has existed, as Wallace Stevens would say, in our descriptions of it, and these have been in the future tense. The trickster, a figure who appears in the mythology of many cultures, is domesticated as an American by incorporating this promissory quality— hence his name Confidence Man. Whereas the traditional trickster exists on the margins of cultural value, deliberately suspending or testing or even flouting the laws that keep things stable,[1] the confidence man assumes his importance by acting out the ambiguities of American ideals themselves. If he has the sly, opportunistic nature celebrated in the folklore of Yankee peddler and Robber Baron, he also shares the hopeful, future-oriented spirit of Thomas Jefferson and William James, who believe that faith is creative and that possibility is one of the major elements of human experience.

Americans divided very early into parties, and the basis was only in part political. Jefferson was quick to place the antagonism of Federalists and Republicans in a broader division that he regarded as permanent in human affairs, between those who fear that people must be surrounded with safeguards and those who believe that people can be trusted to handle their own affairs. Although the immediate basis for this division has to do with ways of organizing a government, Jefferson's repeated emphasis on fear and confidence when he characterized the split suggests that he saw the fundamental contrast not in political strategy but in temperament. Emerson later picked up this contrast and again emphasized its permanence in human nature. He characterized the two sides as the Party of Memory and the Party of Hope, those who feel warned and constrained by historical precedent and those who are buoyed up by the possibilities of fresh experiment. My subject in this chapter is the Party of Hope, Jefferson's party who "like the dreams of the future better than the history of the past," the people for whom confidence is not merely a useful venture but a force to sustain their very well-being. Afloat in possibility themselves, they try to breathe their trust into others, to demonstrate the efficacy of faith. This party has been so numerous in American history, especially in the nineteenth century, that I can treat only selected aspects of it and suggest how many-faceted the promissory tradition has been.

What I want to indicate is how this tradition has sustained and complicated the cultural image of the confidence man. My first topic is "land speculation" as a force and a metaphor in the making of America. Then I will turn to four of the major figures in the promissory tradition—Thomas Jefferson, Walt Whitman, William James, and Jay Gatsby—to explore the strategies and joys of creative confidence.

Before turning directly to the Party of Hope, however, we must note the importance of the doubters. As R. W. B. Lewis has demonstrated in *The American Adam,* it was not simply a yearning for innocence that marked nineteenth-century America but a dialogue about it. In fact, one of the signs that the Party of Hope lived on faith itself was the existence of doubters whose skepticism was as embracing a temperamental quality as their counterparts' hope. "Men seem," as Emerson said, "to be constitutionally believers and unbelievers." When Goodman Brown leaves Faith behind, he does not return a realist; he finds himself living now with Doubt. And although his story is based in Calvinist experience, Hawthorne makes clear that the allegory of Faith and Doubt is not exclusively or even primarily a religious issue. Repeatedly in nineteenth-century American literature the drama of faith and doubt converts religious to psychological experience. The rhythms of Emerson's essays with their moments of buoyancy and their days of bewildered doubt are matched more sardonically by the arguments in Melville's *The Confidence-Man* between constitutional believers and constitutional skeptics. The risk for idealists and believers—both having been nurtured by faith itself—is that if their promise is withdrawn or their generous plans thwarted, they will become cynics. That is one way of looking at the confidence man, who, as Dos Passos noted, has found it's as easy to pass bad checks as good ones.

But knowledge of the ways of the world need not destroy one's faith, and the most characteristic American confidence men are not disillusioned sharpers but experimenters who try to make faith practicable. Franklin, for instance, clearly knew what the world is like, but only in his matter-of-fact celebration of practical techniques can we find any hint of cynicism. In voice, attitude, and assumption he stands at the head of American boosters, confident that bustling activity is progress. He presents a world in which trust pays off, and he promises that anyone can have his rewards by diligence and frugality. Earlier I considered Franklin's model as a self-image; here I would stress that his very promise is an act of creation. The many employers in the late nineteenth century who at Christmas gave their employees tracts based on Franklin's model knew what they were about. The promise is a means of producing a mass of sober, industrious workers. Franklin's individual model thus allows a growing establishment to motivate its ideal subjects. This is how Ralph Ellison sees the promissory model—as the Establishment's means of manipulation. When the Invisible Man enters a dream world under the guidance of his black-trickster grandfather, the briefcase he has been awarded by the leading whites of his community appears filled with nested envelopes, in the innermost of which is the core of the booster ethic as Ellison knows it: "Keep This Nigger-Boy Running."

The Promoter's Vision: Land Speculation and the Making of America

Directly as well as indirectly Franklin was a promoter. The *Autobiography* was not only one of the major how-to-do-it manuals in American history but a promotional tract as well, an instrument to further the development of the new country. This point is made explicitly in the letter by Benjamin Vaughan that Franklin includes before Part Two. Vaughan notes that Franklin's picture of the internal circumstances of his country "will very much tend to invite to it settlers of virtuous and manly minds. . . . I do not know of a more efficacious advertisement than your Biography would give." And among his many projects as booster Franklin included nation booming. Like promotional tracts from Captain Smith's onwards, his "Information to Those Who Would Remove to America" (c. 1782) warns that immigrants will have to work hard for their sustenance but at the same time it offers genuine promise to those who are diligent. For artisans the promise is that the expanding population will require more goods and thus journeymen can quickly become their own masters. For farmers, great tracts of fertile land can be had cheaply on the frontiers. And for investors, the promise inheres in the increase of land values as the growing population fills in and improves wilderness areas. Whereas the earliest promotional tracts had stressed the natural resources of the new country—land, game, fish, and more fancifully, mineral riches—Franklin shifts the emphasis toward human resources. The growing population itself is what makes removal to America and investment in its lands worthwhile. Even the enterprising farmer depends not only on the land but on a nearby market to sell his produce. In such a situation, the more investors the boomer can convince, the truer his promises become. Nation building thus turns out to be a massive game of confidence.

Although many European adventurers had been drawn to the New World by the lure of mines and quick wealth, the primary impetus to settlement was the possibility of land ownership.[2] For one who did not have an estate already, the difficulty of acquiring land and independence in Europe was so great that open lands were a powerful motive to emigrate. And the record of individual and communal enterprise in clearing and cultivating American lands justifies the familiar picture of an industrious people turning a wilderness into a thriving land of farms and towns. But there was another side of the picture which became more and more apparent after the middle of the eighteenth century. If one could rise in the world by saving some of one's earnings, buying a tract of undeveloped land, diligently clearing and developing it, and becoming a rich farmer, one could perhaps get rich more quickly and with far less effort by buying the land cheaply, holding it, and selling it for a profit. The trick depended on one of two conditions: that the improvements of neighboring lands would increase the value of one's own unimproved acreage, or that a fever of speculation would draw so many potential investors as to make prices temporarily soar.[3] Either condition required that instead of laboring directly on the land one work indirectly on other people's confidence. Thus actual settlement and virtually fraudulent land booming were twin features of American development from early seizings of rich bottom land along Virginia's coastal rivers to recent speculation in suburban shopping-center sites.

By the time of the Revolution it had become a commonplace of British observers to see Americans as characterized by speculative fever. Something seemed to happen in the New World environment to make even the staunch New England Puritans, who had planned to use land grants to spread the true religion, begin to usurp and later to auction off town sites, driving newcomers who wanted land to the frontiers.[4] By the last decades of the eighteenth century people came to believe treatises like Franklin's which argued that mere growth of population would inevitably puff up land values, and land speculation became a virtual mania. This wave of gullibility crested in the infamous sale of Yazoo lands (present-day Alabama and Mississippi) by the Georgia legislature in 1795, a transaction in which New Englanders alone risked $2,000,000 on unseen lands. And when the Georgia legislature rescinded the scrip a year after the original sale, the result was not disillusionment but a fresh round of speculation over whether or not the new federal government would rescue investors by backing up the rescinded scrip.[5] From the speculations over frontier lands claimed simultaneously by two or three colonial governments and properly still possessed by the native inhabitants, to the mania over prospective town sites in the Old Northwest, to the mid-nineteenth-century ventures in western lands that might adjoin a new railroad line, there was a series of bubbles for investors, and European visitors repeatedly noted the circulation, restless movement, and boiling agitation of Americans, who seemed to inhabit a fluid world where riches and poverty constantly changed places.

The direct effects of land jobbing have been studied elsewhere,[6] and I will note them only as they illuminate America's development into a confidence culture. One ironic effect of large purchases of land held for future profit was that the tracts withheld from cultivation could choke in or destroy a potential settlement, thus preventing the very population that could have made the investment pay off. The large acreages held by investors tended to drive new settlers still further across the frontier, thereby dispersing individuals more rapidly than would be healthy for the development of civil institutions like schools, a point acutely made by Ray Allen Billington. The frantic efforts of investors to get their property improved and their claims ratified corrupted local politics. Yet the cupidity of speculators and adventurers did spread the population, and the large land companies could provide well-spotted lands, transportation, and credit for potential settlers. For all their venality and unreliability, land speculators were important agents in the development of America.

Indirectly, the effects of land speculation are even more illuminating. The seething turmoil among Americans over new lands, new towns, new railroads was noted by skeptical domestic observers as well as European visitors. Timothy Dwight in his *Travels in New England and New York* attacked not only peddlers but speculators too. In the spread of paper currency after the Revolution, in the Funding System for paying the national debt, in the fairyland sale of western lands, and in the pride of frontier entrepreneurs over hasty transactions, he saw the same thing—the risk that people would be corrupted through the prospect of easy wealth. "In certain stages of society the expectations of enterprising men may, with little difficulty, be raised to any imaginable height. Fortunes, they will easily believe, may be amassed at a stroke, without industry or economy, by mere luck, or the energy of superior talents for business."[7]

Moreover, the people first drawn to western lands formed, in Dwight's view, a dangerous class—restless, prodigal, talkative, shiftless, delighted with innovations. Infected with speculation themselves, they stirred up and confused "regular" societies. They loosened people from settled values and dissociated profit from effort. Hannah F. Lee in her novel of 1844, *The Log Cabin*, hinted at an even more extreme effect of speculation: "A farmer who gets upon this speculating plan seldom grows rich or lives comfortably. Home happiness hardly comes into his account. His house, his stock, even his plunder are mere articles of trade."[8] She implied that in speculation, as in confidence games more generally, all belongings and winnings became mere parts of the game. The reality was drained out of domestic life, material objects, and labor. Mrs. Lee's criticisms also drew on what was becoming a stereotype about speculation—men were the speculators, flighty, undependable, insubstantial, easily gulled, whereas women were, if not precisely skeptical, at least substantial, solid, respectful of real objects and genuine work.[9]

Land speculation did more than unsettle values and cloud perceptions of reality. It bred a certain atmosphere and a set of habits immensely important in American history. Especially in speculation on future town sites, confidence could become a creative commodity. If enough people *believed* that a town would be where the promoter promised, a town *would* be there. People who had already had faith needed to convince others to have faith as well in order to protect their own investments. Such a situation encouraged the belief that one would profit more by promise than by performance. Thus many nineteenth-century railroad companies were actually land companies, whose profit would be realized not by carrying goods but by selling lands adjacent to the projected line.[10] The effect of such an economic pattern on the actual building and running of the railroads themselves is obvious. But the necessity of sharing faith did more than allow fraudulent profits. It created an atmosphere of boom and promise. The habits and the tone of the land jobber spread among his clients and into other areas of American experience. The optimistic note of promise, as virtually all foreign visitors agreed, became the *American* note, and confidence became an icon of the developing society.

Not only land jobbers but Americans more generally were, by the early nineteenth century, disconcertingly apt to *see* what was not yet there. In *American Notes* Dickens lampooned the proud boosters of Washington, D.C., by noting that the mile-long magnificent streets needed only dwellings and inhabitants to be impressive: "One might fancy the season over, and most of the houses gone out of town forever with their masters." Dickens would have seen comparable infatuation in the following bland description of Florida real estate sales by the vice-president of an investment company in 1925: "Lots were bought from blue prints. They look better that way. Then the buyer gets the promoter's vision, can see the splendid curving boulevards, the yacht basin, the parks lined with leaning cocoanut trees, and flaming hibiscus."[11] But there is a serious side. Getting "the promoter's vision" has been one of the most sacred gestures in American history, a measure not only of one's faith but, in certain contexts, of one's "Americanism." The cheerful, energetic buoyancy of the believer became a cultural standard. With so many people mutually boosting the future, it is not surprising that promises and dreams came to seem more real than the shabby present. If Dickens in *Martin Chuzzlewit* would mercilessly expose the fever-and-ague swamps behind the American land boomer's promises, Mark Twain in *The Gilded Age* and Henry James in *The Europeans* were to imply that the long view, the distant prospect, is the American view, and that despite its insensitivity to the squalor in the foreground, it has a charm of its own.

The visionary tradition has been one of the major continuities in American culture, linking land boomers and poets, prophets and profiteers. Even outspoken critics of land speculation easily fall into something of its promissory tone. Thus Timothy Dwight closes his *Travels* with a visionary letter promising the spread of beautiful villages and thriving towns over the interior of the country. And Emerson, Thoreau, and Faulkner, who show how mean and foolishly arrogant it is to grab title deeds to the landscape, also "speculate in land values," for they hope to convince readers that returns to the spirit are more substantial than returns to the pocket. By turning from land sales to the spiritual value of the landscape itself, they simply extend and intensify the magical sense of promise. In the general atmosphere of boosterism and mutual congratulation, "America" itself came to exist primarily in the imagination. As Herbert Croly notes in his acutely titled book, *The Promise of American Life:* "The higher patriotism combines loyalty to historical tradition with the imaginative projection of an ideal national Promise. The Land of Democracy has always appealed to its more enthusiastic children as a land of wonderful and more than national possibilities."[12] Such ratification of the future not only joins speculators with visionaries but also helps account for the paradoxes of actual patterns of land development. The building of the Union Pacific railroad, for instance, was a massive series of swindles, but it was also a great feat of engineering skill and capitalist expansion. The longer view of the future, encouraged by actual accomplishments,

conveniently *overlooked* moral and material blemishes in the foreground.

Among American historians, none has been more keenly sensitive to this doubleness—to both the visions and the fatuities—than
Henry Adams, and I would like to use his perspective as a way of
turning from the promissory tradition in general to the work of one
of its first major proponents, Thomas Jefferson. Inheriting a family
quarrel with confidence men in public life, Adams dissected the
barely fictional career of Senator Silas Ratcliff in *Democracy* and the
actual progress of Gould's conspiracy to corner the gold market during Grant's administration. But John Adams's fiery integrity was
greatly complicated by the time it reached his great-grandson, who
sardonically delighted in historical paradox. Apart from his intelligence and patient care, there were two temperamental qualities in
Henry Adams to make him a superb historian of the Jefferson years.
The first was his expectation of ambivalence, his ability to rest in
seemingly contradictory signs. The second was his sensitivity to the
power of certain beliefs—whether accurate or not—to shape history.

In his brilliant opening chapters of the *History of the United States
during the Administrations of Jefferson and Madison*, he characterizes
the ideals and the state of mind of the American people in 1800. He
notes characteristically the unexamined contradictions in the reports of European observers who saw Americans as sordidly lacking
in ideals and enlarged ideas and yet criticized Jefferson, the exemplar of majority opinion, as a dangerous visionary. Unlike the European travelers who were outraged at the obvious lies and swindles of American land boomers, Adams recognizes the force of the
promoter's vision. "If the Englishman had lived as the American
speculator did,—in the future,—the hyperbole of enthusiasm would
have seemed less monstrous."[13] He discerns how much the typical
American lived by faith—"his dream was his whole existence"—
and how readily the new immigrants adopted the promoter's vision
instead of feeling deceived: "Within a moment, by the mere contact
of a moral atmosphere, they saw the gold and jewels, the summer
cornfields and the glowing continent." And he knows that their
confidence was itself a creative force in American history: "Whether
imagination or greed led them to describe more than actually existed, they still saw no more than any inventor or discoverer must
have seen in order to give him the energy of success."[14]

If the bulk of Adams's *History* is a study of the discrepancies between theory and practice in the Jefferson years, his opening and
closing surveys of American character implicitly turn Jefferson from

quixotic political failure into a genuine representative of the people at large with their grandest ideals and their ambivalences. Thus Jefferson's difficulty in relating his ideas to workable institutions emerges less as a commentary on his own flaws than as a study of American paradoxes, the visionary ideals and the gimcrack expediencies. Jefferson himself is obviously one of the central figures in the promissory tradition. His name has become a synonym for political faith and democratic idealism, and most historians would agree with James Bryce and Woodrow Wilson that his influence in America has been on the spirit and attitudes of the people more than on their institutions. Henry Adams affirmed that spirit as representative of the populace at large, but he also fully elucidated its compromises and its irrelevance in the face of political actualities.

That skeptical realism was his inheritance from his great-grandfather, and John Adams's famous correspondence about aristocracy and democracy with his friend and rival, Thomas Jefferson, helps clarify the bearing of Jeffersonian confidence. To John Adams human perfectibility is an appealing idea but one with no evident relation to the contemporary world. He looks shrewdly and carefully at what is, in order to test all theories, and he salts his observations with asides like "Such has been and such is the world we live in." He agrees with Jefferson that the people elected to government ought to be the best—the aristoi—and that virtue and talents (or genius) are the essential measures. But he also sees that aristocracy in actual practice has five pillars—Beauty, Wealth, and Birth as well as Genius and Virtue—and that any of the first three can overpower the last two in political processes. He notes that the majority of voters are not only overawed by wealth and family name, but ready to be duped by grace, winning airs, cunning, and eloquence. He sees, in other words, why a con man could succeed in politics. More specifically he predicts that the surge of land jobbing and the developing power of banks will generate a new aristocracy to overpower men of virtue and talent.

Thomas Jefferson and the Strategies of Trust

Given that most of what John Adams said turned out to be perfectly true, what can one say for Thomas Jefferson? The difference between the two men involves more than their political ideas. It is a contrast of temperament and stance. Adams looks to the past for precedents; Jefferson looks to the future for possibilities. Whereas the former analyzes what is, the latter speculates on what might be. The soberness and caution of the one set off the other's buoyant faith and enthusiasm. For Jefferson it often seems as if confidence is a sign of health and energy, so that skeptics about human powers and distrusters of the people are sickly and timid, whereas the strong and bold person cherishes the people and ventures on their capacities to handle their own affairs. Again and again he argues that it is better to act out of enthusiasm and confidence than out of doubts and efforts to avoid possible pain. He freely accepts the risks of trying out his faith. It was Jefferson's distinction among the "Founding Fathers" to speak most cheeringly and persuasively in the accents of trust, to identify the strength of a government with the willing support of its citizens.

But in countering the hard-headed realism of John Adams, Jefferson depends on more than mere buoyancy and idealism. He works out strategies by which trust can be developed and by which it can prove itself. In his exchange of letters with Adams as in his two inaugural addresses as President, Jefferson qualifies his faith in the public in two essential ways. The first consideration shows that Jefferson is at heart another land boomer, despite his opposition to speculators and his warnings against large-tract sales of western lands. He identifies American opportunity with the availability of lands, just as Franklin did in his promotional treatise:

> Here every one may have land to labor for himself, if he chooses; or, preferring the exercise of any other industry, may exact for it such compensation as not only to afford a comfortable subsistence, but wherewith to provide for a cessation from labor in old age. Every one, by his property, or by his satisfactory situation, is interested in the support of law and order.[15]

Thus the spreading land to the west not only practically ensures the responsibility of the people; it enlarges their ideas and their visions. It makes them identify with American destiny and believe in American opportunity. Jefferson is an important part of the tradition that culminates in Whitman's effort to describe American character on a colossal scale by enumerating towns and regions of the national landscape.

The second way in which Jefferson qualifies his faith in the people reveals even more about his strategies of confidence. He adapts Enlightenment experimentalism to the growth of a republic. Convinced, like many people of the late eighteenth century, that most perversions and evils in "human nature" are actually the product of corrupt institutions, he wants to try to find out what people would be like if freed of past encumbrances. At his most enthusiastic, he firmly adheres to the fable of American newness, arguing that the

European past is irrelevant to the American future, for its people were degraded by bad institutions. But he holds no illusions about innate goodness or radical innocence. In his first annual message to Congress, he surveys the rapid growth of the country with a view "to the multiplication of men *susceptible* of happiness, *educated* in the love of order, *habituated* to self-government, and valuing its blessings above all price." [16] His point is that people may have the innate capacity to manage their own affairs but this capacity must be nourished. To abolish entail, primogeniture, and a state church, as he did in Virginia, is merely to disencumber the populace of negative influences. They must also be schooled, and they must learn at the local level to take part in political decisions. When their participation has perceptible results, they develop not only political know-how but self-confidence as well.

In Jefferson's visions of the ideal large republic, all citizens would learn self-government in ward organizations and generate in these mini-republics the kind of leaders the nation should have. If information is freely dispensed to all, and if citizens are given the opportunity to exercise and develop their political powers, they will, in this view, *become* worthy of trust. Confidence will create its own object. This is why Jefferson's sense of experiment is so keen, why he loved Washington for "his determination that the existing government should have a fair trial," why both his inaugural addresses envision the new nation in "the full tide of successful experiment." His theme in the political debate of the early republic was thus not only to have faith in the people but to make that faith valid by modifying public institutions so as to nourish their best capacities.

In his idealistic visions, Jefferson is commonly seen by historians as a better judge of ends than of means. In this sense he represents a very different aspect of American confidence from Franklin, who was so engaged with means and techniques that he tended to leave the ends to take care of themselves. Yet this is not to say that Jefferson disregarded practical institutions or had no interest in technical pursuits. If one side of him would produce the stirring vision of the Declaration of Independence, another would return from service as Washington's Secretary of State to manufacture and sell nails so as to finance the redevelopment of Monticello. No one can explore his many contrivances at Monticello without realizing that Jefferson the visionary also belongs in the tradition of American tinkers. He shows a workman's fascination with method, contrivance, and invention. [17] Like Franklin he regards an enterprising, energetic citizenry as intrinsically progressive, and he advises his fifteen-year-old daughter always to keep busy, for the habit of industry and activity will make her cheerful and build her self-trust. Doing is being.

The problem for Jefferson, as for so many of his compatriots, is that the visionary and the tinker are two separate selves. When the political idealist turns to practical politics, he expediently adjusts and readjusts the mechanism, temporarily disregarding the principles that theoretically guide him. The case of Franklin suggests that the American confidence man elevates means over ends. Jefferson allows us to see that the more precise issue is *separation* of means and ends. While the visionary is buoyed up by the larger prospect, the tinker is animated by the pleasure of his immediate gambits.

That duality is also incorporated in the split of city and country. Jefferson's promissory vision is agrarian. He repeatedly characterizes the "mobs" of European cities as hemmed in, brutalized, and irresponsible, whereas the small American farmer, surrounded by open spaces and accessible land, develops a correspondingly larger, more independent character. Yet Jefferson's celebration of bustling activity and of workmen's skills aligns him with Franklin's world, which is emphatically urban. When the two traditions cross, when the visionary promise of new lands combines with the faith that in a fluid urban world one can make a new self, the product is the fully ambivalent American confidence man, at once dreamer and gadgeteer.

Walt Whitman: Vertigo and Vision

Something of that omnivorous confidence—Jefferson's agrarian idealism and Franklin's urban exhilaration—appears in the poetry of Walt Whitman. No American poet has been more concerned with "the promoter's vision." In his preface to the first edition of *Leaves of Grass*, Whitman describes the American bard as one who "sees the solid and beautiful forms of the future where there are now no solid forms." If that sounds like the recipe for a land boomer, listen to the voice he assumes in proclaiming his own divinity:

> Outbidding at the start the old cautious hucksters, . . .
> Lithographing Kronos, Zeus his son, and Hercules his grandson,
> Buying drafts of Osiris, Isis, Belus, Brahma, Buddha,
> In my portfolio placing Manito loose, Allah on a leaf, the crucifix
> engraved . . .

Booster, broker, huckster, prophet—he absorbs and fuses the many styles of American confidence and speaks a language that is the poetry of popular promise. If he often mixes it with something like the dizzying verbal incantation of Ben Jonson's *Alchemist*, it is because such language, too, belongs to the further reaches of the promissory tradition, to orator and boomer, revivalist and hawker of tonics: "My voice goes after what my eyes cannot reach,/ With the twirl of my tongue I encompass worlds and volumes of worlds." Whatever Whitman's ties to Eastern mysticism, the voice and the manner derive from the brash all-American huckster.

His purpose, as well, belongs firmly in the promissory tradition. Whitman tries to do in his poetry what he says in his essays needs to be done—to create a literary language "which leaps overhead, cares mostly for impetus and effects, and for what it plants and invigorates to grow." Testing literature by its "eligibility to free, arouse, dilate," he sees himself as a spiritual booster, a builder of confidence: "I dilate you with tremendous breath, I buoy you up." The ideal poet is to be the agent of the people's faith. He must be alert to the hints of promise in the life around him. In one of his most effective poems, "Crossing Brooklyn Ferry," he manages to blend his own voice as a person in time with the whisperings of some larger possibility inherent in American history. When a listener moves with this voice into its cumulative hintings, the effect is uncanny: "What I promis'd without mentioning it, have you not accepted?"

Whitman is one of the strongest spokesmen for the sheer buoyancy of the Party of Hope. His faith is not a matter of reasoning, argument, demonstration, nor is it quite the same as religious faith that leaps beyond the evidence of sensory experience. It is rather a mood of exuberance, a feeling valuable for its own sake and infectious for others. Like Emerson, he refuses to argue, to qualify, to prove. It is sufficient that as the sun simply shines, he simply makes his assertion and moves on. Like others in the Party of Hope, Whitman suffers periods when the faith withdraws or the exuberance slackens, and there is little he can do about it except try to work it up again or speak forlornly out of his emptiness. As there is no way to argue or explain the state of confidence, there is also no basis within it for distinction or preference. The spirit of enthusiasm eradicates party lines and removes the need for dialogue or adjustment to circumstance. When the visionary mood possessed Jefferson in his first inaugural address, he asserted, "We are all federalists. We are all republicans." And when the same mood possesses Whitman, as in "Crossing Brooklyn Ferry," he suggests through his merging symbols of masts and broad hills the marrying of commerce and an agrarian landscape, as if federalists and republicans had never quarreled at all.

That enthusiastic fusion, of course, has to overlook certain present circumstances, and one can see why Whitman's vision of America in 1855 takes the form it does: "Here is action untied from strings necessarily blind to particulars and details magnificently moving in vast masses." The natural locus for the buoyant faith and for the signs of promise is the future, and like the whole Party of Hope, Whitman looks a long way ahead. Even his approach to the past is like that noted by Herbert Croly in *The Promise of American Life*—to duplicate the future-directedness of earlier generations— but Whitman finds his own characteristic way of doing it. In "Passage to India" he builds on the early efforts to reach the East by going west and shows that with such miracles as the transcontinental railroad, one can reach the seat of humanity's earliest beginnings by simply moving ahead into the future, and when one reaches India one will see *on ahead* Adam and Eve and Columbus still looking to what will be. America, as Whitman says in "Democratic Vistas," counts for its justification almost entirely on the future, and his very metaphor of *vistas* is drawn from the field of land speculation. One of the chief functions of his poetry is to present landscapes to readers, to create in imagination a country that one can move in and identify with: "My left hand hooks you round the waist,/ My right hand points to landscapes of continents, and a plain public road."

But Whitman does not merely absorb and extend the popular style of the land boomer. He recognizes as well the "shoddy gaud and fraud" that had spread in a confidence culture:

> Never, in the Old World, was thoroughly upholster'd exterior appearance and show, mental and other, built entirely on the idea of caste, and on the sufficiency of mere outside acquisition—never were glibness, verbal intellect more the test, the emulation—more loftily elevated as head and sample—than they are on the surface of our republican States this day.

When the best class of the day is "but a mob of fashionably dress'd speculators," the poet needs to indicate something better, and Whitman makes explicit in "Democratic Vistas" a program that had been implicit in his poetry all along. He calls for "an American stock-personality," for "the formation of a typical personality of character, eligible to the uses of the high average of men." Like Franklin he sees the value of a self-image prepared for general popular use, but whereas Franklin's model self has a program of actions, a series of specific styles and capacities, Whitman's "stock-personality" is less definite, less susceptible to a how-to-do-it presentation. It arises from the visionary, not the tinkering tradition.

It answers his call for an enlarged spirit to match and justify the astonishing "material" progress of America.

In part, Whitman's effort merely updates the brooding of the aged Jefferson over the fact that, counter to his expectations, economic, political, and scientific improvements do not seem to have produced moral ones. But for all Whitman's theoretical references to moral development, the quality he has in mind, as is especially clear in the poetry, is a capacity for vision, a receptivity to promise. An enlarged spirit, in other words, is much the same thing as the buoyant confidence of the Party of Hope. Like Jefferson, however, Whitman does not depend on mere temperament and mood; he tries to indicate strategies by which confidence can be developed. As I suggested earlier, he carries to the extreme the idea that larger lands produce larger character. His ideal poet—who anticipates the more general stock personality—incorporates the country, its terrain, its people, its actions and resources. Thus when Whitman wants to describe a spiritually enlarged person, he starts to list cities, occupations, parties, rivers, trees, animals, dwellings, or gestures. To *see* all those things is to broaden one's vision.

But Whitman's strategy is more complex and illuminating than that. To see how his catalogues work and what they tell us about the experience of "confidence," we have to begin with his strange notions about matter and spirit. In contrast with Emerson, he does not see the material and the spiritual as two discrete realms, the first a quite dispensable shadow of the second. Material things and our experiences with them are for Whitman not only perfectly real and substantial but the necessary basis for *all* our experience, just as the accumulation of wealth and railroads and other "internal improvements" forms the basis for American democracy. "Spirit" is not our faculty for entering an independent realm; it is an *accompaniment* of the world of our senses. When our imaginations are excited at our grasp of an object or an event, when we sense that the things we perceive have a "purpose," when we quicken to what seems most inviting in our experience, we show the effects of spirit. Although these spiritual perceptions *hint* at another world or a greater reality, that other world need not exist in itself nor need we try to reach it. Whitman's emphasis is on the sheer thrill of the inner exhilaration, and this is what makes him so telling a representative of the promissory tradition. As he deals with spiritual experience, the agonizing early American distinction between saving faith and excited affections simply dissolves.

Whitman is less concerned with conveying specific spiritual insights than with generating that inner excitement which seems to be the essence of spiritual experience. The very listing of geographical features, for instance, can produce an exhilarating sense of vastness, as any land boomer knows. But more is involved in Whitman's catalogues. In his version of spiritual experience objects seem to become porous so as to convey hints of something else. Thus if he can make objects seem less solid while amplifying our subjective feelings in the presence of these objects, he can poetically simulate spirituality. And in "Song of the Open Road" he defines most clearly his central technique for creating this sense of spiritual wisdom: "Something there is in the float of the sight of things that provokes it out of the soul." To transcend objects, one must unfix them from their solidity, and what better way to do this than to start moving oneself? Whereas the Eastern mystic adopts a lotus posture to meditate and transcend the body, Whitman sets off on the road.

When his catalogues are most effective, as in Chant 33 of "Song of Myself," he is indeed "afoot with my vision." Not only does he rapidly replace one image with another but he suggests the movement between them, thus joining the sense of vastness with the continuity and thrill of motion, which in turn establish the "spiritual" sense of unity and progress. Like the confidence man with his fast talk and constant redirections, Whitman draws the reader along instead of simply describing or narrating. He calls his method "indirection," and he sees the poems as starts of something in readers, not as finishes in themselves. Although he wants to suggest a grand vision, his approach is finally related to that of the gadgeteer who finds process more engaging than product.[18] The visionary capacity is created by the exuberance of movement along the way; it is not simply a response to a completed poem. Whitman does not present his vision, he generates it.

In drawing readers into the process of the poem, Whitman does not rely solely on the voyager's sweep of moving vision. Change, too—sheer fluidity of circumstance—can produce "the float of the sight of things" that seems to provoke wisdom out of the soul. It is in this sense that Whitman echoes Franklin, for he tries to sell his readers not only an abundant landscape but a series of people busy in developing it, a cumulative image of activity, enterprise, and variety. When he notes that "agonies are one of my changes of garments," he indicates the strategy for maintaining confidence in adverse circumstances. One simply holds to the sense of fluidity so that no particular state can fix itself on the spirit. Whitman is as ready as Franklin to enter a series of roles—cultural bard, American Adam, common laborer, nurse, prophet, lover, scapegoat, booster.

His own way of being the jack-of-all-trades is imaginatively to enter many occupations in a catalogue, as in Chant 15 of "Song of My-self." But like Franklin's model self, he preserves through his very shifting of roles a basic detachment from each. As the poetic jour-neys unfix material objects, shape shifting unfixes the self. The con-fidence inspired by seeming to perform so many tasks is dissociated from any particular activity or role, as the spiritual promise in voy-aging transcends any single scene.

The enlarged spirit that Whitman sets as his poetic goal is achieved, then, when the movement and the healthy thrill of change create a feeling of buoyancy:

> My ties and ballasts leave me, my elbows rest in sea-gaps,
> I skirt sierras, my palms cover continents.

In such a state "I see it is true, what I guess'd at." These many qualities in Whitman's poetry—the incantation of names, the voice of promise, the vision of land enlarging character, the participation in a dizzying series of roles, the breathtaking movement over land-scapes of continents—all suggest the same thing. Buoyant faith can be induced like vertigo.[19] It is a purely subjective state, immensely desirable, but quite possibly having no reference to anything out-side the self except in one important sense—it may give a person more power to act in the world. The thrill of confidence as a rush of images is rather like what we in the late twentieth century are fa-miliar with from other sources—montage in cinema and in 40-second TV commercials, travel at high speed in an automobile. Jack Kerouac knew what he was about when he made his twentieth-century descendant of Whitman a fast-talking, fast-driving con man on the road.

William James: Faith Works

It is the possibility that confidence could give power and thereby create what it assumes that lies behind the philosophy of William James. Although he does not try to induce vertigo by movement or by "omnific" verbal play, James belongs as firmly as Whitman in the promissory tradition, and one reason his pragmatism can be simplified as freely as Franklin's social rise is that James, too, grounds his work in popular thought and experience. When we think of James's work as the distinctive American philosophy, we think less of a logical argument than of a set of attitudes—the ten-dencies to test things in action, to focus on future possibilities, to emphasize practical experience. And despite the specialized technical derivation of the term "pragmatism" in the philosophical work of Charles Sanders Peirce and William James, there are good reasons why "pragmatic" so easily took hold as a catch-all name for the expedient, concrete, shifty, technique-loving tendencies in American experience, which Tocqueville long ago noted as oddly isolated from our abstract idealism. In this sense James belongs with the side of Franklin that always enjoyed the sight of workmen handling their tools or the side of Jefferson that made nails, contrived a reading-chair desk, and urged busy-ness and resolution. To validate his theories, he refers to people of practical experience, who love facts more than systems, and he recognizes that he is describing something more fundamentally "popular" than philosophical idealism. Yet when Santayana pointed out in "The Genteel Tradition in American Philosophy" that James "had a prophetic sympathy with the dawning sentiments of the age, with the moods of the dumb majority," he was referring to something more than a belief that whatever works is right.

If "pragmatism" seems to be the philosophy of the tinkering tradition, it draws as much from the Party of Hope. Even when James tests ideas by their practical consequences, he means more than concrete action. He sees that *doing*—taking command or being able to act—generates confidence, and that this in turn makes it possible to do new things. The meaning of an idea or a belief, as he describes it, is not directly its production of active results but its effect on the mind of the believer; what the idea may bring about in that individual is the *capacity* to act. James's theories are the philosophical expression of the Party of Hope. Behind his doctrines and even more noticeably behind his tone there is a long-standing cultural dialogue between skeptics and men of confidence. He speaks, like Jefferson, in the accents of trust, preferring motives of hope to those of fear. Instead of trying to avoid error, he emphasizes the positive seeking of truth and is willing to take risks in order to know. The danger, in James's view, is any rule of thinking that would prevent us from finding or acknowledging certain kinds of truth if they should happen to exist. His enemies, then, are not simply the rationalists and idealists he chastises. Like others in the Party of Hope he adopts a tone of bold assurance to counter the crippling effects of skepticism, deference, complexity, and superstition. He would have us turn from precedents to possibilities. We find almost everywhere in his writings that cheering and vigorous attitude toward experience: "I have often thought that the best way to define a man's character would be to seek out the particular mental or moral attitude in which, when it came upon him, he felt himself most deeply and intensely active and alive." He has Jefferson's generosity of spirit and temperamental affinity to risks.

William James's distinction is to fuse the promissory tradition with the practical one. His basis is the *enabling* power of belief. Faith has practical consequences by enabling, even encouraging, us to act in certain ways. Dropping the static concept of "correspondence" between the mind and the world, he substitutes the idea of "commerce" between our thoughts and the great universe of our experience. An idea "agrees" with reality by helping us to *deal* with it. Briefly, he argues that a belief or an idea is true for us insofar as it enables us to move freely and coherently among our various experiences—not only to act effectively in the immediate circumstances but to discover continuities in our other beliefs and to go on fruitfully to new experiences. This is more or less what he means when he says that an idea "works" or has "cash value." Ideas become instruments by means of which we can both do things and move about in our heads. In contrast, rigid dogmas or absolutes block our actions and fix our minds. James's efforts to make thought and action more limber reach all the way from his philosophical innovations to his theories of psychology and physiology. He would free us from dogmatic or skeptical ideas and from the tyranny of habit as well. In his well-known chapter on habits in *Principles of Psychology* he creates a program as practical and encouraging as Franklin's Art of Virtue. Locating the basis of habit in the most frequently followed pathways of the nervous system, he shows not only how habit helps economize our living but how we can creatively form habits and exercise inner capacities that increase our powers. In both psychology and philosophy he sounds the same promising note—the world is more plastic to our demands than we had thought: "Our only means of finding out is to try."

The buoyancy of the Party of Hope becomes in James's work a basis for action: in our conduct we venture our faith in certain hypotheses, and these can often be *made* true by our belief in them and our positive action on that belief. He shows how confidence can be creative. Not only in personal action but especially in cooperative or social situations—as Jefferson, too, had noted—faith foreruns its own object:

> Who gains promotions, boons, appointments, but the man in whose life they seem to play the part of live hypotheses . . . ? His faith acts on the powers above him as a claim, and creates its own verification.

> Believe that life *is* worth living, and your belief will help create the fact.

> Mental interests, hypotheses, postulates, so far as they are the ba-
> sis for human action—action which to a great extent transforms
> the world—help to *make* the truth which they declare.

Only by having faith, by willingly taking its risks, can we experiment at all and thereby discover the nature of the world and of our
own powers as well. In so arguing, James not only joins the promissory and the practical currents in American life but he exposes the
radical core of Protestant doctrine: we are saved by faith alone, for
without precursive faith we cannot even perform good works.[20]

The popular emphasis on James's practicalism—truth is whatever
works—is misleading and not only because it blurs the intricacies
of his philosophy. It leaves out half of his own "popular" background—the appeal to faith. When he argues that truth is not independent but is caught up in human needs, he means more than
that our ideas must have a practical utility. Many of our needs are
inward, and what we believe in must help us act and must *satisfy*
us too. James anticipates Wallace Stevens's criterion for "the supreme fiction"—"It must give pleasure"—and his definition of the
subject of modern poetry—"the finding of a satisfaction." Such an
idea can, of course, be easily misconstrued, and both writers have
been accused of arguing that we can believe whatever we wish
were true. But satisfaction is a demanding condition for James and
for Stevens. It involves our whole inner state, not only our deepest
wishes and fears but our convictions about how things actually are,
our temperaments and castes, our prejudices and our experiences.
And this complex grounding of our ideas in our particular human
nature lies behind James's approach to religious ideas in "The Will
To Believe" and *The Varieties of Religious Experience*. He shows that
he comes to philosophy from medicine and psychology, for he is
more interested in conditioned than in unconditioned or absolute
ways of thinking.

But there is also a cultural basis for James's approach. Like Poe
and Whitman, he is less concerned with the substance than with
the effects of belief. It has become a commonplace for Americans in
public life to advocate religious belief while avoiding exclusive en-
dorsement of any one sect—it doesn't matter what you believe as
long as you believe something. Such an all-purpose assurance about
the efficacy of faith suggests engagement less with religious doctrine than with the very experience of belief. And James moves to
the heart of this tradition by developing a science of religion, a
doctrine-free study of the effects of faith. As he finds physiological
and philosophical grounds for the cultural habit of seeing confidence as creative, so he finds in his case studies of personal reli-

gious experience a basis for faith. Repeatedly he notes how prayer and the experience of belief actually affect the personal center of energy, giving an influx of power and thereby rejuvenating the self.

In the philosophical work of William James, then, there is a remarkable fusion of popular tendencies. He brings together the booster and the gadgeteer with one eye on the future and the other on practical method. He accounts for a world in which belief is vital but in which individuals are often desperately wondering *what* to believe, so that "truth" becomes a function not of what is but of our *beliefs about* what is. Even James's ambiguities reflect his culture. His effort to bring truth back to a subjective center of experience and to measure its meaning there picks up the widespread concern with the efficacy of faith. And the popular recasting of this idea—truth is whatever can be made believable—produces as culture hero the confidence man, who prepares a role to match the circumstances and who discovers himself in what others can be made to credit about him. This is the cultural habit so acutely assessed in the work of Poe and Melville. Like Melville in *The Confidence-Man*, James endorses the attitude "of looking away from first things, principles, 'categories,' supposed necessities; and of looking towards last things, fruits, consequences, facts." His philosophy makes sense of that novel with its strangely hypothetical approach; it is a philosophy for those who are *in the game*, who are willing to unfix themselves from absolutes and to venture their faith, who understand a doctrine not by its substance but by its consequences. Finally, there is James's view of indeterminism, which "gives us a pluralistic, restless universe, in which no single point of view can ever take in the whole scene." What is this but the fluid world of Benjamin Franklin and Arthur Mervyn, the world only adequately to be known and experienced by the restless role-player or shape-shifter? In this composite of American tendencies, James shows what grounds there are for those who dwell in possibility.

Jay Gatsby: Floating on Air in Promise Land

If William James gives the Party of Hope its characteristic philosophy, F. Scott Fitzgerald provides its hero. *The Great Gatsby* is a book about American promise, and Gatsby himself is marked by "some heightened sensitivity to the promises of life, as if he were related to one of those intricate machines that register earthquakes ten thousand miles away." He moves in a world radiant with imagined possibilities, and his story traces the progress of the promissory tradition. Unlike Jefferson, Whitman, and James, Gatsby is no public spokesman; he does not broadcast the promissory mode, he lives it. He is not a booster but an ideal recipient of boosterism, perhaps even its victim. By the age of fourteen James Gatz had already undertaken the program of Franklin's model self, noting his self-improvement schedule and resolves in the back of his copy of *Hopalong Cassidy*. In the next few years he had gone on from this rather specific course to the more all-encompassing sense of promise itself, spinning out gaudy dreams and finding that they are more nourishing than one would expect. Thus by the time he appears to Nick Carraway, he has combined the self-improvement tradition and the promissory mode. He is the ideal inhabitant of Promise Land.

Fitzgerald's talents are especially suited to this world of promise. He can analyze its illusions and deftly signify the forces that destroy dreams—the crunching boots and the cufflinks made of human molars—but he can also infuse reality with the note of promise: "In his blue gardens men and girls came and went like moths among the whisperings and the champagne and the stars." And his narrator Nick Carraway shares just enough of Gatsby's sensitivity to glowing possibilities so that he can convey something of Gatsby's basic vision. The world Gatsby moves in is well characterized in his feelings about Daisy Fay's house in Louisville:

> There was a ripe mystery about it, a hint of bedrooms upstairs more beautiful and cool than other bedrooms, of gay and radiant activities taking place through its corridors, and of romances that were not musty and laid away already in lavender, but fresh and breathing and redolent of this year's shining motor-cars and of dances whose flowers were scarcely withered. It excited him, too, that many men had already loved Daisy—it increased her value in his eyes. He felt their presence all about the house, pervading the air with the shades and echoes of still vibrant emotions.

Here we have the promissory mode in the intimacy of personal feelings. Gatsby sees the possibilities, not the house itself. He is alive to implications, and this keeps not only his vision but reality as well fresh and vital. The present can only lead into the future; it does not become the past. Moreover, Gatsby quickens to emotions instead of things. The tangible world is merely an evocation of his own and other people's vibrant feelings. We cannot respond to Fitzgerald's rhetoric, especially at the closing of the novel, without recognizing the sense in which Daisy symbolizes for Gatsby and for us some larger promise inherent in American life. In this passage Gatsby is absorbing not only the intimations of Daisy's house but the whole promissory tradition which charges the sensory world with other people's dreams and desires.

Nick, too, responds to the promise in things and people. He recognizes at the outset something special about Daisy:

> Her face was sad and lovely with bright things in it, bright eyes
> and a bright passionate mouth, but there was an excitement in her
> voice that men who had cared for her found difficult to forget: a
> singing compulsion, a whispered "Listen," a promise that she had
> done gay, exciting things just a while since and that there were
> gay exciting things hovering in the next hour.

Daisy is much more than a symbol of ideal promise. She grows out
of another stereotype that Fitzgerald sensed was somehow linked to
the promissory tradition. This stereotype appeared in the Gibson
girl and the retouched photographs of young women at the turn of
the century, in the comments of Europeans and the stories of Americans marrying into foreign aristocratic families, in Henry James's
Daisy Miller and Edith Wharton's Undine Spragg. She was called
"the American girl," and she was marked not only by boldness,
charm, freedom, and wealth but by a provoking habit of promising
what she had no intention of delivering. Thomas Beer in *The Mauve
Decade* and Leslie Fiedler in *Love and Death in the American Novel*
have attacked this figure as in effect a puritanical flirt, a "bitch-
goddess" who tantalizes and then withdraws. But in portraying
Daisy Buchanan, Fitzgerald indicates another side of the issue.
Daisy's appeal, especially to Gatsby, is pure and radiant promise,
not promise of anything in particular but ever-alluring possibility.
She does not, for instance, lead Gatsby on sexually only to run
away, but then again their sexual activity itself seems oddly insignificant. Gatsby would probably say of it what he says of Daisy's
relation to Tom, "In any case, it was just personal."

   In both rhetoric and characterization, Fitzgerald indicates that
Gatsby lives in a world teeming with possibilities, and he is well
adapted to it. He not only hears the hints in his experience, but he
absorbs the pure inner buoyancy of the Party of Hope. Like William
James's true believer who enters into prayer, he experiences an influx of power and energy that makes him highly resilient. And he
can, in turn, radiate this energy to others. He infuses his parties
with the almost magical enticement that Nick senses as soon as he
goes to one. Gatsby's smile is the finest flower of the promissory
tradition:

> It was one of those rare smiles with a quality of eternal reassurance
> in it, that you may come across four or five times in life. It faced—
> or seemed to face—the whole external world for an instant, and
> then concentrated on *you* with an irresistible prejudice in your fa-

vor. It understood you just as far as you wanted to be understood, believed in you as you would like to believe in yourself, and assured you that it had precisely the impression of you that, at your best, you hoped to convey.

It is the expression of vigorous belief as an inner force, but it is also adapted to the social patterns of Promise Land. It recognizes the efforts of others to make certain impressions and to discover themselves in the effectiveness of those impressions, and it celebrates a world sustained by mutual confidence.

Fitzgerald, of course, is interested in what *happens* when the promissory mode is invested in actual experience. Émile Durkheim's distinction between culturally defined goals and socially prescribed ways of attaining them provides a useful approach to Gatsby's situation. From the broader American heritage Gatsby has absorbed both the habit of creating a self and the tone of sheer confidence, the sense of virtually boundless promise. From the narrower social patterns of post-Civil War America, Gatsby has learned that the self to be created is a millionaire and that the substance of promise is to climb into a higher social class. And finally, in the immediate ambience of the late teens and early twenties, he finds the style of life and the kind of person to want—both incorporated in Daisy Fay. All this is summed up in the major crisis of Gatsby's life: "He knew that when he kissed this girl, and forever wed his unutterable visions to her perishable breath, his mind would never romp again like the mind of God." The risk is to contain the cultural promise in the socially available forms, and if Gatsby finds that kissing Daisy does infuse the sensory world with all his dream-wonder—"she blossomed for him like a flower"—he also discovers that his dream and its object are now implicated in history. In other words, he has to buy all those shirts.

For one thing, the vague outline of "Jay Gatsby" has to be filled in more substantially in a way acceptable to Daisy's world. Hence his bootlegging and other mysterious activities to become so quickly a millionaire. Along the road to Promise Land Gatsby has to become a self-made man. His approach to riches, however, has more to do with the success tracts of the early twentieth century that emphasize will, magnetism, and confidence, than with the earlier gospel of industry and frugality. If his need to get ahead could link him with Clyde Griffiths, whose story appeared the same year, Gatsby acts out his compulsion in a radically different way. Whereas Dreiser forces us to plod along heavily in the details of Clyde's activities, the urgencies of his desire, the particular things or persons he wants, Fitzgerald condenses or abstracts the substance of Gatsby's economic rise so as to keep the informing promise in the foreground. Dreiser weighs us down; Fitzgerald buoys us up. In his approach what is material becomes strangely immaterial, and it is hard to imagine a reader any more disturbed than Nick Carraway is at the fact that Gatsby is actually a criminal. What Nick and Fitzgerald admire about Gatsby is that his dream survives its incarnation. Somehow he manages to keep the cultural promise intact through the degradations of "success" in the Gilded Age and the Jazz Age. Surely this is one of the implications of the closing vision in which Nick links Gatsby's dream with the earliest whisperings of American promise and shows, like Walt Whitman and Herbert Croly, how we are borne back into the past by re-enacting our predecessors' dreams of the future.

Yet Gatsby is a crook as well as a dreamer, and although Fitzgerald chooses not to dramatize this side of his career, he clearly indicates how the man of confidence turns into the confidence man. Lured on by the promises he feels in Daisy's world, Gatsby in turn cons her into believing he is something he is not. His smile may indicate his faith in other people's projected images but it is also his own device to inspire confidence. The world of the novel is more than a scene of promise; it is a large game of confidence with people making and testing impressions. Yet if Gatsby thrives on projected images, there is a sense in which those images are not quite false. By emphasizing the world of promise, Fitzgerald suggests that direct social and economic maneuvers are not exactly real, that family background and wealth are less substantial as signs of the self than inner vision. Gatsby's extravagant claims and promises are a far better indication of self than the way he got his fortune. In other words, while Fitzgerald sees how the promissory tradition produces a confidence man, he also shares with us the perspective within which the two become one.

There is another sense in which Gatsby consummates the promissory tradition. On that hot, fateful afternoon of the trip to the city, Daisy tells Gatsby that he always looks cool, that he resembles an advertisement. And he does. In him the inward confidence expresses itself in outer surfaces. He does not wear a mask, he becomes one. The inner self is expressed in the creation of an ideal role, and there is finally no distance between façade and self. When his dream world is shattered, Gatsby cannot experience disillusionment; he simply collapses. The role, in turn, is not strictly personal at all; it grows, like Franklin's model self, out of the possibility of a cultural norm. "If personality is an unbroken series of successful gestures," Nick tells us, "then there was something gorgeous about him." But who ever suggested that "personality" is a series of successful gestures, i.e., an expert game of confidence? All traditional definitions of "personality"—from the quality that makes a person different from a thing, to the cluster of inner dispositions that help determine behavior—depend upon distinction: "personality" is what makes us different from someone or something else. What are we to think, then, of personality as successful gestures, which could presumably be practiced by many others as well? or of Whitman's equally odd notion of "an American stock-personality," and "a typical personality of character"? or of courses in personality building? or of that hack song popular a few decades ago "You've Got Personality"?

This strange American popular usage reveals some implications of the promissory tradition. When you've got personality instead of *a* personality, you've taken on a model instead of realizing yourself. And that model is the outgrowth of the Party of Hope. When "personality" is used in the sense that you ought to have it or develop it, it means, of course, that you get along well with others and are gregarious. But this does not involve adapting yourself to other temperaments or being able to enter imaginatively into other experiences. It means being "nice," cheerful, optimistic. Even more it suggests a certain sparkle and radiance, as if inner energy were gushing out to enspirit others. In a word, "personality" is the buoyancy of the Party of Hope, held up as a social norm. No wonder Gatsby resembles an advertisement.

6

SHAPE SHIFTING
AND SELF-RELIANCE

It might be done, sir, without knowing as much as Doctor Franklin—
it might be done.

—Cooper's Richard Jones

Me, I couldn't think that all was so poured in concrete . . . and maybe
most intolerable the hardening of detestable character, like bone, similar to a second skeleton and creaking loudest before the end.

—Augie March

Heroes do not fix, but flow, bend forward ever and invent a resource
for every moment.

—Ralph Waldo Emerson

Where lies the final harbor, whence we unmoor no more?

—Melville's Ishmael

In a fluid world, full of promise, it is easy to regard self-
transformation as a matter of *becoming*. This is what the self-made
man and the booster do, the one with his heart on the goal and the
other with his head in the future. But there is another side to the
pleasures of self-transformation. For some people, doing and
changing provide intrinsic satisfaction, regardless of the longer-
range consequence. The cultural icon representing this state of
mind is the jack-of-all-trades, and Franklin's purest nineteenth-
century descendant was a shape-shifter. Franklin himself enjoyed
both sides of self-transformation. Eventual success and promise and
immediate dexterity coexisted in the model self and sustained each
other. But as the nineteenth-century compulsion to succeed turned
the self-made man into a caricature of the model self, helplessly

immersed in the economic system, the jack-of-all-trades appeared as an alternative.[1] In one sense his virtues represented another cultural extreme, the tendency to disregard ends entirely in an obsession with sheer facility. His adroitness could take the form of another American style of "innocence"—gadgetry without consequence, or doing things simply because they can be done.

But it is not as gadgeteer that the jack-of-all-trades is most revealing. It is in his attitude toward himself. Of Franklin's descendants, he alone inherits that essential view of the self as an instrument for performance, a tool adapted to many varying jobs. His fascination with the immediate workings of the tool merges with his pleasure as detached spectator of his own performance. If he is good at doing what he does, he is even better at withdrawing from it, and this mobility is what makes him an alternative to the self-made man. Shape shifting keeps him independent.

The same flexibility, however, also raises the question of how the jack-of-all-trades can be said to have any identity at all. Who *is* he? What is the relation of shape shifting to self-reliance? What kind of a self is it that one trusts? Who, as Emerson puts it, is the Trustee? These questions are not merely rhetorical; one cannot read far in the literature of nineteenth-century America without realizing how frequently and how urgently they are raised. It is curious how seldom our most canonized nineteenth-century writers insist on mere *integrity* of the self, how often instead they appeal to such concepts as poise, balance, one's own "orbit." Rather than affirm one's ability to *maintain* an identity, Emerson, Thoreau, Melville, Hawthorne, Whitman, even Henry James, see the need of self-*recovery*, a pulling *back* from something else and feeling one's selfhood in the disengagement. It was not one's integrity that was threatened in money getting but one's flexibility. The role-playing jack-of-all-trades can free himself from any one of his roles, and this means he can free himself from all of them. He merely circulates. In discussing Whitman in the preceding chapter, I noted how his role playing, his journeying, his love of change and process create a feeling of buoyancy that passes for spiritual wisdom. Here I am interested in the sense of the self accompanying that vertiginous movement. And perhaps the metaphor I am seeking can be found in the combination of Whitman's whirling motion, Hawthorne's demand for "poise," and James's concern for one's "orbit." It is possible that the "self" on which one relies as jack-of-all-trades exists as the steadiness exists in a spinning top.

To explore these questions about identity and the jack-of-all-trades, and to see the relationship of this cultural icon to the confidence man, I focus here on three literary shape-shifters—Cooper's Richard Jones, Hawthorne's Holgrave, and Melville's Ishmael—who in their complexity and their variations from each other indicate some of the major significances of the jack-of-all-trades.[2] Then in the last part of the chapter I turn this popular stereotype into a figure of the imagination so as to clarify certain major concerns in the work of Ralph Waldo Emerson. His ideas, in turn, allow us to see more precisely and more extensively the cultural values invested in the jack-of-all-trades.

The Con Man on the Frontier

Cooper's *The Pioneers* is a useful point of departure, for it indicates how booster and shape-shifter unite in a confidence man. Cooper perceived the jack-of-all-trades as a threat, as the representative of a cluster of social tendencies so dangerous and already so well developed in the 1820s that they forced him by revulsion into inventing one of the great heroes of the American imagination. For the more clearly Richard Jones brings out the potentialities of the jack-of-all-trades and the Franklinian model self, the more Natty Bumppo turns from surly frontiersman into the quintessential victim and resister of American confidence men. Before we turn to the many appealing qualities of the jack-of-all-trades, it is well to acknowledge what he can do at his worst.

The Pioneers is about the early development of a frontier settlement in upstate New York. Boosterism and "the promoter's vision" are thus natural issues, especially because of Cooper's concern with his own father's role in the creation of Cooperstown. To some degree Templeton is a fictionalized Cooperstown, and Judge Temple represents not only William Cooper but a whole class of resident promoters, a class Cooper was later to defend outspokenly during the anti-rent crisis of the 1840s. In one sense, then, Cooper had some interest in showing the value of the promoter's vision, sacrifice, and planning. Judge Temple named the spot from which he first "saw" the future settlement Mount Vision, but he is not a mere visionary. He tries to educate his settlers in useful approaches to farming and building, and he helps them through crises. He wants to promote civilization as well as settlement, and he tries to stabilize both economic development and social relations. When he sees the future landscape, it is a harmonious mixture of cultivated areas and natural reserves. Moreover, this is the vision Cooper himself presents to us at the opening of the novel, a distant prospect of a thriving settlement blending in well with an arable landscape under a wise pattern of government. It is close to the visionary prospect at the end of Timothy Dwight's *Travels.*

Like the skeptical Dwight, however, Cooper knew that there was another side to boosterism as well, a side first visible when we get a close-up view of that same "thriving" landscape. For as the returning heiress, Elizabeth Temple, comes down from the hills into the village itself, she sees the half-made roads ending in fields, the disregarded tree stumps, the cheerless and unfinished houses, the ravages of hasty and careless enterprise. Everywhere are signs of the discrepancy between idea and execution—the mismatched wallpaper with General Wolfe's severed arm, the porch of her father's house with its pillars suspended from the portico they were designed to support. This is the stuff of Dickens and Mark Twain in their satires of American boosterism, but Cooper is not trying to show Judge Temple's land jobbing as charlatanism. Instead he presents two different kinds of booster. In contrast with the Judge with his foresight and restraint stands the Judge's "agent," Richard Jones, who carries out the Judge's plans by means of slapdash expedients. Whereas Judge Temple represents civilized enterprise, Squire Jones translates promotion into puffery. As glad-handing shaper of public opinion, publisher of a congratulatory weekly newspaper, promoter of giant exploits, he represents the more familiar and disconcerting kind of booster. And *The Pioneers* could be seen as a contest between two alternative ways of developing a community.

But the opposition between Marmaduke Temple and Richard Jones is more deep-seated than that. They disagree about the essential nature of a human being. In one of the key statements of the novel, Jones characterizes the contrast: "You are of opinion, Judge Temple, that a man is to be qualified by nature and education to do only one thing well, whereas I know that genius will supply the place of learning, and that a certain sort of man can do any thing and every thing." Judge Temple represents an Old World view with which Cooper basically sympathizes. People learn vocations or master trades; they are fitted to specialized tasks; they inherit a certain "station" in life to which they are well suited; and they are arranged in a hierarchy of precedence. In such a view the developing community should contain a diverse group of specialists, each of whom can carry out skillfully certain tasks essential to the well-being of the rest. Furthermore, the arrangement requires a certain stability in the settlers, for if the wheelwright departs for a new country farther west, he leaves a deficiency in the settlement. This is why Judge Temple is so angry at shiftless vagrants like Jotham Riddel.

Richard Jones, in contrast, stands for New World "genius," and he is his own Exhibit A. As architect, veterinarian, miner, songwriter, sheriff, newspaper publisher, he is the supreme instance of the jack-of-all-trades, and the people of Templeton are "accustomed to his 'general agency.'" He sees certain people—a surprisingly large number of them for so small a settlement—as suited to any and every task. And he does not disown any of the disturbing consequences of this belief: DOING is his deity. What can be done should be done, and as largely and hastily as possible. Are there flocks of passenger pigeons migrating over the village? Bring them down with a cannon of buckshot! Are there thousands of bass in Lake Otsego? Drag them all out in a giant seine! He doesn't ravish the landscape because the settlers are in need or because he secretly hates trees and birds. He does it because *it can be done*. He genuinely does not understand the Judge's calls for conservation, foresight, planned development. Immediate action is enough.

When Elizabeth Temple informs him that her father is going to give him an important position in the county, Richard Jones characteristically responds, "Say, is it an office where there is anything to *do*?" He is constitutionally restless. The jack-of-all-trades must always be busy about the settlement, organizing the Christmas service and then hurrying back from it to doctor the innkeeper's mangy hogs. He shows the underside of "enterprise." Cooper shares his fellow New Yorker, Washington Irving's, aversion to frenetically busy people. He shows how the urge always to be doing something makes Jones unstable and reckless. He also sees that the jack-of-all-trades tends to be a meddler: "Mr. Jones invariably made it a point to participate in the business in hand, let it be what it would." More than industrious, Jones is officious, and in his willingness to take on whatever the community needs done, he easily invents things that would be better left undone. In contrast with Judge Temple, who prizes stability, Richard Jones values change and busy-ness for their own sakes.

Unlike the popular American stereotype, Cooper's jack-of-all-trades actually follows the Old World adage of being master of none. Despite Jones's claims to "genius" and his frequent boasts about his accomplishments, he indicates his actual capacities in his first gesture in the novel—he nearly backs a sleigh off a cliff in showing off his ability to turn around his team of horses in a narrow quarry. Cooper repeatedly emphasizes the sloppiness of Jones's work, and he stylizes the contrast between his use of cannons or seines and Leather-Stocking's skill with the single rifle shot or the fishing spear.

But Leather-Stocking's mastery of what he does is the exception in Templeton, and in the opposition between Temple and Jones over "genius," it is clearly Jones's attitude that prevails in the community. As jack-of-all-trades, Jones is himself representative, and he surrounds himself with satellites of similar tendencies. First, there is Billy Kirby, whose massive strength and rough boastfulness are ready for any form of exploitation—chopping down forests, hauling out bass, gouging sugar maples. The French storekeeper calls Kirby a "Jack All-trade." Second, there is Hiram Doolittle, carpenter, petty magistrate, and all-purpose cheat, who is as ready to apply his low cunning to any enterprise as Billy Kirby is to apply muscle. Third, and most extreme, there is the itchy, restless Jotham Riddel, who not only helps create the atmosphere of instability in Templeton but succumbs more quickly than anyone to its wildest promises. In a forceful attack on the jack-of-all-trades and his world of "genius," Judge Temple calls Jotham Riddel "that dissatisfied, shiftless, lazy, speculating fellow! he who changes his county every three years, his farm every six months, and his occupation every season! an agriculturist yesterday, a shoemaker to-day, and a schoolmaster to-morrow! that epitome of all the unsteady and profitless propensities of the settlers without one of their good qualities to counterbalance the evil!"

It is not only because Jones surrounds himself with such assistants, however, that he is representative. He has also correctly gauged the atmosphere and the possibilities of the frontier settlement. It simply doesn't matter that Leather-Stocking is more skillful than any of the residents of Templeton or that Richard Jones does shoddy work. The point is not to do well but to get the credit. "This is a damn'd envious world that we live in," Jones notes, in a wonderful piece of self-caricature, "people are always for dividing the credit of a thing, in order to bring down merit to their own level." The opening quarrel between Judge Temple and Natty Bumppo over who actually shot the deer raises the question that will be raised in one form or another in every human encounter in the settlement. With their eyes always on public acclaim, the people of Templeton exhibit the very antithesis of self-reliance. Thus the jack-of-all-trades works with more than tools and materials; he also manipulates popular opinion. By associating himself with whatever anyone else is doing, Richard Jones *appears* to be one of the ablest men in the settlement, and for those who missed the performance itself, he touches it up in his weekly newspaper.

If Judge Temple would like a stable social order based on precedence, Jones sees that democracy and fluidity create a different situation, which Elizabeth describes comically: "you would not care a fig for distinction, if there were no one in the world but yourself; but as there happens to be a great many others, why you must struggle with them all—in the way of competition." With appearances and positions so uncertain, people start to scramble with each other for prominence, and the restlessness of the jack-of-all-trades is mirrored in the changeableness of the whole settlement. As Elizabeth Temple notes, "Everything in this magical country seems to border on the marvellous." The shape-shifter is well adapted to the opportunities of such a world and thrives on the flow of appearances. It is appropriate that the only genuine criminals in the background of *The Pioneers* are a group of counterfeiters.[3]

Another side of this unstable community is revealed by Cooper's plot in the novel. It is Richard Jones's jack-of-all-trades attitude and its collective effects that motivate the central sequence of events. His notion of universal genius encourages a spirit of restless competition in which people pursue sudden riches as a way to move ahead. Moreover, his desire to have his fingers in every enterprise makes him and his extension Hiram Doolittle both meddlesome and inquisitive. The direct result of his sense of genius is a tendency to pry into the affairs of others, especially if they prefer privacy and thus seem to have something to hide. And it is Jones's and Doolittle's prying into the affairs of Natty Bumppo that sets in motion the major events in the latter part of the novel—the release of Natty's hounds so that he will hunt and kill a deer, the visit to his hut with a finagled search warrant, the nighttime "arrest" of Natty before which he burns his hut, the trial, the escape, and the village's attack on Natty's cave. Regardless of the conventional interests of a love story and of a secret dispute over Judge Temple's or Oliver Edwards's rights to the land, the basic chain of events in the novel involves the persecution of Natty Bumppo by Richard Jones and his assistants.

Furthermore, the rapid growth of minor intrigues into lynch-law passions shows something about the atmosphere of Templeton. Where credit and shifting appearances are so important, everyone seems peculiarly vulnerable to rumor and suspicion. Richard Jones's and Jotham Riddel's own mining enterprise starts the rumor about Natty's secret treasure, but when it returns to them magnified by communal retelling, they are as ready as anyone to act on the hints. It is the atmosphere of competition, the pursuit of riches, the emphasis placed on mere appearances that make the community so erratic and gullible. In this sense the persecution of Natty Bumppo is not merely a symbolic device to show that the coming of civilization drives out the frontier individualist. Cooper has arranged that the hounding of Leather-Stocking be a fully expressive gesture. It arises from the very nature of the community and reveals its worst potentialities. And this aspect of Cooper's plotting is historically quite credible; what seems more contrived is his quick resolution of the difficulty without frontier violence.

But why harass poor Leather-Stocking? Because he sums up what Templeton is destroying. Not only is he a standing reproof (the only consistent one) of the settlers' "wasty ways." He is also the antithesis of the jack-of-all-trades. For all his frontier skills, Natty Bumppo does not have all-purpose "genius." He *is* what Judge Temple merely theorizes about—the product of his own particular nature, background, and wilderness education. He recognizes ineradicable differences in people's "ways," and he announces his own specialty: "The meanest of God's creaters be made for some use, and I'm formed for the wilderness." His sturdy integrity and his patient mastery of his tasks are a sore reminder of the tackiness and posturing that characterize the social order of Templeton. The more Richard Jones comes into his own in this novel and carries Templeton with him, the more clearly Leather-Stocking emerges as the resister of a whirligig, exploitative social world given over to games of confidence. When Cooper's social observation and his darker prophecies produce the fictional character of Richard Jones, his imagination reacts to produce Leather-Stocking, who embodies what the jack-of-all-trades will destroy. For if Natty Bumppo is invented as agent of resistance, he is also seen from the outset as victim. What he demonstrates is Cooper's fear that if American social development continues as the Benjamin Franklins and Richard Joneses have begun it, genuine self-reliance will become an *anti*social virtue.

But if Natty Bumppo actually incarnates some of the basic principles that Judge Temple advocates in his opposition to Richard Jones, why isn't the old frontiersman in imaginative league with the conservation-minded proprietor? Here we come to Cooper's own ambivalence, to the things he could imply but could not quite own up to as the child of the founder of Cooperstown. As should be obvious from Judge Temple's cheery continued employment of Richard Jones as secretary, agent, architect, sheriff, and factotum, his opposition is merely theoretical. At best Temple is to Jones what idea is to the execution of that idea. Jones is the means by which Temple does his work. Cooper repeatedly reminds us that Richard Jones is finally the extension of Judge Temple, that the promoter drags the booster in his wake, that the idealistic developer actually has to employ whoever is available. And one mark of the jack-of-all-trades is his emphatic availability. Richard Jones, in short, sums up the historical actuality accompanying "the promoter's vision." The ideal society with its orderly development and its institutional safeguards easily slips into the slapdash, boastful world of Richard Jones. Even the laws that Judge Temple institutes to make the community stable provide the means by which the very persons who most need to be restrained can persecute the one truly upright man in the settlement. And despite his personal misgivings, Judge Temple tacitly recognizes that opposition to his sheriff's will is useless; he has set in motion a force he cannot control.

It is not surprising that when Cooper foresaw how Thomas Jefferson would gradually slide into P. T. Barnum, he also created an extreme agent of resistance that would capture the American imagination. Like many American writers who want to analyze the present as having fallen away from some more heroic or more integral past, Cooper typifies the change in the arrival of a confidence man.[4] As Melville put it, the extermination of wolves "would seem cause for unalloyed gratulation, and is such to all except those who think that in new countries, where the wolves are killed off, the foxes increase." Natty Bumppo comes to stand for the integrity, the self-reliance, and the mastery that are conspicuously missing in Cooper's Templeton. His existence—fabulous or not—measures the quality of life in the actual pioneering settlement. Insofar as he belongs to a grander past, he also belongs in a disturbing historical sequence. For what does he do on departing from Templeton, but become "foremost in that band of Pioneers, who are opening the way for the march of our nation across the continent"! If the promoter's heir is the shape-shifting booster, his forerunner is the individual frontiersman. *The Pioneers* presents one of the great counter-fables to the myth of American progress: Adam in the wilderness gives way to the con man in the clearing.

Holgrave and Ishmael: Shape Shifting as Salvation

Other American writers in the nineteenth century, however, did not look on the jack-of-all-trades with Cooper's distaste, but rather saw him as both personally and culturally redemptive. The jack-of-all-trades is an alternative figure, and one way to understand these differing attitudes toward him is to note how the terms of contrast change. Hawthorne's version of the jack-of-all-trades—Holgrave in *The House of the Seven Gables*—is characterized through some of the same polarities that produced Richard Jones: stability versus fluidity; continuity with the past versus transformation in the present. But Hawthorne gives a different coloring to these contrasts, making Holgrave far more attractive than Jones. Cooper associates stability with order, integrity, and skill, whereas fluid characters tend to be shiftless, meddling, wasteful, and overly busy. For Hawthorne the fluid characters seem cheerfully active and competent. His images of stability and of the past, on the other hand, settle into ponderous gloom.

The chief source of the constant sense of oppression in reading *The House of the Seven Gables* is Hawthorne's emphasis on sheer weight. The mass of the house itself, the heavy fixity of Judge Pyncheon's corpse sitting in its chair, help to suggest the larger ponderousness of the past, of authority, material possessions, social respectability. And the characters most affected by this weight— Hepzibah, Clifford, even Judge Pyncheon—are given over to stagnant introspection, brooding, morbidity. If that is what permanence and stability entail, no wonder one turns with relief to Holgrave's easy competence and his spirit of encouragement. Although the youngest Pyncheon, Phoebe, is dismayed at his hatred of old things—"It makes me dizzy to think of such a shifting world!"— she is herself so briskly active, so caught up in the possibilities of useful work in the present, that she symbolically joins him as an agent of confidence. His shape shifting and her domestic busy-ness are the chief alternatives to the gloomy fixity of the other characters.

But if Hawthorne is imaginatively disburdening himself of some tremendous weight in this novel, and doing it through a light, flexible jack-of-all-trades, he doesn't entirely break his habit of preferring the substantial to the evanescent. For all Holgrave's appealing resiliency, there is something inescapably superficial about him and about Phoebe too. In a novel tracing the overlong continuance of the past into the present, they seem too easily detached from that past. Like Mather, Cooper, and Eggleston, Hawthorne sets a transient, somewhat superficial present against a graver past and makes a shape-shifting masquerader the descendant of more serious, if scarier, forebears. Hawthorne consistently scorns people who think they can lightly break their ties with the past, whether that past be communal, familial, or personal. Yet to acknowledge the past in this novel does not seem especially helpful for the characters. Holgrave's characteristic image of the Past restates Hawthorne's own preoccupation with weight and bulk in *The House of the Seven Gables:* "It lies upon the Present like a giant's dead body!" Hawthorne may not ultimately believe that the past *can* be escaped or its fixed forms made fluid again, but in this novel he at least acknowledges the value of assuming for a time "that the earth's granite substance is something not yet hardened."

Holgrave's chief theories, which he voices in youthful enthusiasm to Phoebe, have to do with getting out from under the heavy burden of the past. Overtly the issue, of course, is reform, and he sounds like a partisan of Thomas Jefferson advocating a new set of political and social institutions for each generation. In this sense Holgrave is a typical member of the group that Emerson characterized so acutely and yet sympathetically in his 1844 lecture "New England Reformers." But particular social reforms are not finally Holgrave's concern. The almost comic mixture of his associates and his causes suggests that the *idea* of reform is more vital to him than any actual program. And the essence of that idea is fluidity. The arch-reformer is the shape-shifter, who not only re-forms himself perpetually but creates an atmosphere of impermanence in the surrounding world: "He made her uneasy, and seemed to unsettle everything around her, by his lack of reverence for what was fixed."

In this sense, the mission of the jack-of-all-trades is to break up the heritage of the fathers. Like Richard Jones, Holgrave distrusts precedent, familial position, social hierarchy. But he has better reason to than Jones, for not only are the inherited institutions in *The House of the Seven Gables* stuffy and cumbersome, but the personal heritage of his fathers is positively dangerous. Clearly the underlying impulse in Holgrave's attacks on the past is his urgent need to break away from his own Maule-ness. Maule's curse, after all, was not merely a gesture against evil Pyncheons who would have to die choking on their blood. It also reciprocally involved the Maule family in an obsession with helping the curse along, as is apparent in Holgrave's story of the younger Matthew Maule and his entanglement with Gervayse and Alice Pyncheon. And Holgrave cannot free himself of this family burden simply by being aware of it or even by trying to exorcise it in the art of story telling. When the heritage of the fathers is radically tainted, one is perhaps justified in using more desperate measures to dispel it.

The theological type underlying both Maule's curse and the tainted blood line is Adam's fall, and it is in relation to original sin that Hawthorne reveals the essence of his jack-of-all-trades. The danger to Holgrave is that like his ancestors he will become ob-sessed with working his will on Pyncheons, that he will turn into a mere agent and finally a victim of the curse in his own deepest nature. His continued scrutiny of Hepzibah and Clifford and his temptation to hold Phoebe in a hypnotic trance show that this dan-ger is not merely metaphoric. How do we escape such a radical predisposition? More generally, how can we keep from brooding over the inherited limits of our own nature? That was the problem Franklin faced in formulating the Art of Virtue, and certainly his emphasis on what can be gained by practical activity in the present tells us something about Holgrave's own career. Indirectly as well, Franklin provided the useful model, for insofar as the risk is a fix-ation of the self on some inward gloom or guilt, the means of deliv-erance is to unfix the self, to substitute outward action for inward brooding, and to keep that action changing so as to prevent a re-currence of the fixation. For Holgrave, this means turning the he-reditary evil eye of the Maules into one more temporary outward role—that of mesmerist. The jack-of-all-trades, in short, is the relief from original sin.

In one respect Franklin had a number of heirs among mid-nineteenth-century American writers who shared his desire to find some more practical means of clearing away original sin than wait-ing for the entire regeneration of the inward self by God's grace. If the deepest self has been tainted and cannot be conveniently cleansed, perhaps one should dissociate oneself entirely from that kind of "depth." Thoreau makes a very suggestive joke when he tells people who complain about the Fall of Man to get up again and walk. Although he means more than literally standing up, what he is appealing to is the practical confidence that comes from the fact that one *can* stand up again after a fall. The jack-of-all-trades thus figures as a representative of one's freedom from the past, from guilt, from brooding, from all forms of Depth. And his exhilaration in outward performance and change can easily seem a metaphor of his inward health.

Hawthorne is too astute an analyst of the psyche, however, to leave the matter there, for in other contexts he is one of the strong-est spokesmen in the nineteenth century for the continued validity of the doctrine of original sin. Thus, if he cannot resolve the ambi-guity of the "deeper self," he at least poses the problem distinctly in presenting Holgrave. He recognizes that the cultural appeal of the jack-of-all-trades rests on the notion that the self is split.[5] The outer career, which Holgrave calls his "oscillating tendency," does not go in any particular direction. Instead, each of his numerous roles—schoolmaster, storekeeper, political editor, peddler, dentist, mesmerist, packet ship officer, daguerreotypist—appears as an "equally digressive means." While the jack-of-all-trades outwardly revolves among these guises, something else is assumed about his inward nature:

> what was most remarkable, and perhaps showed a more than common poise in the young man, was the fact, that, amid all these personal vicissitudes, he had never lost his identity. Homeless as he had been—continually changing his whereabout, and therefore responsible neither to public opinion nor to individuals—putting off one exterior, and snatching up another, to be soon shifted for a third—he had never violated the innermost man, but had carried his conscience along with him.

The confidence Holgrave inspires—and he is "the representative of many compeers in his native land"—does not arise from people's glimpses of his inner self; it is rather the inference they make from the way he outwardly plays his many roles. The moral issue is not integrity but "poise," and the "innermost man" here seems to be merely Holgrave's ability to maintain equilibrium while changing roles. The innermost man remains independent of the outward activity.

How different a matter is the deep self that inherits original sin and guilty predispositions! Hawthorne is obviously not referring to Holgrave's Maule heritage when he blithely affirms his "conscience" or his "innermost man." What we have here are two fundamentally different notions of human nature. In the one, the deeper self—the psyche—is complex, problematic, full of twists and impulses. It is also subject to analysis and is the part of the self in which the most interesting events take place. Outward actions are often motivated by this deeper self and thus indirectly express it, and cumulative events in the outer world can, in turn, complicate the inner being. Theologically, it is the seat of original sin and possibly of salvation as well. This is the sense of self that informs Hawthorne's best characterizations, especially of Hester Prynne and Arthur Dimmesdale. In the other view of human nature, "the innermost man" is considerably vaguer—it exists as an abstraction, an inference from the outward activity, and its qualities are indicated by clever metaphors based on outward actions, like Thoreau's standing up after the Fall. Despite the metaphors, however, the inner being is neither revealed nor affected by its outward guises. The social independence of the jack-of-all-trades suggests by analogy his independence from original sin and other complicated inborn traits, but his inner self is also separated from his own jack-of-all-trades activity.

The way Hawthorne puts these two notions of human nature together is to juxtapose Holgrave's heritage as Maule and his heritage as Yankee shape-shifter. Despite his "great mobility of outward mood," his playfulness and ease, there is an underlying gravity, a "magnetism," that even Phoebe notices in their first acquaintance. This sober side is the Maule influence, and it is Holgrave's danger, his "depth." Despite Hawthorne's reference to his "rare and high quality of reverence for another's individuality," it does not seem to be love or even conscience in the traditional form that saves Holgrave from his own deeper nature. It is rather his habit of surface variability. Phoebe accuses him of being a heartless observer: "The play costs the performers too much—and the audience is too cold-hearted." And it is true that he scrutinizes others without a corresponding play of affection, that they become to him mental food only. This sounds frighteningly like Hawthorne's "unpardonable sin"—the use in many ways of the mind without the heart. Yet Holgrave is critically different from such characters as Ethan Brand, Dr. Rappaccini, and Roger Chillingworth. If they approach others with their intellects but without their hearts, they also act out some deep inward compulsion which in turn has hold of their minds. In this sense Holgrave's very superficiality is his salvation. His scrutiny of others is genuinely disengaged, like that of Brown's Carwin or Melville's Confidence-Man. When Phoebe goes into a trance during his mesmeric reading of "Alice Pyncheon," Hawthorne argues that to a disposition like Holgrave's "there is no temptation so great as the opportunity of acquiring empire over the human spirit." He could have added, on the basis of the rest of his characterization of this jack-of-all-trades, that to a superficial shape-shifter like Holgrave, *no* temptation can be all that powerful. What finally saves him from obsession, from original sin, from his own deeper nature is that he has dispelled its concentered force in his whirl of activity.

Melville's Ishmael shares that strategy, and Melville is even more emphatic in using circular images to develop the idea. Ahab, the obsessive and driven man, is center seeking. He centralizes all woe and exasperation on one object and becomes himself the central man of whatever scene or subject he enters. Ishmael's "furious trope" about the development of Ahab's monomania expresses the ultimate horror that the shape-shifter tries to avoid: "his special lunacy stormed his general sanity, and carried it, and turned its concentred cannon upon its own mad mark." The jack-of-all-trades, in contrast, is centrifugal. He preserves his general sanity and his freedom from obsession by successively disengaging himself from each role, by knowing how to work from the center outwards into many alternative possibilities. The culminating image of the novel expresses this contrast perfectly: Ahab's concentrated purpose drags him and indirectly his ship and crew down into the mad vortex, while Ishmael rides the outer circuit of the whirlpool until its force is dissipated.

Melville, however, is less ambiguous about Ishmael than Hawthorne is about Holgrave. If Ishmael's variability steadies him and buoys him up, preserving him from certain risks, it has other values at least as important. Shape shifting positively delights him. Not driven by a larger purpose nor even concerned with making his fortune, "quite content if the world is ready to board and lodge me," Ishmael is free to enjoy what Wallace Stevens calls "the pleasures of merely circulating." He handles his various occupations—schoolteacher, merchant seaman, writer, stonemason, whaler—with the easy familiarity of the jack-of-all-trades, and like this figure he amuses himself with adaptation and experiment. "I try all things; I achieve what I can." By crossing book production with anatomy, he invents a new means of classifying whales, and he makes an ingenious, if inevitably futile, attempt to adapt the techniques of physiognomy and phrenology to the reading of the whale. He revels in the cultural habit of tinkering.

He enjoys even more his capacity to enter a role, to play it well, and yet to keep a self-conscious distance from it. *Moby-Dick* is filled with Ishmael's ad hoc performances; he is deliberately showing us what he can do. Often he indicates in a chapter title the role he is going to assume for the occasion: The Carpet Bag, A Bosom Friend, The Advocate, The Mat-Maker, The Hyena. To set off Ahab's demonic anti-social spirit, which is especially evident in his gam with the *Samuel Enderby* of London, Ishmael follows up the chapter with a digression—"The Decanter"—in which he himself later plays the bon vivant aboard the same ship. And the contrived narrative framework within which he tells The Town Ho's Story—the visit with "a lounging circle of my Spanish friends" in Lima—merely stylizes Ishmael's constant delight in shifting his narrative masks and expecting us, too, to enjoy them as performances.

The versatility of the shape-shifter relates to Ishmael's capacities as narrator in another sense as well. Simply to *know* about such a variety of matters, he has to be more people than the easy-going sailor who shipped with the *Pequod* and managed to circle back from an otherwise linear voyage. Thus when he proposes to tell us about the whale's skeleton, he interrupts himself with our natural question: "How is it, that you, a mere oarsman in the fishery, pretend to know aught about the subterranean parts of the whale?" And he obliges our curiosity by constructing a Bower in the Arsacides, where, in visiting "my late royal friend Tranquo, king of Tranque," he was able to walk through a whale's skeleton. Similarly, before discussing fossil whales, Ishmael comically presents "my credentials as a geologist, by stating that in my miscellaneous time I have been a stonemason, and also a great digger of ditches."

Such excursions from the sailor's experience aboard the *Pequod* are not, of course, designed to be directly convincing. They establish Ishmael's credibility in a different sense. His authority derives in part from his reading, in part from his imagination, but chiefly from his capacity to dramatize *himself* in the various human possibilities he tells us about. He knows not only the forms but the pleasures of frontier posturing: "With a frigate's anchors for my bridle-bitts and fasces of harpoons for spurs, would I could mount that whale and leap the topmost skies." He can enter into contention with the visible and invisible worlds—in the chapter "Moby-Dick" he out-Ahabs Ahab in describing the roots of his captain's monomania—but he can equally well picture himself comically plunged in deep thought in a garret in August, with steam rising from his head. On the masthead he is lulled into a pantheistic revery; at the sperm-tub he is suffused with the sentiment of brotherhood; in the center of the Grand Armada he is awed at the beauty and mystery of whales; at the tiller he is demonically possessed by fire; in the capsized whale boat he goes into a funk over the perils of whaling. The point is that all of these postures are credible, all are actual human possibilities. Entering into so many of them, the jack-of-all-trades becomes *more* human.

Ishmael as jack-of-all-trades is both omnivorous and skeptical. He wants to enter *all* experience, to dip into *all* knowledge, but he also knows that he cannot rest in any one guise. The sheer capaciousness of *Moby-Dick*, the cataloguing impulse that informs so much of it, reflects Ishmael's hunger and his restlessness. But the proper posture for dipping into "the Potluck of both worlds" involves restraint as well as appetite. "Doubts of all things earthly, and intuitions of some things heavenly; this combination makes neither believer nor infidel, but makes a man who regards them both with equal eye." The spirit of Ishmael's skepticism and gamesmanship is not to avoid erroneous belief but to remain open to all possibilities.

Finally the jack-of-all-trades is a valuable figure to Melville not merely because he avoids monomania or because shape shifting itself is fun. As Melville pictures it in *Moby-Dick*, the world itself is multivalent. It will not yield to a unitary view.[6] In such a world Ahab's fixation is psychologically damaging and it misreads the world by closing off too much. Ishmael's flexibility, on the other hand, matches an unfixed, multiple reality; it allows him to apprehend more experience. Similarly, his impatience with limits and endings is suited to a world that does not seem to have one goal, one purpose, but many. He argues in "Cetology" that all great works must be incomplete, that he can prepare only a draft of a draft. And the image with which he concludes "Stowing Down and Clearing Up" expresses his characteristic sense of all human inquiry. After the whalers or seekers have captured the prey, gone through the whole tedious process of extracting from it its small valuable essence, and cleaned up after themselves, another whale is spotted and the whole thing begins again. Metaphysical inquiry, in Ishmael's explicit analogy, thus becomes endless, incomplete, cyclic, like the occupations of the jack-of-all-trades.

Personal experience, too, goes through those endless cycles. In "The Gilder" Ishmael recognizes that in this mingled life there is no gradation or progress, that we proceed through the stages of unconsciousness, thoughtless faith, doubt, skepticism, disbelief, "resting at last in manhood's pondering repose of If," only to begin the whole cycle again. It is not only the world that is multiple and open-ended but the self as well. When Ishmael enters all those varying roles, he is doing more than acting out a myriad of human possibilities. He is dramatizing human experience itself as a succession of moods, a theater in which the momentous and earnest attitude of one moment is suddenly and unpredictably displaced by the feeling that it is all part of a general joke. As he gives voice to the insight, the belief of a particular time, he also recognizes that he is speaking from within a certain mood, which will soon yield to another.

Circulating among many occupations, roles, moods, philosophical stances, the jack-of-all-trades thus suggests for Melville the nature of the world and of human experience as well. But is there no resting point, no "final harbor"? Ishmael indicates clearly that no role is the ultimate one, but he does suggest another sort of repose. Penetrating the outer turbulence of the Grand Armada to the inner peace of mother and baby whales, he characteristically finds an analogy: "even so, amid the tornadoed Atlantic of my being, do I myself still for ever centrally disport in mute calm; and while ponderous planets of unwaning woe revolve round me, deep down and deep inland there I still bathe me in eternal mildness of joy."[7] But who is the "I" at the center of the storm, the equilibrium of the whirling top, the unmoved watcher of the endless masquerade? To explore that question, we must turn to the most extensive and philosophically illuminating study of the jack-of-all-trades in our literature, the works of Ralph Waldo Emerson.

The Oversoul as Jack-of-All-Trades

Emerson's cultural importance, like Franklin's, arises from his essential popularity. Both men seized on widespread images and attitudes and put them into more durable form. Franklin crossed the saint's life with the how-to-do-it manual, whereas Emerson uses the popular nineteenth-century forum of the lecture, but in suggestive ways Man Tinkering is another face of Man Thinking. If Franklin gave political and social sanction to certain popular habits that later turned into a cultural game of confidence, Emerson goes on to ratify such habits spiritually as well. He converts the mundane jack-of-all-trades into an image of the transcendental self in the world. To see how he does this, we can follow out the implications of his most explicit reference to the jack-of-all-trades, a passage in the latter part of "Self-Reliance" confirming once again the theme that one keeps upright by gyration:

> If our young men miscarry in their first enterprises they lose all heart. If the young merchant fails, men say he is *ruined*. If the finest genius studies at one of our colleges and is not installed in an office within one year afterwards in the cities or suburbs of Boston or New York, it seems to his friends and to himself that he is right in being disheartened and in complaining the rest of his life. A sturdy lad from New Hampshire or Vermont, who in turn tries all the professions, who *teams it, farms it, peddles*, keeps a school, preaches, edits a newspaper, goes to Congress, buys a township, and so forth, in successive years, and always like a cat falls on his feet, is worth a hundred of these city dolls. He walks abreast with his days and feels no shame in not "studying a profession," for he does not postpone his life, but lives already. He has not one chance, but a hundred chances.[8]

In one sense this is exactly what one would expect in an essay on self-reliance—the contrast of the spoiled, dependent dandy with the ingenious country lad, the reference to quite practical forms of self-help, the emphasis on present accomplishment instead of long-range expectations, the cheerful resiliency of the person who is busy *doing* things. And the fact that the sturdy lad can do so many different things without help seems to multiply his independence; shape shifting has tacitly been crossed with self-reliance.

But when we look again at what Emerson is doing here, the problems appear. *Is* there any legitimate connection between the jack-of-all-trades and the concept of self-reliance? The larger context in which the passage appears only deepens the confusion, for if this passage is just what we might look for in any essay on self-reliance, it is very much not what we would expect by this point in *Emerson's* essay on self-reliance. It is glaringly out of context. But before we dismiss it as mere evidence of the hodge-podge way in which Emerson rigged this lecture out of unrelated fragments of his journals, it is useful to look into the exact nature of the discrepancy and to see what it shows about Emerson's thinking.

Self-Reliance, as Emerson describes it in his most famous essay, is not a matter of farming, peddling, or buying townships. In another passage of this essay he calls such outward gestures "screens" over one's "proper life": "I ask primary evidence that you are a man, and refuse this appeal from the man to his actions." To be self-reliant is to ignore convention, habit, and outward pressure in order to be open to the impulses and laws that come from within. And the less vitiated such impulses are by public usages, the more they will be seen to arise from something beyond the self. The deepest Self on which one relies is not finally personal at all; it is the ground of all people, and it guarantees that if one is genuinely Self-Reliant, one will be speaking and acting for everyone. One can ignore laws because one knows the Law. It is jarring in the context of such spiritual generalizations to be suddenly presented with a New Hampshire jack-of-all-trades as the representative self. The jack-of-all-trades is not, in fact, an image to which Emerson refers very often, at least not as directly as he does here. But indirectly that same shape-shifter is everywhere in his writings. For Emerson, all outward actions and actors turn into metaphors, and what the jack-of-all-trades comes to stand for is his basic conception of the Self in action.

Emerson believes that there are two selves—inner and outer, primary and secondary, a self that IS and a self that DOES. The business of the first is with the ideal and the possible, whereas the second confronts the actual, the concrete, the realized. Although each is an essential part of human experience, the two kinds of self do not, for Emerson, have much to do with each other. As Hawthorne says of Holgrave, the outer roles do not violate "the innermost man." Nor are the qualities of the inner self reliably indicated by outward behavior. As Emerson's seventeenth-century forebears would have put the same idea, one cannot be saved by good works alone, nor can one be confident that good works reflect a gracious disposition. There are *two* selves.

Given this split, Emerson is pretty clear about his preference. For all his trenchant observations of the outer life around him and his everyday conformity to social values, he believes that the inner self is the important one and that the outer self is ultimately inconsequential. Henry Nash Smith has shown how Emerson agonized over a vocation—clearly an *outward* choice—and gradually came to realize that his ideal posture was loyalty to his inner demands, to contemplation, seeing, and being, instead of doing.[9] Ultimately, Emerson would like to see the inner self free of any dependency on the outer one. Nothing is more characteristic of his early essays than his habit of finally dissolving the whole world of externals and particulars in the flood of Spirit or pure Being. And throughout his career he doubted the capacity of the inner self to embody its ideas in the workaday world. "You cannot institute," he says in his essay on Plato, "without peril of charlatanism."[10] Yet if *all* outward activity is mere phenomenon, one cannot discriminate between the authentic gesture and the sham. The outward self can be nothing but a gamesman.

Despite the paean to idealism at the end of *Nature*, however, Emerson knew that it was not easy to disown the outer world or the self that managed to cope with it.[11] In fact, he took increasing interest in this shape-shifting outward self. What is distinctive about Emerson's approach is that he looks at the jack-of-all-trades *from the inside*. This is why the figure so rarely appears in his works in quite the stereotypical form that he presents in the passage I quoted from "Self-Reliance." Instead Emerson sees a playful masquerader cavorting independently around the self that he identifies as ME. Yet he knows that there has to be commerce of some kind between Being and the Doer, and that it is not enough to say merely that Being descends into the world of action for the tropes through which it addresses itself. One of the key questions underlying Emerson's thought is thus precisely the question with which I began this chapter: What is the relation of the outward shape-shifter to the Self?

The first and simplest way in which Emerson analyzes this relationship is to see each outward pursuit as a part of a larger whole. This is a common cast of thought in his writings. Great books, for instance, are the Universal Mind seen through the eyes of a particular scribe, and inconsistencies are merely the many faces of the One. The personal equivalent of the same idea is expressed in the circle imagery so often associated with the jack-of-all-trades: "every path we take is but a radius of our sphere."[12] From this standpoint the problem with any single role is that it is at best partial and thus a diminishment of the self. In "The American Scholar" Emerson relates this idea to the division of labor, recalling a fable that in the beginning the gods divided Man into men:

> The old fable covers a doctrine ever new and sublime; that there is One Man,—present to all particular men only partially, or through one faculty; and that you must take the whole society to find the whole man. Man is not a farmer, or a professor, or an engineer, but he is all. . . . The fable implies that the individual, to possess himself, must sometimes return from his own labor to embrace all the other laborers. . . . The state of society is one in which the members have suffered amputation from the trunk, and strut about so many walking monsters,—a good finger, a neck, a stomach, an elbow, but never a man.[13]

This helps. One can begin to see here why that sturdy New Hampshire lad who farms *and* teaches *and* peddles might represent Man instead of a walking monster. The jack-of-all-trades literally enacts the return of the specialized laborer to the embrace of all other laborers and thus to self-possession as well. He is a concrete representative of Man in the world of men. Furthermore, if each occupation is only a partial putting forth of the Self, and if each person is in turn only one specialized member of the All, then the popular stereotype is also the ultimate spiritual figure. What is Emerson's Oversoul but the Jack-of-ALL-Trades?

When one can identify with the Oversoul, occupy its permanent center, and sense it pouring itself forth into the world in plenitude and variety, the conception of parts and whole expresses well the relation of one's own outward masquerade to one's real Self. But what happens when this inspired view is not accessible and the changing faces appear merely as changes? Often, especially in the later works, Emerson finds himself drifting in the very midst of flowing appearances,[14] and like Franklin he has to assume or discover after the fact that all the roles interlock, that seeming inconsistencies average out into "character" after all. For a world of seemingly endless changes, part-and-whole is too static a figure, and Emerson turns to the concept of tendency. The deeper Self is to the succession of outward roles what the wire is to a string of beads. In order to know the Self through the rotating states of mind, one looks at "the record of larger periods. What is the mean of many states; of all the states?"[15] And the same procedure applies to the observed world as well; the poet is the one who can look at the metamorphoses of matter and see the "direction" that guides the flow.

Although the search for a tendency behind the mutations adapts Emerson's idea of whole and parts to a dynamic reality, it diminishes the importance of spiritual oneness and stresses the immediate experience of change. In fact, once Emerson acknowledges the flowing, he spends more time celebrating impermanence than seeking the law behind it: "The philosophy we want is one of fluxions and mobility."[16] Like Franklin's model self, Holgrave, and Ishmael, he not only fears that fixity will cramp the self but also abhors the very idea of it: "Wisdom consists in keeping the soul liquid, or, in resisting the tendency to too rapid petrifaction."[17] He sees every thought, every image, as a potential prison, and the value of poets is as "liberating gods" who free us from our selves of this hour, who "unfix" the world itself from its present moorings. Without "this elastic principle" people and their labors "become blockish and near the point of everlasting congelation."[18] The horror expressed in that metaphor is matched by Emerson's sheer delight in mutability. "Our love of the real [i.e., the ideal] draws us to permanence, but health of body consists in circulation, and sanity of mind in variety or facility of association. We need change of objects."[19] What is this but a medico-philosophical basis for the cultural restlessness that Emerson so thoroughly shared? From this perspective, what the jack-of-all-trades represents is not plenitude or wholeness but flexibility and change.[20]

The relation of the deeper Self to its successive guises is suggested by analogy to God's actions in the visible world:

> Metamorphosis is the law of the universe. . . . the thoughts of God pause but for a moment in any form, but pass into a new form, as if by touching the earth again in burial, to acquire new energy. A wise man is not deceived by the pause: he knows that it is momentary: he already foresees the new departure, and departure after departure, in long series.[21]

While this journal entry of 1845 tacitly assumes the underlying coherence of God in the creation, there is no suggestion of whole and parts. Note, too, that what is being affirmed here is not direction but departure. If we apply the same figure to the self, what Emerson values is not the larger tendency guiding the masquerade but the shape-shifter's ability to drop one mask in order to don another. Emerson seems to revel in the idea of masquerade. Like Ishmael, he recognizes human experience as a succession of unrelated attitudes: "Our moods do not believe in each other."[22] And he knows that the mood of the moment is also a mode of perception. Thus he relishes the ability to play a variety of parts, to speak in many voices, each of which can convey some new apprehension of truth.

In one sense his most skillfully composed essays (e.g., "Experience" and "Montaigne") can be seen as virtually dramatic exchanges among a variety of speakers—skeptics, believers, free-speaking poets, materialists, transcendentalists. But although more inclusive generalizations usually conclude the essays, no one really "wins" the argument. In fact, the voices do not really argue at all, for they do not listen to each other. What Emerson does is not to arrange a debate nor to argue dialectically but to perform a series of roles. When he assumes a part for the time, he enters it fully and with surprising authority. At his best he does not use straw men. And when he enlarges the method to a whole book—*Representative Men*—he uses each character as a thread of perception on which to resee the world. When he speaks fo Plato, *that* sounds right, and when he speaks for Napoleon, *that* sounds right, too. Like Ishmael, he is showing off his capacity to play one stance or mood after another and to make each convincing.

But at least as important as the ability to enter a role is the capacity to withdraw from it again: "Valor consists in the power of self-recovery."[23] This capacity to withdraw is at the root of the shape-shifter's appeal to Emerson and to his culture: he cannot be caught or fixed in any role. And that detachment brings us to the third and most characteristic way in which Emerson sees the relationship of masquerade to inner Self. In his journal for 1837 he notes that at privileged moments he knows he exists "directly from God, and am, as it were, his organ," but that he also finds himself in the contradictory state, "a surprised spectator and learner of all my life."[24] It is that pure sense of being a watcher, apart, as Whitman says, from the pulling and hauling, that is so revealing. For Emerson's ultimate pairing is the one he introduced in his first major work—ME and NOT ME.

In Emerson's view the NOT ME includes both the whole external world and his own body, his gestures, his masquerade in that outside world. When the inner Self wants to understand itself, to contemplate pure Being, it voraciously takes in the outer world for metaphors, a process that could be described in an adaptation from Freud: Where NOT ME was, let ME be. This is the side of Emerson's thought that Quentin Anderson aptly styles "the imperial self."[25] But psychologically the reverse of this proposition is even more suggestive: Where I thought I was, let ME not be. If the imperial self wants to swallow all experience, what are we to call the

self that needs immediately to disgorge it again and leave it behind? The fact is, that for Emerson the deep Self, the ME is *not*
usually known directly by intuition or primary assurance. It is discovered reflexively by detachment from the NOT ME. And if the
ME is to continue to be aware of itself, the disengagement must be
constantly re-enacted. This is why self-reliance presupposes shape
shifting. The essential gesture declaring one's independence, starting anew, beginning to create a self, is to throw off the old role.
Thus the jack-of-all-trades perpetually celebrates the cultural myth
of renewal. But he also indicates that the myth may rest less on
future promise than on ceaseless disengagement from the past and
the present. One finds the self to rely on in the act of detaching it
from something else. Thus it is one's outward flexibility that assures one of the deeper Self's very existence.

Emerson stresses this psychological discovery in an amusing passage in *Nature:*

> Certain mechanical changes, a small alteration in our local posi-
> tion, apprizes us of a dualism. We are strangely affected by seeing
> the shore from a moving ship, from a balloon, or through the tints
> of an unusual sky. The least change in our point of view gives the
> whole world a pictorial air. A man who seldom rides, needs only
> to get into a coach and traverse his own town, to turn the street
> into a puppet-show. The men, the women,—talking, running,
> bartering, fighting,—the earnest mechanic, the lounger, the beg-
> gar, the boys, the dogs, are unrealized at once, or, at least, wholly
> detached from all relation to the observer, and seen as apparent,
> not substantial beings. . . . Turn the eyes upside down, by look-
> ing at the landscape through your legs, and how agreeable is the
> picture, though you have seen it any time these twenty years!
>
> In these cases, by mechanical means, is suggested the difference
> between the observer and the spectacle—between man and nature.
> Hence arises a pleasure mixed with awe; I may say, a low degree
> of the sublime is felt, from the fact, probably, that man is hereby
> apprized that whilst the world is a spectacle, something in himself
> is stable.[26]

What a picture—as comic as Christopher Pearse Cranch's drawing
of the "transparent eyeball"! A man doing somersaults across the
landscape to convince himself that the world is going flippety-flop
while something in himself remains stable! Here is the reduction to
the absurd of the self as a whirling top; yet its very extremity is its
subjective truth, as any child knows while doing cartwheels, swinging, or twirling in place. Emerson is as keen as Whitman on setting
the self in motion to create a new sense of the world. But where

Whitman's vertiginous movement induces a feeling of spiritual buoyancy ("the float of the sight of things"), Emerson's chiefly convinces him of his own detachment. As more and more of the seemingly substantial things around one are turned into mere spectacle, "unrealized," shown to be NOT ME, something else in the self is felt as that which is *not* the NOT ME.

That view from the serene and inviolable center is Emerson's legacy. At certain happy moments he is given to know that he and the ALL are one, and that every outward role or event simply adds to the Spirit's multifarious showing for its own benefit. For that mood, the jack-of-all-trades is the Spirit's outward type, the exemplar of plenitude and wholeness. Even during the longer days, however, when such spiritual identification does not occur, when there are no grand flights, Sunday baths, or tootings at the weddings of the soul, Emerson holds to that central view. The fluidity of events, the metamorphoses of nature, the changings of mask and mood are so many reminders of all that is NOT ME. In his flight from one role to another, the jack-of-all-trades can represent this view as well, enacting the perpetual disengagement of something in the self from the NOT ME.

For Emerson the mundane habits of shape shifting, gamesmanship, and self-help thus ironically provide assurances of the ME, from whose vantage point all such outward activity is purely inconsequential. Yet he is not simply playing a shell game here, nor is he alone in crossing materialism and idealism, in using the practical, self-reliant jack-of-all-trades as the basis for spiritual vision. James Russell Lowell disparagingly called Emerson "a Plotinus-Montaigne" with "a Greek head on right Yankee shoulders, whose range/ Has Olympus for one pole, for t'other the Exchange," but such dualism has been widespread in American culture, and Emerson's treatment of the jack-of-all-trades helps suggest why. This icon develops value by contrast, by what it is *not*—not limited or shrunken, not obsessed or guilt-ridden, not stodgy or fixed, not stuck in inherited roles. The jack-of-all-trades is a figure in flight: flight from every outward mask and flight as well from a deeper, brooding inwardness. He does not suggest the values of looking *beneath* the surface or *behind* the mask but of rising *above* the surface, "transcending" temporary appearances. By this evasiveness he provides the psychological equivalent of spiritual vision—the detachment of something from the spectacle. Even in mastering the games and masquerading skillfully at the Exchange, he keeps his distance and thus, by inference, his spirituality. He can only be authentic by constantly freeing himself. "Yet, what is my faith?" Emerson asks in describing the inner life of the jack-of-all-trades. "What am I? What but a thought of serenity and independence, an abode in the deep blue sky?"[27]

That strangely nebulous assertion hints at the answer to a question that must be troubling my readers by now: What does the jack-of-all-trades have to do with the confidence man? Cooper's *The Pioneers* shrewdly reveals how, *in practice,* the one slides into the other. Yet there is more to the issue than that and more also than the merging of confidence man, jack-of-all-trades, and trickster in the general figure of the shape-shifter. Both confidence man and jack-of-all-trades are role players who delight in technique and in the capacity to make a role convincing. But the jack-of-all-trades is essentially not a public figure, and that would seem a critical difference between him and the confidence man. Another basic difference is that the jack-of-all-trades seems more innocent. In fact, the differences are related. The jack-of-all-trades seems more innocent because he does not try to do something *to* someone else—he simply does as he does. Or so he assumes. In Emerson's account of the inner life of the jack-of-all-trades, the public is not quite real anyway. Nothing one does outwardly has more than a shadow existence, and one of the central values of gyration and shape shifting is to "unrealize" the familiar world. To say that the jack-of-all-trades is "innocent" is merely to restate his own sense that his actions are morally indifferent. When social, economic, and political experience becomes mere spectacle, one cannot take one's actions or relations seriously. The public world turns into a game space, and Melville's *The Confidence-Man* shows us the consequences of that attitude.

What is important to the jack-of-all-trades? Not quality but facility. Whether we think of material goods or social consequences, the products of his actions seem unreal to him, not worth much of his time, energy, or attention. What matters is the doing itself, the proof of his varied capacities. And if the public measure of his tasks—quality—must be disregarded, so must integrity, the private measure. No outer gesture expresses the true self; no role is authentic. Instead we discover the true self by disengaging from each role. If for Franklin being is doing, for Emerson doing is being. Inside the whirl of activity is the spiritual equilibrium, "a thought of serenity and independence, an abode in the deep blue sky." When quality and integrity, as measures of the self, give way to facility and detachment, we are not only in the confidence man's game space but in his mind as well. He gathers to himself several seemingly innocent American icons—self-made man, booster, jack-of-all-trades—and shows what can be done in the open-ended world they share. That is why he is so hard to disown.

7

A SOLITARY PERFORMANCE
AT WALDEN POND

Everything turns gray when I don't have at least one mark on the horizon. Life then seems empty and depressing. I cannot understand honest men. They lead desperate lives, full of boredom.

—Victor "The Count" Lustig

The New England character is essentially anti-Diogenic; the Yankee is too shrewd not to comprehend the advantages of living in what we call the world; there are no bargains to be made in the desert, nobody to be taken advantage of in the woods.

—Charles Frederick Briggs

How long before our masquerade will end its noise of tambourines, laughter and shouting, and we shall find it was a solitary performance?

—Ralph Waldo Emerson

The nearly simultaneous publication of P. T. Barnum's autobiography and Thoreau's *Walden* prompted an anonymous reviewer in *Knickerbocker* to compare the two men as "Town and Rural Humbugs." Like most nineteenth-century commentators, he emphasized Thoreau's quirkiness—in this case, what he construed as a diet of beans—rather than his vision or his integrity; yet by noting the "diametrically opposite" lessons of these two books, he suggested something important about *Walden*. Barnum demonstrated the gullibility of the public; Thoreau showed how to avoid shams, even though they paid better than realities. "If ever a book required an antidote, it is the auto-biography of Barnum, and we know of no other so well calculated to furnish this antidote as the book of Thoreau's."[1] And that is how Thoreau comes down to us—as an antidote. Emerson noted in his younger friend's personality what is also apparent in the voice of *Walden,* a certain military nature, a need for a fallacy to expose, "as if he did not feel himself except in opposition." If American society was by the mid-nineteenth century becoming overly hospitable to illusions and confidence games, Thoreau was one of its most trenchant critics, and few books would seem less appropriate in a study of the confidence man in America than his *Walden.*

Even as critics in the twentieth century became more receptive to Thoreau and turned from his eccentricities to his insights, his artistry, his organic vision,[2] they still responded to him as an alternative. And indeed the Thoreau who is most audible in *Walden* sounds like the antithesis of a con man: "I perceive that we inhabitants of New England live this mean life that we do because our vision does not penetrate the surface of things. We think that that *is* which *appears* to be." While Barnum was advertising the gaudiest costumes, Thoreau was noting that the emperor had no clothes. He saw through passing shadows to bedrock truths, and he constantly distinguished means from ends. He would have architecture and clothing develop organically from one's character, so that life would not be a masquerade or a game but an earnest "business."

Insofar as nineteenth-century American illusionism had its roots in attitudes associated with Benjamin Franklin's model self, Thoreau seems deliberately to invert these attitudes. Franklin turns Puritan pieties to secular habits; Thoreau uses business language as a metaphor for a new spirituality. Franklin's model self lives in a crowded, urban world; Thoreau finds himself when he is isolated in the natural world. Franklin likes systems, adjustments, cooperative efforts; Thoreau prefers a radical individualism. Whereas Franklin's model self develops complexity and power through its increasing connection with social systems, Thoreau's whole experiment at Walden begins in the effort to disaffiliate himself from the busy commercial world. At the heart of these contrasts is a disagreement about appearances. One of the major qualities of the model self in Franklin's autobiography is that he exists among appearances and lives for and in public performance. Although he knows only too well that the outward semblance may be misleading, he understands the practical value of the impressions one makes. Self-creation thus involves a concern for how one appears to others, and some of the recommended techniques of self-development are frank manipulations of others' beliefs.

Thoreau, in contrast, despises appearances. He sees the problem of his society as its inability to look behind the outward show. He seems to have no interest in creating a self for public performance.

In fact, in his preference for permanent truth he argues that one should not put oneself into *any* relation to the given social order, neither support it, exploit it, nor resist it:

> A saner man would have found himself often enough "in formal opposition" to what are deemed "the most sacred laws of society," through obedience to yet more sacred laws, and so have tested his resolution without going out of his way. It is not for a man to put himself in such an attitude to society, but to maintain himself in whatever attitude he finds himself through obedience to the laws of his being. . . .

This statement in the "Conclusion" of *Walden* utterly rejects that kind of self making which has any regard at all for public impressions. But it comes at the end of the greatest handbook in our literature on how to *get* oneself into a certain attitude toward society. Although it may seem by the end of the book that Thoreau has all along been at peace while only society was "the desperate party," the process of attaining such a perspective demands deliberation and ingenuity. And Thoreau draws readers into this final perspective not by directly conveying his own vision but by re-enacting the steps to it.

Walden is a visionary book, but more fundamentally it is a guide to extrication. It tells how to get out, how to work free. Whatever peace may reside deep within the self, we must use wit and dexterity to come to it. A person cannot simply lie back, resign himself to his mood, unlock at all risks his human doors, or unclench the floodgates. For all Thoreau's audacity at speaking as an outsider to the social world, he knows that we actually start out inside, encumbered, and that we must make our way deliberately to freshness and "innocence." Once we see *Walden* as this long act of disengagement, some otherwise paradoxical qualities of the book begin to make sense. Why, for instance, should the spokesman for spiritual integrity dramatize himself as a witty shape-shifter? If the true self is free, why do we need so much analysis and denunciation of social customs? What does Thoreau's experimentalism have to do with his belief that all outward phenomena are mere shadows? Why does he need to measure the length and breadth of the pond, producing that suspiciously neat formula about finding the greatest depth, in order to make a generalization about the depths of human nature? What, in short, is the relation of his Emersonian concern for higher laws to his Franklinian penchant for practical demonstration?

Such discrepancies are usually treated as matters of rhetoric, as if the issue were how to convey to one's busy, materialistic neighbors the truths of the human spirit. Thoreau's Yankee gamesmanship thus seems a strategy for reaching his audience, and his practical suggestions merely a lure to his real subject. But *Walden* is more than a skillful selling of the visionary life to people who drive a hard bargain. It is a re-enactment of self-discovery. And the model self—as articulated by Franklin and developed in practice in the nineteenth century—plays a critical role in that process. What allowed Franklin to align himself with the powers of the world becomes for Thoreau the means to work free of these very powers. He shows how the strategies of creating a self for the marketplace can also be used for discovering the self *to the self*. In breaking his ties to a society of con games, he draws on the same gambits and values that built up such a society in the first place.

To see how this is so, we must begin with the similarities of *Walden* and Franklin's *Autobiography*. Both books open in worlds where people are enslaved and indebted, where their material difficulties are compounded by their tendency to labor under old beliefs and prejudices. Both writers assume that a person's preliminary need is to be free of such a situation, and they acknowledge that in the first instance the problems are quite practical. Both test precisely what is necessary for human survival, and both are interested in finding the minimal ways of satisfying these needs, so that most of the self can be freed for something better. Each treats the self as an instrument that can be experimentally improved so as to function well in the world. Whatever their differences in defining the higher ends of life, both encourage a clever, efficient approach to the solving of concrete problems. They live by their wits. Franklin and Thoreau know that their readers want practical advice more than moral exhortation. They draw on and reinforce the how-to-do-it tradition, breaking down their experience into well-defined steps. Many readers regard Thoreau's tabulation of the costs to build his house as an elaborate joke on his neighbors, but clearly there is something infectious in his example. It is the experimental accessibility of these two lives that makes them initially engaging, and both Franklin and Thoreau know how to capitalize on this appeal to build up confidence in their readers. The larger optimism of both writers is rooted in their ability to do things successfully and to show others how. The do-it-yourself Self comes with detailed instructions.

Thoreau's relation to Franklin is, moreover, only one aspect of his more extensive grounding in popular traditions. His earliest critics may have missed his artistry and his vision, but they were alert to the popular side of his nature.[3] Repeatedly they noted his Yankee notions and his tendency to play games like the legendary peddlers. The recurrent phrase "a Yankee Diogenes" suggests that they responded to his quirkiness not as a personal but as a cultural trait. And indeed Thoreau is more than a product of his contemporary New England with its high-brow transcendentalism and its peddler folklore;[4] he deliberately draws on popular stereotypes and uses them to carry on his own sort of neighborliness. When he warns designers of houses "to exercise a little Yankee shrewdness" lest they end up with a prison or a mausoleum, he is not making fun of his neighbors' cultural heritage but using its persistent values to remind them of the risks of conspicuous consumption. He knows that officially his America is dominated by a work ethic but he also knows, as Mark Twain and Barnum do too, that there is a deeper current of resistance to work, a wish to get by on as little effort as possible, and he appeals to this feeling by his own emphasis on ingenuity.

When he begins his account of his life at Walden by answering the questions his neighbors have asked, he is, as most of his commentators note, actually spoofing them for asking the wrong questions. But his intimacy with his neighbors is greater than that. First, he spends enough time answering their "very particular inquiries" to show that he respects their curiosity. Second, he recognizes that Yankee quizzicality is part of their heritage, a game that he can not only respond to but play himself as well. Repeatedly he introduces questioners of this mode of life only to turn the game around; Thoreau makes as many "very particular inquiries" into his contemporaries' lives as they do into his. In this sense his playfulness is neighborly, an enactment and celebration of regional manners. Before taking himself out of relation, he is quite deliberately and systematically putting himself *into* relation with his peers.

It is more than popular manners that he shares with his neighbors. Thoreau also draws on popular aspirations, especially the vogue of "self-culture."[5] Like his neighbors, he assumes that the aim of life is the development of the self, and he is far from a purist. *Walden* illustrates the whole heady mix of nineteenth-century self-improvement—the practical forms of self-reliance, the manipulative arts of self making, and the intellectual and spiritual developments associated with "self-culture." In a late journal entry Thoreau voices an attitude that had informed *Walden*. He argues that success is something higher than acquiring property, that one approaches it by "trying to invent something, to be somebody,—i.e., to invent and get a patent for himself."[6] Despite his persistent attack on the cult of the self-made man for distorting essential values, he avidly appeals to its rhetoric, its personal promise, its delightful sense that the self is plastic. The easy confidence of self making is paradoxically most evident in Thoreau's fear that if he went into business, he would of course end up doing "a good business" and thus find himself trapped by success. He must use his wits *not* to succeed.

Thoreau thus both attacks and reinforces the image of the self-made man. His kinship with the other nineteenth-century descendants of Franklin's model self is more open and unqualified. "If I seem to boast more than is becoming," says Thoreau the booster, "my excuse is that I brag for humanity rather than for myself." He does not propose to write an ode to dejection, "but to brag as lustily as chanticleer in the morning, standing on his roost, if only to wake my neighbors up." Like Jefferson, he would rather confirm people's hopes than console their fears. The "Conclusion" of *Walden* has nearly as zany a mixture of exhorting, confident voices as Whitman's "Song of Myself," ranging from the Vedas to the tinker's advice on the gallows. And the whole book is inventive at selling real estate in Concord. The same spirit that was hopefully naming remote American villages Cairo and Ithaca appears in Thoreau's characterization of the Walden mosquito as an Iliad and an Odyssey, singing its wrath and wanderings.

His connection to the jack-of-all-trades is even more marked than his boosterism. "I have as many trades as fingers," he tells us, and he delights in showing how many things he can do. If raising beans is a rare amusement, "which, continued too long, might have become a dissipation," he can without leaving the bean field slide into theoretical agriculturist and then again into preacher. Even in his aloneness, Thoreau discovers a self by his ability to shift roles, turning mason to get his chimney up and poet to celebrate its smoke. The shape-shifter, however, seems to Thoreau as much as it does to Emerson merely an outward kind of self:

> I only know myself as a human entity; the scene, so to speak, of thoughts and affections; and am sensible of a certain doubleness by which I can stand as remote from myself as from another. However intense my experience, I am conscious of the presence and criticism of a part of me, which, as it were, is not a part of me, but a spectator, sharing no experience, but taking note of it, and that is no more I than it is you. When the play, it may be the tragedy, of life is over, the spectator goes his way.

Since Thoreau gives more attention than Emerson to the skills of the outward shape-shifter, his sense of doubleness is even more emphatic. When he walks back from town through the woods on dark nights, he retires inside himself with his thoughts, "leaving only my outer man at the helm." [7]

Whatever calm and permanence there may be in that deeper self, however, the shiftiness of the outer man is closer to the central values of *Walden*. As much as any nineteenth-century jack-of-all-trades, the "I" of *Walden* abhors fixity and heaviness. He may not wish to travel to the ends of the earth, but he wants to be ready to depart at any moment. The saddest sight he can imagine is a man dragging so much furniture behind him that he is at a dead set. In contrast, the model self is light and mobile. He can change shape, location, and attitude at a moment's notice. This same flexibility he wishes to restore to the surrounding world as well. Repeatedly Thoreau makes solid-seeming *things* porous and fluid. The ultimate vision of the shape-shifter appears in the ecstasies of "Spring" when the granite earth itself starts to flow, turning from dead history to living poetry. When Thoreau justifies his departure from Walden Pond, he does so in terms that help us understand the restlessness of the jack-of-all-trades:

> I left the woods for as good a reason as I went there. Perhaps it seemed to me that I had several more lives to live, and could not spare any more time for that one. It is remarkable how easily and insensibly we fall into a particular route, and make a beaten path for ourselves.

The references to several more lives to live seems related to the omnivorousness that Ishmael and Emerson display as jacks-of-all-trades, but Thoreau's primary emphasis is not on the yearning to take in all experience but on the fear of that beaten path. He wants always to move on, to break free.

I said earlier that *Walden* is not only a visionary book but a guide to extrication. Having shown how thoroughly the self in *Walden* is grounded in the popular traditions of the model self in the nineteenth century, I want now to examine why this model self was so important to Thoreau, what help it could provide in the art of disengagement. Like Edgar Allan Poe, Thoreau bears not only interesting specific relations to the American confidence man but a more general relation to the primitive trickster figure, especially the Winnebago trickster, Wakdjunkaga.[8] The trickster begins his adventures by breaking the implements and customs of the tribally familiar world and then wanders in a place of shifting boundaries, where all relations and habits have to be renegotiated. Poe acts out this impulse by playfully dissecting the senses and the mind. Thoreau acts it out by systematically breaking his ties to the social and economic world. The essential gesture of *Walden* is disengagement, and it is not an easy task. In "Where I Lived, and What I Lived For" Thoreau describes himself as in a remote place, "behind the constellation of Cassiopeia's Chair, far from noise and disturbance," but the distance he goes and the newness he seeks are not products of travel. He does not voyage; he imaginatively severs his relations. The passage on Cassiopeia's Chair may seem lofty and peaceful, but we must remember that it immediately follows Thoreau's razzle-dazzle spiel as a "real estate broker," letting farms pass through his hands and his head without getting his fingers "burned by actual possession." To gain his distance, open his vision, and return to an original fluidity, Thoreau does not meditate, he plays games.

In brief, Thoreau uses the model self to make explicit his ties with his neighbors, to turn them into play, and thus to break them. Once he has done this, the logic and the imagery of the book would suggest that the model self should turn into mere metaphor and then should be left behind as cocoon or shell so that the regenerated and purified self could pass on. Thus the cantankerous trickster of "Economy" should be displaced by the congenial, mellow, philosophic friend of "Former Inhabitants; and Winter Visitors." But this development, although partially enacted in *Walden,* is neither so simple nor so complete as it appears. The model self will not be downed so easily, and once Thoreau draws on some of its popular values, he finds himself celebrant as well as critic of his culture.

The very idea of a model self had a peculiar appeal in nineteenth-century America. Beyond tangible rewards, it offered something even more democratic—a personality available to many. As Thoreau puts it, "I trust that none will stretch the seams in putting on the coat, for it may do good service to him whom it fits." And the pleasures of entering into this stock personality did not entirely depend on one's achieving the official rewards of affluence and reputation. In fact, the powers of the model self could become so intrinsically satisfying that gaining riches would seem a mere figure of speech to convey some essentially inward accomplishment. Thus when Thoreau saw how often the model self was degenerating into a slave of those superficial goals—"the mass of men lead lives of quiet desperation"—he did more than repudiate his culture. He set about to reinvigorate the model self in all its sprightly poise and humorous detachment, precisely the qualities that Franklin had associated with it in the first place. What he attacks in *Walden* is not the concepts of "enterprise" and "business"—these he finds exhilarating—

but the rigid, unenterprising application of these concepts. And once the model self is reinvigorated, its powers cannot be fully left behind by the ecstatic, semi-mystical self who emerges from the cocoon in "Spring" and "Conclusion." The butterfly is still a playful shape-shifter.

James Russell Lowell said something of Thoreau that clarifies the importance of the model self in *Walden:* "He was forever talking of getting away from the world, but he must be always near enough to it, nay, to the Concord corner of it, to feel the impression he makes there."[9] When Thoreau at Walden playfully cuts his ties to the familiar world, he is doing more than freeing himself from convention; he is also *discovering* a self in his own facility. In the most obvious sense, he can survive on more efficient terms than his neighbors, but more generally he can play their games better than they can. His independence and superiority are not intrinsic qualities, nor are they achieved once and for all at a certain point; they are processes that must be constantly acted out, and two-thirds of *Walden* is given over to these processes.

The often-remarked seasonal structure of the book is chiefly apparent in the later chapters beginning with the approach of winter in "House Warming." Prior to that, the structure is dialectical. The self moves back and forth from society to solitude, from "The Village" to "The Ponds," and then from "Baker Farm" to "Higher Laws." The regenerative power of the natural world comes from its being an alternative to the social, and the self at the center of *Walden* is marked less by his pure identification with the natural world than by his extraordinary dexterity at moving to and from it. The *personality* in the book is most distinct and engaging in precisely those contexts where Thoreau is at once getting away from Concord and feeling the impression he makes there.

In essential ways *Walden* deals with borderline experience. The frontier that Thoreau moves to, between civilization and the woods, is also the frontier between inherited models and open experiment. It is a place where all compacts need to be redrawn, and where techniques of living can be imitated, jerry-built, or made entirely new. It is also a place in which the self perpetually re-enacts the drama of disengagement. When the train passes Walden at the beginning of "Sounds," Thoreau criticizes it for creating the illusion that material progress is all there is, but he also celebrates the confidence and adventure of commerce, using them as standards by which to measure his neighbors' sluggishness. Like Whitman, who bases his spiritualism on "the float of the sight of things," Thoreau feels exhilarated by the list of products the train is carrying by, the mixture of smells, the movement and exchange of objects. Finally, when the train has passed, it *makes* the silence and aloneness at Walden. In these many ways it typifies the busy social world that is so essential to Thoreau's self-definition in *Walden,* the public scene in which and against which the model self gains identity.

It is characteristic of Thoreau, then, that he should start his account of "I" by talking about "you" and "they." The "I" of *Walden* develops identity in a scene where most people live lives of penance, pushing about their "inherited encumbrances." Thoreau wants to be free of those encumbrances, but he also wants to *feel* his freedom, and this he does in the very process of extricating himself. Like Emerson, he finds himself by detaching something from the NOT ME. In the first instance, this impulse is carried out in his taking inherited habits apart to see how they work and what they are for. When he accidentally scalds his yeast and thus finds that he can make bread without it, he notes that "my discoveries were not by the synthetic but analytic process." He enjoys stripping things away, doing without, for as he eliminates one non-essential thing after another from his life, he continues his self-discovery by clarifying all that is NOT ME.

"I went to the woods," Thoreau tells us, "because I wished to live deliberately." This is more than a matter of doing without superfluous things. The self in *Walden* wants *all* gestures and relations to be the product of choice. In order to undo his conventional ties or at least to accept them in a fresh act of deliberation, he must first make them explicit, put them out where they can be scrutinized as something separate from the self. Thus when he visits "The Village," he traces out a series of possible relations between his neighbors and himself: they are a colony of animals with interesting habits; they are a "gauntlet" through which he must pass; they are the "State" that imprisons him; they are people more likely to get lost in the woods than he is; and individually they are beings who can be trusted if he leaves his door open. By such playful manipulation, he keeps each relation tentative and shows that he himself is separate from all of them. He does not want any part of his life to be entangled in assumptions of which he is not aware. Like Franklin's model self, he wants his life clear, explicit, under control. And his infectious confidence is grounded in his demonstrated capacity to make a self, a home, and a world: "I know of no more encouraging fact than the unquestionable ability of man to elevate his life by a conscious endeavor."

Thoreau's how-to-do-it approach is one way of making his life deliberate and detaching himself from the conventions that would bind him with his neighbors. Another is to turn these bonds into games. Thoreau plays a series of self-conscious roles in *Walden*, setting his own life off against alternative models, like the Woodchopper and John Field. But there is more to his changing of masks than proof of his superiority to others. He enjoys the experience of slipping out from under easy labels and trite categories. Like Robert Frost, he amuses himself with Yankee inscrutability, keeping his attention secretly on his neighbors so that he can always evade their names for him: when a neighbor knowingly taps and lifts the shell, the pea is gone. Thoreau feels his own freedom and ranging possibility by listening to the inadequate comments of travelers passing his bean field: "Beans so late! peas so late!" "Corn, my boy, for fodder." "Does he *live* there?" The human race provides Thoreau with a comic spectacle that clarifies the wisdom and substantiality of his own life choices. "I went there frequently," he says of Concord, "to observe their habits."

This is how the model selves in *Walden* and Franklin's autobiography are most revealingly alike. They live in competition. Holding out their own procedures as examples for others, they nevertheless find themselves surrounded by incompetents, and in a hundred ways each illustrates his own practical superiority to the timid and the trapped, the people who "sit" risks instead of running them and who have old notions stuck in their heads like maggots' eggs. Thoreau's Yankee shrewdness, which he sees as a gift like Calvinist election, is most conspicuously set off against the immigrant inefficiency of John Field, who came to America to get coffee and tea and meat, and now finds himself enslaved by this pursuit. Although Thoreau talks to Field as to one who wants to be a philosopher and who could learn from a model life, he assumes that "the culture of an Irishman is an enterprise to be undertaken with a sort of moral bog hoe." The ineffectual and desperate John Field is not in *Walden* to be enlightened; hs is there to set off Thoreau's own cleverness, mastery, and wit.

The episode with John Field is the longest version of something Thoreau does often in *Walden*. He dramatizes himself in encounters with others, and these are either contests or games. When a man asks him if he can really live on vegetable food alone, Thoreau replies that he could live on board nails. When his tailoress resists his request for a particular garment by arguing that "They do not make them so now," Thoreau responds, "It is true, they did not make them so recently, but they do now." His procedure here is typical and instructive. He begins by analyzing the implications of her statement, making her assumptions about "them" explicit. But he does not answer her in this analytic mode, for he is at least as interested in showing that he can play the game in her own cryptic language as that he can understand its bearings. The master game-player knows each game in play, estimates its hazards, and adapts to it. And Thoreau presents himself as such a master. His effort to keep on top of "the rules," his deliberateness, his detachment, and his sense of play all come together in his being a gamesman.

The gamesman in turn is the virtuoso of disengagement. "Let not to get a living be thy trade but thy sport." The problem with desperate lives is that they have no play in them, and Thoreau is at least as concerned to restore the playfulness as to repudiate the basic economic ventures. Instead of criticizing his neighbors' interests in practical enterprise, he shares them, demonstrates his own proficiency, and then rises above them to turn them to play:

> My purpose in going to Walden Pond was not to live cheaply nor to live dearly there, but to transact some private business with the fewest obstacles; to be hindered from accomplishing which for want of a little common sense, a little enterprise and business talent, appeared not so sad as foolish.

The gamesman is a practical transcendentalist, whose wit turns solid things porous. At times the effect is dazzling and quite deliberately so:

> In imagination I have bought all the farms in succession, for all were to be bought, and I knew their price. I walked over each farmer's premises, tasted his wild apples, discoursed on husbandry with him, took his farm at his price, at any price, mortgaging it to him in my mind; even put a higher price on it,—took everything but a deed of it,—took his word for his deed, for I dearly love to talk,—cultivated it, and him too to some extent, I trust, and withdrew when I had enjoyed it long enough, leaving him to carry it on. This experience entitled me to be regarded as a sort of real-estate broker by my friends.

That is one of the great passages of fast talk in our literature. In its demonic verbal energy, it reminds us of Melville's *The Confidence-Man*, and the resemblance is more than superficial. The protagonists of *Walden* and *The Confidence-Man* are both expert players who unmoor the familiar world and float it before our eyes. They accept their opponents' counters but change the game by unfixing the references and values of words as signs. They are keen observers of human transactions as gambits, and they know how to transfer plays from one game to another, so that from the "real-estate broker" Thoreau makes a transcendental prophet. For both protagonists, words and actions are always latent puns, and the art is to keep the significance flexible. They punish their opponents for being so literal, for treating shells as essences instead of covers in a shell game. Thoreau and the Confidence-Man are experts at dislocating clichés and canceling out the usual sense of phrases, showing that speech is a convenience for those who are hard of hearing.[10] The Confidence-Man knows that we have to see him in many guises and many gambits before we can free ourselves of the preconception that he is out for sordid monetary gain, and Thoreau knows that people have to go fishing many times "before the sediment of fishing would sink to the bottom and leave their purpose pure." In this sense both figures use games to purify human activities, to discard the mere outward issues and rise to a perception of the essential forms.

The problem with such an approach to human activity is that instead of making spiritual discoveries directly, the gamesman simulates the excitement of such discovery by shuffling conventional shells. His emphasis is not on the new insight but on the clever devaluation of the old labels. Even in the closing sentence of *Walden* this mode of tricking up an insight lingers to complicate the ecstasy: "The sun is but a morning star." If *Walden* is a handbook on how to extricate oneself from a desperate and trivial world, the game-playing self that provides the model of such disengagement also provides the basis for one of the most persistent pleasures of reading the book: the fun of getting out from under. Furthermore, the "I" of *Walden* shares another important quality with Melville's Confidence-Man—each celebrates his own identity in the reflexive act of outgaming others and keeping free of their preoccupations.

The difference between *Walden* and *The Confidence-Man* as studies of gamesmanship is that Melville's is a purely public book. His protagonist exists only in social exchange and social roles, whereas Thoreau's games are finally not social at all. In a series of imagined and stylized encounters, he confronts *in himself* the representatives of society and works out his victories over them and thus his separation from them.[11] Game playing is a private act in *Walden*. It is, nevertheless, still game playing, and it is just as important in establishing a sense of the wily, dexterous, free self as it is in *The Confidence-Man* and in Franklin's *Autobiography*. Can there be such a thing as a confidence man all alone, or a model self in the woods? In an important sense, the confidence man is always alone. Even in a crowded urban world, he does not develop love, friendship, close personal ties. His social relations are not complicated entanglements but deliberate maneuvers. Thoreau at Walden provides the defining image of the private trickster who is ultimately alone, who chooses all his relations with others, who feels himself in his superior facility, even when the clever games take place in his own head.

As booster, self-made man, Yankee trickster, gadgeteer, gamesman, gentleman living on his wits for next to nothing, huckster of Walden's sacred water, shrewd scrounger of the benefits of civilization, Thoreau shows how the model self could draw in the whole spectrum of popular values that made the confidence man a secretly attractive image in mid-nineteenth-century America. Perhaps with all that game playing and juggling of cultural stereotypes, it wasn't so lonely at Walden Pond after all. Perhaps when Thoreau returned from the village to his isolated house, he even did what Poe says every diddler does:

> He grins when his daily work is done—when his allotted labors are accomplished—at night in his own closet, and altogether for his own private entertainment. He goes home. He locks his door. He divests himself of his clothes. He puts out his candle. He gets into bed. He places his head upon the pillow. All this done, and your diddler *grins.*

The joy of *Walden* is that Thoreau knows how to share his grin with us.

III

*Tricking Tricksters:
Survival in a Confidence
Culture*

8

INSIDE THE GILDED AGE:
P. T. Barnum, Tom Sawyer, and Huckleberry Finn

'Cuteness is held in such great esteem that the fact of being egregiously cajoled and fooled out of our money is lost sight of in admiration for the shrewdness of the man that can do it.

—*Knickerbocker review of Barnum*

It doesn't seem reasonable that people would be so gullible. I have often marveled at the number who seem to be waiting for someone to come along and take their money. Beyond the normal, greedy desire to make easy money or to get something for nothing I can't explain it.

—*Joseph "Yellow Kid" Weil*

Hustlers of the world, there is one Mark you cannot beat: The Mark Inside. . . .

—*William Burroughs*

At about the time of the Civil War, the role of the confidence man in American culture changed significantly. The earlier part of the nineteenth century had been a period of powerful affirmations. Personal confidence went along with cultural expansion; creative faith made new settlements and new selves; crude realities in the here and now were imaginatively displaced by what Whitman calls "the solid and beautiful forms of the future." In such a context the model self summed up for the individual the sense of promise and possibility that sustained the whole culture. If its virtues—flexibility, manipulation of appearances, game and role playing—would ambiguously converge with those of the confidence man, this did not yet appear to constitute a danger. For one thing, the very atmosphere of collective faith that eventually gave the confidence man his name highlighted the joyous, affirmative side of self-creation. And although self making was collectively celebrated, it was presented strictly as an *individual* program. Outside the developing self seemed to be merely a tabula rasa of open possibilities—faceless gulls, unimaginative stick-in-the-muds. The human world within which one made it appeared unreal or at best unrealized. The confidence man may already have become a culture hero, but under these conditions he remained very much a covert one.

Just at the peak of this period of faith, however, the con man moved into the open. In 1849 people learned his name and thus could talk about him and his game; in 1855 Barnum published the first version of his how-I-did-it autobiography; and in 1857 Melville published *The Confidence-Man*. The new explicitness was soon accompanied by an even more important change. The confidence man ceased to be strictly an individual model. Once he became an officially recognized possibility, he also provided a collective description. Individuals were no longer projecting themselves before a not-quite-real audience of suckers, for everyone else seemed to be trying to do the same thing. After the Civil War the confidence man multiplied and began to appear as culturally normal. And with that change came the swelling protest as well. Whatever his joyous affirmations, the con man now had an unmistakably sour side.

Between those who continued to celebrate the possibilities of self-creation and those warning of its hazards, a kind of cultural dialogue emerged, both sides of which were often recapitulated in one work, like *The Rise of Silas Lapham*. But the more interesting versions of this dialogue went beyond the issue of whether the confidence man was a good or a bad model for the self. Some writers, most conspicuously Mark Twain in *Huckleberry Finn* and William Faulkner in the Snopes trilogy, recognized that in a culture where everyone is trying to make it by self-promotion and gamesmanship, the chief issue is no longer how to succeed but how to survive. Both of them took for granted what Melville had implied in *The Confidence-Man*, that social relations in a confidence culture are contests in which one wins or loses, that to relate to others at all one must accept the gambit and play the game. Instead of simply denouncing such a situation, they adapt a new kind of hero to it, not an innocent self free of masks but a rogue-survivor who takes part in contests of trickery to salvage something in himself that has no name and no official value in a confidence culture. My subject in these two chapters is that rogue and the issues of his survival.

A world in which everyone was assumed to be out to trick everyone else was not exactly a new phenomenon or perception after the Civil War. Such a situation, for example, is projected in the world of Southwestern Humor with its pranks, frauds, fights, and contests of boasting.[1] And the hero of such a world—most engagingly represented in Simon Suggs and Sut Lovingood—frankly acknowledges the terms of it and exploits its fluidity with little inward pretension of goodness or piety. If Simon and Sut believe they are superior to others, it is simply because of skill in the game: bolder stratagems, more skillful impersonations, shrewder reading of motives and weaknesses, less befogging platitudes, more imagination and dexterity. And there is so little humanity in their worlds for one to sympathize with, that one can admire the central rogues on their own terms, enjoying their devious energy and finding in their minimal integrity something of a moral triumph—at least they know what they are doing. Of course the world of Southwestern Humor is carefully isolated from the "real" world of its writers and readers, at least officially. It is sealed off in a seemingly distant, crude frontier, often framed by a narrator whose class superiority keeps the characters amusing but not threatening. And the comic techniques make the characters not quite human. The story occurs in a game space; the sanctions that would ordinarily check our admiration of the rogue do not operate. Thus he plays on a latent regard in his readers for an out-and-out trickster.

It is this potential sympathy that is so revealing, for it is anarchic in two senses. First, it negates moral perception. To enjoy the exploits of the rogue, one must prize clever dexterity while ignoring the pain, loss, and anguish of his victims. Second, one's sympathy for the rogue is anti-social. Unlike Franklin's model self and its descendants, who are formless initiates, more or less free to create their terms of relation to a given social order, the rogue has been stamped already as lower class or outcast. He is a social alien. Resentment and fear may thus motivate his pranks, but in a more important sense these pranks are gambits for survival. His energies are the stirrings of an intractable self whose role is to resist the specific threats from other greedy and deceitful people and more generally to subvert those social institutions that confuse and nullify one's deepest feelings. Despite his unruly origins and habits, then, the rogue of Southwestern Humor can salvage something of value in a culture given over to the officially more respectable con games of the self-making man. He is the direct ancestor of Huck Finn and V. K. Ratliff, and the spiritual grandfather of such contemporary rogue-survivors as Heller's Yossarian.

But there were other worlds than that of Southwestern Humor in which one had to watch out for con men. Why, for example, is it so conventional a practice for chronicles of American men on the make—Benjamin Franklin, Arthur Mervyn, Ragged Dick Hunter, Silas Lapham—to feature in the background frauds, swindles, and con men?[2] Evidently the eastern urban business world, if not quite so harum-scarum a place as the fictional Southwestern frontier, has its share of devious practices too, and the shrewd maneuvers of the central characters play off against a murky background that both justifies their cunning and lends to their own relative scruples a moralistic veneer. Another figure of folklore and popular convention belongs to this world and helps one to understand it, the Yankee peddler, whose notorious sharp practices give new color to the principle of *caveat emptor*. He differs from the rogue of Southwestern Humor in many ways, but the most pertinent here are that his acumen is primarily oriented toward trade and that his license is based not in an isolated subworld of scoundrels and fools but in a portion of the everyday world set aside for trickery.

P. T. Barnum and Tom Sawyer: Boys Will Be Boys

This latter point is a critical one in that repository of Yankee-peddler lore, P. T. Barnum's *Life*. Barnum is one of the great examples and analysts of the confidence man in America, and his treatment of his own emergence is highly instructive. His boyhood he presents as dominated by the spirit of his grandfather, Phineas Taylor, a lover of such practical jokes as giving his grandson of age four a deed of land, gaining the support of the family and neighbors in boosting for eight years the lad's expectations of this "promised land," and then allowing the boy of twelve to discover that Ivy Island is a barren swamp. In retelling the peddler anecdotes in which his grandfather is so often a cagey participant, Barnum stresses that trickery is more essential than riches. In the world he projects, business is assumed to be a contest of wits, and the general spirit of fun eases the pain of having been "sold."

There is in Barnum's stress on contests of trickery an air of apology, an effort to prove that human nature needs quite an arena of humbug. It comes out in his description of his grandfather's group of friends who each agreed that any of them who took a joke wrong would forfeit twenty dollars. It comes out in his selection of incidents to relate, his readiness to tell not only his triumphs but his own experiences of being tricked. And it comes out in his frank assessment of clerking in a dry goods store in Bethel, Connecticut:

> The hatters mixed their inferior furs with a little of their best, and sold us the hats for "otter." We in return mixed our sugars, teas, and liquors, and gave them the most valuable names. It was "dog

eat dog"—"tit for tat." Our cottons were sold for wool, our wool
and cotton for silk and linen; in fact nearly everything was different from what it was represented. The customers cheated us in
their fabrics: we cheated the customers with our goods. Each party
expected to be cheated, if it was possible.

The principle Barnum is driving at, however, is not that this is a
dog-eat-dog world, but that within certain limits the economic loss
can be offset by the fun. One is, in effect, paying to be entertained.
He can be quite explicit about revealing the tricks of his trade, "for
the public appears disposed to be amused even when they are conscious of being deceived." Barnum combines the pieties of the self-
made man with the acuity of the Yankee peddler and then colors
both with the grandiloquence of the showman to demonstrate that
the American public not only venerates figures whom it would not
be polite to acknowledge as con men but also enjoys and pays to be
duped by an acknowledged artist of deception. In Barnum the confidence man appears in one of his most characteristic and revealing
guises, not as shady operator but as puffing promoter, boldly con-
fessing to one hoax in order to keep his name in the headlines
while carrying out the next one, using such audacious advertising,
glaring posters, and exaggerated pictures that the very concept of
truthful representation pales before the dazzling energy and fun of
the invention. Barnum appeals to three apparently distinct but
really convergent qualities in the public—an admiration for sharp-
ness in trade, a respect for self-reliance, and a yearning for amusement. These are among the basic components of a confidence culture.

It is not accidental that the circus and the show appear prominently in *Huckleberry Finn*, for Barnum's world is part of the complex dialogue that produced the novel. The mediary, of course, is
Tom Sawyer. The author of *The Adventures of Tom Sawyer*, despite
his much emphasized background in the West and the South, was
in important ways a resident of Hartford, Connecticut, and Tom's
qualities have as much to do with the worlds of P. T. Barnum and
Horatio Alger as with the conventions of Southwestern Humor or
the patterns of life on the Mississippi. This approach helps one understand Tom's role in *Huckleberry Finn*, which becomes much
clearer when it is seen not as a follow-up but as a reconsideration
of *Tom Sawyer*. The earlier novel is a boys' book, both in its osten-
sible audience and in its assumptions. It grows out and extends the
sentimental concern for children following the Civil War,[3] and one
of its functions is, as the Preface puts it, "to try to pleasantly remind adults of what they once were themselves." This fact is essen-

tial, for in *Tom Sawyer* the Barnum-like tolerance for good tricks is compounded with nostalgia and an acceptance of the principle that boys will be boys.

Between author and reader and between adult world and boy there is a covert celebration of pranks, imaginative escapades, and wholesome lies (Judge Thatcher says that Tom's deceit in taking Becky's punishment for the torn page in the schoolmaster's anatomy book is "a lie that was worthy to hold up its head and march down through history breast to breast with George Washington's lauded Truth about the hatchet!"). Beyond its evident sex typing (as Tom points out, "Girls' faces always tell on them. They ain't got any backbone"), this attitude lays on boys two beliefs—that there is a certain arena set aside for the tricks of boyhood, and that many of the rascally qualities apparent in such escapades are precursors of the traits desirable in an independent, enterprising man. When these beliefs are compounded with the others prevalent in the rags-to-riches paradigm, one sees what Mark Twain means by saying, "There were some that believed he would be President, yet, if he escaped hanging."

Tom Sawyer's appeal depends on this curious combination of popular assumptions. On one side, his escapades belong to the arena set aside for boyishness. Like Barnum's world of canny trade and his later world of showmanship and spectacular hoax, it is an arena in which the cleverness of the dodge justifies it. Tom's elders unofficially reward the playful subversion of the very constraints they have officially imposed. On the other side, Tom is attractive because he embodies several of the orthodox qualities of a young man who will Go Far and Make Something of Himself—energy, initiative, quick imagination, natural leadership, independence. If he does not quite exemplify the other stock virtues of thrift, diligence, and hard work, it is not because of laziness or lack of foresight. Rather he shows that the one thing his culture admires more than hard work is the ability to get around it. As Barnum blandly puts it, "I wanted to do business faster than ordinary mercantile transactions would admit." Thus when Mark Twain characterizes the results of Tom's great whitewashing scheme in the culturally approved formula—"from being a poor poverty-stricken boy in the morning, Tom was literally rolling in wealth"—he is not so much spoofing the ethic of Franklin and Horatio Alger as indicating how that ethic converges with the popular admiration for cunning enterprises and with the tolerance for playfully relaxed principles among "boys."

The confidence man, we need to remind ourselves, did not get to be a representative American by appearing primarily as a sleazy riverboat operator or a spurious revivalist. Richard Nixon surely did not see himself in the guise of Melville's Charlie Noble or Mark Twain's Colonel Beriah Sellers or Adams's Senator Ratcliff but rather in the engaging and basically innocent pattern of a Horatio Alger figure, and if some people would now look on him as an example of the con man as President, many others still see him as Ragged Dick, triumphant in adversity through his own pluck and then tragically deprived of his success. This ambivalence of popular values lies behind the appeal of Tom Sawyer.

It is not only Tom's charm, however, that illuminates his culture. He is himself representative. Despite his rebellions and resistances, as most commentators have recognized, he accepts the deeper values of his social order. Both his affirmations and his recalcitrance are so conventional that Mark Twain could easily ask readers to see themselves in Tom. But it is another aspect of Tom's representativeness that takes us to the interior life of a confidence culture, and we can locate it in the complex implications of his most famous enterprise. Whitewashing, for the co-author of *The Gilded Age*, is obviously a symbolic act. Tom's success at making other boys pay him to do his fence painting depends on the dazzling manipulation of appearances. His finical, studied showiness in touching up the fence combines with his fast talk to make the other boys look again at their familiar assumptions—"Does a boy get a chance to whitewash a fence every day?" The suggestion here is that values and personal desires are easily created or transformed by the skillful operator.

But what about Tom's own values? After he has seen the fence thoroughly whitewashed and is "rolling in wealth," he gets an apple from Aunt Polly along with edifying praise for his "virtuous effort." Then he trades his spoils for Sunday School tickets and turns in enough of them to earn that rare and, for him, unlikely prize, a Bible. He evades the work of whitewashing the fence and uses his profits to evade the work of memorizing 2,000 verses of Scripture, a neat paradigm both of the way to easy wealth and of the communal whitewash that converts wealth to piety. It's a wonderful joke until one asks what Tom Sawyer *wants* with that Bible. "It is possible that Tom's mental stomach had never really hungered for one of those prizes, but unquestionably his entire being had for many a day longed for the glory and the éclat that came with it."

This statement is the key to Tom Sawyer and his world. If his friends can be duped into actual labor by a play of social appearances, Tom is himself as willing to disregard substance and to settle for mere aura. Tom, his friends, and his elders inhabit a world in which all objects and actions are transfigured by collective attitudes. These characters do not *see* or *feel* without the intervention of something abstract, public, and insubstantial. When the young "pirates" leave for Jackson's Island, the river itself is invisible, displaced by "the wild sea" and the last look at the scene of "former joys." The thunder storm recedes as phenomenon to be replaced by echoes of literary storms at sea and by metaphors of battle.[4] Emotion itself has less to do with personal experience than with the assumed participation of others. Thus Joe Harper quickly tires of the pirate escapade on Jackson's Island: "Swimming's no good. I don't seem to care for it, somehow, when there ain't anybody to say I sha'n't go in." This statement goes beyond Mark Twain's familiar concern with the pleasure of what is forbidden. It implies that even the intimate sensations of physical pleasure depend finally on communal patterns. Joe does not own his own body.

Tom's motives constantly involve this imagined public. He does not envy Huck Finn for his freedom or his idleness but for "his gaudy outcast condition." He knows that while he and the other "pirates" are assumed drowned, they are "the envy of all the boys, as far as this dazzling notoriety was concerned," and this is an adequate reason to continue the deception. Tom's dependence on books and romantic "authorities" is often stressed, but we need to notice that his orthodox imagined adventures have a common purpose and closing—the glorious return to the community. It is not primarily participation in romantic adventure that he wants—as opposed to Don Quixote or Emma Bovary—but public effect: envy, glory, notoriety, or more complexly, pity and grief from those he wishes would love him.

Curiously enough, the novel does not ridicule, it ratifies this pattern of glorious return. Tom's adventures may be phony but his gaudy receptions are as real as such things can be; they are quite satisfactory. In this sense, as in many others, the novel presents no basis for measuring the hollowness or duplicity of these public emotions. Gilding and whitewash are not, in the world of *Tom Sawyer*, deceptions or false coverings but rather substitutes for actual experience. What Mark Twain testifies to is the wonderful capacity of people not only to be gulled but to stay gulled. Once values, beliefs, feelings, and desires are all dissociated from anything substantial or personal, there is no basis for disillusionment or exposure. The stir of appearances *is* reality, and "showing off" is the very essence of social activity. Tom Sawyer's kind of confidence man is the exemplar of such a world in two senses. Where glory is dissociated from substance, reward from accomplishment, the con man's manipulation of appearances is simply the skillful extension of all social performance. On the other hand, his reward is often as insubstantial as his achievements, and his satisfaction with tinsel and gaudiness shows that he not only thrives in a world of appearances but inwardly shares its values. Among the victims of his shell game is often himself. When Tom imagines himself drowned as a fitting retribution for those who unfairly punished him, he chokes up over his own fancied image. His feelings, like those of others, are not so much experienced as worked up.

Mark Twain had already dealt with this representative figure in an adult and national context, and the continuities between Colonel Beriah Sellers of *The Gilded Age* and Tom Sawyer are revealing. Despite the emerging pathos of Sellers, he is a man of confidence with an imagination and a verbal art to match Tom's: "The Colonel's tongue was a magician's wand that turned dried apples into figs and water into wine as easily as it could change a hovel into a palace and present poverty into imminent future riches." And like Tom, he can work up his own feelings as readily as those of others. When his young auditor, suffering from cold, accidentally opens the isinglass door of the Colonel's stove and learns that the cheerful glow is produced by a tallow candle, Sellers is disconcerted for only a moment before he spreads himself into a scientific disquisition to the effect that "What you want is the *appearance* of heat, not the heat itself." The point is that Sellers is not exactly caught in a deception, for he seems genuinely to have convinced himself that he does not suffer from the cold, as more generally he does not actually *see* the present poverty of his life. The confidence man's commodity is confidence, and one of the most effective ways to create it is to possess it. When we recognize that the inwardness of Colonel Sellers, Tom Sawyer, and their world is thoroughly susceptible to persuasion, that gilding is for them enough, we can also leap a century ahead and understand why it is not exactly ironic that the leading political cry after Watergate was not that we restore integrity and effectiveness to public institutions but that we restore the people's confidence in government.

The Numskull's Masquerade

We are now in a position to see, in the development of the American con man, what a momentous gesture it was to turn from Tom Sawyer to Huckleberry Finn, from that world strangely compounded out of Benjamin Franklin and P. T. Barnum, Horatio Alger and The Gilded Age, to that of the rogue. To notice Tom's lack of inwardness is to be reminded that the autobiographies of Franklin and Barnum, like the lives of Alger's characters, are also peculiarly free of psychological complication. This dissociation from feeling and pain, his own and others', is what makes it possible for Tom to be brutal but never cruel. In contrast, the world of Southwestern Humor, which must be isolated from reality for readers to be amused, thrives in itself on the possibilities of pain. Sut Lovingood's cruelty is the product of his awed and lively awareness of feelings; on being kicked in the backside he catalogues his own sensations as minutely as he imagines the feelings of the horse he hits with a board. And Mark Twain recognized that from the dazzling insubstantialities of Tom's world, he had to descend to the frank viciousness of the frontier in order to recover humanity. From Sut's cruelty he ironically derives Huck's compassion, for Sut at least knows what he feels.

"You don't know about me, without you have read a book by the name of 'The Adventures of Tom Sawyer,' " Huck tells us, and what it means to be a real individual in Tom's fabricated world appears immediately in the reworking of motifs from the earlier novel. Tom's yearning to die temporarily in order to have a showy return to society reappears in Huck's obsession with death as a means of escape. The flight to Jackson's Island, the storm there, the steamboat cannonade to bring up the supposedly drowned bodies, and the furtive return to the town to see what is going on are all repeated in the early chapters of *Huckleberry Finn* with the obvious variation that they are no longer play. The virtually stylized contrasts between passages describing the river, the island, and the storm in the two novels are not solely the result of escaping fictional stereotypes and landscape conventions through the freshness of report in vernacular language. Huck's language simply registers the fact that he is in touch with his own feelings and sensations. That he *sees* the river at all measures his deviance from Tom's world. And loneliness, which in *Tom Sawyer* is the occasional result of unfair persecution or lack of appreciation, reappears for Huck as the primal inner state.

Huck's true self emerges and develops on Jackson's Island and in the drifting down the river, so that the renowned natural description in this novel doubles as an act of characterization. As is often noted, Huck symbolically dies to the social world in order to be reborn in the natural and personal world, and this motif expresses the inner substance that makes Huck so different from Tom and Tom's world. It is the very existence of this inner self that accounts for the radical re-examination of the con game in *Huckleberry Finn*, for it produces experiences that make little sense in Tom's world—disillusionment, antagonism between mask and self, discrepancy between fiction and reality. Huck's "numskull" tendency to look enthusiastically for the camels and elephants that Tom promised or to rub a tin lamp for the genie is of a piece with his close observation of the natural world; he actually *has* feelings and perceptions that are not simply worked up by fabrication. This authenticity gives him access to a new view of the social world as well. It is scarcely noticeable, for instance, that *Tom Sawyer* takes place in a slave culture. Huck, in contrast, not only can see the world of blacks and the actualities underlying many other social fictions, but can learn that other people, even Jim, also have feelings.

The essential loneliness of Huck Finn expresses the isolation of this personal and substantial self from a confidence culture, a world in which all communal experience turns on fictions and confected feelings. The condition of Huck's relation to others is the con game, and it is as natural for him to lie in society as to tell the truth of his own sensations.

> I says to myself, I reckon a body that ups and tells the truth when he is in a tight place, is taking considerable many resks, though I ain't had no experience, and can't say for certain; but it looks so to me, anyway; and yet here's a case where I'm blest if it don't look to me like the truth is better, and actuly *safer*, than a lie. . . . it's so kind of strange and unregular . . . it does seem most like setting down on a kag of powder and touching it off just to see where you'll go to.

For all its apparent comic irony, this is serious and practical analysis. Huck is less naïve than disconcertingly clearsighted about both the natural and the social world. He sees not only that Tom and everybody else lie but that human relations turn on the *effects* of words, that speech in society is a contrivance to work up more or less predictable feelings. This is why truth is both "unregular" and risky. Huck can shrewdly anticipate the practical workings of his improvised stories, but to tell in public what he really is *would* be like setting off a keg of powder. There are, then, two Huck Finns, and his loneliness measures both his isolation from society and the distance between inner self and mask. This doubleness is the basis of Huck's complexity. If the periods on the river and the raft with Jim develop his true self, his exact feelings, and his "heart," the rest of the novel—far greater in bulk—dramatizes his relations to the social world. It is in this masquerade that Mark Twain reveals the endowments and dangers of the con man as agent of survival.

It is a simplification to see the antithesis of the novel as between a personal reality of feelings and a social world of illusion, for that world of lies and contrivances, as Huck knows perfectly well, is as real as his sensations, and most of the people in it seem to believe most of the fictions' that support it, including many of their own. It is a world grounded in lies—Christianity, gentlemanliness, and democracy cloaking violence, crude selfishness, and slavery—and the characters have the uncontrollable habit of converting painful or problematic realities to fictions. Buck Grangerford turns the grotesque feud into a comic condensation, and the Arkansas townsmen translate the murder of Boggs to an amusing mime. The impulse is dual—to keep reality at a conventional distance, and to dress it up in masquerade. On the one hand, Mark Twain captures the wonderful buzz of communal talk, especially at the Phelps farm, that begins in bizarre events and gradually deflects and reshapes them into something familiar or acceptable. On the other hand, reality may be more dull than disconcerting, and when the mass of people seem "grateful for the noise," there is always an audience for Tom Sawyer's romancing and for the histrionics of the King and the Duke.

It is worth noting that within two days the people of Bricksville yearn to set a dog afire, enjoy the spectacle of Boggs's comic anger, serve as fascinated audience for the shooting of Boggs, share bottles with those who can mime the death of Boggs, join a lynching party, attend a circus, show up in small numbers for spurious Shakespeare, and pack the hall for a Men-Only performance by the Royal Nonesuch. Clearly there is a demand for those who can dress up reality, a demand that P. T. Barnum assessed accurately. Even pathos and outrage seem right on the edge of buffoonery, for serious issues can be so easily deflected into spectacle. When the sordid hoax of the Wilks family is disrupted by the arrival of a second set of "heirs," the townspeople run up, responding with joyous laughter: "You pays your money and you takes your choice!"

So pervasive is this habit of deception that it becomes the assumed basis of human relations. Tom and Huck trick Jim at the beginning of the novel. Pap Finn tricks the new judge with his pious reform. Huck pretends to be Tom Sawyer, and Aunt Sally tricks Uncle Silas by concealing him. Then Tom pretends to be Sid Sawyer who pretends to be a stranger and kisses Aunt Sally. Through such repeated episodes all social behavior emerges as comic horseplay. The actuality of sensation, feeling, interior selfhood is kept at such a distance by this fictionalizing that most of the characters seem to have forgotten it.

In such a world, where the normal human being is both manipulator and victim of fictions, those two arch con men, the King and
the Duke, must be seen not as peripheral freaks but as stylized exemplars. They help characterize the suckers they exploit, for their
methods depend on a massive public willingness to settle for trum-
pery. As the King recognizes, they have the fools on their side, and
that is a big enough majority. Even in flight, as they first appear,
the King and Duke remain representative, for they mark that fine
line of ambiguity between the toast of the hour and the scapegoat.
There is no essential difference between the crowd that pays $465
over three nights for the Royal Nonesuch and the crowd that tars
and feathers the performers. As in the world of Southwestern Humor there is too little moral contrast between con man and victimized crowd to quibble over. Even when Huck voices his harshest
overt judgments of the King and the Duke at the beginning of the
Wilks affair, he refuses to single out the two scoundrels for his condemnation. If he describes their initial performance as "enough to
make a body ashamed of the human race," he also watches the
women goading each other into a mechanical sequence of tears and
says, "I never see anything so disgusting." He is less soured by the
rascality of his two frauds than by the general situation within
which it can be so effective.

The King and the Duke are representative in more direct ways as
well. As they vie to establish fictive identities and the manners that
should support their roles, they provide a parody of rights and
privileges in a democracy, which are gained neither by birth nor
strictly by merit but by effective persuasion and show. Their claims
to royalty highlight the larger situation in which all identities are
merely claims. We never do know who they are. They hint at the
underside of the self-made man and self-reliance, the freedom to
become whatever others will believe. As they prey on others, they
illustrate not what energy and diligence but what spunk and audacity will do in a protean society. The jack of all trades becomes the
shape-shifting diddler, a reminder of how many occupations can be
made to turn on the evasion of work.

The cultural promise that one can make a self by shrewdness and
diligence has, then, in the world of *Huckleberry Finn*, soured into a
battle of con artists. To preserve one's psychic and moral integrity,
one must either drop out entirely or win at more skillful deception.
This is Huck's dilemma. Insofar as the con man is a social norm,
Huck is, within certain limits, a very good one. He skillfully adapts
to circumstances, as when he builds out of Mrs. Loftus's penetration of his feminine disguise his own new role as runaway appren-

tice. He accurately intuits the self-interest and capacity for deception in the people he encounters, and when he needs to deceive
them in order to escape or to do what his heart demands, he
quickly manufactures the right dodge.

But there is more to Huck's skill as trickster than his deliberate
maneuvers in an emergency. He virtually sports masks by instinct.
His recognition that lying is the basis of social relations accompanies a series of habits that link him with the King and the Duke. He
adjusts to circumstances so easily that more seems involved than
his caution or his hard-headed realism. He is one of the great
shape-shifters in our literature. As the Duke calls upon a series of
culturally ingrained habits in summarizing the many occupations
he has entered—"most anything that comes handy"—so Huck appeals to this pragmatic spirit in arguing against Tom's romantic
principles: "if a pick's the handiest thing, that's the thing I'm ago-
ing to dig that nigger or that watermelon or that Sunday-school
book out with; and I don't give a dead rat what the authorities
thinks about it nuther." The complication of this ethic is that it
enters moral decisions as well. Huck resolves the dilemma of
"right" and "wrong" about turning Jim in as an escaped slave by
recognizing that both make him feel bad and one is more trouble
than the other: "So I reckoned I wouldn't bother no more about it,
but after this always do whichever come handiest at the time." Of
course Huck's sound heart practically qualifies the outright expediency of his resolution, but the point is that he habitually adjusts
his identity, his motives, his judgments, and his plans to the circumstances. As he approaches the Phelps farm to rescue Jim, he
does not have a plan "but just trust[s] to Providence to put the right
words in my mouth when the time come." This is exactly the procedure the King used in approaching the Wilks affair, even with
the reference to "Providence." As the King pumps information out
of the countryman in the canoe, Huck pumps information out of
Mrs. Loftus, the boatman, Mary Jane, and Aunt Sally, and, like the
King, he wants it in order "to find out who I was." Identity, in
other words, becomes a matter of what others can be made to believe.

These extended parallels between Huck's shifts and those of the
King and the Duke show how thoroughly one side of his nature is
caught up in the circumstantial world of the con game.[5] The confusing thing about such a world is that moral and sentimental issues are deflected by the basic game patterns. As the King and the
Duke command a certain respect by their sheer manipulative en-

ergy, Huck himself can disengage principle from practice by his dexterity. It is not his decision to do whatever comes handiest that really resolves his dilemma with the slave traders but his skill in the con game as he convinces them that a family with smallpox is on the raft. Even Jim is torn between gratitude for Huck's loyalty and admiration of his ploy: "But lawsy, how you did fool 'em, Huck! Dat *wuz* de smartes' dodge!" The con game has its own terms, whereby the most detached and shrewd player draws our approval. The game also has its own impetus. The more Huck plays games in society, the less clearly he can hear the voice of his inner self. The slippery practicalism that makes him successful threatens to destroy any consistency of value or intention.

The results for Huck are disturbingly apparent during the Wilks episode. Although he initially expresses his scorn over the two frauds and cannot very well carry off his own part in their hoax, he sees no need to resist until Mary Jane's sentimental kindness to him suddenly makes him feel "so ornery and low down and mean, that I says to myself, My mind's made up; I'll hive that money for them or bust." But even when he has discovered a new motive for action, he shifts his grounds repeatedly in calculating the practical consequences of each possible strategy. At one time he is primarily concerned about the entanglement he could get himself into; at another, he indirectly argues that he has to go along with the King and the Duke because of the danger to Jim. The entire sequence of his motives, his judgments, and his plans in Chapters 26 through 28 gives one little reason to admire him for his honesty, compassion, straightforwardness, or judgment. In fact, the more reason he has to despise the King and the Duke in this episode, the less harshly he expresses his estimate of them, for he has become thoroughly engaged in gamesmanship himself.

The risk for the rogue-survivor, then, is not only that he may lose his game but that he may lose the inner self in the sheer juggling of masks. If he is a boy, he may become, like Tom Sawyer, a "composite" being, fabricated out of social fictions with no personal interior left at all. Huck might, in other words, *become* Tom Sawyer. The possibility arises repeatedly in the novel, especially when Huck is engaged in an active enterprise. He thinks about Tom as a model when he contrives his "death" to escape from Pap, and as he yearns to board the *Walter Scott*, he argues to Jim that Tom Sawyer would never pass up such a chance. Even when he has completed his elaborate arrangements for the counter-hoax of the King and the Duke at the Wilkses', Huck thinks about how much more style Tom would have thrown into the scheme. Thus it is not surprising that he is glad to discover who he is at the Phelpses', for "Being Tom Sawyer was easy and comfortable."

What does it mean for Huck to play Tom Sawyer and for Tom himself to reappear at the end of the novel? It results in a complex judgment which cannot be fairly reduced to the standard assertion that the last fifth of the novel is a letdown, a cop-out, or a travesty. For if Tom's reappearance has the effect of converting all the risk and joy and agony of the river journey back into boyhood play, the intervening experiences, both the personal ones of Huck and Jim and the sordid social ones involving the King and the Duke, give new meaning and irony to the gilded world of Tom Sawyer. Tom is still playing the same games and tricks, and the Aunt Sallys of the world are still describing them as "about what a body might expect of boys," but it is now apparent that there is something terrifying about Tom's emptiness and about the social habits that encourage it. Tom becomes the secret agent of a society of fictions, and his mission is to convert Huck's and Jim's problems into an extended joke, and thus to evacuate Huck's major affirmations of all their radical content. For Tom to take over with his conventional imagination is for his world to reappear in its actuality and its power. Tom's games and tricks are no less real, after all, than the frauds worked by the King and the Duke, and at the end the squalidness of their world has crossed with the cloying playfulness of his. Faced with the problem of trying to relate the inner reality that Huck and Jim discover on the raft to the social world of games and lies, Mark Twain recognized that the split was irreconcilable. As Tom puts it so well with inadvertent puns: "When a prisoner of style escapes, it's called an evasion."

In the buffoonery of the ending, then, Mark Twain dramatizes the problem of crossing from Huck's sensory and intuitive honesty to the social world as given. The only way of getting from Huck's world to Tom's is "letting on," and Huck is as willing as Tom to acknowledge the need—"Letting on don't cost nothing; letting on ain't no trouble." But there is more to the ending of the novel, and in the formal problem of bringing the adventures to a close Mark Twain indicates the implications of Huck's double nature. Our very expectation of an ending in fiction is the strongest expression of our capacity to follow a story in time, to remember and anticipate, to wish and to fear. It is an acknowledgment of the importance of action, both as a sequence of things happening and as a developing field in which the stories that characters tell themselves are gradually modified by other stories and other characters.

But to look at Huck Finn in this way is to misconstrue his nature, for in basic ways he neither develops with an action (in contrast, for example, with Captain Ahab) nor defines himself in time by telling inner stories. Rather than try to accomplish something or get somewhere, he is concerned to preserve himself; he prefers freedom and ease to "adventure" and would gladly forgo glory if he could only be let alone. As the river voyage leads nowhere definite,[6] so his primary experiences, alone and with Jim, take place outside of time: "Two or three days and nights went by; I reckon I might say they swum by, they slid along so quiet and smooth and lovely." Of the two quite different ways that Huck might define what he is doing on the river—"floating with Jim" or "freeing a nigger"—he clearly sticks to the former, and there is no projection of a desired end in this experience. It ought simply to continue. Thus the basic gestures of Huck's inner self are flight and evasion followed by survival and rest. Against this aimless, idyllic continuity appear the occasional segments of narrative dominated by a direct intention. It is well to remember that the plan to leave the raft at Cairo and go up the Ohio River is casually announced only one chapter before it becomes impossible. The anticipation of an ending, then, has little to do with the inner, substantial Huck Finn.

On the other hand, the contrast between freedom and adventure is basic to the novel. If the world of adventure suggests the romantic stylizations and gaudy lies of Tom Sawyer, it also represents the possibilities of action, assertion, conflict, principle, and change. To free Jim, for instance, *is* an adventure, regardless of how the action is dressed out. Simply to acknowledge a line of intention or to try to accomplish something is to participate in adventure. This novel, then, suggests that the very possibilities of doing something or getting somewhere are all entangled with the conventional story patterns of gaudy fiction or social pretension. The figure of the con man, out to create a self or cause a stir or make a fast buck, presides over these possibilities, and when Huck needs to assert himself or to achieve something in the social world, he plays the con game. But in contrast with the elaborate projects of the King and the Duke and Tom, Huck's actions merely involve escape and survival. He does not primarily wish to free Jim but to continue to experience freedom with him, and it is only the intrusions and graspings of others that force him into adventures at all. If he is not a young man on the make, neither is he a rebel or a seeker—when he has to, he drops out and flees. Thus the very necessities for action and adventure at the end of the novel are as alien to Huck's nature as Tom's attempts to dress them out in romance.

But when Huck finds himself of necessity playing "Tom Sawyer," it is with certain important differences. Even the active, masquerading side of Huck remains relatively close to the inner being, and this is nowhere more apparent than in his overall spirit of accommodation. His characteristic posture toward both the natural and the social world is passive wonder. Not only does he observe clearly and exactly but he basically accepts what he sees. While he may wonder at it or question it, he does not resist or recast his perception. His social shape shifting and his grasp of whatever comes handiest under the circumstances are the counterparts of his tendency to adjust to things as they are. As he gets used to the widow's way at the beginning of the novel—"they warn't so raspy on me"—and then readjusts to his life in the cabin with Pap—"It was pretty good times up in the woods there, take it all around"—so he finds a practical compromise between the widow's notion of "stealing" and Pap's notion of "borrowing." His very acceptance of Tom's "principles" is the evidence of his own lack of principle. His practicalism and his accommodation, his concern to smooth people's roads "down here below" even with lies and inconsistencies, all suggest a core of Huck that cannot be destroyed even when he sports the mask and accepts the assertions of Tom Sawyer.

His kind of confidence man differs fundamentally from that of Tom Sawyer and the King and the Duke. In contrast with them he accepts and even elaborates on the condition of outcast or orphan. Instead of trying to make something of himself in society, he plays roles merely to be left alone. His masks are neither showy nor imported—he cannot, for instance, fake an English accent—and thus he can wear them without deluding himself by his own rhetoric. Although he understands as shrewdly as the King, the Duke, or Tom the capacities of people to be deceived and to have their feelings and beliefs worked up by a clever operator, he does not share their tendency to fall into the same trap by coming to believe only what they promote themselves to be. He retains his awareness of his real feelings and sensations. His posture as rogue, then, is not simply the mask he must wear for his relations to a confidence culture but also a reflection of his inner nature. Its shiftiness corresponds to his spirit of accommodation; its expediency, to his concern for immediate feelings as against abstract principles; its slippery evasiveness, to his desire for peace and rest. It is this kind of consistency between mask and inner being that allows Huck to survive more or less intact even through the masquerade and foolery of the ending.

But if Huck as rogue is a figure of survival in a confidence culture, there are severe qualifications on his potential heroism. He is a minimal survivor, and we must neither sentimentalize his moral qualities nor underestimate the value of that minimum he represents. He is not a champion of blacks or a righter of wrongs. On the one hand, it is not in his nature to interfere or to try to change things; he wants to leave people alone. On the other hand, he does not have the qualities needed for interference. He lacks the conceptual power to rise from his immediate experience to broader recognitions; although he learns that *Jim* has feelings and deserves loyalty, he continues to see other blacks stereotypically, and he certainly cannot move from his personal awareness to a larger critique of a slave-holding society. Moreover, his lines of intention are short; he acts for immediate ends, not for distant or complex goals. Yet Huck's limitations are indirectly related to his culture. He lives in a world where the possibilities of principle, idealism, and social action itself have all been pre-empted by official fictions and successful con games, and those who act in the name of abstract virtues or intangible rewards delude others and themselves.

The occasion in which one is most tempted to overestimate Huck's moral qualities is when he decides in Chapter 31 to free Jim and thus to "go to hell." This famous episode is often taken as the major crisis in Huck's development, the point beyond which he should never again be able to see things in quite the same way. But he comes to no ultimate recognitions. Like most of his inward broodings, this entire meditation is simply a strategic adjustment to circumstance. Everything has been "all busted up and ruined" by the selling of Jim back into slavery, and Huck is characteristically seeking something practical to do about it. He thinks of writing to Miss Watson so that she could take Jim back and make things softer on him since he has to be a slave again anyway. Only when Huck comes to his third reason for rejecting this pragmatic option—he wouldn't be able to face people in his town again—does his mind wander into the socially contrived dilemma in which he must either deny his heart or go to hell. Moving as his choice finally is, it remains a digression. Huck's notion that "I'd got to decide, forever, between two things" is as inflated and alien to his nature as is the concept of "the plain hand of Providence slapping me in the face." The same social order that prevénts serious political perception also garbles moral issues in a stereotyped rhetoric. Huck's language here bears no relation to his feelings or his circumstances. He is not the kind of person at any one moment to decide "forever" between two things. He preserves his immunity from warped social principles by being immune to principle itself.[7]

But in this immunity he retains his own feelings, and if all his moral conduct seems reducible to what comes handiest under the circumstances, at least one of those pressing circumstances is the urging of his heart. Huck does not reach a grand moment of self-recognition in Chapter 31 and then fall beneath himself in the remainder of the novel. Both Tom's contrivances for the "evasion" and Huck's meditation about going to hell are instances of gaudy, irrelevant, socially encouraged fictions overlaying Huck's basic nature. He accommodates them for the moment, but he can also slip out from both without ultimately deluding himself. The survival of the rogue does not represent the possibilities of heroism or of exemplary and selfless moral conduct. All he retains is his clarity about what he sees and feels and his ability to distinguish these from the forms of the encompassing masquerade. But given the threats to even this small clarity, the temptations to disregard imperatives from one's feelings because they have no lawful names, it is not a bad remainder. The minimum that Huck stands for appears best in his own plaintive words on being welcomeed into the "mighty nice family" of Colonel Grangerford, a pack of dogs at his heels and three shotguns in his face: "I don't want nothing, sir. I only want to go along by."

9

DIDDLING ON A
LARGE SCALE:

Robber Barons, Snopeses, and V. K. Ratliff

We are now taught to believe that legerdemain tricks upon paper can produce as solid wealth as hard labor in the earth.

—*Thomas Jefferson*

You can't keep such men down. . . . . I don't believe that by any legislative enactment or anything else, through any of the States or all of the States, you can't keep such men down. You can't do it!

—*William H. Vanderbilt*

People will tell you that crime does not pay. Perhaps that is right. But it paid me handsomely. I feel that I have lived a thousand years in seventy.

—*Joseph "Yellow Kid" Weil*

Huckleberry Finn presents a world in which everyone plays con games and the trick is to preserve one's own identity. In that sense conning is collective for Mark Twain. In every other sense it is still personal, small in scale, easy to grasp. Yet by the time this novel was published con games had become not only widespread but also large and complex. The Robber Barons were in their heyday, and although *Huckleberry Finn* may present a telling *symbol* of life in the Gilded Age, it does not analytically represent the new scale of conning. In fact a good part of its appeal depends on its nostalgic evocation of a simpler way of life in which personal gestures were still at the center of interest. In the last third of the nineteenth century, in contrast, American economic life fundamentally enlarged its scope; American fiction, journalism, and sociology developed a new approach to the new reality; and American confidence games followed suit. When Poe analyzed the ingredients of diddling in 1843, he emphasized minuteness. The diddler works on a small scale. "Should he ever be tempted into magnificent speculation, he then, at once, loses his distinctive features, and becomes what we term 'financier.' " A financial operation, Poe said, is "a diddle at Brobdingnag." Poe knew, of course, that a diddle at Brobdingnag is still a diddle and that a financier is still a con man, but he had a point. Diddling on a large scale does change its nature. And so does the impulse to resist it. Huck Finn's style of survival was not suited to the world of Vanderbilt and Gould.

Conning in Systems: Analysis as Collusion

One of the most important historical developments in America during and after the Civil War was the consolidation of resources. In the development of a massive transportation system, especially through the railroads, in the growth of corporations and trusts to fund the extraction and production of natural resources, especially in the steel and oil industries, and in the acceleration of finance capitalism, there are variants in the same basic process—the organization of separate enterprises into large complex systems. And in that burgeoning network of systems one either took one's place as a small part of a larger process or learned to think in systems in order to comprehend the economic transactions and perhaps master them. In either case one experienced one's very identity *in relation* to larger systems. This is why *Huckleberry Finn* seems anachronistic in comparison with Howells's *The Rise of Silas Lapham* and James's *The Bostonians,* both published within a year or two of it.

In fact if one component of American Realism nostalgically celebrated the distinct qualities of regional experience as these were being eroded through the systematizing of American life, another component developed strategies for representing the new systems themselves. In subject matter, for instance, there was an enlargement of the scale of action—many people were involved, their lives were entangled with a pervasive environment, and in the background loomed immense forces and systems. In treatment, too, the new reality registered its impact, for novelists began to approach complex social and economic developments in a carefully analytic way, as if it were essential to explain, in almost scientific precision, the operations of larger systems in their characters' lives.

These changes appeared in the novel of manners as novelists analyzed social dislocations so immense in scope that they reshaped the very idea of individual personality—James in *The Bostonians,* Howells in *A Hazard of New Fortunes,* Wharton in *The Custom of the*

Country. Business novels portrayed economic developments so vast and complex that the individual had either to retreat or to become a new self, altered to match the powers he manipulated—Howells in *The Rise of Silas Lapham,* Dreiser in *The Financier* and *The Titan.* The changes appeared as well in Henry Adams's sour analyses of giant political swindles in *Democracy* and *The Education of Henry Adams.* In the same turn-of-the-century period, the social sciences burgeoned, as if in response to the necessity of thinking analytically about social systems. Thorstein Veblen's widely read *Theory of the Leisure Class* and *Theory of Business Enterprise,* for instance, explained the con man's world of conspicuous appearances and profit without production as the inevitable outgrowth of capitalist economics.

All these writings testify to a new order of reality and a new way of thinking about it, a sense that people are best understood in their connections with complex systems. The scientific curiosity informing this approach could, however, slide over into outright fascination, and it is with this possibility in mind that we can turn to the primary cultural dialogue about confidence men at the turn of the century—the confrontation in the popular media between Robber Baron and Muckraker. Despite their moral antagonism, the two parties in this dialogue shared the same basic sense of reality. Both understood the possibilities of financial and political operations on a scale that would baffle less imaginative or audacious minds (even Silas Lapham reached a point in his economic career where his sheer bewilderment counted for more than his moral scruples). Both were fascinated by the technical intricacies of such massive maneuvers. Both saw that complex economic forces could actually be grasped and directed by individual people. They differed only about the purposes for which resources were to be seized and organized—private exploitation or public improvements.

From every perspective—muckrakers, apologists for the Robber Barons, attentive public—a good deal of glamour surrounded the captains of industry and investment (consider the very metaphors one inevitably uses). One can see this clearly in the two popular histories that gathered and systematized the research of the muckrakers—Gustavus Myers's *History of the Great American Fortunes* (1909) and Matthew Josephson's *The Robber Barons* (1934). Both writers regard their subjects as a band of cutthroats and plunderers, but like Huck Finn at the Wilkses', they are outraged more by the overall situation than by the individual deeds of a Gould or a Vanderbilt. On the one hand, they warn the public that "the vast labyrinth of the modern marketplace" will produce inevitable harm and that individual misdeeds are basically determined by the economic system that makes them possible. On the other hand, the magnitude of that system enters into the fascinating image of those individuals who seem to master it. Thus it is not Jay Gould but social institutions that should be blamed for the fact that someone as clever and bold as Jay Gould could understand the industrial system well enough to tamper with it at the critically weak points (this is the bearing of Josephson's suggestively entitled chapter "Mephistopheles"). The portraits drawn in these two histories are products of that new sense of character emerging at the end of the nineteenth century: personal gambits are analyzed directly in relation to general economic and social forces; the self is at once an extension of these forces and potentially a temporary master of them. Andrew Carnegie summed it up from an insider's view: "This bigger system grows bigger men."

Were these bigger men also confidence men? In many ways they obviously were. The world of Barnum's boyhood merges easily with the world in which Vanderbilt and Gould tried to out-trick each other for mastery of the Erie Railroad. Both Barnum's autobiography and Myers's and Josephson's histories are repositories of diddling lore, formal collections of trickster tales that have often already attained some notoriety through word of mouth or through rumors in the popular media. After Josephson tells how Daniel Drew's sayings "were repeated everywhere and his more famous tricks were rehearsed by younger disciples," he goes on to recount himself the "handkerchief trick" in which Drew "accidentally" dropped an Erie stock order out of his handkerchief and gulled the would-be opportunists who picked it up into buying heavily. And Myers repeatedly veers from denunciation to a fascinated analysis of con games. Sometimes he even celebrates the qualities of success in a world of such contests, as when he says of Commodore Vanderbilt's setbacks in the Erie battle: "The veteran trickster had never before been overreached; all his life . . . he had been the successful sharper; but he was no match for the more agile and equally sly, corrupt and resourceful Gould."

But in other ways Poe was right in arguing that when a diddler engages in magnificent speculation he loses his distinctive features. Apart from their occasional outright tricks, the Robber Barons do not seem to resemble earlier American con men until we recognize that like so much else, the confidence game, too, was altered by the new reality of immense, interlocking systems. Personal contests gave way to larger transactions in which one could scarcely identify the victim or assign the blame. The con man no longer engaged in one hoax at a time, each with its clear point of triumph. Instead he played several intertwined games at once, the gambits in one taking on different values in another.[1] In both these senses it became much harder even to figure out what the con man was up to, and this difficulty was compounded by the fact that his operations were entangled with the larger institutions and systems of the economy. Thus the confidence man threatened the community itself, not simply a group of individuals. To follow his operations at all, one had to analyze them within the intricacies of a complex system, and then one ran the risk—as we have seen with Myers and Josephson—of having one's outrage dissolve in fascination. The very community that was threatened showed a peculiar appetite for tales of trickery. It was not simply wish fulfillment that made the cult of success and the muckraking revelations about it so popular. As Poe and Barnum knew so well, exposé itself had enormous public appeal. One could always find a market for stories of how the public or the government was hoaxed. Thus *History of the Great American Fortunes* was published with a dust jacket that could have been written by Barnum himself: AN AMAZING EXPOSÉ OF THE GREATEST FINANCIAL GIANTS OF AMERICAN HISTORY.[2]

Of course the muckrakers did make a historical difference—the Greatest Financial Giants did have to learn to behave with somewhat more decency and restraint. But what I have been summarizing is a pattern in which con men and their antagonists turn out to be interlocked in a network of complicity with the public delightedly applauding the show. It was the muckrakers, after all, who provided the public with the titillating details that showed how truly audacious and cunning the Robber Barons were; they inadvertently filled in the popular mythology. One of the central continuities of American culture is summed up in the image of all those people flocking to Barnum's American Museum to see whom he would fool next and how he would do it.[3] The ironies and difficulties of such a situation require a more complicated model of survival than Huck Finn. To cry out "Fraud" does not end the show, it swells the audience. And if we step back to laugh off the whole situation as absurd, we ignore the genuine communal values that may partly explain the apparent foolishness. On the other hand, a truly analytic approach has its own risks. When we analyze large-scale con games as complex distortions of an economic system, we may become so scientific that we describe "actions" on a scale that our imaginations refuse to recognize as human. Thus our very precision could preclude those responses of feeling and judgment that we reserve for the human agent and the personal gesture. Both laughter and analysis, then, could suggest that the situation is not *our* problem at all.

Snopes Watching

But our collusion is so central a part of the problem, especially when con games become systemic, that to ignore it is hardly to survive at all. And this is one of the major issues underlying Faulkner's Snopes trilogy. Faulkner recasts the larger cultural dialogue I have noted in the terms of his own fictional county: Robber Barons reappear as Snopeses; muckrakers re-emerge in the actions of Gavin Stevens, Chick Mallison, and V. K. Ratliff; and the colluding community of witnesses is dramatized in the men on the store porch in Frenchman's Bend and the ladies and gentlemen of Jefferson. This condensation provides the basis for one of those invaluable acts of fiction making that confront the unimaginable developments of contemporary history and convert them into shapes that we can recognize once again as human. The complexity is still there, along with the intertwining of human gesture with economic and social institutions, but the participants are all recognizable as human beings, and their mutual entanglements are too evident to be ignored. Thus we not only see Flem Snopes's actions as tamperings with communal systems, but we recognize the supposedly innocent onlookers as essential participants in his rise. And more personally we find ourselves implicated in his accomplishments by our very capacity to follow his transactions with delighted interest.

The model of survival in this more complicated con-game world is V. K. Ratliff. Because of Faulkner's clear inclusion of all terms in a cultural dialogue, however, we cannot see Ratliff alone (as we often can Huck Finn); he is always a counter-term to Flem Snopes or a participant in communal interpretation. And he himself gradually comes to recognize this as well—it is his complicity. In fact, Ratliff enacts for himself within the fiction the larger process of imaginative understanding that underlies the novels themselves. He knows the systems of Frenchman's Bend and Jefferson as only an expert gamesman can, and he sees how Flem manipulates those systems. He tries to warn his neighbors and even tries to beat Flem at his own game. But he also reflexively discovers his own collusion and rises even higher to a perception of the still-viable public values that led him and others astray. Ratliff's game playing thus becomes a form of humanism, and it is this imaginative humanism that represents the basis of survival in the world of Snopes.

Faulkner summed up the analytic activities of muckrakers and titillated public in his own memorable form—Snopes watching. This is essentially a communal occupation in the trilogy. Faulkner transmits much of the story through collective anecdote and speculation, making his very subject that communal engagement, as the titles *The Hamlet* and *The Town* suggest. The novels deflect the focus from the scene of action to the scene of telling or interpretation and we learn more about his would-be analysts than we do about Flem himself. Flem's rise is only the indirect subject; what emerges directly is the hamlet's or the town's knowledge of his rise, or, more often, their shrewd guesses about it.

We see Flem's rise from the point of view of those threatened by it. But this formulation suggests a sense of fear and resistance which is usually not part of the communal interpretation. More often the tellers show a certain comic pleasure in explaining or hinting at what Flem is up to. Their smugness and delight come from their ability to discover patterns in Flem's conduct, and these patterns have been defined by the institutions and beliefs of their community. What the tellers reveal in trying—and often failing—to interpret Flem's conduct is not Flem's character but the values and systems of Frenchman's Bend and Jefferson. Flem is, in this sense, the raw material out of which they make stories and images reflecting their collective preoccupations. *They* raise the questions and determine the kinds of interest that allow us to follow Flem's story in the first place. Thus if Flem's own maneuvers gradually take over communal institutions, the communal stories through which he is interpreted convert him to the image of those institutions, making a perfect circle of collusion.

What kind of a world, then, is reflected in Snopes watching? It is a world in which the primary pleasures—for men—are trading and talking. Economic transactions provide the central patterns of the narrative: monetary threats, exploitation, exchanges of value.[4] But the most celebrated form of exchange in Frenchman's Bend is a crossing of trade and talk, and we can see the bases of it in the oddities of the talking. Often it seems like idle gossip, even nosiness, but the art of the talk is to tell good stories. These, in turn, have several functions. Immediately, they amuse listeners and reaffirm a communal system of values. They transmit news about other people and more distant communities. And they reduce the unknown or the outrageous to familiar forms, as when the chaotic energy of the spotted horses is gradually contained in the anecdotes told about them on the store porch. But as in Melville's *The Confidence-Man*, the stories are often told for an ulterior purpose; they make points in the transactions of storyteller and audience.

Thus Ratliff's opening story about the burning of Major de Spain's barn changes Jody Varner's scheme from how he can exploit Ab Snopes's dubious reputation to how he can save his own barns.

The art of story telling in Frenchman's Bend has one special twist that helps define the world of Snopes. It is based on indirections, understatements, innuendoes. While the teller seems open, even garrulous, he carefully avoids committing himself at certain key points, leaving the full narrative and its impact for the listener to discover by inference. Thus Jody breaks into Ratliff's narrative:

> "And so he burnt it," Varner said. "Well well well."
> "I don't know as I would put it just that way," Ratliff said, repeated. "I would just put it that that same night Major de Spain's barn taken fire and was a total loss."

This element of concealment in the midst of apparent openness is one of the major qualities celebrated in the world into which Flem makes his way.

As the teller hides his purposes and leaves his key points unstated, so the parties in a trade conceal their fears and desires. In Frenchman's Bend, and later in Jefferson as well, men are expected to wear masks, and the game of trading—whether goods or tales—turns on the effort to cause and detect a loss of composure. When Jody, for instance, rides out to see Ab Snopes on an apparently casual visit, Ratliff's story about barn burning has broken his mask; his voice is "too loud still, he could not seem to help it. I got too much to think about to have time to watch it, he thought, beginning at once to think, Hell fire." The outside narrator's descriptions of the characters reflect the importance of these masks. Repeatedly he notes the difficulty of one man's telling whether another man is looking at him. And at critical moments of exchange he emphasizes that "there was nothing in his face" or "there was something." When Ratliff shows Flem a threatening note from Flem's cousin Mink, "he saw it—an instant, a second of a new and completer stillness and immobility touch the blank face."

Trade is a pleasure in Frenchman's Bend because it is a game. To conceal motives and feelings—to bluff—is essential in that game.[5] But the game and the use of masks are so much a part of communal mores that they become a collective pattern of behavior. Men in Frenchman's Bend take for granted that they are in contests with each other. Lump Snopes exaggerates this assumption by his "unflagging conviction of the inherent constant active dishonesty of all men, including himself," but he does provide a crude insight about the world into which he moves. The action of *The Hamlet* opens with Jody Varner meeting Ab Snopes and immediately searching out a way to take advantage of him; it closes with Flem's victory in the tricking of Ratliff. And to stress the extent to which contests form the basis of human transactions, Faulkner occasionally moves from the wary outsider's point of view to an inner glimpse of the gamesman's mind in action: "Because I believe I done it right. I had to trade not only on what I think he knows about me, but on what he must figure I know about him, as conditioned and restricted by that year of sickness and abstinence from the science and pastime of skullduggery."

Because the contests are so widespread, they become more than an amusement. Men in Frenchman's Bend test their prowess and prove their identities in these contests. Ratliff and Will Varner, for instance, earned their communal respect by special skill in "the science and pastime of skullduggery." That is why Flem Snopes's arrival seems to each of them a personal challenge:

> "I think the same as you do," Ratliff said quietly. "That there aint but two men I know can risk fooling with them folks. And just one of them is named Varner and his front name aint Jody."
> "And who's the other one?" Varner said.
> "That aint been proved yet neither," Ratliff said pleasantly.

Knowing that their own local reputations are at stake, and assuming, like everyone else, that Flem is also in on the contests, both men eventually rise to the challenge and get themselves more entangled in Snopesism than they bargained for.

Is Flem in on the same contests? Both the villagers' financial transactions with him and their stories about him are predicated on the belief that he is. But they can't be sure. And this uncertainty increases their vulnerability because their own games are so widespread that they *must* take for granted the participation of other players. A subtler con man in such circumstances not only recognizes that the other party is trying to trick him but sets up his own game on that basis: "maybe Ab was so busy fooling Pat that Pat never had to fool Ab at all." Surrounded by game-players, the most effective con man can virtually leave them to work out their own schemes and their own undoings. Thus Flem begins his career simply by being in the road when Jody returns from his frightened visit to Ab. It is Jody who does the talking and the maneuvering that lead to his being usurped as heir to the Varner system. In such circumstances, the more elaborate and subtle one's suspicions, the more thoroughly one can fool oneself. This is the most obvious sense in which Snopes watching becomes an act of collusion, especially as the men crowd around the spotted horses to see what Flem is up to and whom he is trying to trick now.

The imaginations of the onlookers, however, do not produce all the imagery surrounding Flem. Faulkner, too, as master image-maker, introduces his own patterns to make Flem and his world more imaginable and significant to readers. And the most important of these patterns in *The Hamlet* characterizes a peculiar quality of both human relations and the physical setting in the world into which Snopeses erupt. From the opening description of French-man's Bend onward, Faulkner stresses the impermanence of human accomplishments, the fluiditity of boundaries, states of being, def-initions. The Frenchman's plantation has reverted to a jungle, his house is being dismantled for firewood, and the very record of his claims is fading in the Chancery Clerk's office. The outward signs or appearances by which identities might be established are comi-cally dissociated from their proper references and set in a bewilder-ing drift: "Federal officers went into the country and vanished. Some garment which the missing man had worn might be seen—a felt hat, a broadcloth coat, a pair of city shoes or even his pistol—on a child or an old man or woman." As often as possible Faulkner repeats this kind of image: Jody Varner's discarded suits can be seen walking down the roads on the backs of the family's black retainers; Labove's football shoes are worn by his grandmother in her rocker; Varner's suitcase comes and goes with the honeymoons of his children; I.O. Snopes's clothes never fit or even indicate his body. What we confront here is a blurring of identity, a world in which appearances are almost ludicrously fluid.

The source of this fluidity is not entirely clear, but at least part of it is related to the transition from bartering to a cash economy. Ac-cording to Ratliff,

> When a man swaps horse for horse, that's one thing and let the devil protect him if the devil can. But when cash money starts changing hands, that's something else. And for a stranger to come in and start that cash money to changing and jumping from one fellow to another, it's like when a burglar breaks into your house and flings your things ever which way even if he dont take noth-ing.

Since the townsmen's feelings are entangled with these systemic issues, the economic changes become psychological changes as well. The significance of such disconnected and free-floating ap-pearances is that they provide the ideal situation for a confidence man. I.O.'s constant proverbs function like the con man's fast talk:

they separate language from its moorings and loosen the listener's hold on the familiar world. Flem goes even further, making herds of cattle appear and then reappear fatter somewhere else; buying and selling parts of two blacksmith shops in so bewildering a way that even Ratliff loses sight of the possible profit; and later in Jefferson making substitutions for the brass fittings in the power plant, apparently pilfering the brass, only to repay the town for its estimated value. In such a world of razzle-dazzle, the spotted horses are a peculiarly appropriate basis for a con man's trick, combining the entertainment value of P. T. Barnum's circus world with the now-you-see-it-now-you-don't quality of Frenchman's Bend itself.

The men sitting on the porch of Varner's store and spinning out their tales of tricky trade are thus only too ready to be Flem's victims. As with the King and the Duke in *Huckleberry Finn*, the outright con man emerges as both exploiter and exemplar of communal habits. In the larger narrative development of the trilogy Faulkner dramatizes this convergence as a virtually symbiotic relationship in which neither Flem's nor the townsmen's actions can be understood without the other. But immediately the convergence is simpler and more evidently ominous, for if the communal game is to conceal one's feelings in a contest, the secret condition of success is to have so little behind the mask that one cannot be caught. It is this communal emphasis on reading masks that turns Faulkner's comic-grotesque descriptions of Flem into something sinister: "His face was as blank as a pan of uncooked dough."

The young Flem Snopes has, in fact, the ideal qualification for immediate success: he seems to have nothing inside at all. Clearly he has none of the tacit civic beliefs and restraints that bind people together in communities. The Snopes clan more generally overawes Frenchman's Bend because it is so hard to find what it is a Snopes will not do. The fear that Ab will burn barns prompts Jody into giving Flem his start, and Lump's open willingness to lie in court ends the suit of Mrs. Armstid against Flem. But Flem himself is neither so violent as his father nor so base as his cousin. He is more abstract. And this is true not only in relation to particular depravities but also in relation to social habits. Flem, like Melville's Bartleby and Emerson's primary Self, is "not particular." He cannot be explained or characterized by "secondary testimony," by conformity to social usages, or by conventional labels. Flem reduces to the absurd the American image of the "new" man who enters history stripped of collective beliefs and customary placings, ready to be fleshed out by the circumstances and opportunities that turn up.

But Flem is missing more than these subtle bonds with other people. He seems to have no feelings or desires at all. In Yoknapataw-pha's games of trade he has nothing to lose. This is the quality that Ratliff seizes on in his first full imaginative definition of Flem's character—the fable at the end of Book Two of *The Hamlet* when Flem goes to Hell and meets the Prince. Ratliff's Hell is organized around pretty much the same values as Frenchman's Bend—understatement, trading and contests, challenges, saving of face. Flem's soul has disappeared, and when he comes to settle for it the Prince discovers that Flem can't be bribed or threatened. As he falls screaming to the floor, this heir of the First Confidence Man shows that not even devils can move a soul-less man:

> *"Then what do you want?" the Prince says, "What do you want? Paradise?"*
> *"I hadn't figured on it," he says. "Is it yours to offer?"*

This soul-less quality, so frightening at the outset of the trilogy, undergoes some complications as Faulkner looks longer into Flem and his world. There is already in *The Hamlet* a potential pathos in Flem's nature—to be without feelings is to be without pleasure. And as the exchange in Hell illustrates, Flem does not even know what he wants. He is surprisingly close to the world of Tom Sawyer in this sense, pathetically dependent on a communal system of desires to suggest what he should himself care for and go after. He gathers money, but he is also *like* money, dissociated from intrinsic value and adapted instead to what people have agreed to believe in. Despite his ruthless gathering of wealth, Flem cannot be described as greedy—the term is too passionate. Eula Varner Snopes comes perhaps closest to characterizing this side of her husband's nature when she describes his visit to the Memphis furniture store to find out how to furnish a house suitable for the rising vice-president of a bank. Flem knew he had to have something but had to learn from the salesman what it was and how much it was worth.

Thus while the Snopes-watchers try to guess what Flem is up to, he is himself groping his way toward knowledge of what he should have. The same emptiness—or abstractness—that makes him invulnerable in contests, also leaves him blank until he is filled in by communal desires and interpretations. The community's stories about Flem are not detached reconstructions of his conduct after the fact; they are active shapings of his character and his gambits. Flem may not tell stories himself, but he is not stupid or deaf. He listens to what others hypothesize about his plans and often tends to become what they suspect he may be. More importantly, he listens to their tones of envy and yearning to learn what is valuable. Although he cannot enjoy Eula Varner, he does marry her, and he takes the Old Frenchman's Place as a dowry apparently because he, like Ratliff, assumes that if Will Varner owns it, it must be a good thing. And he finally moves into de Spain's mansion even if he has nothing to do in it but sit alone by the fire, chewing air.

The moral ironies of Flem's development come from this reciprocal relation with the community. The villagers and townspeople cannot tell stories about Flem or about their own aspirations without creating the patterns that gradually shape him. And he in turn cannot assume power in the local economic and social systems without becoming civilized in the process, constrained in his own conduct by the necessities of the system, and concerned in turn to make the behavior of other Snopeses less "out and out unvarnished." He can only learn what to want from the people around him. The process is easy enough to follow—for both villagers and readers—when the question is simply what he should possess, and Flem's acquisition of such things as cattle, land, store, blacksmith shop, restaurant, even Eula, makes him seem like merely a monster of rapacity. But material possessions are only the outward and preliminary approximation of what is finally a far more abstract pursuit. One of the major issues of Snopes watching in *The Town* is thus broached by Ratliff's sense that Flem is after something new, something more than money. He compares guessing what Flem is doing to watching the bushes shake and not knowing which way the varmint in them will be running when it breaks into the clearing. He twice hints to Gavin Stevens what "the clearing" is—it's not only what Flem is after but where you can finally *see* him. What he is after in fact is a place where you *can* see him, where his own situation will coincide with the community's image of value. "But this-here new thing he has done found out it's nice to have, is different. . . . You got to work at it steady, never to forget about it. It's got to be out in the open, where folks can see it, or there aint no such thing." When Gavin persists in missing the point, Ratliff finally names Flem's object—respectability. But his own more abstract hints about Flem's purposes are a reminder that even "respectability" is merely another example of things Flem seeks because people seek them, the things that have no existence or meaning except as folks can see and want them.

Respectability is, in this sense, rather like currency, and Faulkner explores the convergence of the two in dealing with the problems of trust and credit. Flem's early successes arise in part from his unwillingness to be taken in by an act of faith—he refuses to give credit in the store—but once he has begun to accumulate his own fortune, he must shift fundamentally his attitude toward other people and toward civic institutions. When Faulkner analyzes Flem's relation to the bank in *The Town,* he moves to the heart of his larger assessment of social systems. He shows how one of the most respected economic institutions can be understood as a massive game of confidence, gradually made credible by complex communal developments.

As Gavin Stevens speculates in Chapter 17, Flem began by seeing banks like frontier inns, always open to depredations, just as he had earlier been concerned primarily with the problems of *getting* money. Now that he must face the problem of *saving* it, he begins to see more complications. The normal condition of a bank is "a steady and decorous embezzlement" in which the cleverness of the looters maintains the public illusion of solvency, even at the point of transference of the "yet-intact disaster" to the looters' successors. Furthermore, the older a bank is, the more time it has had "to adjust itself to the natural and normal thieving of its officers and employees which was the sole reason for a bank," so that its longevity protects it from the particular frailties of its present staff. After the scandal of Byron Snopes's robbery of the bank, Flem solicits the vote of Will Varner to make Manfred de Spain the new president, and not only to save his own money:

> he not only affirmed the fact that simple baseless unguaranteed unguaranteeable trust between man and man was solvent, he defended the fact that it not only could endure: it must endure, since the robustness of a nation was in the solvency of its economy, and the solvency of an economy depended on the rectitude of its banks and the sacredness of the individual dollars they contained, no matter to whom the dollars individually belonged, and that rectitude and sanctity must in the last analysis depend on the will of man to trust and the capacity of man to be trusted . . .

Both in analysis and in the newly adopted clichés of civic rectitude, this passage reflects the essential transformation from brigand to pillar of society.[6] Like Tom Sawyer's white-washing scheme and its follow-up, it provides a paradigm of one of the more disconcerting laws of social development: that no swindler or criminal can continue to be successful on an ever-increasing scale without becoming more or less respectable in the process, even concerned to maintain public decency and deference to the law.

Flem thus arises as exploiter of communal institutions, takes shape and purpose from communal interpretation, and becomes civilized by adjustment to the very systems he takes over. This symbiotic relationship suggests that although he poses a danger to certain individuals—displacing Jody, for instance, as Will Varner's heir—he does not really destroy the larger structures of the village or the town but rather adapts to them. Yet this constitutes the gravest threat of all, for we find it easier to cope with an outsider than with one of us.

Survival in the world of Snopes is a complicated problem. Too many "good" people are implicated in Flem's successes for us simply to say they got what they deserved, and although Ratliff when exasperated calls them "the folks that cant wait to bare their backsides" to Snopeses, he has too much affection to disregard them. Furthermore, the institutions and values that allowed Flem to succeed cannot be thrown out with the offender, for then there would be no community left. Personal survival—preserving one's psychological and moral identity—is entangled with communal survival, and both require complex imaginative understanding. When Flem takes advantage of communal habits, such as the prevalence of trickster contests, one must learn precisely what went wrong and how one was possibly implicated. The con games of Frenchman's Bend stop being fun when Flem enters them. The pride of a contest constrains normal tricksters—even the Texan, Buck Hipps—from exploiting a helpless madman like Henry Armstid, but for Flem there is no more pride than fun. What we see in this instance is that trade for Flem becomes impersonal and joyless; it loses its meaning. Yet such a perception reflexively clarifies some genuine values in Frenchman's Bend's institutions. And that is what Snopes watching at its best is all about—the active affirming of those values without which human activity loses its significance.

V. K. Ratliff: Complicity, Survival, and Play

The best of Snopes watching is carried on by V. K. Ratliff. He is the agent through whom we finally can follow Flem's story. He is enough of an insider in Frenchman's Bend to know thoroughly the economic and social patterns that Flem moves in on. Trickster, trader, tale-teller par excellence, Ratliff not only embodies but heightens and purifies the basic habits of the village. He can imagine tricks and tell stories to suggest the complexity of Flem, and he knows enough about the people and their history to provide patterns of interpretation that reflect the village. Yet he is personally representative in another way as well. He makes the habits and systems of Frenchman's Bend look good. For him the contests of trade and tale telling are genuinely pleasurable, and the game of concealment is made all the more admirable by having to play across his comic garrulity. His way of taking part in the communal games makes the games themselves appealing and sets off by contrast the methods of Flem Snopes.

It is not simply as community representative that Ratliff helps us follow Flem's progress. There is also a more detached side of Ratliff. It is apparent first in his wandering. He traverses four counties selling sewing machines and carrying news, gossip, advice. He deals with women as well as men, gaining access to a world of lore and feeling closed off to the other men around him. As he easily crosses boundaries, serves as regional herald, skillfully manages the rituals of dealing with strangers, uses words craftily, and straddles that uncertain ground where commercial exchange and stealth blur into each other, this itinerant Mississippi sewing-machine agent resembles the Greek god Hermes.[7] He is both insider and outsider, and there is something godlike in his mastery of games. It comes from his capacity, like that of Melville's Confidence-Man, to recognize patterns, to shift perspectives, to enlarge his imagination to encompass the grander contest within which the entire immediate game is merely a gambit. This capacity is what makes Ratliff continue as announcer and interpreter of the game in play in *The Town* and *The Mansion,* even though Gavin Stevens and Chick Mallison, the other major Snopes-watchers, are much more closely affiliated with the community in Jefferson. In the subtleties, hypocrisies, and innuendoes of urban socio-economic life, Ratliff's frontier gamesmanship allows him to look behind what others regard as gauche behavior and to perceive the essential gambits, the manipulations, the achievements of power. He poses the primary questions and hints at the issues through which Flem's games can be interpreted.

Yet Ratliff offers hints more than full explanations. He expects others to complete the interpretations for themselves. This may be a carry-over of the tale-telling patterns of Frenchman's Bend with its emphasis on concealment and understatement, or it may be the modesty of a country boy in town, and one who had already lost badly in his own game with Flem. But I suspect there is more to Ratliff's indirectness. He had to learn bitterly for himself how his own desires and schemes set him up for victimization by Flem. Now he seems to know that others will have to learn for themselves, too. And this is not because experience is the best teacher. It is rather that self-discovery *is* the essential discovery to make about Flem's rise. Flem is not finally much of a game-player. His method is not illusion but collusion. He depends absolutely on the playing of others, as in letting Gavin Stevens go to extraordinary and rather foolish efforts to make Eula Snopes respectable, a gesture that gives Flem in turn a far stronger position in Jefferson. What the other characters need to learn is less what Flem is like than what they themselves are like, or more precisely, what aspects of themselves Flem draws out. And these reflexive discoveries belong not only to characters within the trilogy but to author and reader as well. As we read these novels and think we are following Flem's rise, we repeatedly collude with the characters in projecting sordid fictions to make him imaginable, and the surprising changes in his story force us back to re-examine our own assumptions. Even Faulkner, in the Preface to the final volume of the trilogy, acknowledges his own self-discoveries during the period from 1925 to 1959 in which he worked on the Snopes material: "the author has learned, he believes, more about the human heart and its dilemma than he knew thirty-four years ago; and is sure that, having lived with them that long time, he knows the characters in this chronicle better than he did then."

Ratliff's own story is the finest model within the fiction of such self-discovery. This is the essential way in which he helps us "follow" Flem's story, not by having it interpreted for us but by witnessing what it is *like* to follow Flem's rise, to stake his pride on opposing him, to discover his collusion, and to rise above the ensuing cynicism to affirm all that is nevertheless best in himself and in his community. From the outset of *The Hamlet*, before he knows *himself* very well, Ratliff perceives Flem as a challenge. It becomes virtually a game for him and the other villagers to make up stories that will explain the inscrutable newcomer. The challenge is also personal. Ratliff automatically assumes that the only pattern within which he can relate to Flem is a contest of trade, and his comment to Will Varner that they are the only two people around who can deal with Snopes shows how soon he has inwardly accepted the challenge. Yet we should also note that Flem, who at this point scarcely knows Ratliff, has not issued any such challenge. The idea exists in Ratliff's mind; it is his way of imposing a significant structure on the well-nigh shapeless Flem (whom Faulkner repeatedly compares to putty or raw dough). And it is a powerful enough idea to govern Ratliff's behavior throughout *The Hamlet*.

It takes some time, however, before Ratliff acts on the challenge. First he sees and then hears of Flem's series of minor exploitations in Frenchman's Bend and asks the other villagers if they aren't going to do something about it. Thus by the time he enters the lists himself against Flem, he has not only personal pride but a sense of civic responsibility at stake. The first direct contest between Ratliff and Flem takes place in Chapter 3 of Book One, and it involves, among other things, a contract for fifty goats that Ratliff picked up from a northerner who started a goat farm without goats. By following this transaction in detail, we enter fully into the socio-economic complexity of the trilogy,[8] see how confidence games changed in the age of the Robber Barons, and participate in Ratliff's own reflexive discoveries about games and stakes.

He begins his game with elaborate indirectness. Knowing that Will Varner would be sure that some of what he gives Flem would contain burnable property known to be in Flem's name, he visits the Chancery Clerk's office and learns of the farm where he then discovers Mink Snopes as tenant farmer. By fast talk and byplay between Mink and his wife about his cousin Flem, Ratliff "sells" Mink a sewing machine for two notes drawn on Flem, one for $20 with a threat about hay barns, the other for $10 payable to *Isaac Snopes or bearer*. The next stage of Rattliff's preparation is to draw Flem into a contest by letting him overhear that he could himself buy the fifty goats that Ratliff knew about when he originally bought his contract. Thus before even approaching Flem directly, Ratliff has arranged that Flem should seem to have the advantage over him while he himself should secretly have a leverage on Flem. He can thus open the personal transaction by announcing, "You beat me." For this maneuvering he is rewarded by one instant when Flem's mask changes slightly as Ratliff shows him the $20 note from Mink, and Flem does exchange it for the goats, leaving Ratliff a $5 profit when he collects on his contract.

What has Ratliff won in the game so far? Although he has made a profit of $5, he has sacrificed the $12.50 profit he would have made by not bringing Flem in at all on the purchase of goats. Ratliff is at least as concerned with "the pleasure of the shrewd dealing which far transcended mere gross profit," and he has demonstrated that he can not only deal with Flem but profit at it and make Flem lose his self-possession, if only for a moment. But Ratliff is playing for still more complicated stakes, as is clear in his own evaluation of the game: "I went as far as one Snopes will set fire to another Snopes's barn and both Snopeses know it, and that was all right." The deeper game is one of resistance or containment, and the preliminary strategy is to find out how Snopeses operate, what they fear, what they will and will not do. Ratliff is willing, as in this instance, to sacrifice "mere gross profit" in order to test his own assumptions about Snopesism.

But there is another stage of the game. So far Ratliff has not only outguessed Flem but also remained disengaged behind his mask while Flem loses composure. He now introduces the second note, the one payable to *Isaac Snopes or bearer,* and Flem's jaw stops chewing even longer. When Flem goes out to produce Ike, however, it is Ratliff whose inner self bursts into the game: "Then something black blew in him, a suffocation, a sickness, nausea." Flem's exploitation of his idiot cousin's $10 inheritance proves more than Ratliff can accept, and he burns the $10 note instead of collecting on it and thereby allowing Flem to use it once more. This time Ratliff has lost, although the extra $10 would anyway have been his commission on the sewing machine he sold to Mink. More than that. Ratliff gives Mrs. Littlejohn, Ike's keeper, the $5 he made on the goat deal, the $10 of Flem's note to Ike, and the three years' interest on that note. This scrupulously economical way of assuring that his economic transactions will not infringe on the innocent costs Ratliff $11.80. He has also lost in the game of trade, for Flem has demonstrated that he can get at Ratliff's inner life at least as effectively as Ratliff had gotten at his. But in the larger game of gathering Snopes lore, Ratliff has been successful again, for he can add retrospectively to his guesses about what Snopeses will do: "I never went on to where that first Snopes will turn around and stomp the fire out so he can sue that second Snopes for the reward and both Snopeses know that too."

Ratliff's summary to himself of what he has learned in the game is also reflexive, for what he pieces together is not only a new explanation of Snopes behavior but also a correction of his own imagination. His game plan had been based on the crude preliminary assumption that the way to frighten one Snopes is with another one. Now he finds that his own guesses were inadequate, that his imaginative projections of threats and counter-threats did not encompass the unforeseen baseness of Flem's behavior nor its reliance on the laws of the community. Aside from learning that Flem could disrupt his own self-control in the game, Ratliff has also discovered that the game-playing savvy on which he had prided himself is not yet adequate to explain or predict Flem. This is the bearing of his message to Will Varner, alluding to his earlier boast that his own prowess with Flem was still to be tested—"it aint been proved yet neither." Although Ratliff still perceives Flem as a personal challenge, he has lost his playful assurance about coping with him or understanding him. For some time after this episode his dealings with Flem are only secondhand and they show Ratliff to be both more cautious and more desperate than he had been.

Ratliff can still resist Snopesism in smaller ways, as in successfully cajoling Eck and I. O. Snopes to stop Lump from selling peepshow tickets for Ike's lovemaking with the cow. But he fails to discover an adequate interpretive pattern for explaining Flem. His most imaginative effort is the fable he inwardly constructs at the end of Book Two in which Flem turns up in Hell to settle for his soul. The story clarifies one important matter—that Flem has no soul. But this is to say that the very model Ratliff has relied on to give Flem significance—the Faustian pact with its pattern of temptation and soul-selling—has itself lost its meaning. Flem has displaced the framework within which evil makes sense. And Ratliff does not find it much easier to account for the acquiescence of the other residents of Frenchman's Bend. He unsuccessfully tries to goad them into resistance or at least wariness, as when he chides them before they attend the auction of the spotted horses. And his failures bring out a more savage and desperate side of Ratliff which is apparent at the beginning of Book Three when he bitterly parodies I. O.'s proverbs, ridicules Will Varner's meekness, and caricatures Flem's sexual impotence. Ratliff is losing his self-control, and it finally gives way entirely in his outrage over Henry Armstid's loss and injury in the auction of spotted horses.

Such is the frame of mind in which Ratliff enters his second direct contest with Flem, the closing episode of *The Hamlet*, when he, Bookwright, and Armstid buy the Old Frenchman's Place from Flem after "discovering" three buried sacks of coins on it. This time the initiative is Flem's, but in contrast with Ratliff's complex gambits in the goat deal, Flem begins with one of the oldest and simplest cons in existence—the salted mine. All the complexity comes from Ratliff's maneuvers and motives, and the discoveries to be had in this episode concern Ratliff himself almost exclusively. Why could he be so easily conned? One of his motives is simple greed for buried treasure, as is apparent in his frenetic digging and his quarrels with his partners. In a more complex way his skill as a gamesman undoes him, for his reading of others' motives assures him that Will Varner would not have hung on to the Frenchman's Place for so long if he hadn't known some secret value in it. Then, too, there is in Ratliff's mind the long-standing notion of a challenge with Flem. And finally his bitterness at Flem and pity for Armstid make him want to help Armstid, a motive that he denies so vehemently as to raise doubts.

Almost as soon as Ratliff trades Flem his half-ownership in a restaurant—ironically the basis for Flem's move from Frenchman's Bend to Jefferson—he begins making discoveries about himself and his transaction. Long before he realizes that he has been conned, he recognizes his own greed and shames himself back into more balanced behavior. The clearest sign of his having lost to Flem in this contest is not a monetary matter, however, but a personal one. Ratliff has given over to economic compulsion. Not only does he lose his characteristic self-control and shrewdness but he enters Flem's own world where food becomes tasteless, where the sun gives no pleasure, where human company is a burden. This is the nadir of complicity, and in it Ratliff discovers himself. He puts aside his obsession with Flem as a challenge and with economic contests as the sole mode of being. Instead he deliberately cooks and slowly relishes a meal, thus beginning to repossess his own pleasures. And even before he has directly faced the fact of being conned, he starts talking again in the old way, "anecdotal, humorous, his invisible face quizzical, bemused, impenetrable." Before he has to call himself a fool, in short, he stops being one.

Many of the very qualities that make Ratliff vulnerable to Flem are actually strengths: his compassion for Henry Armstid, his anger at Flem's power over the village, his nausea over the exploitation of Ike. Without such feelings Ratliff would be a diminished human being. What is admirable about his game playing is not merely his skill or his canniness; his masquerade plays across a substantial inner being, and the tension between feeling and game energizes the game itself. In fact the very humor, understatement, and indirection in Ratliff's talk are ways of playing on such undeclared feelings. His recovery, then, is a restoration of balance, a recognition of how he had let the contest world usurp his personality. It is also a gamesman's recovery, a recognition that what happened between him and Flem was only a game after all.

This may sound like a way of trivializing the issue, a cynical approach to a serious moral problem. But it is actually a way of reaffirming communal values. Ratliff's complexity as a game-player is not unique. He may be more skilled, but he is not different in kind from the other men in Frenchman's Bend. Their contests of talk and trade involve the same multiplicity as Ratliff's: a tension between the said and the unsaid, between the playful form and the genuine feeling. The habits that Flem takes advantage of—the concealment, the masquerade, the assumed contests—actually coexist with other qualities that bind people together. The fun of the unspoken, after all, depends on a great deal being playfully spoken around it. Thus when Ratliff reflexively discovers his own complicity with Flem and learns what it has made of his own character, he is in another sense recovering the community as well. This is why Faulkner dramatizes the recovery as a mutual gesture between Ratliff and Bookwright. And the final ratification of their recovery is a game. They bet on whose sack of "treasure" planted by Flem actually has the earliest minted coin. Instead of rejecting their habits of contest and masquerade because Flem has distorted and exploited them, they restore to game playing the values that Flem Snopes will never share or even recognize. Their closing game is fun, it imaginatively resolves a problematic situation, and it allows the two men to share a deep if unspoken bond. Flem has only superficially won the game, for these survivors have won back the game playing itself as a genuine form of communal pleasure.

The real threat that Flem poses, then, is not monetary but psychological and social. By drawing people through their very institutions and habits into collusion with him, he tends to drain the significance from communal patterns and to empty the individual gamesmanship of human feeling. The problem of survival is not only to recover the collective values and personal feelings but to keep these more substantial matters in a healthy, playful relationship to the old story and game patterns themselves. As long as Ratliff's resistance to Flem is bitter and retaliatory, he is losing to Flem whether he succeeds or not. It is when he comes back to his bacon and coffee, his warm sunshine and anecdote, his whole comic game playing, that he emerges triumphant even though Flem takes over his restaurant.

Something like that has to take place for readers, too. In order to contain Flem we must imaginatively share in the affirming of all that he threatens. Flem's rapacious, shapeless, and seemingly boundless powers must be restored to human scale, and this means that both Snopes-watchers and readers must see Flem precisely *in relation* to civic institutions and to communal values. Thus Faulkner helps us "place" Flem through a system of contrasts. Flem is set off against the playful world of talk and trade in Frenchman's Bend, against the urban traditions and social nuances of Jefferson, against the lush fertility of the landscape and of the human sexual energies projected in Eula Varner. When we recognize these contrasts, we can determine Flem's significance through what he violates or threatens.

Faulkner sets Flem off not only against the special values of Frenchman's Bend and Jefferson but against a more general and more radical set of human values as well, and these he ironically embodies in two other Snopeses, the idiot Ike and the killer Mink. Ike has the simple unmediated feelings so conspicuously missing in Flem. His love and his wonder take no account of social patterns, whereas Flem can only mimic the yearnings of others. But it is Mink Snopes who provides the major antithesis to the successful con man, Mink the "cottonmouth Snopes," the nemesis, the patient, stalking, enraged reminder of what Flem has betrayed. He is a loser for reasons as unrelated to merit as those which determine Flem's successes. Whereas Ike cannot understand "the rules" and Flem simply takes advantage of them, Mink takes them at face value. In fact, this two-time murderer turns out to be one of the most painstakingly law-abiding people in the world of the trilogy. Yet a world organized so that Flem can make it by his methods does not provide much opportunity for one of the "tenant and cropper kind," who depends only on hard work, integrity, and "rights." What Mink reveals by contrast to Flem is not so much basic human feelings as a basic deference to social order, a radical sense of fairness, playing straight (note his dogged and desperate uprightness in playing checkers with his constitutionally dishonest cousin Lump).

When he goes after Flem for not helping him avoid or escape prison, he is thus acting out of more than personal retaliation, or as he characteristically puts it, the right to "get his licks" too. He is also expressing a bewildered resentment at the modes of success in a confidence culture, where people *use* rather than *obey* the rules. He envies, even admires, but cannot understand Flem, who has somehow figured out how to cope with "Them" and thus to rise in the world. What for Flem appears as a system to be mastered and then exploited looks to Mink more simply like "Them"; he must either accept what They have determined or assert his own fierce will in an act wholly outside the patterns of the con game.[9]

One of the measures of Faulkner's own range of compassion is the amount of sympathy he can generate for these two unlikely Snopeses. As we are drawn into temporary identification with Ike and Mink, we find our imaginations using and thus reaffirming those capacities for feeling that Flem threatens to make meaningless. And Ratliff's sympathy for both characters re-enacts that same affirmation within the fiction. But the things that we seize on through Ike and Mink—love, wonder, simple sensations and feelings, fairness, integrity—are not enough. In one sense the Snopes trilogy is about the survival of the old truths, the things of the heart, that Faulkner so often celebrates in fiction and in public speeches. But in both threat and recovery these three novels are more culturally specialized than a litany of the timeless virtues would suggest. Flem is not an outgrowth of the whole modern world or of acquisitive capitalism in general. He emerges from and exploits a special version of competitive capitalism, one which emphasizes trade as a contest of tricks, in which bluffing and concealment and game playing are taken for granted, and in which the public fascination at successful con men turns into collusion. And if the threat is specially adapted to a confidence culture, so is the affirmation, for what Faulkner and Ratliff celebrate in these novels is not simply the persistent truths of the heart but a special way of bringing them into play.

Ike and Mink are conspicuously missing a sense of humor. So is Flem. So, for that matter, is the entire Snopes clan. And yet for all the poignancy of Ike and Mink and the horrifying emptiness of Flem, the Snopes novels are essentially comic. Furthermore, the comedy is not merely in the author's overall vision of his world; it is shared by the Snopes-watchers as well. It is at the very root of their communal habits and values. Their concealment behind masks is related not only to the poker face but to the deadpan, and the fun of their stories and their tricks turns on the complex play of their shared but unspoken feelings across their actual words and gambits. Game playing in both trade and talk is a radically comic activity in Frenchman's Bend (and only to a slightly lesser extent in Jefferson as well). It is a complex balancing act and can only be played fully when the self is in balance internally and when there is balance as well among the players. Flem with his absolute imbalance— all economic strategy and no feeling—completely distorts the games. He makes it necessary that one go to an opposite imbalance like Ike's—all impulse and no economic or social form—to restore one's feelings. But only when one can be playful with one's feelings again is the balance truly restored, as Bookwright and Ratliff demonstrate together at the end of *The Hamlet*. If Ratliff is a master at this kind of balance in his oral tale telling, Faulkner creates his own authorial version of it in several cases, the most extraordinary being his account of Ike's love affair with the cow, which is simultaneously a deeply moving story of desire and wonder and an outrageously bawdy burlesque of chivalry.

The centrality of play in the Snopes trilogy suggests both how Ratliff resembles Huck Finn as a survivor in a confidence culture and how he differs. *Huckleberry Finn* and the Snopes novels grow out of the premise that con games have become a way of life. With the realm of social relations given over to trickery and factitiousness, Mark Twain and William Faulkner fear that human activity might lose its intrinsic value and that individuals might become disconnected from their inner selves. Role playing is the problem, but it is also the solution, for both authors dramatize survival as a self-conscious playing of roles. It is literally *self-*conscious for Huck and for Ratliff, because it involves what Huck calls "playing double," playing the public role while remaining aware of the self behind the mask. When other characters wear masks and forget who they really are, and when social patterns emphasize tricks and fabrications to the degree that inner experience is almost excluded, it becomes necessary as a gesture of survival to descend to the roots of the self—to wonder and pain and joy and sympathy and sensation—in order to restore some substance to human experience. Playing double, then, is engaging in the public games while keeping in touch with this more radical seat of authenticity. For both Huck and Ratliff it is a strategy for bearing intact through a factitious world something too genuine to be tricked up, feigned, or bargained away.

But for Huck Finn playing double is a subversive activity. Mark Twain sees the genuine self as an anti-social or pre-social being whose validity needs periodic reaffirmation outside society altogether. The only truly communal bonds revealed in *Huckleberry Finn* develop between Huck and Jim when they discover that away from society they can expose and share substantial feelings, a process that would shock and outrage the other people around them. Huck's repeatedly stressed innocence is the product of Mark Twain's assumption that the true self can exist only outside social experience. "Playing double" would seem to qualify this innocence, to mire it in complexity. But Huck is so uncritical, so little given to analysis or to strategic thought that even his role playing seems innocent. Playing double is necessary for Huck, but it is not something he wishes to do. It is in fact not playful at all. *Huckleberry Finn* is certainly as funny a book as *The Hamlet*, and yet Huck himself has almost no sense of humor. Mark Twain's deeper sense of comedy comes from the radical discrepancies he sees, the distance between pretense and actuality. He shares that comic vision with his readers but not with his characters. Just as Huck's inner self remains distant from his social experience, Mark Twain's sense of division and duplicity keeps him distant from the social world he projects, even though he imaginatively brings us in very close to Huck and to Jim as individuals.

Faulkner, who is at least as concerned with collusion as he is with duplicity, does not maintain that same distance. He and his readers frequently share the villagers' and townspeople's curiosity, apprehension, and amusement. When Ratliff plays double, it is not a subversive activity but a communal one. And Faulkner's comedy in turn dramatizes communal bonds within the novels and allows readers to share in the characters' own sense of mutual fun. At their best the games of Frenchman's Bend and Jefferson are not fabrications substituting for real human feelings. The understatements, the innuendoes, even the deliberate hazarding of one's pride and desire in the economic market, all presuppose a healthy range of unspoken feelings. These are literally brought *into play* in the games. They give the vitality and edge to the outward sporting. In this sense game playing and contests of trickery are the manners of Yoknapatawpha County, the forms through which individual feelings can be contained and expressed, brought into public play, and thus connected with the feelings of others. Without this unspoken realm of feelings, the game becomes an empty pattern of manipulation, like overt manners imitated by an outsider who is blind to the feelings and values underlying them. For Flem, of course, that is what the game is like, and his expertise at empty manipulation tends to make the games themselves seem meaningless.

The art of survival, then, is not to keep clear of the games but to restore the balance and complexity and communal pleasure to them. Ratliff's virtue is not that he feels more deeply than other people but that he preserves a range of feelings and enough balance among them so that he can play on them. His detachment and flexibility as a game-player are humanistic. If social activity is patterned as a series of games, to know the game in play is to recognize the issues of conduct. And one's capacity to determine the stakes of various games is also one's ability to recognize relative values. Whereas Huck Finn finally has to trust to his feelings, realizing that he will never really *know* what is wrong in his world, Ratliff has far greater self-consciousness about what is ultimately at stake. And since the roots of the self grow intertwined with the roots of the social in his world, his self-awareness is communal as well. Long after he has given up overt contests with Flem, he continues enacting in his own talk the playful gamesmanship of the community, because he knows that if that is preserved Snopesism cannot prevail. By sharing in the spirit of his play, Ratliff's auditors and Faulkner's readers discover that Flem is not omnipotent, that to risk nothing is to win nothing. It is not even to play the game. If the Snopes novels explore the complicated hazards of collusion with a confidence man, they also suggest that collusion has its roots in communal habits of playing together. As long as that kind of play continues, the Snopes-watchers can't lose.

IV

"Something Further
May Follow
of This Masquerade":
Contemporary Conning

10

PLAYING FOR REAL

Campaigning is symbolic, i.e. it is not what the candidate actually
does as much as what it appears he does.

—Nixon political staff manual, 1968

If so many do the same wrong there maybe is something to it that's
not right away apparent.

—Augie March

Something is happening here, and you don't know what it is,
Do you, Mr. Jones?

—Bob Dylan

Have Americans lost their confidence? Opinion polls, news analysts, and worried presidents tell us so. If one thinks about the
question, of course, it loses its edge. How could one test whether
Americans have lost confidence? in what? since when? Yet the
question seems plausible, and that is a reminder of how often the
issue of confidence has been identified with American life. And
whatever else we have lost in the decades since World War II, we
have hardly lost confidence men. In our fiction and sociology, our
pop culture and do-it-yourself psychology, the con man keeps appearing as the agent of popular values. His earlier guises—jack-of-
all-trades, booster, gamesman, rogue—are still viable, and he provokes the same mixed response, the admiration and doubt, the exhilarated faith and the knowing laughter.

There are aspects of contemporary life, in fact, that make the confidence man even more obviously a center of value than he was in
the past. With the growing relativism about moral codes and the

widespread loss of deference to official public beliefs, there are fewer temptations for the confidence man or the authors re-creating him to disguise what he is doing. Confidence games are treated now with an easy, often delighted straightforwardness, as is clearly illustrated in the popular film *The Sting*. "Con" appears more often as a term of admiration. Earlier it had been a common strategy for writers like Brown, Howells, Mark Twain, and Faulkner to split good con men from bad ones. Now it seems less necessary to project into a fiction the inconsistency between the public's overt and its covert attitudes. Con men now not only appear in a zany mix of styles, but they simultaneously carry on criminal activities and redemptive ones. Writers seem to be freer than in the past to indicate in a single character the paradoxically compounded qualities of the confidence man.

But if the con man can now appear more openly, the world in which he acts is also more threatening. Beyond its moral malaise, its uncertainties about right and wrong, American society in the last forty years has developed in three special ways that affect the nature of the confidence man. The major change involves the spread of official collective con games, institutional scripts that systematically replace personal experience with public illusion. That development is my subject in this chapter. The kind of con man who represents redemption in such a world bears close relations to the rogue-survivors discussed in Part III. Like them he outcons official self-making confidence men and thus preserves something authentic in himself. But because he is surrounded by such heavy-handed illusion, his playfulness and lightness of mind are pressed to new extremes. If it was good to be shifty in a new country, it has now become imperative.

The contemporary world has also been overlaid with the authority of media images. Life seems to have become so complicated that many people have succumbed to personal despair, a running down of energy and a shrinkage of will. The kind of confidence man who confronts that situation differs in style from the rogue-survivor. He more closely resembles the boosters described in Chapter 5. In this sense he is the purest contemporary manifestation of the original promise-land spirit that gave rise to the American trickster as "confidence" man. But he is surrounded by such diminished selves and such pressures to despair that he enacts the old verbal magic in much more desperate ways, often becoming sordid and callous himself as he tries to keep the faith. This contemporary booster is my subject in Chapter 11.

Finally, for the more metaphysically oriented, the contemporary world presents a special kind of problem. With the spread of collective illusions and media images, the undermining of public faith by operations like the Tonkin Gulf resolution and Watergate, there is a strong temptation to turn utterly cynical, to look at public life as ultimately without meaning. This is, of course, the temptation that prompted Melville's *The Confidence-Man* over a century ago. If all human transactions are games, how can one expect anything to be authentic? Melville's solution was to take the game seriously *as a game,* and this delicate demanding approach has been updated in some interesting ways in the last twenty years. It is my subject in Chapter 12.

Con Games as Collective Reality

Something happened to American gamesmanship after the crises of the 1940s. There was nothing new in the spectacle of con men competing with each other to act out the promise of American life. For nearly a century such games had appeared as the covert content of the official success ethic. But in the 1950s the con games turned into group performances and game playing emerged as the official ethic itself. Melville could have subtitled *The Confidence-Man* "the presentation of self in everyday life." It took a contemporary sociologist to use that very title, and one of the illuminating things about Erving Goffman's *The Presentation of Self in Everyday Life* (1959) as both product and description of the fifties is that there is nothing sardonic, covert, or audacious about it. Goffman quite simply argues that mutual conning is *and should be* the basis of social life. Noting that one's activity in the presence of others "will have a promissory character," he assesses communication as if he were glossing Melville's novel. It is a game of concealment, discovery, false revelation, an "interplay of poses," in which "the individual's initial projection commits him to what he is proposing to be and requires him to drop all pretenses of being other things."

To feel the force of Goffman's argument we must begin with his assumption that in modern social relations full information about people and their backgrounds is unavailable and we must rely in its stead on cues, expressive gestures, status symbols "as predictive devices." Again the analysis is a straight extension of what Melville saw about social relations "in a new country," but the rapid movement and turnover of modern social relations do carry to a new extreme the familial and class dislocations characteristic of the European settling of America. The point, for Goffman, is that in such circumstances, "reality" is inaccessible; what one has is appearances. There is at best "a statistical relation between appearances and reality." That premise gives Goffman his basic metaphor—reality as dramatic performance. He argues that social activity, especially in its collective or institutional forms, is a more-or-less deliberate performance aimed at sustaining a certain limited definition of the situation. Performers tend to form teams who cooperate in maintaining the illusion, and ordinarily the audience as well is strongly interested in keeping up the special version of the situation implied by the performance. "Furthermore, in so far as the expressive bias of performances comes to be accepted as reality, then that which is accepted at the moment as reality will have some of the characteristics of a celebration. To stay in one's room away from the place where the party is given . . . is to stay away from where reality is being performed." Once "reality" is performed, in other words, it entails certain complicated obligations, and much of Goffman's book is an analysis of these. One has, for instance, the right *to expect* responses appropriate to the role one projects (or, less abstractly, the mark is obliged to be conned if the con man puts on a good performance). The audience, in turn, has the right to an effective and reasonably consistent show, there being an "etiquette of misrepresentation." In circumstances where appearances are so important, where reality is only what is performed, the impressions one gives are rightly to be treated as claims and promises, and this is the source of the moral urgency in Goffman's analysis.

The key point in the moral argument, however, is not that one should actually *be* what one's performance seems to claim; what is morally necessary is that one sustain the performance itself. Backstage information, secrets of the performers, discordant gestures are not to be seen as hints of the reality behind the illusion; for Goffman they are simply threats to the definition of the situation that the performance is all about. Both the performers and the audience have a tactful interest in preserving the show. Goffman devotes a chapter, "The Arts of Impression Management," to the techniques of avoiding the principal types of "performance disruption." It reads like a cross between the etiquette book and the compendium of diddling lore. One might assume that in such a world—where reality and appearances are inverted, where morality is theatrical, where people's primary duty is to reinforce their mutual illusions—the category of "impostor" would be meaningless, but not for Goffman. An impostor is one "who makes it impossible for his audience to be tactful about observed misrepresentation."

Goffman's argument shows how the con game turned into an official ethic, and his implications tell us a great deal about the background world against which contemporary fictional con men play their own games. First, Goffman indicates why public relations experts are so important in our world. Since performers are less concerned with meeting the many standards by which self and product are judged than they are with "engineering a convincing impression that these standards are being realized," they need experts to study audience susceptibilities. The performers become "merchants of morality." They develop a strong sense of loyalty to the team of fellow performers, in comparison with which the audience seems rather abstract, less than human. From the perspective of Goffman's book, it would be more than appropriate for H. R. Haldeman to move from public relations to the White House staff; it would appear an act of moral service.

Yet if Goffman's analysis of performance seems to encourage con games as the legitimate base of social transaction, his approach to our moral responsibilities in performances changes the situation significantly. When performers are morally obligated to keep up the show, and when the audience is duty-bound to abet the performers and tactfully conceal their mistakes, the enterprise scarcely resembles the sprightly gamesmanship formerly associated with con men. Goffman is uneasy about the feeling of exhilaration that may accompany a controlled and inventive game; he is too intent on the risks of "performance disruption." In his vision of collective social action, all those illusion-makers carry out their tasks with the utmost seriousness, always fearing gestures or words that might spoil the show and thus watching each other with the same nervous dread that they feel about their own pretended roles. Even when common sense would tell them that the game is up, when an old-fashioned con man would switch gambits to adapt to a fluid reality, they feel both moral duty and loyalty compelling them to sustain the performance. We might expect Goffman to use con men as explicit models, given his premises about social relations, but he overtly and firmly disapproves of them, and I suspect it is this issue of moral seriousness that determines his judgment. He sees the real crime of the confidence man as robbing us "of the belief that middle-class manners and appearance can be sustained only by middle-class people," a kind of metaphysical spoiling of the show. Goffman's joyless antagonism toward con men is most clearly expressed when he warns that "the cynic, with all his professional disinvolvement, may obtain unprofessional pleasures from his masquerade, experiencing a kind of gleeful spiritual aggression from the fact that he can toy at will with something his audience must take seriously."

And finally the audience *must* take the show seriously because it's all they have. When the situation is confused with the performer's implicit definition of it, when reality becomes appearance, both audience and performer lose their faith in a self or a reality outside the show. A good con man would not make this mistake. Thoreau expresses the essence of the shape-shifter's integrity: "When the play . . . of life is over, the spectator goes his way." Goffman gives us the inverse: "A correctly staged and performed scene leads the audience to impute a self to a performed character, but this imputation—this self—is a *product* of a scene that comes off, and is not a *cause* of it. . . . the characteristic issue, the crucial concern, is whether it will be credited or discredited." All one is, in Goffman's analysis, is the thing that concentrates on sustaining correct appearances.

I have dealt with *The Presentation of Self in Everyday Life* at some length because it provides so illuminating an account of the background world of contemporary con games. Directly, it clarifies the collective conning that is taken for granted as social performance; indirectly, its etiquette-book tone suggests the timid earnestness of the performers. It sounds like an apology for Watergate, prophetically written more than a decade in advance: Goffman clarifies the public-relations approach of the White House staff; he predicts that the performers would doggedly and sincerely maintain their honor and team loyalty; and he implies that conning the public—even successfully—would be no fun at all. The televised "inside stories" of Watergate and of the Equity Funding Corporation insurance scam featured a series of "innocent" young men who seem to have stepped out of Goffman's pages. They are aspiring, technically able, seemingly incapable of independent moral judgment. They participate collectively in what they know are giant hoaxes, and they feel loyalty to the other performers and obligation to embellish and sustain the show. Con men of the most helpless kind, they merely play prescribed roles in what seems to everyone involved someone else's game.

In *The Auctioneer* (1975) Joan Samson explores the other side of Goffman's world, the mutual fear of "performance disruption," the eagerness of the audience to help sustain the show. The Auctioneer is con man Perly Dunsmore, who sees a future in the past and gradually takes over a New Hampshire village so as to auction off its old goods to nostalgic tourists. His strategy is to suggest the town's need for an expanded police force, which would be supported by voluntarily donated old furniture or implements to be auctioned off to visitors. Perly himself comes straight out of American traditions as booster, medium of exchange, fast-talk artist whose secret is to get all solid and fixed things into movement once again: "Balanced lightly on the toes of his boots, Perly stood perfectly still like an axis around which pasture, pond, and woods—even the other three adults—revolved." But the force of Samson's novel comes not from its title con man but from her portrayal of the psychology of his victims. She tells the story from the perspective of one of the townspeople, revealing their uncertainty, their mutual suspicion, their sense of being surrounded by "deputies." These are the results of their reluctant efforts to sustain a performance they know to be false, and eventually collective fear drives them to abet that performance with their own violence. Perly's closing speech emphasizes his sense of simply being part of a collective experience: "But you folks just wouldn't let me quit. . . . All I did was float along on the crest of the wave. And a wonderful ride it was—the most American experience anyone can have. It's like the very eye of a hurricane— where the sellers and buyers come to terms." His last words are a direct warning from a skilled con man to people who, like Goffman's audiences, fear disruption of the performance more than anything: "Just remember this. . . . Whatever I've done, you've let me do."

Joseph Heller's *Something Happened* (1974) is also about such collective anxiety. This novel is indirectly a tribute to the cultural value of confidence, for it shows what happens when this resilient inner energy, so often celebrated in American literature, is unaccountably drained off. Bob Slocum is an unconfident man, who gets the willies when he sees closed doors. He conveys in the intimacy, personalism, complexity of fiction what it is like to live in the world sociologically analyzed by Goffman. He works in Market Research, trying to find reality if he can and then helping disguise it, working closely with Public Relations to convert "whole truths into half truths and half truths into whole ones." Like Goffman's performers he is loyal to the team, self-consciously practiced in the arts of deception, careful not to believe so thoroughly in what he says that he stops attending to his duty to engineer a convincing impression. As in Goffman's book the essential reality in Heller's novel is corporate—social life has taken on the organization mentality that became dominant in the fifties. And Heller has here invented a mode of characterization suited to such a world, a way of giving life to a statistical figure. Slocum as narrator is both outside and inside himself. He sees himself as others see him, but he goes beyond Silas Lapham and Clyde Griffiths in this sense, for he also sees himself in public terms, virtually as part of "them." Repeatedly he tries to fulfill the expectations they/he have/has of himself. His inside and outside views of himself interpenetrate so completely that they fuse. His position in the company becomes a position in the law of statistics.

The traits of mimicry, deception, and shape shifting associated with traditional con men now appear in a more pathetic form, for Slocum's personality involuntarily conforms to those around him. "I always dress well. But no matter what I put on, I always have the disquieting sensation that I am copying somebody; I can always remind myself of somebody else I know who dresses much that same way." The point is that such mimicry is far from unique. Bob Slocum's corporate/individual point of view is also individual/corporate, a representation of how others around him in turn think of themselves and of Slocum him/them-self. Slocum's attention to clothes, protocol, and suitability extends to others' attention to the same things in a mutually supportive system of fabrications. And what is the result of all this eyeing of each other? Fear, loss of confidence. All social relations among unconfident confidence men turn on who gets the whammy on whom. And like the self postulated in *The Presentation of Self in Everyday Life*, Bob Slocum has so little confidence in an identity outside the present performance that he emerges like a cry for help. "I often wonder what my own true nature is. Do I have one?"

Catch-22

How does one get help when something this awful has happened? Imagine a scene . . . Two con men are up a tree together, the one costumed appropriately for his game, the other naked; one cheating, lying, and rationalizing in the orthodox ways, the other improvising; the first failing by his successes, the second triumphing in failure. The pair has had varying names in American literature, among them Tom Sawyer (or the King and the Duke) and Huckleberry Finn, Simon and Augie March, even Charlie Noble and the Cosmopolitan. But for now dress the straight con man in a carefully arranged military uniform (difficult after climbing a tree) and call him Milo Minderbinder. Call the naked, unaccommodated man Yossarian. Yossarian is in the tree to watch the burial of his gunner, Snowden, who was torn apart when Yossarian's plane was hit. He is naked because Snowden was all over his uniform. Milo is up the tree because he needs help. With characteristic enterprise he has cornered the market in Egyptian cotton, and now no one wants to buy. He cornered the market because he saw the opportunity to do it, and Milo, like Melville's Charlies Noble, has a knee-jerk response to the hint of illegitimate profit, "his eyes, as though he were in the grip of a blind fixation, burning feverishly, and his twitching mouth slavering." Yet, like the performers in Goffmanland and Watergate, he does what he does with "industrious sobriety" and self-righteousness. He is uneasy about Yossarian's not wearing his uniform and even more uneasy about his simple explanation, "I don't want to," which has as little relevance to a conformist, principled world as Bartleby's "I would prefer not to."

Yet Yossarian can help in Milo's dilemma about the cotton—he suggests selling it to the government. After Milo makes this bald proposition palatable to himself by camouflaging it in the alternative principles that the government has no business in business and that the business of the government *is* business, Yossarian adds that Milo could *bribe* the government to buy the cotton. Now Milo must combine the two principles that bribery is against the law and that profit making isn't, to deduce that "it can't be against the law for me to bribe someone in order to make a fair profit, can it?" Yossarian's final suggestion is that Milo can say that national security depends on "a strong Egyptian-cotton speculating industry," which Milo does say.

> "You see?" said Yossarian. "You're much better at it than I am. You almost make it sound true."
> "It is true."

This scene not only suggests a great deal about Heller's earlier novel *Catch-22* (1961) but it clarifies the importance of a figure like Yossarian in the collective conning world I have been describing. Milo and Yossarian come from fundamentally different con-man traditions, both pressed into new extremes. The contrast in styles can be summed up by saying that Milo is serious but covert and that Yossarian is open but playful. They inhabit a world of so many catches and lunacies that one can only be serious and principled by being duplicitous and secretive, whereas to be open one must be playful. The one con man retains the deft maneuvers and persuasions of the game (Milo is brilliant at razzle-dazzle transactions and fast talk), but he loses the sense of a game in play. The other remains flexible, detached, and playful but without inventing selves or making fast profits. Yossarian knows how the public world works and makes his suggestions to Milo in open play. Milo cannot accept them, for they do not fit his principles, but he can convince himself that they do. Milo gains money and power; Yossarian, for all his dangers, has fun.

The lunacies and dangers in the novel pertain in the first instance to military organizations in wartime, but apart from the grotesque physical consequences of official plans and errors, the background world of this novel closely resembles that of *Something Happened.* Both are worlds of collective timidity, where, with a few striking exceptions, people act on the basis of nervous guesses about others' judgments. People identify each other so thoroughly with military rank or organizational position that bureaucratic procedures seem to take over the powers of volition. In this way the collective fiction assumes its own momentum, like the memos that keep coming back to Major Major with added memoranda for still another of his signatures until he starts signing "Washington Irving" to break himself from the cycle. General Peckem playfully invents the term "bomb pattern" and soon Colonel Cathcart is obsessed with making his pilots drop their bombs close together for good aerial photographs. He sends them on a mission which Peckem, from another vantage point, sees is unnecessary, "But that's the way things go when you elevate mediocre people to positions of authority." Major Danby, in turn, forced to convey the orders to the pilots themselves who wonder about the point of the mission, argues, "Look, fellows, we've got to have some confidence in the people above us who issue our orders."

But mediocrity is everywhere and confidence is scarce. The variants of frightened, earnest characters make up a gallery in *Catch-22:* Major Major, who was promoted by an inevitable computer error and who flees his office when anyone is coming; Major Danby, who envies vegetables because they do not have to make decisions; the Chaplain, who keeps wondering what it is all about and wishing in panic "for something like a mask or a pair of dark glasses and a false mustache to disguise him." Most revealing, because of the influence of his actions on the pilots in his command, is Colonel Cathcart, who desperately wishes to please those above him. He keeps tables of "Black Eyes" tallied against "Feathers in My Cap." But because he cannot know for sure what the generals think and because they themselves detest and therefore contradict each other, Cathcart's "feathers in his cap" keep turning out to be "black eyes," and his inner monologue proceeds through endless sentences from *but* to *although* to *however* to *then again.*

Heller's organization of the book indicates how matters develop in a world of such timid, other-pleasing characters. Instead of following the course of an action or tracing someone's intention, Heller moves through snowballing digressions from character to character and from episode to episode, coming back to certain key events over and over in fragments seen from many perspectives. This is not a matter of psychological patterning (as in *The Sound and the Fury*) nor of impressionist narrative (as in *Lord Jim*) but an indication that there are no completed, coherent actions, and more important, that there are no lines of intention. General Peckem's joke becomes Colonel Cathcart's desperate imperative becomes Captain Yossarian's imminent peril. Yossarian's superstitious moving of the ribbon on the field map as if Bologna had been captured leads his superiors to assume Bologna *has* been captured and to cancel the mission to bomb it, which leads Major——de Coverley, who always rides in state into newly captured towns, to disappear from the base and from the book. No one has the plan. There is no goal. The course of action is a series of misinterpretations, partial messages, irrelevancies, snowballing like Heller's digressions into accidental atrocities. With most of the characters trying to cooperate in or enhance the performances they assume others are engaged in, no one seems to take the responsibility to use his own judgment or his own will. Milo's gargantuan scams in the name of "private enterprise" and Cathcart's multiplying number of bombing missions per pilot in the name of patriotism are the characteristic extensions of this factitious world. In the absence of volition, the order of events is circumstantial.

"Yossarian was willing to be the victim of anything but circumstance." To survive in his world it is necessary to master circumstance. But to do this, one has to have a different sense of one's self and of the collective fabrications than most of the characters in *Catch-22*. Yossarian's distinctive qualities are all related to each other. He does not wish to please others and to be promoted through their favor. This frees him from accepting their ideals and plans and principles—their fictions. Viewing events with this freedom, he is quicker than the others to spot fortuitousness and circumstantiality. And viewing other characters without their own moralistic fabrications, he is quicker to see what they are and how they are likely to act: "Between me and every ideal I always find Scheisskopfs, Peckems, Korns and Cathcarts. . . . When I look up I see people cashing in." When he cons people—as in getting himself repeatedly hospitalized for an undiagnosable liver complaint—he knows what he is about. As a good gamesman he keeps track of the game in play and remains detached from it. He also adapts freely and tests what will and will not work under the circumstances. After seeing that the embarrassment of his superiors forces them to promote him for defying orders by flying in twice over a target because the bombs were not dropped the first time, he refuses to fly any more missions at all and forces the even more embarrassed officers to promote him again or look foolish to *their* superiors. He experimentally learns how things work in a world of collective timidity.

Yet despite his clear view of accidents and illogic in military affairs, he repeatedly insists that "somebody was always hatching a plot to kill him." This may seem like paranoia—another kind of fiction—but his logic in believing in such plots reveals the central saving quality of Yossarian. The characteristic general disasters of modern life (food poisoning, enemies shooting down planes) seem to be things that happen *to everybody*, but Yossarian remembers that they are done *to somebody*. Hence, the Germans and the Colonels and the Cook are trying to kill *him*. Yossarian's secret is that he takes it personally. He remembers that there is *a person* who feels and suffers and thinks and chooses. No matter what rationalizations and ideals and scenarios others may try to put him in, Yossarian has an unanswerable reply—"It's my self."

He is as clearsighted about that self as he is about the absurdities of others. He does not look on at himself from what he imagines as others' points of view, and thus he is free of the timidity that characterizes both *Catch-22* and *Something Happened*. But he is scared to death of flak. He knows what it can do; he knows how *he* feels about it; and he takes personal responsibility for getting himself as far from it as he can. Like Huck Finn, he stays in touch with his own feelings and needs in a world of confected emotions. He has enough confidence in his own feelings and reactions to acknowledge them as his own without shame. Psychoanalysis—the study of what one has repressed so as to appear as one feels others would expect—does not work on Yossarian. All the impulses that Major Sanderson wants to uncover as secret and unconscious—sexual aggression, hatred of authority figures, survival anxieties, inability to adjust to war—are in fact Yossarian's overt, conscious motives. In the world of *Catch-22* it is all too easy to become the man in white, a mass of bandages with a mouth hole, a tube for entering fluids and another for exiting wastes, a name and a military rank, about whom Dunbar yells, "There's no one inside!" There is someone inside Yossarian.

The value of Yossarian to others who need help is clarified by Colonel Korn: "The men were perfectly content to fly as many missions as we asked as long as they had no alternative. Now you've given them hope, and they're unhappy." Yossarian is the embodiment of alternative. It is the essence of his gamesmanship to remember that there is another reality than that defined by the rules, another self than that performing the immediate role. His whole sense of play—turning up naked at the ceremony promoting him to captain—depends on this knowledge that there is something else than the present scenario. And his awareness of choice also enables him to reject the snowballing absurdities around him: "Someone had to do something sometime." In offering an alternative, Yossarian is more than an evasive survivor, he is a bearer of confidence. In the closing scene he has sunk to near despair over the enclosing trap of his situation, but the Chaplain tells him that Orr—another pilot, seemingly crazy, and assumed dead in the crash of his plane into the Mediterranean—has in fact paddled a life raft to asylum in Sweden, thus showing that his apparent simplicity was the calculated series of ploys of an arch con man. Orr (whose name is alternative) projects possibility and choice into a seemingly closed situation. Whether he actually got to Sweden or not doesn't matter; the mere story is enough to inspire confidence and action, to restore Yossarian's sense of the personal edge. This is exactly how Yossarian himself works as a character throughout the novel. As he sits naked in that tree, he offers the alternative of playful self-awareness to a world of serious frightened confidence men.

Yossarian inherits the style of survival associated with Huck Finn—the openness, the awareness of personal feelings in a tinsel world, the final recourse to flight from "them." Both are good con men in the rogue style, but there is an important difference. Huck is more of a masquerader than Yossarian. His shape shifting helps him to escape from difficulties, but it also relates him to a masquerading public with whom he engages in a virtual contest. Yossarian's games involve even more disengagement than Huck's. Huck's inventiveness and adaptability are replaced by Yossarian's playfulness, for Yossarian cannot risk even Huck's degree of participation in a lunatic world. Where Huck unknowingly mocks his social order by trying to reason in its terms—seeing Jim's children, for instance, as belonging to another—Yossarian playfully reduces his social order to its essential lunacies: a strong Egyptian-cotton speculating industry is critical to domestic security.

The tone of this contrast is suggested by a statement of Augie March's, which in turn illuminates the nature of the con-man survivor in the contemporary world: "And this lightness of mind—I could have benefited from the wisdom about it that the heavy is the root of the light." Augie explains his remark by noting that the graceful comes from what is deeply buried and that lightness of laugh comes from heaviness of heart. But despite the specialized allusion to the quality of humor associated with Yiddish folklore,

Augie's own experience shows another application of his principle. Lightness of mind, nimble playfulness, fluidity and detachment, are rooted in the necessities of psychic survival in a world of heavy, overly serious people who cannot recognize the games they play and the fictions they stage. Yossarian is only one among many contemporary fictional heroes who exemplify such lightness. He is the best pilot in his squadron in evasive action, but he has important predecessors in running, dodging flak, and turning ponderous realities to play. Two slightly earlier figures—Augie March himself and the Invisible Man—show the complex genesis of modern playfulness. And like Yossarian they are set off against other types of confidence men.[1]

Invisible Man

In Ralph Ellison's *Invisible Man* (1952) one of the key issues is whether to align oneself with "the forces of history" or to run and dodge them. One impulse in the novel is to live life earnestly, to subscribe to the old American faith that historical processes and personal success are bound together. But the opposing impulse is at least as strong—to see how racism negates the success ethic and how contemporary life more generally makes many traditional pieties absurd. From these contradictions in belief and tonality, Ellison puts together a virtual survey of con-game styles. The self-making, promissory model of the confidence man is gradually displaced in *Invisible Man* by a game-playing evasive rogue who lights up the coal-cellar margins of the modern world. The ultimate terms of the novel's dialogue about con games are posed by the protagonist's grandfather in the opening chapter. On the one side is his cryptic and disturbing death-bed advice to his descendants: "I want you to overcome 'em with yeses, undermine 'em with grins, agree 'em to death and destruction." On the other side is the message that he shows in a dream to the Invisible Man as the secret content of a series of envelopes nested inside the briefcase given by him by the town's leading white citizens along with a scholarship to the state Negro college: "To Whom It May Concern. Keep This Nigger-Boy Running."

Like the Invisible Man himself, we need to understand the second message before we can begin to grasp the implications of his grandfather's advice. "Keep This Nigger-Boy Running" is a neat paradigm of a confidence culture. The promise of personal success impels the Invisible Man in his early experiences to try to align himself with "the forces of history." Like the figures in Goffman's world and in Heller's novels, he has to believe in the collective fiction, to play his accorded role carefully in the collective performances, and to avoid "performance disruptions," like the meeting of Boston trustee Norton with country-blues-singing, incestuous Jim Trueblood. As Bledsoe puts it, "You're black and living in the South—did you forget how to lie?" The stories that the Invisible Man tells himself to chart his own aspirations show his readiness to adopt the general success myth of the Horatio Alger-Booker T. Washington sort and also his willingness to subscribe to the immediate roles suggested by the present collective drama. He will rise by doing well in a Tuskegee-like black college, pleasing the trustees and the white community; he will rise by returning to the college after being tested and improved in his work in New York City; he will rise from the basement to the offices of the Liberty Paint Factory by pretending that the introduction of black pigment makes white paint whiter; he will rise to power in the Communist-Party-inspired Brotherhood by translating party doctrine to effective public speech. He is only too eager to play the right role and to believe in the right reality as defined by the current script. He notes at the outset that he has always had someone to tell him who he is. And certain of his talents seem to suit him for the Goffman world— he is bright, adaptive, agreeable, convincing as an actor-speaker.

One of the most persistent qualities of the Invisible Man is his experimental adaptability. He unthinkingly goes with whatever works; only when something fails does he begin to think it through. Although he does not believe that humility is the key to progress for blacks, he uncritically continues to say it because it is effective, especially with whites. When he much later discovers how useful dark glasses are in allowing him to pass through crowds unnoticed, he sees how this fact will help him with his "plan" and only then realizes that he doesn't have a plan. Such discoveries are characteristic. "The plan" takes shape as the Invisible Man almost instinctively seizes on what's available. When other members of the Brotherhood accuse him of opportunism, they are more right than he will acknowledge, for all along he has identified more with the organization and his possibilities within it than he has with the political-economic cause it espouses. His very power as a public speaker derives from his quick response to what works with his audience.

The Invisible Man's adaptability is thus quite a different matter from, say, Huck Finn's. It implies that his sense of who he is will basically issue from the effectiveness of his present role. In a critical moment he seems to reclaim part of his genuine nature by daring—

despite the culinary training of his college—to eat yams openly on the street. Yet the same character who asserts "I yam what I am" needs only to hear encouragement for his own public speeches and he is ready to reformulate the principle: "I am what they think I am." Despite his growing acceptance of his own past and of his personal feelings, the Invisible Man is repeatedly prepared to become the self that others seem to think he is. Being, as a public speaker, the focus of all those eyes and ears seems to fuse a new personality for him. Such willingness to accept an identity given by others is characteristic of many whites in a confidence culture, as shown by *The Presentation of Self in Everyday Life* and *Something Happened.* What makes the Invisible Man's experience distinctive is the other side of the issue, the fact that unless his identity does register with someone else, he doesn't exist. And the basic premise of the novel is that since black people's identities do not register with the whites who represent power and social prestige, they are invisible.

The development of the novel, then, traces the series of roles through which a nobody tries to register as somebody. What appears at first as mere opportunism and expediency is actually the Invisible Man's continuing effort to make enough impact to seem real. He has double reason for believing in the College and later in the Brotherhood. On the one hand, he needs personal affirmation in his current role, and on the other hand, the institutions themselves offer idealized, publicly useful actions as their scripts. What distresses the Invisible Man is to learn that what he himself has been so earnest about is frankly seen as manipulation and lies by the men in power in these institutions. Dr. Bledsoe in the College and Brother Jack are self-aware performers in Goffman's sense who pride themselves on technically successful staging. Bledsoe tells the Invisible Man how he manipulates white trustees, how he controls what they will see, how he ingratiates himself by playing nigger, and how his motive is personal power. The Invisible Man ought to be used to such conning, for he has been doing it himself, as in the first chapter when he speaks accommodationist principles of Booker T. Washington's Atlanta Exposition Address to a white audience while his own mouth keeps filling with blood from the brutal, humiliating fight they have forced him into with other black boys. But he doesn't acknowledge that it is conning. His mind has been short-circuited by the fact that the ploy apparently works. Bledsoe's and Jack's frankness about running organizational games of confidence shocks the Invisible Man, and although he tries to continue his performances in the College and the Brotherhood with their strategies in mind, he finds that their combination of pragmatism, idealism, and cynicism is a style he can't adopt.

The promises that seem to be available to him in the College and later in the Brotherhood do "keep this nigger-boy running." Even the revelations that the governing agents of the organizations are cynical manipulators do not dampen the Invisible Man's desperate faith that he can align himself with "the forces of history"; he merely recognizes that these forces are a bit more tarnished than he had guessed. But the Invisible Man's real problems in his chosen organizations are not matters of disillusionment, cynicism, men parading as idealists. They are matters of perception. The reality of a power-hungry manipulative man at the controls of a high-minded enterprise like the education of southern blacks may slightly jar with the appearance of selfless devotion, but it still accords with the larger script in which the values and goals of the school are so all-important that they justify certain compromises. But what of the realities entirely excluded from that script? What about Jim Trueblood, the delightful, disreputable storyteller who has made more money since committing incest with his daughter and telling about it than he had in mere farming? What about the madcap revelries of shell-shocked black veterans of World War I in the saloon The Golden Day? The problem with the story one tells oneself of a future rise in the world is that it locks one into the reality circumscribed by the story, and even the game-playing Bledsoe and Brother Jack are fixed within the narrow fields of their institutional realities.

In *Invisible Man* Ellison invents a brilliant form to record the transition from traditional stories about self making to a post-war fluidity in which a new style of hero appears. Much of the novel is dominated by familiar novelistic patterns—the protagonist charts his course by telling himself stories; circumstances reinforce, complicate, or break down the stories; he is disillusioned, adapts the story, and carries on. These stories (within the College, the Paint Factory, the Brotherhood) are aspirational, and the Invisible Man's self-interest makes him terribly earnest in telling them and identifying himself with them. But the book is full of nodes, experiences that neither confirm nor deny the stories but have virtually nothing to do with them. They are, from the Invisible Man's perspective, intrusions of utter chaos into an orderly life—the visit to Trueblood's cabin, the comic apocalypse at the Golden Day, the fight and electric shock treatment at the Liberty Paint Factory, the eating of yams, the sight of Tod Clifton hawking Sambo dolls, the accidental discovery of Rinehart, the Harlem race riot. Ellison's

technique in these episodes is as modernistic as it is elsewhere traditional—he uses elements of nightmare, surreal exaggeration, symbolic landscapes, grotesque characters, and unbridled comedy.

It is the interplay of the two modes that defines the form of the
novel. What we experience is the effort to live by a plan and the
repeated disruption of the plan. The career-based Horatio Alger
model, with which the Invisible Man so desperately wants to identify himself, is brought up against experiences for which it has no
names. This alternative experience thus appears fluid and chaotic.
But the phenomena within the chaotoc experiences are neither absurd nor unreal—they are a challenge to the Invisible Man's perception of the world and of himself: "the mind that has conceived a
plan of living must never lose sight of the chaos against which that
pattern was conceived." At precisely the moment in which he feels
most threatened and disoriented (because the current script is being
disrupted), he is actually opening his vision, releasing his energy,
and enlarging his field of action. He sees that the world is possibility. And in these moments he edges his way into a new shiftier
style of conning, much closer in certain respects to the traditional
trickster of folklore and myth.

If the traditional story telling stresses the possibility of aligning
oneself with "the forces of history," the alternative mode suggests
something else, like the group of young black men wearing zoot
suits and reading comic books with rigidly formal gestures:

> who knew but that they were the saviors, the true leaders, the
> bearers of something precious? . . . What if history was a gam-
> bler, instead of a force in a laboratory experiment, and the boys
> his ace in the hole? . . . For they were outside, in the dark with
> Sambo, the dancing paper doll . . . running and dodging the
> forces of history instead of making a dominating stand.

The zoot suit is a parody of downtown styles. The strategy of conning here is the put-on. To run and dodge the forces of history is
to turn the world into play and thereby to remain in touch with a
reality outside the official performance. The zoot-suiters reinforce
the advice which the Invisible Man had earlier heard without understanding from a black doctor, whose own unwillingness to play
the expected roles had landed him in a mental institution: "Play the
game, but don't believe in it—that much you owe yourself. . . .
Play the game, but play it your own way—part of the time at least."

The extreme of such fluid game playing is Rinehart, whom the
Invisible Man discovers near the end of the novel and can't quite
shake from his mind. Rinehart does not exist as a character. He is

merely a mask and a set of roles. The Invisible Man learns about Rinehart in the most convincing way by putting on a broad-brimmed hat and a pair of dark glasses and thus *becoming* Rinehart. As people on the street greet him in different ways, he fills in the various roles of Rine: runner, gambler, briber, lover, Reverend. It is the inner experience of being taken for Rinehart that clarifies for the Invisible Man the nature of this shape-shifter and his world. "His world was possibility and he knew it. . . . The world in which we lived was without boundaries. A vast seething, hot world of fluidity, and Rine the rascal was at home." If Rine represents pure shape-shifting exploitation, in which one moves others without being moved oneself, he also represents open possibility and a new sense of the self. What can integrity mean in "a world in which Rinehart was possible and successful?"

It is the Invisible Man's experience of chaos and play, of put-on and Rinehart, that gradually opens his mind to the significance of his grandfather's advice to overcome them with yeses. Something of this altered state of consciousness is suggested by the Invisible Man's discussion of invisibility and Louis Armstrong's music in the Prologue. Invisibility, he says, gives a different sense of time. "Instead of the swift and imperceptible flowing of time, you are aware of its nodes, those points where time stands still or from which it leaps ahead. And you slip into the breaks and look around." From the perspective of one who is trying to keep the beat, to follow the melody, or analogously to pursue the aspirational story line, such nodes are simply disruptions, threatening moments of chaos. And that is the first effect of the absurdist intrusions in Ellison's plot, for through the Invisible Man's urgent narration of what he is trying to do, we as readers are also attuned to following the orderly story. But gradually we learn, like the Invisible Man himself, how to slip into the breaks and look around. Rinehart lives in the breaks; by mastering what seems chaotic he demonstrates that fluidity is not pure chaos, but his heartless masquerading is not Ellison's ultimate model. The Invisible Man is interested in the melody as well as the breaks, in the orderly, historically relevant plots as well as the purer perception available during performance disruptions. But he has to learn a style of being—even a part of himself—suited to the nodes, so that instead of feeling threatened, he can slip into them and see things freshly, put on dark glasses and laughter. The result is a kind of double consciousness, a con-man actor engaged in the plots of "history" and a more fluid shape-shifter who dodges history and thus preserves the alternate rhythms of his own being and of other realities than those celebrated in the current script. Such literal duplicity seems to be what his grandfather was advocating.

In 1958 Ellison wrote an essay "Change the Joke and Slip the Yoke" to correct the impression that *Invisible Man* is based on a trickster archetype and that the grandfather is a variant of the "darky entertainer."[2] He argues that his themes and patterns of action are not derived from African folktales or even primarily from Afro-American traditions;[3] the use of mask and theatrical, the stress on possibility, are to Ellison associated with America itself, a "land of masking jokers." And he argues, as I do elsewhere in this book, that the trickster is not directly relevant; it is archetypal, not suitable to the "time-haunted" novel, and it is archaic, not adjusted to the particular complexities of the modern world. But when he quotes Karl Kerenyi's theory about that archetype (in Paul Radin's *The Trickster*), Ellison reveals something essential about the Invisible Man's consciousness:

> Disorder belonging to the totality of life . . . the spirit of this disorder is the trickster. His function in an archaic society, or rather the function of his mythology . . . is to add disorder to order and to make a whole, to render possible, within the fixed bounds of what is permitted, an experience of what is not permitted . . .

The Invisible Man's experience in the breaks of his story is supremely modern and yet archaic as well, a confrontation with contemporary disorder and a reactivation of sources of energy and insight deeply locked within the self. Far from representing a racially distinctive state of mind, this agent of disorder and wholeness is potentially universal. Playfulness, put-on, and life "in the breaks" are experiences of other contemporary trickster-survivors as well, like Yossarian and Augie March. In this sense, the Invisible Man's final words are right: "Who knows but that, on the lower frequencies, I speak for you?" What is distinctive is the Invisible Man's multiplicity, which derives from Ellison's own complexity. The protagonist exists neither as self-making, upwardly mobile confidence man nor as evasive, shape-shifting dodger of history but as a composite of the two. The interplay between two distinct modes *is* his state of consciousness. The disruptions make him more keenly alert to the expectations and roles in the dominant collective games; his earnestness about the current scenario, in turn, helps him feel both the terror and the elation of a more fluid existence. He incorporates within his own present self the historical genesis of a new style of con-man survivor.

The Adventures of Augie March

The Invisible Man can thus continue to think and talk about historical accountability while he lives alone in a coal cellar. Augie March doesn't have that kind of ambivalence. Bellow's protagonist can never feel as strongly as Ellison's the attraction of *being somebody* within the forces of history; he cannot sustain one role, one performance, one hope as long as the Invisible Man and thus he is less surprised when the performance is disrupted. Glimpses of historical greatness—he sees Trotsky in Mexico—are all Augie has or wants. He travels the edges of "history," and when he misses the Decoration Day Massacre in Chicago by dropping his temporary role as union organizer, he recognizes that he is not destined to navigate "by the great stars": "I just didn't have the calling to be a union man or in politics, or any notion of my particle of will coming before the ranks of a mass that was about to march forward from misery." Augie's idea of the "forces of history" does not exhilarate him; like Henry Adams he sees such lines of force too readily arranging human beings as a magnetic field arranges a dust of metals. He wants his particle on the periphery.

To become somebody, to create a self with historical significance, is a central motif in the promissory tradition, and Ellison records the complication of that tradition as it is transmitted to the modern world. Augie March's roots are in a different set of American values. He would understand the modesty of the speaker in Emerson's poem "Days," who passes over the kingdoms and stars that are among the Days' offerings and takes instead a few herbs and apples. Except for the syntax, Emerson could have said what Augie says: "there may gods turn up anywhere." The idea is that the commonplace is not only sufficient, it is divine. Augie describes himself as "a sort of Columbus of those near-at-hand." Unlike Ellison, who derives the contemporary con man's lightness of mind from the collapse of promissory plots, Bellow takes for granted that such plots are outmoded and sets about to fashion a style in which one can not only survive the modern world but experience it piece by piece. For this purpose, he draws on and fuses two of the major alternative traditions of American con men, the omnivorous jack-of-all-trades and the rogue-survivor. And he adjusts the styles of Emerson and Huck Finn to an urban social world, so thick with human artifacts that one can no longer fall back on nature or spirit for a sense of what is real. In *The Adventures of Augie March* (1953) shape shifting is more than a means of survival. It is a mode of being. In fact it is the essence of identity and discovery.

For a modern urban rogue, Augie March shows surprising affinities with Ralph Waldo Emerson. He rises at times to the "triumphant life" and sees how the world of daily facts recedes. He intuits a seemingly permanent reality within, and he is as ready as Emerson to call off other duties "in the inspiration of the day" or to feel "the axial lines of life" running beneath the confusion of appearances. But it is not Augie's fate to sit still long enough for such contemplations. Like the jack-of-all-trades, as I noted in Chapter 6, he reaches for the eternal, the real, the axial lines, not by retreating from the phenomenal world but by immersing himself as variously as possible in it. Thus although he often speaks like the Emerson of first principles, he is closer in spirit to the Emersonian shapeshifter. He acts out Emerson's advice and proves it still useful: "Be a football to time and chance, the more kicks the better so that you inspect the whole game and know its uttermost law."

Augie March brings his sense of a grander world into this world at hand by refusing to specialize. It becomes both a joke and a complaint among his friends that nothing is good enough for him, that he will always be campaigning "after a worth-while fate." His response to the division of labor is to try as many things as possible, for he fears limitation. He does not disdain the everyday world, but his "nobility syndrome" keeps him from resting in any one corner of it. One of his friends describes him in Emerson's own words about the ultimate shape-shifter beyond the fall of man and the division of labor: "You want there should be Man, with capital M, with great stature." This posture for Augie is not theoretical, nor is it bolstered by philosophy. It is, from the start, a radical penchant of his temperament. He is changeable, varietistic, diffuse. "I touched all sides, and nobody knew where I belonged." On one side, Augie as jack-of-all-trades is a seeker, omnivorous, idealistic, restlessly transforming himself so as to be as many parts of Man as possible. On the other side, again like Emerson, he is detached. His fear of limitation and specialty expresses itself through discontent with every role as a possible trap. He feels his self in the act of disengaging it from the present pursuit.

Yet Augie's shape shifting has a very different quality from what Emerson celebrated. It is suggested by his words about his complicated "courtship" with the rich and almost promiscuous Lucy Magnus: "But I enjoyed all that was allowed and to that extent I remained myself." In addition to being omnivorous, diffuse, and detached, this speaker is accommodating. He is more radically experimental than the jack-of-all-trades, for he tests at each moment not only what will work but what he can get away with. More important, he acknowledges what Emerson never would—the *primacy* of the world out there. This is the side of Augie March that seems more obvious and appropriate, his kinship with Huck Finn. He is fluid not merely in testing out many roles but in constantly adapting himself to the situation. Like Huck, he usually appears in a passive relation to others—they command him, punish him, dupe him, create roles for him. Neither a trickster nor an honest man by heart, Augie says it depends on which way he is drawn. He is constantly subject to outside influences and tells us finally more about them than about himself. Instead of trying to flee or to change the world around him, Augie accepts it as it is: "I don't want to tamper with anyone else." But if Augie seems in this sense all too ready to take the shape of the situation, there are limits to his acceptance. The ease with which he is influenced indicates how superficial the influence will be. Augie March does not adapt himself to the current scenario as fully as the Invisible Man or Bob Slocum or Goffman's organization performers do. For all his fluidity, open-endedness, and accommodation, he remains stubbornly himself.

What the jack-of-all-trades shares with the rogue-survivor is the ability to shift shapes and yet to keep free of the world. Augie is at once tougher than Huck Finn and more accommodating than Emerson. He lets the world do what it will to him, and he enters gladly into the present situation. But something he holds back. In con-game terms, if he willingly gives his faith, he never risks much on it. In one sense this tendency makes Augie appear heartless. Like the early American con men, Benjamin Franklin and Arthur Mervyn, he disengages himself too easily. To be so devilishly pliant is to have little at stake. He even recognizes this quality in himself when Thea Fenchel leaves him in Mexico and he thinks back over his sentimental relations. Why, he wonders, has he not had money or profession or duties except to keep free so as to be a sincere follower of love? Now he discovers that all his Emersonian negativity was not a means to an end, for he is as easily detached from love as from everything else. Disengagement proves to be his characteristic, not his strategy. Like Emerson and Franklin, he finds that nothing is a fate good enough, nothing deserves his full enthusiasm or commitment, nothing is so special that he will specialize in it.

Augie's detachment, however, is not heartlessness. One of his would-be mentors, William Einhorn, comes closer to the mark in saying something that Augie thinks back on again and again— "You've got *opposition* in you. You don't slide through everything. You just make it look so." In contrast with Heller's Bob Slocum, who wonders during his own adjustments whether he even *has* an inner nature, Augie wonders where his inner nature is directing him. But the force of opposition he can always feel in himself. Something tells him that he is above or outside any role the world has to offer him. This is not a matter of naming wrongs, attacking the present world, assuming a political or moral stance. Nor is it a matter of pride, of walking through the world with his nose in the air. Augie accepts the world and even humbles himself before it, taking its kicks as readily as its gifts. He is in opposition because he never forgets that he is opposite the world—it is many things but he is another thing. This is what keeps his pliancy so healthy: "all was vague on my side and yet it was also very stubborn."

Emerson and Huck Finn also remembered or intuited that they were opposite the world. What makes Augie distinct and modern is that there is no larger reference for his inwardness. Huck Finn could be himself in the natural world. It presented him with uncontaminated sensations and with scenes somehow akin to his deep but unnameable feelings. It also provided an alternative place within which he could have a human relationship not mediated by social games. Emerson, too, turned to the natural world as the outward semblance of his inwardness—it furnished him tropes for his intuitions, and through its sublime laws and the surrounding inclusiveness of its horizons, it suggested the spiritual oneness with which Emerson felt his own kinship. And as with Huck Finn, the natural world served Emerson as a realm separate from the social world, where he could go to have in the first place those intuitions about his true self. Augie March rarely gets "outside of the busy human tamper." His world is almost entirely artificial, and he knows the consequences: "you can't lie down so innocent on objects made by man. In the world of nature you can trust, but in the world of artifacts you must beware." In such a world there can be no period of pastoral innocence to forerun the complicated adjustments of maturity. One has to cope from the outset with "deep city vexation."

In this overshadowing world of artifacts, shape shifting is more than a strategy, it is identity. Emerson and Huck Finn had two selves. One—the real one—they experienced in the natural world. The other—the shape-shifter—they presented to the social world. Thus their social relations involved a complicated masquerade, and the inner and outer selves played games. Without that separate natural world to nourish an original state of innocence, Augie cannot play double. If he has a continuing identity—a seat of "opposition"—he must experience it in the very way he engages in roles and fictions. Augie is not preserving something else (like Huck

Finn's true feelings) through the strategies of masquerade. Nor is he descending with a gamesman's delight from the true world of spirit to the sideshow events around him. For Augie March there is only the one world. His restless entering of role after role demonstrates his appetite for the sundry things of that world. His withdrawal in turn preserves his detachment. The yearning and the independence may resemble Emerson's spiritual qualities, but for Augie they represent a style that affirms the concrete variety of *this* world and that defines a self who can revel in it. Thus Augie can encompass the discrepant styles of the jack-of-all-trades and the rogue-survivor without contradiction. He moves through the world with the former's restless yearning and the latter's amoral accommodation, ever humble before the scattered offerings of the day and never quite satisfied with them.

How different an approach from his brother Simon's urgent efforts to make something of himself. Like Yossarian and the Invisible Man, Augie March is characterized by contrast with familiar types of confidence men who are identified with dominant patterns in the social order. In fact, in *The Adventures of Augie March* con games form an even more overt part of the background world than in *Invisible Man* and *Catch-22*. In 1920s Chicago, with its bootleggers and swindlers and bookies, it is not surprising to have one character ask Augie, "What's the matter, are you honest?" There is Grandma Lausch, the Marches' boarder, whose desire for Simon and Augie to get ahead in the world is coupled with elaborate stratagems to hoax the welfare administrators. There are the Kleins, whose scams and scavenging and giddy generosity evoke the milieu of "Yellow Kid" Weil. There is William Einhorn, gambler, shady investor, manipulator of the larger institutions of his day, whose appetite for experience knows no moral boundaries and cannot even be contained by his life in a wheelchair, and who tutors Augie in how to take advantage of a world in which the old prescriptions fail. But the major example of a confidence man to set off Augie's style is his brother Simon. Like Tom Sawyer and Milo Minderbinder, Simon March is full of principle. His "English schoolboy sense of honor" and his official desire to rise in the world contrast early with Augie's moral flexibility. It is this sense of honor that sets him up for the socially available goals and the socially acceptable means. Thus without Augie's detachment, he sets about to ingratiate himself with the wealthy Magnuses. He buys the right clothes, develops the right tastes, adapts himself to the right manners so that he will *appear* to be accepted, for appearing successful must precede success itself.

But Augie also recognizes in his brother the nearly suicidal mania of his pursuit. Simon is so earnest that he is the victim of his own sense of possibility. When Augie and Simon dress for Simon's wedding in the "governor's suite" of a big hotel, they "come into a view of mutability," but for Simon this view compels him to rise because he can, whereas for Augie mutability involves *all* possible changes, up, down, or, more likely, sideways. Yet temporarily Augie can play roles as well as his brother. He can court Lucy Magnus, model sporting clothes with the Renlings, hunt iguanas with an eagle. He has far greater range in impersonation than his brother and correspondingly less belief and persistence in each role. But the major difference is that conning for Simon March is a socially expected means to a socially dictated end. For Augie, to play the role is merely to participate in the world, the more roles the better. His adventures lead nowhere, for there is no larger purpose. Shape shifting, adaptation, impersonation are the styles through which Augie confronts the world. They make up the form of life itself.

The form of Bellow's novel is adapted to this style of life. The more or less aimless sequence of adventures is an old staple of fiction, the very essence of picaresque narrative. But Augie's experiences are so broken and disrupted—or he is so permeable to distractions—that the "adventures" never quite get going. To experience *plot* in *The Adventures of Augie March* is always to experience *someone else's* plot.[4] In *Invisible Man* other people's scenarios become the protagonist's own plot lines and we follow long sequences of development with anxiety and anticipation as well as a growing sense of irony. The local scenarios in *Augie March* never become *the* plot (one measure of this effect is how extraordinarily difficult it is to grasp and to remember the novel *as a novel*). Particular wishes and strategies come to be identified with particular characters; they do not define Augie himself but merely shape his experience of the other fascinating people around him. Chapter 12 illustrates such experience. Augie has, with some success, been courting Lucy Magnus, the even richer cousin of Simon's rich wife. He plays a role written by Simon to the apparent satisfaction of Lucy. Meantime, Mimi Villars, a woman in Augie's apartment, needs an abortion, and Augie, with his usual desire to please, has been trying to help her. The two plots cross on New Year's Eve when Augie has to miss a family party with Lucy in order to help Mimi to a hospital, where he is then seen by another cousin of the Magnuses who spreads the story that Augie himself was Mimi's lover and thus breaks off Augie's courtship. The point is that in all this entanglement of plotting, secrecy, erroneous impression, Augie himself is basically untouched.[5] The collapse of plots around him leaves him no worse off than he was and not even especially troubled.

The simple fact is that Augie does not live in stories nor does he organize his experience by telling them. He is surrounded by characters who do. The other characters repeatedly draw Augie into their scenarios. There is something "adoptional" about Augie, "the sign of the recruit under which I had been born." Grandma Lausch plots a social rise for him; Jimmy Klein plans to rake off money in the department store's Christmas promotion; Joe Gorman draws Augie into a robbery; the Renlings dress Augie as a son; Simon projects a joint success in the world of the Magnuses; Thea Fenchel's script for Augie includes making movies of iguana hunting with a trained eagle. And such script writers are also costume designers. The Renlings, Simon, and Thea spend a good deal of time literally dressing Augie for his roles, and part of his impersonative skill is that he seems able to carry off any style of clothing. In this world of fabrications, where everyone tries to convert others to his or her personal plot, Augie is the perpetual, able recruit who cannot be too disappointed when the scenario breaks down.

Disruption of the other people's performances could be said, in fact, to save Augie by freeing him from fabrication. But such evasion is not the primary point. Survival of the self is not enough. Neither a cynic nor a misanthrope, Augie does not try to avoid the performance. Rather, like Melville's Cosmopolitan, who says that life is a picnic *en costume*, he wants to enjoy the show. For all the sordid and selfish aspects of Augie's world, his and our experience of it is primarily exhilarating, and the cause is in Augie's approach to it. Like Melville's protagonist, he finds the human world around him utterly fascinating, but instead of tricking people into being more themselves, he participates in their worlds on their terms. He explores what it is to be human by immersing himself in the various roles and circumstances in which people act out their humanness. This strategy appears self-negating; Augie is more interested in the world around him—its crusty details, complications, quirky personalities—than in his own nature. He serves as a fine center of perception, alert and mobile, ready to engage in the stories at hand. First-person narrative is essential to his approach, for as in the case of the Invisible Man, what is interesting is how the shape-shifter experiences his world, engaging and freeing, entering a plot and leaving it. Thus Augie not only tells us about the appearances and the temperaments of the people around him but he acts out, for a time, their longings and illusions, shares their secrets and disguises.

Yet Augie's self is not negated by his transferring of interest to a primary world out there. How it persists is indicated by one of his clearest statements of theory:

> Everyone tries to make a world he can live in, and what he can't use he often can't see. But the real world is already created, and if your fabrication doesn't correspond, then even if you feel noble and insist on there being something better than what people call reality, the better something needn't try to exceed what, in its actuality, since we know it so little, may be very surprising.

Augie has the kind of identity an explorer has, not dependent on what he seeks or on any particular thing he finds. He is most himself in the very act of exploring. The formal brokenness of the novel suits Augie's style, for it forces us to be, like him, absolutely engaged in the jaggedness of the moment, not stepping back for larger interpretive surveys, expectancies, and fabrications. And that is where Augie's lightness of mind comes in. Whereas the promissory version of the confidence man was suited to a self and a country in the making, a place of open possibilities, Augie's version of the jack-of-all-trades–survivor knows how to live in a world already made. In his ability to impersonate and then move on, to shift both appearance and principle so as to engage in the momentary game in play, he meets and explores his world and celebrates his own resilient self. He knows that if you want to "try out what of human you can live with," you have to be ready at every moment to be "thrown for fair on the free spinning of the world."

11

FAITH ON THE RUN

We've all certainly got our money's worth every time he fleeced us, haven't we? . . . I feel *compelled* to defend my friend's honor as a good old red, white, and blue hundred-per-cent American con man.

—*Ken Kesey*

There he is on the midway, Grack the Frenchie, talking for his count-store or his zoo, while the loudspeaker clamored under his come-on with a *hee hee hee* and a *ho ho ho* . . . This was the big show, if they only knew it.

—*Herbert Gold*

Do you think we believe it.

—*Gertrude Stein*

Traveling light, like Yossarian, the Invisible Man, and Augie March, may be our central strategy of survival. It allows us to preserve our own reality in a fabricated world and yet to participate playfully in that world. We must be adaptive, resilient, and detached, like nineteenth-century shape-shifters. Traveling light is a way of facing the external world and keeping flexible. But in the American tradition of confidence men, flexibility was not the only central virtue, and dealing with the outside world was not the only art. Even more characteristic than the shape-shifter was the buoyant bringer of faith, who depended less on strategy than on charismatic force and who was less concerned with the surrounding world than with his own radiant energy.

The confidence men who carry on this tradition in the present differ markedly in style from Yossarian, the Invisible Man, and Augie March. In their brashness and frenetic gesturing they are more conspicuous, they take up more space. And they seem oddly out of date, as if they still believe things it is no longer fashionable to believe, or as if they were charlatans who didn't hear the show was over. They influence other people less by gambits and masquerade than by direct personal appeal. On the other hand, they are far less sensitive to the individual needs of other people. They make promises like the nineteenth-century booster, not as contracts but as creative gestures. The faith they appeal to is not directed toward something else—faith in God or faith that the railroad will run by one's land. It is reflexive. A person with "faith" in this sense is healthy, expansive, and energetic.

Although such a state of faith is a personal experience, it can also be shared. That is what the word confidence is all about. The person with extraordinary, buoyant, all-purpose faith and its accompanying energy can radiate this inner state to others. He is, in the purest sense of the term, a confidence man, a sharer of faith. In his presence something almost sacred takes place. But since there is no sacramental ground for him, no elevating official ritual, his touches of divinity are encased in more squalid circumstances, and he is as likely to appear in a carnival as in a church. He is often a cheat as well as a prophet. What is the appeal of the auctioneer's incantation, the carnie's fast talk, the medicine show's razzle-dazzle, the booster's verbal magic? We enjoy such performances even while we doubt the showman's specific promises, for they refresh the mind and renew the world. They excite and exhilarate us. Perhaps the tonic will not cure warts, and perhaps the tract of land is actually two feet under water, but the real promise is of another kind. If we share the con man's faith, allow ourselves to ride his words into his imagined world, we may literally be transported and thus tap a corresponding source of energy within ourselves.

Such free flowing of energy can only be temporary, but even when we fall back to our mundane reality and find his promises not literally fulfilled, we may still recollect the state to which the confidence man lifted us. This is why Nick Carraway maintains his loyalty to Gatsby, why Huck Finn doesn't give up on Tom Sawyer, why Arthur Mervyn's disillusionment does not end his ties to Welbeck, why Mark Twain couldn't simply laugh off Colonel Beriah Sellers. And it is in releasing such inward energy—by nature beyond good and evil, outside cultural bounds—that the modern confidence man most clearly approximates the archaic trickster. But the pressures toward doubt and diminishment are so great in the contemporary world that the shared moments of energy get abruptly cut off. The con man becomes in turn more desperate to recover his own faith and more extreme in his gestures of trying to share it. Even the most enthusiastic of his disciples find good reasons for discouragement. The fate of the contemporary booster shows what has happened to the old American promise-land spirit.

Neal Cassady

The personal energy that the confidence man can share has been particularly infectious for Americans in the closely related forms of fast movement and fast talk. Both were carried to new extremes in post-war America by Neal Cassady (1926–68),[1] a figure who illuminates our world as P. T. Barnum illuminated his. As the model for Dean Moriarty in *On the Road*, the "secret hero" of *Howl*, the sledgehammer-flipping, speedrapping, manic driver of the Day-Glo bus labeled "Further" on which Ken Kesey and the Merry Pranksters helped spread a new culture in the sixties, Cassady occupied a position of considerable influence. What makes him important for an understanding of a confidence culture is the nature of that influence, the peculiar legends that grew up around him, the styles and images that clung to him. Cassady became a culture hero of a special sort, one who combines personal energy and speed, breathless talk and enthusiastic belief. In a diminished and skeptical world, he temporarily makes credible again the old American faith in the future, but it is now a madder faith tied up with a way of moving through the world, and it requires constant recharging, as if the booster has become not only a con man but an extension of the world of automobiles and electricity.

In every context Cassady is a figure of virtually boundless energy. Images of his life in the forties and fifties repeatedly involve a nearly nonstop "schedule" in which he splits his life between two women, learns to write from Kerouac, talks with Ginsberg, nurses a broken thumb and a broken nose cartilage, repairs tires faster than anyone else in the business, and turns up in the lives of his friends with more and more new plans and mad gestures. Then, as Houlihan in Kesey's *Over the Border*, Cassady keeps appearing as the force to GO, the zany driver and talker who can rig a tire change on a bus without a jack, hotwire a car with paper clips, repair an accelerator with a coat hanger, coast backwards down a hill without brakes when the gas runs out, anything to keep the show moving. Descriptions of Neal Cassady inevitably stress his feverish activity, as if his whole body were wired to a high-power cell.

Speed was Cassady's obsession. Acquaintances spoke of him as the fastest man alive. He ran instead of walking, honed his reflexes for quickness, drove fast so as to keep on the very edge between control and adventure. Tom Wolfe's description of his coasting the Further bus down mountain roads without brakes is typical: "For all his wild driving he always made it through the last clear oiled gap in the maze, like he knew it would be there all the time, which it always was." Gary Snyder theorized that Cassady's appeal was like that of the 1880s cowboy, except that since the frontier had been closed in, the taste for limitless space now expressed itself in faster and faster speed. But the outward motion was coupled with inner rapidity, and the nonstop driving was both literal and metaphoric. Tom Wolfe relates Ken Kesey's theory of the time lag between sensation and reaction, 1/30th of a second if you are the most alert person alive. Kesey's point is that only by artificially altering consciousness can one close that gap; but what is interesting is the place of Cassady here, for despite his use of miscellaneous drugs (speed especially), he personally represented the closest one can come on one's own power to joining sensation and reaction. Like Emerson, he would alter consciousness if he could without a little help from his friends, so that Wolfe describes him "fibrillating tight up against the 1/30th of a second movie-screen barrier of our senses, trying to get into . . . *Now*—"

"Now," however, was not exactly the state of consciousness Neal Cassady represented, nor was it the meaning of his obsession with speed. Wolfe comes closer to it in tracing the Merry Pranksters' "Superhero thing" to one of the primary feelings of being Super-kids in the Post-War, "with the motor running and the adrenaline flowing, cruising in the neon glories of the new American night." Such cruising keeps the world out there light, fleeting, insubstantial, and thus preserves its air of promise. Cassady, in his autobiography, re-creates the feeling: "Signs, signs, lights, lights, streets, streets; it is the dark between that attracts one—what's happening there at this moment? What hidden thing, glorious perhaps, is being passed and lost forever." But the effect is also inward, the sheer exhilaration of movement and thus of power. And where the two cross—where the promissory fleeting world fuses with the cruiser's inner ecstasy—was Cassady's domain: "my mind's gears were shifted by unknown mechanism to an increase of time's torrent that received in kaleidoscopic change images, clean as the hurry of thought could allow, rushing so quickly by that all I could do was barely catch one before another one crowded . . ." That is the state of consciousness that Neal Cassady represented and that his driving, his letter writing, and his talking created for others.

In Chapter 5, I showed how such experiences of vertigo are re-

lated to Whitman's style of promise and movement. Cassady inten-
sified the feelings by speeding up, because in the new technology
the open road was neon-studded and he could travel it at rates
Whitman couldn't dream of. He related to the world out there as to
something going past. At its most exciting it consisted of experiences, things, people rushing by pell-mell so that each thing was
briefly seized on before being lost forever. Kerouac describes the
effect as "rushing through the world without a chance to see it,"
but Cassady puts the matter differently in his autobiography: "eyeball kicks are among the world's greatest." And the style applied to
more than the world of objects and people. Kerouac's biographer,
Ann Charters, says, "Neal, with his intensities and enthusiasms,
burst in and out of ideas, coming to them, throwing them in the
air, dropping them behind him and hurrying on to the next one.
He made Kerouac feel thick and heavy. . . ."

If the contemporary world involves rapid changes, perpetual
complications, overturnings of the familiar, or what Alvin Toffler
calls "the kinetic image," Neal Cassady had a way of riding its
changes for thrills. Instead of worrying about disruptions of the
present scenario, he delighted in the making and revising of sched-
ules and thrived on the breathless movement from one situation to
another. This attitude Kerouac captures perfectly in *On the Road*
when Dean and Sal learn that a hitchhiker who was going to give
them gas money after arriving at his aunt's cannot keep his promise
because his aunt shot her husband and went to jail. Dean revels in
the entanglement: "Think of it! The things that happen; . . . the
trou-bles on all sides, the complications of events—whee, damn!"
Such embracing and such celebrating of things as they are recall the
style of Augie March. Both Augie and Neal Cassady move through
endlessly complicated, often squalid worlds with wide-eyed acceptance, too fluid to linger long enough for a situation to go really bad
on them. Cassady's letters and autobiographical fragments veer
from event to event with the erratic, plot-exploding approach of
Augie March.

But there are critical differences between Augie March and Neal
Cassady. Cassady emerges in his autobiography, his letters, the accounts of his friends, as a person more fascinated by the flowing
through of situations than by each one in itself. In this sense he
was more inwardly involved than Augie, less exhilarated by the
world out there than by his own movement through it. His hyper-
activity, his driving, his quick reactions, his fleeting enthusiasms
all point to the same ideal conception of experience: the world is
moving and so is the self. Each thing, person, idea, situation ap-

pears within the consciousness only to be rapidly displaced by the next one. William Burroughs describes Cassady as "the very soul of this voyage into pure abstract, meaningless motion." Whether the cause is running, driving, accelerating the sense of time, or falling into emotional and social complexities, the result is a thrilling mixture of personal ecstasy and a perpetually promising (because perpetually arriving) world.

That conception of a world in rapid motion can be generated in another way as well, and Neal Cassady was an expert at it. Cassady the driver was also Cassady the talker, and every reminiscence of him registers the excitement of his endless monologues with their staccato bursts of energy. The speed of his driving and of his reflexes was matched by the speed of his talk so that the compulsive words could be as infectious as the mountain rides without brakes. Tom Wolfe metaphorically suggests the fusion of Cassady's styles:

> Cassady is a monologuist, only he doesn't seem to care whether anyone is listening or not. He just goes off on the monologue, by himself if necessary, although anyone is welcome aboard. He will answer all questions, although not exactly in that order, because we can't stop here, next rest area 40 miles, you understand, spinning off memories, metaphors, literary, Oriental, hip allusions. . . .

The various re-creations of these monologues indicate that they were basically narratives of events and emotional entanglements, so rapid and disgressive, so full of mishaps and mad scramblings, as to suggest that Cassady in words was always trying to catch up with Cassady in action, or as he put it in his autobiography, "my mind was thinking such thoughts that soon I actually thought of how at last I could tell you on paper perhaps the knowledge of action—But later." Pointless as they may have been, however, Cassady's monologues did more than set the world spinning in a listener's head. Like the con man's fast talk, they promised something, too. Ken Kesey emphasizes this in his tribute to Cassady: "Only through the actual speedshifting grind and gasp and zoom of his high compression voice do you get the sense of the urgent sermon that Neal was driving madcap into every road-blocked head he came across."

Neal Cassady was a confidence man. He knew how to use his fast talk for his own ulterior purposes, as in the trial run of the "Further" bus when by prestidigitation and patient bewildering monologue he convinced a suspicious policeman that a nonexistent handbrake was perfectly functional. His letters and reminiscences dwell with adolescent pride on his ability to con girls, and his wife Carolyn remembers the art as more generally practiced: "He could talk and would talk with anybody and instantly they felt that he really cared about them. . . . Now part of that became conning, he learned how to use that to con. He was a master at getting you to think that he knew exactly where you were and what you needed and he could always supply it." John Tytell, in *Naked Angels,* sees Cassady's conning as a compulsion, a "habitual need to persuade people to act." But coupled with his fast driving, his urgent monologues, his sense of a world in promising motion, Cassady's direct conning takes on the ambivalence of a longer tradition of American confidence men. The people who remember his conning remember it as an attractive, well-nigh a spiritual, quality. His old Denver friend Jim Holmes describes him in terms that Nick Carraway could apply to Gatsby: "The man was very, very energetic and very personable and he would—I don't think intentionally—but he would actually flatter you, your ego, in such a way that he would almost immediately be liked. . . . I don't think it was a put-on. It was a technique, however. But it wasn't a con." And that is where Cassady the man turns into Cassady the legend, the figure who would drive seventy-two hours straight across country because he had heard about a man with a vision; who would gravitate from Kerouac and Ginsberg to Kesey and become an exemplar to two generations of American experimenters.

What people saw in Neal Cassady's feverish activity was simply a modernized version of a very familiar American type, the protean, yea-saying bearer of confidence. He came into the lives of Jack Kerouac and Allen Ginsberg as a persuasive force to move out, to speed up, to experiment, to risk meeting life in a mad rush of frenzy. His driving and his talking made people experience a world in motion as a world full of promise, and his own restless energy seemed the ideal personal style with which to confront it. In contrast with the "absurd hero" of modern existentialism or the nihilistic spirit so often assumed as the appropriate response to the post-1945 world, the Neal Cassady legend draws on the affirmative, joyous, activist traditions of American values. Tom Wolfe contrasts this spirit, complicated by Merry-Prankster put-ons, with the spirit of Eastern mysticism:

> this 400-horsepower takeoff game, this American flag-flying game, this Day-Glo game, this yea-saying game, this dread neon game, this . . . *superhero* game, all wired-up and wound up and amplified in the electropastel chrome game gleam. It wasn't the Buddha

> . . . satori is passive, just lying back and grooving and grokking
> on the Overmind and leave Teddy Roosevelt out of it.

And one of the last pictures in *The Electric Kool-Aid Acid Test* is Neal
Cassady, wheeling into an Acid Test dominated by the Eastern-
oriented Calliope Company which had replaced the Merry Pranksters, Neal's eyes jumping around, the others staring at him in passive tolerance, Neal saying, "Hey! Don't you want to *do* anything—
get it started, you understand—slide it around—" and finally kick-
ing and flailing out the door by himself.

He was, Kesey says, "one hell of a hero and the tales of his exploits will always be blowing around us." That is the other thing
about the Cassady legend, the dimension of the heroic. Throughout
The Electric Kool-Aid Acid Test, which traces Kesey's experience as it
fuses with and becomes affected by a virtual group consciousness,
Cassady is the one figure who remains distinctly himself, an individual whose qualities—alertness to the moment, instant flexibility,
deadly competence—may be collective ideals, but who always practices them in a personal style. His endless seeking of something in
the "new American night," his infectious energy, his dazzling
drive talk merge in a figure who restores an older promise-land
spirit to the strategies of survival in the Post-War world. And unlike the Invisible Man and Augie March, who told their own stories
of play, evasion, shape shifting, and discovery, Neal Cassady in
legend becomes someone *told about*, a figure who can bring buoyancy, energy, and daring to someone else. In his major legendary
form, Neal Cassady becomes a full-scale, fully ambivalent confidence man as hero.

On the Road

Sal Paradise, the narrator of Jack Kerouac's *On the Road* (1957), sees
the book's central character, Dean Moriarty, as a hero in a variety
of American styles—the spirit of the West, the energetic mover and
doer, the cowboy, the Whitman-like enthusiast, "that mad Ahab at
the wheel" compelling others at hissing, incredible speeds across
the country. But the subsuming model for the Cassady legend is of
the American hero as a confidence man:

> He was simply a youth tremendously excited with life, and though
> he was a con-man, he was only conning because he wanted so
> much to live and to get involved with people who would other-
> wise pay no attention to him. He was conning me and I knew it
> (for room and board and "how-to-write," etc.), and he knew I

knew (this has been the basis of our relationship), but I didn't care
and we got along fine. . . .

In Sal's usage, "con-man" is a phrase of admiration—"the holy con-
man with the shining mind," "a great amorous soul such as only a
con-man can have"—and the novel explores the meaning and value
of a confidence man in modern American life.

Sal Paradise is essential to the creation of a con man as hero, for
someone has to register that radiant energy, someone has to receive
and interpret it, almost like a priest. A less prissy Nick Carraway
discovering a more frantic Gatsby, Sal responds enthusiastically to
Dean Moriarty: "I could hear a new call and see a new horizon."
Something of Dean's mad faith is transmitted to Sal whenever they
are together—"somewhere along the line the pearl would be
handed to me." On his own Sal tends to brood and his imaginative
energy runs down, but each time Dean appears or sends a summoning letter—even if in the guise of a frightful Angel or the
Shrouded Traveler—Sal perks up and sets off, as if Dean were a
tonic for a tired soul. He instills the energy to move, to do, to dare
getting off dead center, and more important, he encourages Sal to
believe. Once Dean enters his life, Sal becomes a devotee of Promise Land, alert to the hints of place names and prairie nights—Denver and San Francisco are jewels in the "Promised Land." "Beyond
the glittering street was darkness, and beyond the darkness the
West. I had to go." He and Dean share the vision of the country as
an oyster for them to open, and Sal repeatedly re-enacts the promissory quest, as in calling Hollywood "the ragged promised land,
the fantastic end of America."

The point is that Sal sees in Dean's frenzy and racing and hot-
wired talk what Nick Carraway sees in Gatsby's colossal pretense—
the underlying faith: "the road must eventually lead to the whole
world." All the frantic gestures and leavings behind of charred
ruins, the zany risks and tangled pronouncements appear as merely
the superficial forms through which Dean expresses his urgent vision, his effort to come to IT. Dean talks about IT as Emerson talks
about the pure Poem in the Mind of the One:

> Here's a guy and everybody's there, right? Up to him to put
> down what's on everybody's mind. . . . All of a sudden some-
> where in the middle of the chorus he *gets it*—everybody looks up
> and knows; they listen; he picks it up and carries. Time stops
> . . . everybody knows it's not the tune that counts but IT.

Dean, in Sal's re-creation, is a visionary and an enthusiast. When
he races compulsively about the city in the night, digging the

streets, digging the jazz players, digging the intellectuals and the criminals, we are to believe that he is restlessly seeking IT in its many passing manifestations. The world pouring past the car window is merely the rush of appearances, and to perceive them in a rush is to come closer to what is beyond them. Thus as Dean and Sal race through experience they are doing a kind of high-voltage meditation, "our final excited joy in talking and living to the blank tranced end of all innumerable riotous angelic particulars that had been lurking in our souls all our lives."

It is this enabling faith that transfigures the outward gestures and style of Dean Moriarty. What could easily appear to others as restlessness, undependability, a mere compulsion at every moment to GO, turns out to have a metaphysical basis as Sal interprets it: "we all realized we were leaving confusion and nonsense behind and performing our one and noble function of the time, *move*." The world of particulars and appearances is a world of hassles and misleading entanglements, and much as Dean delights in complication, he leaves it behind on the road, rising above it, cruising past it, seeing beyond it, restoring his sense of control and order and personal authority. This is the inward content of Dean's obsession with speed, the promise behind his fast talk. He does not try to make people believe precisely what he says; they usually recognize that he is "making logics where there was nothing but inestimable sorrrowful sweats." Instead, he offers them a ride, no destination, you understand, but fleeting glimpses of IT through the rush of visions. "There's always more, a little further—it never ends." This is the sense in which Dean the con man has and shares "the tremendous energy of a new kind of American saint." And the American traditions, both popular and intellectual, that celebrated such bearers of faith and energy were precisely what gave Kerouac the perceptual framework to look beyond Neal Cassady and see Dean Moriarty and to look beyond both and see . . . IT.

Yet Dean Moriarty is, of course, a criminal. He is that kind of con man, too, a compulsive thief of cars who spent much of his youth in jail, a "change artist" of the first order who could wish a parking-lot customer Merry Christmas "so volubly a five-spot in change for twenty was never missed." Like Gatsby and Augie March, however, he can mingle with the criminal world and yet not become of it. Augie manages this by detachment. Dean Moriarty and Gatsby actually transfigure criminality itself. Dean has a "native strange saintliness to save him from the iron fate." In his first visit to Sal, Dean appears different from the down-putting, sometimes tedious intellectuals of the East and different from its criminals as well—

"his 'criminality' was not something that sulked and sneered; it was a wild yea-saying overburst of American joy." By racing in society instead of putting it down, Dean somehow redeems crime. As long as he can be a bringer of faith and a celebrant of energy, he can without blame be the more exploitive kind of con man as well.

Or at least he can in Sal's eyes. Like so much American literature of the nineteenth century, *On the Road* divides the world into believers and doubters. There are people like Carlo Marx (modeled on Allen Ginsberg) who ask disturbing but finally wrong questions:

> Then Carlo asked Dean if he was honest and specifically if he was being honest with *him* in the bottom of his soul.
> "Why do you bring that up again?"

Carlo brings a demand for personal sincerity and for intellectual point that runs counter to Dean's whole mode of being. When he asks the book's central question—"Whither goest thou, America, in thy shiny car in the night?"—Sal and Dean have nothing to say: "The only thing to do was go." The other skeptics in the book are more practical in their demands. They look to Dean's outward behavior instead of his beliefs and lose patience with him. "Con-man Dean was antagonizing people away from him by degrees." His former friend Ed Wall "had lost faith in Dean." His cousin tells him, "Now look, Dean, I don't believe you any more or anything you're going to try to tell me." In San Francisco the old gang turns on him for his irresponsibility, his carelessness, "his enormous series of sins," and when Sal tries to argue that "he's got the secret that we're all busting to find," Roy Johnson replies that Dean is "just a very interesting and even amusing con-man." Even Sal has his days of doubt, losing faith when Dean leaves him moneyless on the streets of San Francisco to pursue his own pleasure, recognizing "what a rat he was" when Dean deserts him sick in Mexico at the end of the book. But underlying the vacillation of feeling, when Sal knows better than to *believe* Dean, is a constant belief *in* Dean. "I told Dean I was sorry he had nobody in the world to believe in him. 'Remember that I believe in you.' " From one perspective Dean cannot be trusted to keep his word or his loyalty. From another he can be counted on to turn up again and again with promise and exhilaration, to radiate his tremendous energy to others, to give them a good time just by being himself. On a deeper level Sal is responding to Dean not only as a modern American con man but as an archaic trickster whose primal energy crashes through all cultural bounds: "Bitterness, recriminations, advice, morality, sad-

ness—everything was behind him, and ahead of him was the ragged and ecstatic joy of pure being."

One Flew Over the Cuckoo's Nest

Ken Kesey's *One Flew Over the Cuckoo's Nest* (1962) makes that
same division of the world into believers and doubters, so that the
same confidence man appears alternately as the source of faith and
energy and as a reckless charlatan. And Randle Patrick McMurphy
bears a curious relationship to Dean Moriarty. Kerouac's novel obviously influenced Kesey, both in the hero's personality and in his
potential invigoration of others—"Whooee!" Then there is the uncanny power of prediction whereby Kesey's evocation of the literary
personality of McMurphy could summon Kerouac's own model,
Neal Cassady, into the life of Kesey himself. As Tom Wolfe records
it, "yes, Neal Cassady had turned up in the old cottage, like he had
just run out of the pages of *On the Road.*" McMurphy, to be sure, is
not Neal Cassady, nor is he even that close in overall style to Dean
Moriarty. For Tom Wolfe, McMurphy is simply Kesey himself,
trying to get others "to move off their own snug-harbor dead center" and out to "Edge City." The strange gravitation between Kerouac and Cassady and Kesey is rather to be explained by their common attraction to centers of energy, buoyancy, and faith. The
imaginations producing Dean Moriarty and R. P. McMurphy were
guided by the same cultural heritage, the same values, the same
basic icon of the confidence man. Kerouac draws from the slightly
more esoteric strain of that tradition—the philosophical biases of
Emerson and Whitman—whereas Kesey draws on pop culture
models—the gamblers, the western bullroarers, the auctioneers and
revivalists and sideshow barkers. But the core is the same.

When Kesey divides the world into believers and doubters, he is,
like Jefferson, Emerson, and William James, celebrating strength,
health, and bigness, and associating them with faith. "Society
everywhere," says Emerson, "is in conspiracy against the manhood
of every one of its members." Kesey dramatizes that premise by
figuring the modern world as a mental hospital, the function of
which is to keep the patients docile and to convince them that they
need help. The men on the ward are rabbits because they believe
they are rabbits, or more precisely, they doubt that they are men.
The modern issue of psychological maladjustment is thus recast in
nineteenth-century terms as a deficiency of personal faith and inward energy. The mission of the hero as man of confidence is to

bring faith and energy to the loonies and thus to convince them that they are sane and healthy after all.

But before turning to Randle Patrick McMurphy as con-man hero, I want to take up a disturbing implication of the way in which both Kerouac and Kesey divide believers from doubters. It has to do not only with the place of women in these novels but with the whole relationship of women to the cultural heritage of confidence men. Emerson's phrase "conspiracy against the manhood" is politer than McMurphy's phrase "ball-cutters," but they amount to the same thing, and no matter how much we allow "emasculation" to be merely a metaphor of *human* diminishment, the root of the matter is a threat to men. All the patients in McMurphy's ward are men, and the dominating power against them, the embodiment of social forces, is one of the most misogynist-inspired creatures in our literature, Big Nurse. Throughout *On the Road* as well the social complications and threats that Dean must periodically flee are governed by the presence of women and the issue of whether men have any responsibility toward them. It is the "ladies" who attack him most vociferously at his nadir in San Francisco. Insofar as both Dean and McMurphy need to stir others off dead-center and loosen them from socially constraining assumptions, the inhibiting forces are associated with women.

One way to be con men of their style is to con woman after woman and, by turning them to mere objects of conquest, to declare one's independence of them and of the social entanglements they represent. The con man also needs to keep independent of affectional ties. "No one to *care* about," says the narrator of McMurphy, "which is what makes him free enough to be a good con man." Women, in other words, are associated with all the forces of Doubt. They expect one to be responsible for one's actions, to consider their practical consequences, to keep one's promises literally. They expect one's affection to continue and to nourish a sense of personal responsibility within a socially respectable pattern of life. To put such emasculating issues behind, to turn from practical matters to visionary ones, to become a Man again by faith is thus implicitly to escape women.

There are, to be sure, some confidence women—Mary Baker Eddy being one of the most impressive and multifaceted—but not very many. And part of the reason is the dialectical position of women in relation to the stereotypical con man. Kerouac and Kesey simply bring to a blatant extreme what was there all along—women in the background representing the normalcy *against* which the confidence man is defined. Exploited women form the necessary support for free-wandering con men, defining a "home" to return to and representing the practical, conventional demands that one must periodically escape. And although they may be foolishly conned in minor ways—Tom Sawyer's tricks on Aunt Polly or Neal Cassady's quick seduction of a bewildered girl on a bus ride—they are at core the most rigid of doubters, for they cannot rise to the purer visionary faith that ostensibly justifies and transfigures the more squalid acts of the con man. It is still possible to read confidence men as *human* abstractions rather than *male* ones and thus to see how the values and gambits and faiths they represent can be applicable to women as well as men. But some authors—Kerouac and Kesey among the most striking—make it very difficult to forget that when a con man brings others energy and faith, he is restoring their MANhood.

To point out such a limitation, however, does not exhaust our job, for unless we go on to see exactly how attractive the literary con man can be, we will underestimate the force and complexity of the traditions he represents. Thus while recognizing what is wrong with McMurphy and with what he stands for, we must also acknowledge how impressive and ranging a con man he can be. He is the jack-of-all-trades, keeping flexible, running and dodging the forces of history, proving that "a moving target is hard to hit." He keeps clear of social habits and determinations by his very multiplicity, "logging, gambling, running carnival wheels, traveling lightfooted and fast, keeping on the move so much that the Combine never had a chance to get anything installed." Like Neal Cassady and Augie March, he cannot keep still. He talks, winks, and swaggers like a car salesman or a sideshow barker, and he loosens up his listeners as an auctioneer does before the bidding starts. He is also a gamesman, and Big Nurse characterizes him from the start as a "manipulator." McMurphy doesn't deny it but prides himself on being "a top-notch con man" who knows and plays on exactly what the mark wants. He contains the whole range of con-man styles from rogue-survivor to booster, from carnival gambler and capitalist to Jeffersonian bringer of faith: "Nobody's gonna convince me I can't do something till I try it." And his effects are as ambivalent as the protean tradition he embodies—no one is fully conned by him, but everyone smirks about what he pulls off. No one is sure whether he's crazy or simply playacting, but they "get a big kick out of going along with him."

McMurphy's specialty is fast talk. His spiels show the same frantic variation of subject as Dean's and the same continuing energy, like a dynamo. The voice itself is often more important than what he says. He makes the institutional walls ring with his early morning singing, and he keeps his individual voice playing at a high enough level to compete with the electronic circuitry and taped-in music of the hospital. But the voice is also full of promise. When he wants to encourage his auditors he talks like a rollicking auctioneer, "spinning his tale about how it would be." And along with the energy and promise, there is also in McMurphy's talk a ready resistance to control. In a world easily made submissive by complicated assumptions and restraints, his "brassy talk" defines an alternative.

But the world that McMurphy stumbles into in the psychiatric ward is more complicated than Dean Moriarty's, and the conflict of believers and doubters turns into an actual contest. It is, first of all, a world like that of Goffman's *Presentation of Self*. The patients and staff are self-consciously engaged in collective performances, they fear "performance disruption," and they are made timid by loyalty to the show. The haste with which Harding and others attempt to restore the official script—the analytic language of psychotherapy—after McMurphy calls the group meeting a "pecking party," illustrates their devotion to the fiction and their fear of an alternative reality. In such a context McMurphy's frankness and swagger, his Old West self-reliance, could be just the therapy to restore the victims of mutual fabrication to a sense of themselves. But there is a twist. In Goffman's world the performance is all. In *One Flew Over the Cuckoo's Nest*, as in Eric Berne's *Games People Play*, the performance is merely the mask of a deeper set of games. And these games are in the end deadly. The strategies of psychotherapy dress out a raw confrontation of power, and if one disrupts the performance too violently, that power can be exercised through electric shock or even lobotomy. The narrator's seemingly paranoid descriptions simply translate the action from the terms of the accepted scenario to the actualities of power play: "For forty-five minutes they been chopping a man to pieces, almost as if they enjoyed it." In such a context, the Wild West showdown is out of place, and McMurphy quickly learns that he "is going to be cagey after all."

Believers and doubters are thus regrouped, for the doubters timidly believe in the value of the collective performance while the believers boldly state that it is a sham. And the two parties engage in a contest. As in *The Confidence-Man* "the rules we play by" are that as long as we keep composure and self-control, we can insinuate anything to try to make the opponent lose face. The cowboy hero with the quick draw needs to become the con-man hero with "a trigger-quick mind," and McMurphy not only accepts the challenge but characteristically plans to turn it to profit by betting that he can get Big Nurse's goat. Overtly the contest between Mc-Murphy and Big Nurse is a personal challenge—who can make the other lose face? Beneath the barbs and innuendoes is a battle of power, individual energy challenging institutional forces. And in a broader sense the competing parties represent opposing attitudes toward human nature. Big Nurse expertly plays on hidden weaknesses, like Billy Bibbit's fear of his mother's opinion. She regards McMurphy's brashness as self-serving pretense. Her doubt of human strength is so great that it becomes a rigid belief in the opposite: "He is simply a man and no more, and is subject to all the fears and all the cowardice and all the timidity that any other man is subject to." McMurphy, in contrast, believes that timidity is merely superficial acceptance of the collective performance. Like Jefferson and Emerson, he looks beneath the deaf-and-dumb shows, the rabbitlike docility, to the secret strength residing in all people, and his interest as a man of confidence is in how to tap this hidden power in the other men on the ward. Thus the contest quickly shifts ground from personal barbs to collective manipulation. With the loonies as a test case, the issue is which view of human nature is right. Big Nurse will try to prove that the men are weak, and McMurphy, against collective odds, institutional machinery, and long-settled habits of docility, will try to prove them strong. Or looked at from a neutral starting point, Big Nurse and the hospital want to diminish the selves of the inmates—"cure," "adjust," "control"—whereas McMurphy wants to expand them.

The plot of the novel traces the stages of this contest, with its steadily shifting terms, its changing issues, its raising of the stakes. As Kesey reveals the intricacies of institutional control, he is also exploring the range of ways in which the confidence man figures as an alternative. For with each alteration of the game, "confidence man" assumes new connations, and McMurphy himself is subtly drawn back and forth from braggart to exploiter to collective hero to scapegoat to saint.

Part I ends with his first genuine victory when he turns the pseudo-democracy of ward decisions to something more like real democracy by getting a majority vote to watch the World Series on television and then leading a collective put-on in cheering before a blank TV screen. And the confirming detail is that Chief Bromden, assumed deaf and dumb, casts the tie-breaking vote, first saying to himself that McMurphy must have wired his arm to make it rise and then admitting (which was McMurphy's whole point) that he lifted it himself.

But the triumph is brief, for Big Nurse sets about to undermine the heroic front McMurphy now wears to the men. Her secret is time. Once McMurphy learns that she personally determines the length of his commitment, he becomes edgy and appears frightened and selfish to the others. What began as play has turned to a matter of life and freedom for McMurphy, and the first result is that he becomes self-regarding. When he learns, however, that most of the inmates, unlike himself, were voluntarily committed, that they are afraid of freedom, he comes into a new phase of confidence. The swagger and boldness return, but instead of simply radiating one man's spirit, they now become self-consciously exemplary gestures. With Whitman's representative brashness in tearing doors from their hinges, and with Thoreau's enspiriting reminder that there is a fork in the road where others only see a gap in the paling, Mc-Murphy puts his hand through the Nurses' Station glass to get a pack of cigarettes, as if for a really confident man the rules didn't exist at all.

In Part III of the novel, McMurphy has implicitly accepted re-sponsibility for the other inmates. His challenge is to blow them back up to full size. In this part of the novel, Big Nurse is in the background; in the foreground, especially during the fishing trip, is McMurphy's most overt radiation of the confidence man's energy to those around him—"his relaxed, good-natured voice doled out his life for us to live." Not only is he practically sacrificing himself (each gambit that irritates Big Nurse will prolong his commitment), but he seems to be more and more exhausted by the effort of invig-orating others, as if his energy were literally being transferred.

Once the inmates return to Big Nurse's domain, however, the image of McMurphy as self-sacrificing, heroic builder of confidence gives way to the alternate image of a confidence man as self-serving exploiter. Why would a "seasoned con" risk a longer stay in the hospital? Why has all the money in the ward gravitated to Mc-Murphy? Big Nurse raises those questions, but there is ample ground in the men's own suspicions for the questions to grow and become serious. Even Chief Bromden comes around to interpreting McMurphy's moves as a classic con game when McMurphy builds up the bets about whether one man can lift the control panel (a feat he has already secretly seen the Chief do). The point is that Mc-Murphy really does intend to profit by his exploits; he even boasts about the fact when challenged by the other inmates. He is not a Simon-pure self-abnegating hero but a confidence man whose mo-tives and appeal are ambivalent. Since he has kept his promise (by training and encouraging the Chief to restore his size and strength), why can't he profit by it as well? Haven't the inmates, as Harding argues, got their money's worth each time they were fleeced? It is because of such ambivalence that the conflict of belief and doubt continues so long and so urgently. To *believe in* McMurphy (like believing in Dean Moriarty) is to affirm inner strength and to rise above petty suspicions; to worry over his profit, to mistrust his motives, to see "confidence man" as exploitive charlatan is also to doubt human strength. If the belief is strong enough, it will coexist with a knowledge of the gambler's gains, just as the boldest confidence men can proudly confess to profiteering and make it part of their appeal. When McMurphy learns that the inmates do not yet have this kind of belief in him, that they view his winning with lingering suspicion, he moves beyond the con game entirely for the final, direct, brutal, self-destroying challenge to collective power.

It is thus essential to Kesey's representation of the confidence man that he be engaged *in a story*, and this is Kesey's major difference from Kerouac. Dean Moriarty's experiences and effects could go on and on because he embodies chiefly a style, an attitude, a vision, a set of continuing possibilities. McMurphy, on the other hand, is in a contest. The significance of his character is enmeshed in a complicated plot. Because of this, *One Flew Over the Cuckoo's Nest* provides implicitly much more commentary than *On the Road* about opposing forces and the sometimes crippling relations between them. Dean is a "hero" in the modern sense of embodying a style to be envied and emulated. McMurphy is a "hero" in the more traditional sense of engaging in a heroic action.

There is another side to his heroism as well, and we can get at it through Emerson. Like Bellow and Kerouac, Kesey is bringing Emersonian doctrines into the contemporary period. But instead of characterizing an omnivorous, detached jack-of-all-trades or hinting at the Oneness beyond all riotous angelic particulars, he picks up the popular theme of self-reliance and the motif of the Fall of Man from magnificent divinity to weakened conformist. The potential power of Randle Patrick McMurphy is that, as in the case of Emerson's heroes, all others feel like him deep inside. The buried king, the lost giant, is still there. Chief Bromden may feel small but in actuality he is enormous, and McMurphy sees it at once. The Chief, in turn, responds to McMurphy as to a full-sized man—he wants to touch and to share that power. And if McMurphy is "always *winning* things," from Emerson's perspective and Kesey's as well, such winning is a representative gesture. The ultimate money's worth that the inmates can get for being fleeced is the feeling that something better within themselves is also the winner, than an act of faith is an act of strength.

It is in this virtually Emersonian sense that McMurphy is a hero. He acts out the bigness, the energy, the self-reliance that is there in everyone. This is why the book turns more and more from Mc-Murphy's own personality to the uses that are made of him, the legends that grow up around him. Big Nurse is forced to keep McMurphy on the Ward instead of sending him off to Disturbed, because the legends grow too fast in his absence. And Chief Brom-den recognizes near the end what McMurphy must have felt all along, how the hungry, weakened faces of the men pull and drain at a strong man. Their collective needs force McMurphy to wink and grin and laugh long after the humor has been parched between the electrodes. McMurphy now has his own role to play out, his legend to live through, and the Confident Man needs to persist in the never-ending battle with institutional shrinkers even when the individual Randle Patrick McMurphy has been lobotomized into a "crummy sideshow fake."

This is why Chief Bromden needs to kill McMurphy's shell so as to keep the legend from being spoiled, to keep the men from learn-ing the lesson taught by Snowden in *Catch-22*, "The spirit gone, man is garbage." Like Nick Carraway and Sal Paradise, Chief Bromden is both narrator and high priest of the confidence man as cultural deity. He is the primary recipient of McMurphy's energy, the agent who most clearly registers the best effects of the con man as hero. In passing from deaf-and-dumb, fog-enveloped Chronic to actor in Ward games to giant who literally takes the controls into his own hands, throws them through the mesh of artificial regula-tions, and runs free into the countryside, the Chief enacts the major character transformation that is McMurphy's gift, but he goes be-yond Nick and Sal in not merely recording his own vacillations of faith and doubt but in indicating that there are *two realities*. The Chief is paranoid. He believes that the Combine installs control de-vices in people, that the hospital staff spreads fog through the vents when the patients are difficult, that Big Nurse can swell up to three times her size and strength when angry. Such visions confirm his insanity and suggest his unreliability. They also confirm his weak-ness. "Combine" thinking is a symptom of smallness. He recog-nizes that McMurphy is trying to drag him out of the fog, where he feels safe, into the open where he'd be "easy to get at." Mc-Murphy's therapy (as against the style practiced by Big Nurse) would eliminate such thinking and restore a true perception of per-sonal responsibility. Thus the formal progress of the book from heavily paranoiac fantasies to more and more accurate accounts of events shows indirectly the therapeutic value of McMurphy, and even locally we can see how the Chief's fog is dispelled each time McMurphy starts talking.

But Chief Bromden's paranoid fantasies are true. What seems distorted and insane at first, gradually reveals itself as keen perception of how institutional power works. There may not be a Combine and They may not have installed control devices, but there may as well be and They may as well have. What seems hallucination is often simply the Chief's narration of the actual game plan instead of the script that disguises it from the others. The fog is more than merely a metaphoric way of indicating how the regimen of drugs and rules affects a mind. And the *belief* in a Combine is one sure indication how institutional codes and procedures shape the individual's view of the world. In other words, McMurphy may be right that individuals have untold strength inside if they only dare to tap it, but what he is up against is just as real as he is, a reality of a different order. The Chief is a valuable narrator precisely because he can perceive accurately in both modes. He can recognize the forces in the modern world that make fantasy the best approach to fictional realism. He can see why McMurphy can never win once and for all against such a reality. But he can also respond to the old-fashioned individualism of McMurphy, the world of heroes and challenges and will power. As his own narration veers back and forth from dream vision and conspiratorial fantasy to personal gambits and challenges, he indicates formally how these alternative realities come together.

The story of McMurphy is in one sense a story of triumph, for he succeeds in drawing out the potential power in several people who believed they were rabbits. But in the personal sense it is a story of heroic defeat, a gesture that may have some of the magnificence of Ahab's defiance (recalled by McMurphy's white-whale underwear) but also the inevitability of personal failure before so persistent and ubiquitous a force. It is not a story of survival, and McMurphy does not represent survivor styles of conning. But Chief Broom does. Long before McMurphy's arrival, he has devised a mode of getting along in a threatening world, even to the extent of ferreting out the secrets of staff power. Like Ellison's Invisible Man, he has learned racially the styles of invisibility. After recognizing that whites consistently treat Indians as if they were deaf and dumb, he learns to mirror their preconceptions to his own advantage, being allowed, for instance, to sweep a room in which the staff is discussing the patients and mapping strategies. But such survival is minimal; the Chief retains his perception and his memory but hardly his self-respect or volition. The form of the novel brings a booster-hero into the life of a con man-survivor, and the effect of McMurphy on the Chief is to make him just big enough, self-respecting enough, confident enough to run like hell.

12

IT'S JUST A GAME

All that we reckoned settled shakes and rattles; and literature, cities, climates, religions, leave their foundations and dance before our eyes.

—*Emerson*

He puts me in mind of one of these cars running along the street with a radio in it. You can't make out what it is saying and the car aint going anywhere in particular and when you look at it close you see that there aint even anybody in it.

—*Faulkner*

Although the style of Dean Moriarty and R. P. McMurphy—based in personal faith and radiant energy—differs from the shiftier, more survival-oriented strategies of Yossarian, the Invisible Man, and Augie March, they all share a sense of playfulness. Confronting a world already made, a world teeming with fabrications, they manage to live in it by turning it to play, ridiculing its assumptions, making its rules into games, spinning it on their tongues. They are masters of the put-on, a style of conning that combines mimicry, game playing, and many-layered perception. "It never occurs to [them]," as a disillusioned acquaintance of Dean Moriarty charges, "that life is serious and there are people trying to make something decent out of it instead of just goofing all the time." Indeed not. Not when they know the collective distortions of "seriousness" and "decency" in a factitious world. Instead, they become, like Dean, the HOLY GOOF. Play keeps them detached; they can join in the scripts of a made-up world without being overwhelmed. But play has that element of holiness as well. It keeps them faithful to their own inwardness, and it provides occasions for the release and celebration of personal energy.

Playing games is essential to the con man's art. The more mastery he shows, the more he turns reality itself into a game. (Not only is "confidence man" an American coinage; the phrase "confidence game"—so well expressing the mixture of promise and play—is an American usage, in contrast with the British idiom "confidence trick.") But such play is risky. Those who perceive everything as a game walk on the edge of vacancy. As modern boosters like Moriarty and McMurphy, riding high on their own promises, can collapse at any time in despair and indifference, so the pure game-player might lose all sense of meaning and turn cynic or nihilist. The proliferation of game patterns in American popular culture during the last decade or two increases the temptation. On the one hand, the heightened appeal of the gimmick, such as an ex-con teaming up with a cop to trap criminals by con games, quickly gives way to a sense of the emptiness behind it, thus shortening the distance between exhilaration and nihilism. On the other hand, as game playing is absorbed by the popular media, it loses its distinction as a style. When it was possible to watch *Rockford Files*, ring-around-the-collar ads, and Watergate hearing excerpts within a single two-hour period, it became more and more difficult to stay aware of the differences between them. This chapter surveys some versions of pure game playing in the last twenty years, first noting the nature of the attraction it has had in American pop culture, and then exploring the ways in which John Barth keeps his game-players in *Sot-Weed Factor* from falling into the abyss.

Game Playing as Pop Culture

If Goffman's *Presentation of Self in Everyday Life* records the most desperate extensions of con games in public—the collective performance in which people are caught up without control or initiative—Eric Berne's transactional analysis restores the sense of play, of choice, of individual adeptness. *Games People Play* (1964) is the master instance of pop psychology, the skillful crossing of science with popular culture, and the grounds of its popularity reach into the same American values that produced a confidence culture. First of all, there is a special quality of language that employs fast talk. To say that Berne uses racy colloquialisms as a way of reaching a mass audience, as in his very title, gets at only half the case. For these blunt, accessible, often witty namings of psychological strategies ("Now I've Got You, You Son of a Bitch") are played off against a highfalutin "scientese," an elevated diction that connotes authority, respectability, expertise. The result has something of the appeal of the King and the Duke's garbled Shakespeare, the veneration of learning, the mockery of learning, and the delight at turning intimidating knowledge into a game: "That every individual (including children, the mentally retarded and schizophrenics) is capable of objective data processing if the appropriate ego state can be activated (neopsychic functioning). Colloquially: Everyone has an Adult."

In a similar fashion, Berne appeals, as do Franklin and Poe, to a cultural delight in breaking down complex actions, feelings, states of mind into simple, formulary steps. The entangled personality, which Freud could not schematize without shadings and overlappings, reappears in distinct segments (Parent-Adult-Child) and easily followed transactions. And the knotty socio-psychological situations in which we often find ourselves turn out to be easily diagrammed (and thus, by implication, easily controlled). The diagrams themselves give away the basic game that Berne is playing, for as we look at three circles in a line with shifting arrows to indicate which "ego state" is in play, we are witnessing one of the simplest and most durable of cons, the shell game. The gamesman sets up a situation, and the trick is to figure out which shell is hiding the pea, which ego state is really "it." The potentially threatening uncertainty of social transactions is thus converted to play.

And behind these conversions of complex to simple, of threatening to do-able, is one of the most persistent bases of American confidence, the how-to-do-it approach. What Berne likes about transactional analysis is that it adapts more readily than orthodox psychoanalysis to self-examination, as if Freud were being recast by Franklin, Emerson, and William James. Berne develops, both in *Games People Play* and in his later essays, lectures, and pep-talks,[1] a brassy tone designed to enspirit others with his own assurance: "So that's the way to practice psychotherapy. Like you find a splinter and you pull it out." Such confidence building—the stress on what you can do—is essential to Berne's whole self-help approach, for what he sees deeper inside people are winners and losers. He readily identifies psychotherapy with poker in that they are games of skill which some people believe are games of luck. The winners believe in the skill; they want to cure or be cured. The losers believe it is merely luck; they continue in a losing situation because they don't really want to be cured. Like Jefferson and William James, Berne is out to enspirit the winners, not to console the losers.

To emphasize the do-able is thus to emphasize the winnable. The exasperating psychological encounter turns out to be a game in which one wins or loses. Like the ulterior contests in Kesey's Cuckoo's Nest and the exchanges aboard Melville's *Fidèle*, it requires wit, knowledge of the game in play, shrewdness about motives, and detachment. Although Berne believes that people can move, at times, beyond games (he defines intimacy with Melvillean indirectness as "a candid, game-free relationship"), the emphasis of his therapy is rather on learning to play the games well. "The criterion of a true 'game cure' is that the former Alcoholic should be able to drink socially without putting himself in jeopardy. The usual 'total abstinence' cure will not satisfy the game analyst." What keeps people from playing well is either that the ulterior transaction remains unconscious (they don't know the game in play) or that one ego state "contaminates" another (they don't play with sufficient detachment). Psychological health is restored when they become good game players: "they now had the option of playing or not playing this game, as they saw fit, where formerly they had no choice but to be drawn in. This option was the net therapeutic gain." In fact, if the social pleasures and individual payoffs outweigh the complexity of motives, and if the players can acknowledge their motives without cynicism, the game is a "good game." Another way of putting it is that socially problematic encounters *are* games as soon as all the players recognize them as such and start to play for fun.

In all these ways Eric Berne's transactional analysis is the psychological theory of a confidence culture just as James's pragmatism is the philosophical theory. And Berne expresses the fact himself with an overtness characteristic of the modern period. He draws examples, theory, and terminology from David Maurer's *The Big Con*, defining a game as "a series of moves with a snare, or 'gimmick.' " By the time he updates the game theory in *What Do You Say After You Say Hello?*, he has made psychological transactions indistinguishable from the gambits of "Yellow Kid" Weil and *The Sting*, showing like Melville what a potent model the con game can be:

> Since an ulterior transaction means that the agent pretends to be doing one thing while he is really doing something else, all games involve a con. But a con only works if there is a weakness it can hook into, a handle or "gimmick" to get hold of in the respondent, such as fear, greed, sentimentality, or irritability. After the "mark" is hooked, the player pulls some sort of switch in order to get his payoff.

Such an easy, delighted acknowledgment of how amusing con games are has also been characteristic of popular entertainment in the seventies. The gimmick of several TV series—such as *Rockford Files, The Switch, Feather and Father*—is to employ con games in the solving or punishing of crimes. By making the best con artists "good guys," these series free themselves from moral issues in order to play on the public's appetite for diddles. A more complex and interesting case is the Academy-Award winning picture of 1973, *The Sting*. The same pair of male buddies—Paul Newman and Robert Redford—who had glamorized Old West outlawry and turned it to play in *Butch Cassidy and the Sundance Kid*, here glamorize the underworld of big-time con games and reveal the persistent delight with which Americans have greeted skilled con men. Again part of the gimmick is to free movie-watchers from moral qualms by sentimentalizing the issues. The basic plot turns on revenge for a victimized black family man. The protagonists are midwestern small-time con artists who boldly take on the eastern syndicate. Their assistants are sentimentally attractive, each secretly a good or kindly person who has been exploited. Paul Newman plays a con artist without an action, a knowledgeable and skilled manipulator who needs a good motive to pull together and use his ranging talents. And the chief examples of con work in the film involve victims far more sordid and deceitful than the con artist. But such stylizations to evade moral judgment are merely the film's trimming. The core is good gamesmanship, which is self-justifying. In contrast with the police, who are unattractive heavies, slow-moving and easily tricked, and the syndicate operatives, who represent an amassment of joyless power, the central con men are quick-witted, nimble in spirit and movement, playful. And although the revenge motif, coupled with the syndicate's effort to kill Robert Redford, give the plot an edge of anticipation not directly related to con games, the real point is to win by skillful conning. The closing exchange confirms the point: a successful con may not finally be enough, but it comes awfully close.

There were several popular con-man films in 1973: *The Sting, Paper Moon, The Heartbreak Kid*. The clustering may not have been coincidental, for con games were very much in the public eye as the real meaning of the 1972 presidential election began to be unfolded. And as if the *fact* of political trickery were not bad enough in itself, both the operations and the operatives were being exposed as ugly, graceless, and mean. If Tom Sawyer had, as Mark Twain predicted, conned his way into the presidency, he would at least have done it with flair. Thus while the political activity surrounding Richard Nixon was tarnishing the image of con men and of presidents, too, gradually forcing Americans to believe that they would actually prefer an honest chief executive, the popular culture was busily restoring the lightness, skill, detachment, and play that properly belong to the confidence man as American hero.

The Sot-Weed Factor

The ultimate instance of fictional gamesmanship, in which history itself appears as an entanglement of con games, is John Barth's *The Sot-Weed Factor* (1960). And since Barth uses contemporary perceptions of open-ended play in order to retell the story of the settling of America, showing that in the end was the beginning, his book makes an appropriate conclusion to my study. The mysterious author of the 1708 poem *The Sot-Weed Factor*, whose name Ebenezer Cook may have been a pseudonym, provides the occasion for Barth's reinvention of one stage in the inventing of "America." Barth's Ebenezer, a dilettante and would-be poet, is forced to leave England in 1694 to administer his father's tobacco plantation in the colony of Maryland. He begins in utter aimlessness, assumes a tentative identity as "Poet Laureate of Maryland," crosses the Atlantic, and enters on a series of adventures while trying to find and to possess his promised estate. In outline, this is the story of the making of an "American," the transition from Old World to New. Furthermore, some of Barth's major issues—the search for a purpose, the constant fabrication of identity, the dislocation of historical "facts" from their meanings—suggest that coming to terms with the New World is also coming to terms with contemporary experience. The theme of promise appears in its root form, the arrival of the innocent in a country that refreshes credulity and that can be initially perceived only through the rubrics of fantastical voyage literature, the golden cities and willing slaves. And side by side with the imaginative possibilities is the actual world of imposture.

Barth's New World is colonial, and this is essential to its modes of relationship. Far from the mother-land—the seat of authority, certainty, reliable measures of people—the colonies are open to fakery. The standards and fashions are determined in a distant land, whereas in the immediate foreground people have to guess about each other's credentials. They are systematically removed from authenticity, and they learn to behave accordingly. Thus from Barth's perspective the settling of the New World is not a confrontation with a new landscape, new peoples, a fresher atmosphere. Rather it is something that *happens to* Old World relationships, a sliding around of old habits and beliefs. Ebenezer Cooke's most enthusiastic poetry about the New World can only be written when he has not yet seen it, when it can exist simply as an imagined reconstruction of the past. Similarly, he is *named* "Poet Laureate of Maryland" by Lord Baltimore, but this is not the same thing as *being* Poet Laureate, for Baltimore has lost his own credentials and can only hope to become proprietor again sometime in the future. Furthermore, as we learn later, "Lord Baltimore" was not even Lord Baltimore but Ebenezer's tutor in disguise. Nevertheless, Ebenezer Cooke's dubious credentials as Poet Laureate are lost, stolen, recovered, copied, and forged, quite as if they were "real." Thus New World identity emerges chiefly as an element of play introduced into Old World positions.

Such displacements are even more obvious when one considers what happens to personal relationships as soon as people leave England. Drawing on the familiar world of picaresque narrative where class lines are fluid and identities are repeatedly mistaken, Barth carries the conditions to an extreme and projects them as the nature of the New World. Thus the opening gambit as Ebenezer leaves England is for his valet, Bertrand Burton, to pose as the master and to carry it off so successfully that Ebenezer himself is forced to play the servant. In part Bertrand succeeds through sheer brass and talent for mime: "There's no great trick to this *gentleman* business, that I can see; any man could play the part that hath a ready wit and keeps his eyes and ears open." But the real secret is public uncertainty. While Ebenezer argues that a "gentleman" can be known by another through a thousand signs—that class, in effect, is fate—Bertrand recognizes an actual open-endedness in which "gentlemen" do not behave like gentlemen and can be easily gulled.

If the Atlantic passage introduces the theme of social fluidity, the arrival at Maryland merely compounds it. The first social bargain Ebenezer Cooke strikes is to exchange a sonnet for passage across the Choptank River. When the trip proves much easier than the boatman had indicated in stating his fare, Ebenezer will not be outdone in trickery, for he admits the sonnet was not of his own making. And then to get the best in a contest of gullings, he adds that it wasn't even a sonnet; to which the boatman replies that the body of water they just crossed was not the Choptank River either. Such trickery occurs everywhere in Barth's Maryland. A redemptioner of indentured servants is quite likely to be sold as a servant himself when a clever servant manages to exchange positions. And courts of law do not correct the swindles, they provide a more fertile field for them. In a summary picture of New World land transactions Ebenezer Cooke buys from the judge the right to pass judgment at the first trial he sees, and what he manages to do is legally transfer his own estate to a scoundrel.

As a fictional gamesman, Barth is especially interested in the intellectual consequences of such fluidity. All theories of identity are systematically disrupted. Henry Burlingame, the tutor, presents Ebenezer early in the book with familiar reasons to doubt the memory, the subjective sense of who is who: it has breaks, it can't be proved, it is selective, it colors facts, and it may lapse entirely. But sportive argument has less force than sportive experience, and as Ebenezer finds his own principles and integrity repeatedly subject to the trickster impulses of his self-interest, he begins to feel that Burlingame is right. Despite having staked his identity on being Virgin, Poet, Laureate, he learns to play the valet when he is threatened with walking the plank if he persists in claiming to be the Laureate; he augments the game when he learns that the villainous Coode is looking for the Laureate; he deserts his love Joan Toast and breaks his pledge to his sister Anna when his slippery ethics provide him with rationalizations. And he is surrounded by people who behave the same way: "The world's a happy climate for imposture."

Burlingame's point, however, is not to malign the world but to teach a new way of confronting it. "I wished only to establish that all assertions of *thee* and *me*, e'en to oneself, are acts of faith, impossible to verify." That clear echo of Melville's *The Confidence-Man* is no accident. Barth's novel not only restates Melville's thesis that all New World social relations are acts of faith, but it draws from the situation some of Melville's philosophical implications. Like Melville, Barth shows how one must be hypothetical in such circumstances, ready to play with ideas and selves instead of being fixed in principle. Indeed, the adventures of Ebenezer Cooke, for all his hilarious outward entanglements, are chiefly inward—radical shiftings of opinion, knowledge, anticipation, belief. If the world about him is a razzle-dazzle place, his inner image of it is even slipperier, and one of his special talents is to multiply alternatives in his imagination. For any given predicament, he can produce a catalogue of diverse feelings, each with different consequences, as when he fails to carry out his attack on the maiden in the rigging during the Rape of the *Cyprian* (Book II, Chapter 15) and learns that the giant pirate who did swive her got deadly French pox for it. Ebenezer not only lists six contradictory feelings about what happened but also mitigates the guilt of his earlier desire by learning that the woman was no virgin to begin with and then, since he *thought* she was a virgin, shows how his desire to join her in pollution only augmented his original purity of motive. Such ethical and emotional variety becomes, for Ebenezer and for Barth, too, a game with paradoxes.

If daily life, in Melville's and Barth's New World, is carried on by games of confidence, reality itself is for Barth a series of fabrications, and history becomes indistinguishable from fiction. Like Melville's protagonist, Henry Burlingame is adept at leaping, hypothetically, from the immediate gambit to a larger and larger model:

> The difficulty is, e'en on the face of 'em the facts are dark—doubly so if you grant . . . that an ill deed can be done with good intent, and a good with ill; and triply if you hold right and wrong to be like windward and leeward, that vary with standpoint, latitude, circumstance, and time. History, in short, is like those waterholes I have heard of in the wilds of Africa: the most various beasts may drink there side by side with equal nourishment.

As Ebenezer Cooke approaches Maryland, he hears one version after another of the colony's past, and the parties in it keep sliding about in allegiance and implication. Thus the very mode of narration builds one's suspicion about "history," much as the local games keep one wary about "identity." Throughout the novel, Ebenezer has to assimilate staggering new sets of facts, and at the beginning of Part III Burlingame (now in the person of Nick Lowe) rearranges the very polar stars through which Maryland history could be arranged as a moral drama. Now the put-upon Lord Baltimore is projected as the arch-conspirator in a Catholic plot against the English, and the treacherous John Coode turns out to be a force for independence and resistance to evil. Such developments of the narrative reinforce the notion that reality itself is simply play.

How do you get on in a world like that? Barth's complex picture of the making of Americans suggests three fundamentally different strategies, and the novel shows them playing out against each other. The first response—the most facile and obvious—is that of Bertrand Burton, the valet. He takes what he can get. If moral ideals are in practice dispensable, if integrity serves merely as a ploy, if all people seem what they are not, then why shouldn't a clever mimic make the best of it and rise if he can by using whatever devices work? Bertrand's success at conning others depends not simply on his mimicry of manner but on his insights about what actually impresses people. He plays to their weaknesses and uncertainties, reading in them his own absence of scruples. When Ebenezer truthfully protests that the reason he refused to pay a hired whore was that he fell in love with her, and when he rightly denies having turned papist to please Lord Baltimore, Bertrand winkingly treats such principles as simply clever gambits for getting on in the world. It is his low estimate of others' motives that makes him assured in his practical conduct; he cons people through their weaknesses, not through his own strength. One of the standard assumptions about confidence men—and it often is applied to Melville's novel—is that they are radical cynics. Bertrand Burton has an important place in *The Sot-Weed Factor* because he is the perfect instance of cynicism. By projecting an outright cynic in his novel, Barth can thus indicate the cynic's limits—Bertrand is finally bound by what's available—and clarify that his two major con men, with their creative imaginations and relishing of possibility, represent a spirit far removed from cynicism.

Instead of simply accepting the actual decay of principle in an open-ended world and taking what one can get, it is possible to confront open-endedness in a more celebratory way. For Barth, a climate that is good for imposture is also good for invention, and one of the essential values linking his novel with Melville's is the power of imagination, the capacity to spin out new stories, alternative feelings, fresh principles, perhaps even new worlds. Much of the bulk of *The Sot-Weed Factor* comes from a series of bawdy comic stories, in direct narratives of the characters, in secret diaries they read, in history that they learn. Barth draws here on the old durable world of story, of Petronius and Boccaccio and Cervantes, and pays tribute to the playful tone and the energy of invention. His own characters swim "in an ocean of story." They are able rhetoricians and fabulators who can play upon the language for sheer pleasure. Ebenezer's exasperated command to his voluble valet could be taken as the book's motto: " 'Sheart, man, pass o'er the history and commence thy fabrications!" This spirit, manifested in the narrative energy of *The Sot-Weed Factor*, is what keeps the skepticism about historical "truth" from becoming a burden.

The chief celebrant of this view within the novel is Henry Burlingame III. Part of his radical difference from Bertrand appears in how they use mimicry. Bertrand can "pass for" a gentleman. Burlingame *becomes* Lord Baltimore, Peter Sayer, John Coode, Timothy Mitchell, Nicholas Lowe. In one remarkable scene near the end of the novel, his very facial features, expressions, and voice change before an assembled courtroom. Not only does he play roles with a specificity of imagination that leaves Bertrand bewildered, but he plays an astonishing variety of them as well. And his styles sum up those of a range of earlier confidence men. Like the Emersonian jack-of-all-trades, he plays many parts as a way of embracing the whole, arguing that alternative courses are but two paths to the same end. A "cosmophilist" who will not rest in any mere corner of the world, Burlingame can develop as much genuine enthusiasm as Emerson for the union of opposites, the love of the whole fabric of creation. But despite his projected existence in the late seventeenth century, he is as modern as Augie March in embracing the whole through intricate particularities, by entering into and thus loving the diverse quirky roles that add up to the world. When Burlingame early lost his innocence—his belief that the world would conform to his ideals—he did not turn cynical. He committed himself instead to the world as given, learned to worship the betraying snake, and longed to taste every fruit in the garden.

If the voracity of this approach links him with Emerson, the playfulness of it joins him with Melville's Confidence-Man, and he is closer to this figure than is any other character in contemporary literature. Both are seen from outside as mysterious characters who undergo such radical transmutations that one doubts the existence of an inner identity to string the beads together. Both revel in multiplicity. Both are master storytellers and game-players who can keep track of their moves as they shift games or leap from story to principle to metaphysics. And they are agents of our knowledge, showing what their worlds are like, not by exploiting them but by playing them out with restless energy and curiosity. What Ebenezer says of Henry Burlingame and one of his brothers applies to Melville's hero as well: "each in his own way, came rootless to the world we know; each hath a wondrous gift for grasping it, e'en a lust for 't, and manipulates its folk like puppeteers." What Burlingame represents is the possibility of pure, resilient, flexible living in an open-ended world. He is the endless seeker, the explorer of trial personalities, whose protean existence promises perfect mastery of his world.[2] His general love of the world and his specific, if at times ambivalent, personal love of Ebenezer give him an inwardness that we aren't exposed to in Melville's protagonist, yet both of them are in the end too mysteriously and too completely game-players to seem quite accessible as human models. Ebenezer puts the matter touchingly near the end: "my friend hath passed into realms of complexity beyond my compass, and I have lost him."

Henry Burlingame remains, nonetheless, a major influence on Ebenezer Cooke, for he tutors him in the ways of the world. And his central lesson, or rather strategy, is one that he taught early—to learn history by impersonation. When Ebenezer and his sister Anna were studying history with their tutor, they dramatized it and took on the various roles for play. In Ebenezer's mature life, actual history cannot be distinguished from what he learned as Burlingame's tutee, for most of the significant people he encounters in his adventures—Lord Baltimore, Timothy Mitchell, Nicholas Lowe—turn out to be his tutor in disguise. If this approach gives one, as it were, an inside view of historical action and builds a love of the world, it also has more troublesome consequences. On the one hand, it makes all actions and passions seem equally arbitrary and unreal. Ebenezer is as adept as Poe at imaginatively projecting sensations for a potential event—the feelings, say, of drowning—but he can no more believe in his own actual here-and-now immersion in it than he can ultimately believe in the Roman Empire. Similarly, Ebenezer comes to suspect that such historical figures as the arch-antagonists John Coode and Lord Baltimore *exist* only in Burlingame's impostures, as Rinehart in Ellison's novel exists only through the Invisible Man's impersonation of him. People are roles, and all is play.

On the other hand, playacting his way into history gives Ebenezer Cooke such a taste for multiplicity and such a keen awareness of alternative roles—professional, temperamental, philosophical—that he can see no reason to choose one instead of another. Confronted with choice, he freezes, and the more attractive the various options are, the more likely he is to be gagged and immobilized by them. Barth's fiction repeatedly deals with the problems that Alvin Toffler analyzes as a consequence of living in a society of overchoice—sixteen options for the style of a "common notebook"—and Ebenezer hovers over the Pit; the sheer variety of possible motions causes utter fixity.

What encourages Bertrand to be cynical and Burlingame to revel in multiplicity, thus threatens to keep Ebenezer Cooke stymied. Bertrand takes the first identity available; Burlingame explores so many identities as to enfold the whole; Ebenezer, disabled by equally attractive options, runs the risk of having no identity at all. What saves him is another aspect of New World possibility, the theme of promise. Ebenezer Cooke belongs as fully in the promissory tradition of American confidence men as Henry Burlingame does in the gamesman tradition. His way out of the abyss of inaction is to project an ideal role for himself. In the early chapters of *The Sot-Weed Factor* Ebenezer is moved about aimlessly from possibility to possibility, victimized by chance attractions because he has no impetus of his own. His story proper begins when a comic wager in a tavern—whether the silent man is a better poet and lover than is the glib talker—forces him into bed with the popular whore Joan Toast, and he rises from his own actual failure of performance to assume an ideal identity: he is Virgin and Poet. And when he talks to "Lord Baltimore" prior to leaving for his father's tobacco plantation in Maryland, he adds the third element to the fabrication—his Laureateship. In treating this episode and its effects, Barth reaffirms the power of the promissory mode. Like Whitman, Ebenezer Cooke identifies himself with the promised land that will be the ideal subject of the promised poem: "Only think on 't! A province, an entire people—all unsung! . . . 'Sblood, it dizzies me!" Like Jefferson, Cooper, and the promotional pamphleteers, he spins out the hyperbole of New World settlement: "The courage and perseverance of her settlers in battling barb'rous nature and fearsome salvage to wrest a territory from the wild and transform it to an earthly paradise!" And, like Franklin, he argues the practical utility of his own promissory description: "Moreover, 'twould paint the Province as she stands today in such glowing colors as to lure the finest families of England to settle there; 'twould spur the inhabitants to industry and virtue, to keep the picture true as I paint it. . . ."

Of course, Barth won't let such poppycock pass. Baltimore-Burlingame, on hearing it, spins out a counter-history of the province as "a string of plots, cabals, murthers, and machinations." And Ebenezer's subsequent experience of Maryland is so disillusioning that he finally cries out, "What glory, to be the singer of such a sewer!" and writes the first version of "The Sot-Weed Factor" as a damnation of New World behavior. But the ideal fabrication has its point. Although Ebenezer knows that his Laureateship is a fraud, or at best a mere promise, since Baltimore has no power to bestow it, he begins to act *as if* he really were a Laureate. The promised identity is as enabling to him as Franklin and William James had predicted. He assumes his new identity, feels the enthusiasm and inspiration of one who has scaled Parnassus, and turns from bumbling, reticent drifter to assertive and articulate poet. Even though he retches over the actual prospects and has "dank night doubts," he finds in his fictive identity the stimulus to real action, like Gatsby. He had learned from his tutor the game-player's strategy—to impersonate the actual. Now he takes identity and impetus from his own variant strategy—to impersonate the ideal. Thus in contrast with Bertrand's con-man-as-exploiter and Burlingame's con-man-as-game-master, Ebenezer Cooke exemplifies the Man of Confidence idealized, the self made over in a genuine and enduring Act of Faith.

Another way of looking at these three alternative approaches to an open-ended New World, is to see them as motivated, respectively, by cynicism, by experience, and by innocence. Part of Ebenezer's ideal identity, after all, is as Virgin, and his ideal subject is "a virgin territory." Ebenezer's innocence is one of the most fertile sources of comedy in the novel, partly because it leads him to such silly misreadings of events, partly because it subjects him to Burlingame's tricks, and partly because it is unreal—he would readily surrender his sexual virginity in several episodes if he only could. But he is innocent in more serious ways as well, and Barth is exploring the long-standing American preoccupation with innocence. Burlingame raises a question that troubles a great deal of American literature, especially in the nineteenth century: "But what on earth hath a virgin to sing of? . . . Yet 'tis a mystery to me, what ye'll sing of save your innocence."[3]

Barth, however, also knows the answer to this question—the virgin poet can sing of what will be. Promise Land, like the virgin's experience, exists *in the future*, and thus the innocent poet is its ideal singer. Ebenezer Cooke's verse projects an imagined future instead of interpreting actual occurrences. Reality depresses him. His poems are written before the experience they record; their function is "to describe the great event that lay ahead." If this makes them inaccurate, even unintentionally sarcastic, in relation to Maryland history, it also gives them another kind of realism. Ebenezer knows the general experience of anticipation that is so essential a part of New World history, and his innocence ratifies and prolongs that feeling. Such innocence is, in practice, destructive. Before Ebenezer can truly learn "what folly it is to judge ere ye know the facts," his ridiculous intervention on the side of "justice" in a Maryland law court victimizes Joan Toast (alias Susan Warren), his sister Anna, his father, his tutor, and himself. When he grasps this at the end of the novel, he regards innocence as a crime, "whereof the Knowledged must bear the burthen. There's the true Original Sin our souls are born in: not that Adam *learned*, but that he *had* to learn—in short, that he was innocent."

But regarded psychologically, that same innocence has another face. It makes Ebenezer radically impressible and open, like Augie March, to alternatives. The innocent exists prior to experience and thus prior to choice. His options are still open. His world is perpetual possibility. Paradoxically, the American Adam has something to do with the American con man after all. Once he has been disillusioned about his innocence because of its disastrous practical effects, Ebenezer works out an ethic for the poet that imaginatively unites virgin and game-player. The poet "must fling himself into the arms of life" but hide his heart away; he "must engage himself in whate'er world he's born to, but shake free of 't ere it shackle him." In aping the dress and manners of those about him, playing "at love, or learning, or money-getting, or government—aye, even at morals or metaphysic," he must always remember that it is "but a game played for the sport of 't." The poet's virginity is the gamesman's detachment. Tutored by the arts of Melville's Confidence-Man, the New World poet still preserves his innocence and indeed gives his tutor in turn something to live for, fictions that have tenfold the substance of one's own poor shade of a self. And as these two styles of American confidence men reinforce each other, gamesman–shape-shifter fusing with booster-idealist, they sum up the paradoxical tradition that produced Franklin and Emerson, Jefferson and Augie March, Whitman and Gatsby and Huck Finn—the tradition of confidence men busily renewing the New World.

Which may satisfy those who wish
to reach a conclusion or at least come to an ending

Aside from bringing this book full circle, back to Melville and back to origins, Barth's *Sot-Weed Factor* makes a fit conclusion in another sense. It represents a state of mind related to that in which I wrote the book, and thus it allows me to confront my own implication in it, to turn the critical apparatus around and focus it on my own situation. Melville was my starting point in the order of thought; he produced the model, and laid bare the essential transactions through which I could recognize how representative the confidence man was. But in the order of understanding, a Barthian state of mind came first. As Wallace Stevens's snowman needs a mind of winter to regard the icy landscape and not think of human misery in it, so one needs a gamesman's mind, a pure and untroubled relativism, to read *The Confidence-Man* and not be utterly appalled. Melville himself was so agonized by his insights that he shrouded his book in images of gloom and closed it with the protagonist snuffing the last light. He displaced and overlaid his subject with various religious-philosophical debates, and these in turn dominated earlier readings of the novel. What Barth represents esthetically and intellectually is something that has become more widespread socially during the last decade—an extreme relativism of mind and morals, an acceptance of multiplicity and pluralism that makes such anxieties as Melville's a matter of historical curiosity. The political equivalent of this state of mind is the capacity to find some humor in the story of Richard Nixon (remember him?).

What I am suggesting is that this book could not have been written or even contemplated in, say, the 1950s or the 1930s. Its "truths" are not permanent; I would recast that formulation by saying that its models are timely. It allows us some access to ourselves in the present and some fresh recognition of important traditions in the literature of our past, patterns of value that ultimately encouraged the very game-playing promotionalism in which we now find ourselves engrossed. The state of mind I have been talking about is given splendid articulation in Barth's novel; he allows us to trace its consequences and to play with its possibilities. It has its roots, however, not in imaginative literature but in developments of the material modes of production in our society. Why, during the writing of this book, did I inadvertently find myself imagining dust jackets for it? Why, in his most absorbed and sacramental moments of play, does my son *repackage* his Star Wars action figures, as if the setting in which they truly belonged was not an imagined space venture but the concrete plastic and word-image and trademark wrappings in which he had first seen them and which he now painstakingly and inventively reduplicates with shirt-cardboards and Saran-Wrap? In a rapidly changing social structure, children inhabit the new world first, and I have learned from his bolder gestures that he and I are doing the same thing, that we think and feel in ways patterned by a consumer-oriented state of the productive forces in which the central thing produced is packaging.

The material packaging of toys and books is of course only one phase of such production. The proliferating displays of items in markets, the promotion of them in advertising, the swelling claims made about such non-"objects" as movies and rock concerts and presidential campaigns are closely related elements of a packaging economy. And even in the "detached" world of academia, curricula more and more resemble supermarkets down the aisles of which students push their shopping carts in an agony of over-choice (the professorial metaphor of the cafeteria completely misses the point, whereas the student metaphor of add-drop period as "shopping" hits it); professors find themselves producing gimmicky course titles to repackage the old notes in a more palatable wrap; and the process of evaluation (in grades and letters of recommendation) absorbs the dominant promotion-oriented tone of hyperbole, so that it is as hard to find a D as it is to find a jar of SMALL olives. In such a social situation, with the mind daily numbed to less than truthful representation, habituated to heavy promotion and "media hype" and ceaseless transformation of products, the question is no longer how one could come up with so audacious a proposition as that the con man is our hero. The question is, How could one *help* suspecting it?

But before I reinsert myself so completely into the book as to begin writing my own reviews and claiming that the book wrote me, I want to say one last thing about the confidence man. I have been dealing here with the relationship between personal gestures or states of mind and their social context. The confidence man brings to focus the whole paradoxical question of individualism in the American past. The premise of my study is that conditions in the developing American social structure were especially suited to confidence men. To the degree that the con man both enacts popular values and employs the available techniques in the historically given situations, he is a product of social forces, even a predictable product whose very recurrence in our literature demonstrates how regularly he is produced. Yet the techniques of production in his instance have specifically to do with making and packaging a self. The illusion that the con man generates and sustains is that the self is *not* produced by history, class background, economic forces, or the ideological glosses of these but rather that the self deliberately produces itself. And this is not simply a matter of declaring one's personal priority and independence, like Faulkner's poor Ike Mc-Caslin in the commissary fatuously pronouncing "I am free." It is the experience of turning social manners, habituated gestures, and badges of appearance back into *self-conscious gambits*, so that one's very capacity to play roles proves one's detachment.

Over and over the confidence man experiences his isolation from the social matrix by being able to play himself. Over and over he unrealizes other people by turning his relations with them into maneuvers. Perhaps this is one of the reasons why the model of the con man finally doesn't apply easily or extensively to women. And perhaps this radical, constantly re-enacted isolation explains why, after all the fun and promise, after the dazzle and exhilaration of the confidence man, one senses a disquieting emptiness. Maybe Melville closed by snuffing the light because he knew that if he turned it up, no one would be there.

NOTES

Introduction

1. A quick illustration is provided by Jay Robert Nash, *Hustlers and Con Men: An Anecdotal History of the Confidence Man and His Game* (New York, 1976), p. 274. A stranger named Mel Greenburg appeared in Lexington, Virginia, claiming to be a casting director for an epic film. He managed to get several young women of the town to parade before him nude to try to qualify for roles, and as he left, he stuck the town for a series of bad checks. A citizen's evaluation of the experience (needless to say, a male citizen) was: "We'd never seen a real con man before and we feel proud to have been in on this one." See "Queen for a Day," *Newsweek* (July 1, 1974).

2. This is the approach of Susan Kuhlmann in *Knave, Fool, and Genius: The Confidence Man as He Appears in Nineteenth-Century American Fiction* (Chapel Hill, 1973). She notes certain convergences between the qualities of the confidence man and those of the pioneer, and she indicates the ways in which American authors have used con men—who know the foibles of their times—as comments on American society. Kuhlmann is especially helpful in defining the frontier conditions that favored con men in American life and in showing how rhetoric as a salable commodity provides the common denominator of westward settlement and con games. By basically adhering to the dictionary definition of confidence man, however, she underplays the role of confidence and limits her study to more or less shady and secondary characters.

3. There is, of course, a risk of moving too far in the other direction: of making the con game so inclusive an activity that it loses touch with its most obvious form and ceases to signify anything. A good corrective to this tendency is David W. Maurer's *The American Confidence Man* (Springfield, Ill., 1974), which is a new edition of his well-known book of 1940 *The Big Con*. Maurer's subject is con men of the official sort, the professional criminals, and he knows them and their games and their language very well. Like W. C. Fields, he sees the principle of the con game as "you can't cheat an honest man." What Maurer gets at so brilliantly is the extended com-

plicity between con man and mark, and this principle has explanatory powers that reach far outside the explicitly criminal version of the con.

4. See R. W. B. Lewis, *The American Adam: Innocence, Tragedy, and Tradition in the Nineteenth Century* (Chicago, 1955). Many other central works in American Studies have dealt with the interrelated concepts of wilderness, frontier, pioneèring, innocence: Henry Nash Smith's *Virgin Land: The American West as Symbol and Myth* (Cambridge, 1950); Leo Marx's *The Machine in the Garden: Technology and the Pastoral Ideal in America* (New York, 1964); Edwin Fussell's *Frontier: American Literature and the American West* (Princeton, 1965).

5. The basic tracing of this historical development was done by Paul Smith, "*The Confidence-Man* and the Literary World of New York," *Nineteenth-Century Fiction,* 16 (1962), 329–37, and Johannes Dietrich Bergmann, "The Original Confidence Man," *American Quarterly,* 21 (1969), 560–77. Excerpts from the *Herald* and from Duyckinck's essay are conveniently reprinted in the Norton Critical Edition of Melville's *The Confidence-Man,* ed. Herschel Parker (New York, 1971), pp. 227–28.

6. See Paul Radin, *The Trickster* (New York, 1956), with essays by Karl Kerényi and Carl Jung.

7. See Victor W. Turner, "Myth and Symbol," *International Encyclopedia of the Social Sciences* (New York, 1968), pp. 576–81.

8. For especially helpful analyses of the nature of the picaro and of his literary genre, see C. Guillén, "Toward a Definition of the Picaresque," *Proceedings of the Third Congress of the International Comparative Literature Association* (The Hague: Mouton & Co., 1962), pp. 252–66; Robert Alter, *Rogue's Progress: Studies in the Picaresque Novel* (Cambridge, Mass., 1964); Ulrich Wicks, "The Nature of Picaresque Narrative: A Modal Approach," *PMLA,* 89 (1974), 240–49.

9. This is the one limitation of a book from which I have learned a great deal for my subject, Richard Boyd Hauck, *A Cheerful Nihilism: Confidence and "The Absurd" in American Humorous Fiction* (Bloomington, Ind., 1971). He gives an excellent account of the centrality of faith and confidence in American experience, and he says especially perceptive things about Franklin, Mark Twain, and Faulkner. His paradoxical title is an effort to acknowledge the American promissory tone, but it is ultimately self-canceling, for instead of emphasizing the feeling of opportunity, he stresses the encounter with absurdity, so that the characteristic gesture is not really self-creation but whistling in the dark.

10. Roger Caillois, *Man, Play, and Games,* trans. Meyer Barrash (New York, 1961), p. 7.

11. Originally I had intended to do considerably more with American writers as con artists. The subject is almost inevitable, for who are the most systematic and suggestive makers of belief but literary artists? But three considerations kept me from carrying out this plan. First, those other chapters would have made an already long book monstrously long. Second, Warwick Wadlington published *The Confidence Game in American Literature* (Princeton, 1975), in which he analyzes the works of Melville, Mark Twain, and Nathanael West as complicated transactions of confidence between

reader and writer, analogous in important ways to the implicit motives and strategies of the more conventional con game. Third, and most decisive, I recognized that since *all* imaginative literary works are transactions of confidence between writer and reader, the selection of certain of these transactions as privileged for my study would be more arbitrary than the selection of certain social gestures for analysis as confidence games. What Benjamin Franklin does in Philadelphia is more distinctive as a social gesture than what Henry James does at the end of *Turn of the Screw* is as a literary gesture.

Chapter 1

1. Daniel G. Hoffman, *Form and Fable in American Fiction* (New York, 1961), p. 281. Compare R. W. B. Lewis, Afterword to *The Confidence-Man* (New York, 1964), p. 265, who sees the prose as canceling itself out.

2. See Elizabeth S. Foster, Appendix to *The Confidence-Man* (New York, 1954), pp. 376–77. The Appendix is a study of manuscript drafts, stylistic revision, and order of composition. Together with the Introduction and the Explanatory Notes, Foster's work in this edition constitutes the most thorough single study of the novel.

3. Warner Berthoff, *The Example of Melville* (Princeton, 1962), p. 166.

4. Allen Hayman, "The Real and the Original: Herman Melville's Theory of Prose Fiction," *Modern Fiction Studies*, 8 (1962), 221.

5. See John W. Schroeder, "Sources and Symbols for Melville's *The Confidence-Man*," *PMLA*, 66 (1951), 363–80; Herschel Parker, "The Metaphysics of Indian-hating," *Nineteenth-Century Fiction*, 18 (1963), 165–73; and Foster, Introduction.

6. The extent to which Emerson is caricatured in Mark Winsome has been well documented. See especially Egbert S. Oliver, "Melville's Picture of Emerson and Thoreau in 'The Confidence-Man,' " *College English*, 8 (1946), 61–72; Foster, Introduction and Explanatory Notes; Herschel Parker, "Melville's Satire of Emerson and Thoreau: An Evaluation of the Evidence," *American Transcendental Quarterly*, 7 (1970), 61–67. One should not carry this identification too far. Winsome presents only some of Emerson's ideas; others are mouthed to quite different purpose by the protagonist as herb-doctor; and still others shape the serious argument of Chapter 44. And the ideas about the segmentation of inner and outer selves are not peculiar to Emerson—he merely states memorably what had become a cultural commonplace.

7. In this novel the Confidence-Man's gestures are circumscribed by our merely human world. He shares less of Satan's ultimate wiles than of the "post-Providential, fallen omniscience" of the criminal hero—Richardson's Lovelace or Balzac's Vautrin. See Anthony Winner's fine development of this concept in "Richardson's Lovelace: Character and Prediction," *Texas Studies in Literature and Language*, 14 (1972), 53–75. The criminal hero's activities reveal the fallen nature of the human world; yet he possesses satanic knowledge and control of fallen creatures, the strategic gift of the novelist who wants to probe that world.

8. This point is made by R. W. B. Lewis, Afterword to *The Confidence-Man*, pp. 271–72, who argues that the Confidence-Man's motive is to trick each person he accosts into announcing his own moral and intellectual nature; other characters are lit up by him. Lewis sees the Cosmopolitan as Everyman, fusing all human potentialities, demonic or divine, and summoning mankind to choose.

9. For another argument that the Confidence-Man is a special kind of hero, related to the peculiar insights of the novel, see Paul Brodtkorb, Jr., "*The Confidence-Man:* The Con-Man as Hero," *Studies in the Novel,* 1 (1969), 421–35. Brodtkorb also sees the protagonist as essentially consistent, the Masquerade as encompassing everyone, and the novel's emphasis as on a reality limited to appearance. In assessing the ontological basis of the book, however, he argues that there is no such thing as character, that role playing is the fundamental human condition, that man cannot be separated from role, and that the novel does not try to make this separation. Such a nihilistic extension of Melville's experiment obscures the dramatic gamesmanship with character that is the novel's *modus operandi.*

10. See Roy Harvey Pearce, "Melville's Indian-hater: A Note on a Meaning of *The Confidence-Man,*" *PMLA,* 67 (1952), 942–48; Herschel Parker, "The Metaphysics of Indian-hating"; and Edwin Fussell, *Frontier,* pp. 303–26.

11. See Fussell.

12. See Egbert S. Oliver, "Melville's Goneril and Fanny Kemble," *New England Quarterly,* 18 (1945), 489–500; Harrison Hayford, "Poe in *The Confidence-Man,*" *Nineteenth-Century Fiction,* 14 (1959), 207–18; and Oliver, Foster, and Parker (see note 6 above). Elizabeth Foster qualifies Oliver's assertions about Fanny Kemble, disputes his identification of Thoreau with Egbert, and expands his identification of Emerson with Winsome. Parker adds to the documentation of Melville's reference to both writers.

13. See Paul Smith, "*The Confidence-Man* and the Literary World of New York," *Nineteenth-Century Fiction,* 16 (1962), 329–37; Johannes Dietrich Bergmann, "The Original Confidence Man," *American Quarterly,* 21 (1969), 560–77; Michael S. Reynolds, "The Prototype for Melville's Confidence-Man," *PMLA,* 86 (1971), 1009–13.

14. Three annotated editions are helpful in locating such allusions: Elizabeth Foster's, already cited; H. Bruce Franklin, ed., *The Confidence-Man* (Indianapolis, 1967); Herschel Parker, ed., *The Confidence-Man* (New York, 1971). Parker's edition also contains background material and an annotated bibliography (through 1970) by Watson G. Branch. See also John Seelye, Introduction to *The Confidence-Man* (San Francisco, 1968), pp. vii–xl.

Chapter 2

1. Poe's work has been approached from so many perspectives that rather than indicate my position in the overall critical terrain, I will simply point out the three essays that most helped me get to where I am: William Carlos Williams, "Edgar Allan Poe," *In the American Grain* (New York,

1956), pp. 216–33; Terence Martin, "The Imagination at Play: Edgar Allan Poe," *Kenyon Review*, 28 (1966), 194–209; James M. Cox, "Edgar Poe: Style as Pose," *Virginia Quarterly Review*, 44 (1968), 67–89. The three essays come at Poe in quite different ways, and it was the juxtaposition that proved especially suggestive to my own thinking. Martin indicates the seriousness of play and games in Poe's work. Cox shows the centrality of impersonation and doubling. All three share the recognition that Poe was inescapably both artist and buffoon.

2. Allen Tate, "Our Cousin, Mr. Poe," *Poe: A Collection of Critical Essays*, ed. Robert Regan (Englewood Cliffs, 1967), p. 43. (A lecture given in 1949.)

3. This attitude must not be confused with literary jingoism. Poe was scathing toward such patriotic boosterism as the Young America movement (see Perry Miller, *The Raven and the Whale* [New York, 1956]). As William Carlos Williams argues, Poe was radically, not superficially, of a "New World."

Chapter 3

1. For a fuller treatment of Franklin's use of patterns from Bunyan, see Charles L. Sanford, "An American's Pilgrim's Progress," *American Quarterly*, 4 (1955), 297–310; and David Levin, "The Autobiography of Benjamin Franklin: The Puritan Experimenter in Life and Art," *Yale Review*, 53 (1963), 258–75.

2. See W. T. Brannon, *"Yellow Kid" Weil: The Autobiography of America's Master Swindler* (Chicago, 1948), esp. Ch. 28. Weil repeatedly stresses the fundamental dishonesty of his victims, who wanted to fleece others.

3. *The Papers of Benjamin Franklin*, ed. Leonard Labaree et al., 18 + vols. (New Haven, 1959–), XII, 135. His delight in such hoaxes and in the vagaries of public credulity is one of many qualities Franklin shares with Edgar Allan Poe. Poe, too, as editor and writer, helped serve the literary needs of the nascent republic by boldly disregarding finical distinctions between plagiarism and promotion. Both men were keenly alert to the demands of popularity. And both writers showed, like the best magicians and con men, what David Levin, writing about Franklin, calls "disarming candor about techniques of influence and persuasion." *In Defense of Historical Literature* (New York, 1967), p. 61.

4. *Benjamin Franklin* (New York, 1938), p. 782.

5. *Israel Potter* (New York, 1974), pp. 71–72.

6. See Max Weber, *The Protestant Ethic and the Spirit of Capitalism*, trans. Talcott Parsons (New York, 1930). For related influences of Quaker teachings on Franklin's business ethic, see Frederick B. Tolles, "Benjamin Franklin's Business Mentors: The Philadelphia Quaker Merchants," *William and Mary Quarterly*, 4 (1947), 60–69.

7. *Papers*, I, 75.

8. For an excellent discussion of the *Autobiography* from this perspective, see Robert F. Sayre, *The Examined Self* (Princeton, 1964), Ch. 1. He sees the *Autobiography* as a series of self-conscious roles entered into both by the

actor and by the narrator. A quite different approach to Franklin's role playing is in John F. Lynen, *The Design of the Present* (New Haven, 1969), pp. 119–52, see esp. pp. 136–37. Lynen sees the role playing as a self-conscious response to the distance between eternal verities and the time-limited perspective of the human actor. In this view Franklin knows that we need generalizations in order to act meaningfully, and yet that our generalizations can only be provisional. The self plays a role and must believe in it at the time; in the longer experience the approximations show enough continuity that we find a persistent self who is *wearing* all those masks and that we are also assured there *are* principles of which the temporary rules of conduct can be approximations.

9. Franklin's own unnerving ability to compartmentalize his feelings and roles is apparent in his "Account of Negotiations in London" (1775) when he dismisses the personal insults of the English ministry: "besides, it was a fix'd Rule with me, not to mix my private Affairs with those of the publick . . . I could join with my personal Enemy in serving the public, or, when it was for its Interest, with the Publick in serving that Enemy." *The Writings of Benjamin Franklin,* ed. Albert H. Smyth, 10 vols. (New York, 1905–7), VI, 347. Presumably several other permutations could with equal propriety be admitted to that last clause!

10. "Experience," *Works,* 12 vols. (Boston, 1904), III, 59.

Chapter 4

1. Among many discussions of backgrounds and influences for Franklin's *Autobiography,* the following present useful summaries and are conveniently available: Chester E. Jorgenson and Frank Luther Mott, eds., *Benjamin Franklin: Representative Selections,* rev. ed. (New York, 1962), pp. xiii–cxli. Leonard W. Labaree, et al., eds., *The Autobiography of Benjamin Franklin* (New Haven, 1964), pp. 1–19. These essays in Esmond Wright, ed., *Benjamin Franklin: A Profile* (New York, 1970): Whitney Griswold, "A Puritan on Prosperity"; Frederick B. Tolles, "Quaker Business Mentors: The Philadelphia Merchants"; John F. Ross, "The Character of Poor Richard: Its Source and Alteration"; David Levin, "The Autobiography of Benjamin Franklin: The Puritan Experimenter in Life and Art"; and I. Bernard Cohen, "The Empirical Temper of Benjamin Franklin."

2. For a fuller treatment of the Yankee peddler as a popular motif, see Richardson Wright, *Hawkers and Walkers in Early America* (Philadelphia, 1927); Constance Rourke, *American Humor* (New York, 1931), Ch. 1; Walter Blair, *Native American Humor* (New York, 1937), pp. 17–62. Daniel Hoffman joins Benjamin Franklin and the Yankee under the rubric of a shape-shifting American hero, who moves through metamorphoses without deeper changes in character and who feels his identity in his successful use of the powers of change. I have benefited from his suggestions in "The American Hero: His Masquerade," *Form and Fable in American Fiction* (New York, 1961), Ch. 3.

3. The prevalence of this cultural image is apparent in *The Memoirs of the Notorious Stephen Burroughs of New Hampshire* (published in 1811). Burroughs, a con man, imposter, counterfeiter, and jailbreaker in the late eighteenth century, tells his own story as a series of disasters, failures, false public accusations, bunglings, and generally miserable feelings, and yet in his travels he repeatedly hears diverting stories about himself as a charming and irresistible deceiver. Clearly the general desire for a certain kind of popular idol reshaped the incidents of Burroughs's experience in public anecdote as much as he himself may have recast them in another way for his confessions.

4. Timothy Dwight, *Travels in New England and New York*, ed. Barbara Miller Solomon, 4 vols. (Cambridge, Mass., 1969), I, 223, and II, 34.

5. Frances Trollope, *Domestic Manners of the Americans*, ed. Donald Smalley (New York, 1949), pp. 302, 370. The book was published in 1832.

6. *Apostles of the Self-Made Man* (Chicago, 1965), Ch. 2. Throughout my discussion of the self-made man I have profited from Cawelti's book. See also Irvin G. Wyllie, *The Self-Made Man in America* (New York, 1954). For the influence and image of Franklin in the nineteenth century, see Louis B. Wright, "Franklin's Legacy to the Gilded Age," *Virginia Quarterly Review*, 22 (1946), 268–79, and Richard D. Miles, "The American Image of Benjamin Franklin," *American Quarterly*, 9 (1957), 117–43.

7. Joseph "Yellow Kid" Weil tells the story of "a natural-born con man," Colonel Jim Porter, who was so thorough a role-player that he *lived* in each role. Some of his friends amused themselves by introducing him at a large party as the owner of an island in Florida, and they outfitted him for his role with a Stetson hat and a cutaway coat. The Colonel had soon convinced *himself* that he owned the island and so made others believe it as well, to the delight of his friends. He later played, or more accurately, became, roles set by the Yellow Kid in elaborate con games, but it was the Yellow Kid who had to design the games. Colonel Porter is to the master con man, Joseph Weil, what the self-made man is to Franklin's model self. See *"Yellow Kid" Weil*, Ch. 7.

8. See Cawelti, Ch. 6; Wyllie, "Epilogue"; and Kenneth Lynn, *The Dream of Success* (Boston, 1955), pp. 23–26.

Chapter 5

1. See Norman O. Brown, *Hermes the Thief* (Madison, Wis., 1947), esp. Ch. 1; and Paul Radin, *The Trickster* (New York, 1956), esp. the essay by Karl Kerényi, "The Trickster in Relation to Greek Mythology." Victor W. Turner's essay on "Myth and Symbol" in the *International Encyclopedia of the Social Sciences* (New York, 1968) treats myths as "liminal phenomena" concerned with a state that is "betwixt and between," "where the elements of culture and society are released from their customary configurations and recombined in bizarre and terrifying imagery." Such disruptions expose elements that are more universal—biological, psychological, or spiritual. Trickster tales are especially adapted to throwing this marginal experience

into relief, for tricksters are threshold personalities: "They behave as though there were no social or moral norms to guide them" (p. 580). Turner's analysis makes clear why tricksters in mythology and folklore have an element of the primitive and the universal about them; they are suggestive analogues to the confidence man, but there are profound differences between characters who inhabit more or less sacred myth and those who are generated in the popular lore of modern literate societies. The American "confidence man," as I imply throughout the book, is more interesting and revealing as the exemplar of certain clearly definable preoccupations of a specific culture than he is as a guide to the shadowy ground where the Many become One. For an alternative approach see Warwick Wadlington, *The Confidence Game in American Literature* (Princeton, 1975), especially the highly suggestive discussion on pp. 3–23. Wadlington, too, notes "a national preoccupation with trust" and sees that "In the national iconography, Americans are peddlers of assurance." Yet his discussion of the confidence man essentially equates him with the more universal trickster and employs him as a basis for investigating marginal phenomena in literature, which Wadlington analyzes as a series of transactions of confidence between author and reader.

2. See Louis B. Wright, *The Atlantic Frontier* (New York, 1951), Ch. 1.

3. A useful summary of versions of land speculation in American history is A. M. Sakolski, *The Great American Land Bubble* (New York, 1932).

4. See Ray Allen Billington, "The Origin of the Land Speculator as a Frontier Type," *Agricultural History*, 19 (1945), 204–12.

5. Sakolski, Chs. 2 and 6.

6. Ibid., Chs. 6 and 8. Billington's article cited above is an excellent study of these effects.

7. Dwight, *Travels*, I, 158. It is interesting to note that this was precisely the experience of the New England con man, Stephen Burroughs. After failing repeatedly in his urban ventures as his reputation followed him and blasted his prospects, he set off for the Georgia frontier, earned his passage money by quick turnovers of land investments (only to have it stolen from him), dropped his work as rector at a school to take part in the feverish Yazoo land sales, worked for Robert Morris, the famous speculator and "financier of the Revolution," until Morris's disastrous failure brought Burroughs back to Philadelphia and a land office business, all of which gave him enough profit finally to return to New Hampshire and manage a farm. See *The Memoirs of the Notorious Stephen Burroughs of New Hampshire* (published in 1811). It forms a sardonic companion piece to Dwight's *Travels*.

8. Hannah F. Lee, *The Log Cabin* (Philadelphia, 1844), p. 173. Quoted in Cawelti, *Apostles of the Self-Made Man*, p. 49.

9. This stereotype was not limited to women's novels. It is elaborated in Mark Twain's *The Gilded Age* and it forms a central conception for narrative values in Faulkner's Snopes trilogy.

10. Sakolski, Ch. 13.

11. Quoted in Sakolski, p. 338.

12. Herbert Croly, *The Promise of American Life* (New York, 1909), pp. 2–3.

13. Henry Adams, *History of the United States during the Administrations of Jefferson and Madison,* 9 vols. (New York, 1891), I, 172.

14. Ibid., I, 174.

15. *The Life and Selected Writings of Thomas Jefferson,* ed. Adrienne Koch and William Peden (New York, 1944), p. 633.

16. Ibid., p. 328; my italics.

17. For a fuller study of the importance of this side of Jefferson's character, see Horace M. Kallen, "The Arts and Thomas Jefferson," *Ethics,* 53 (1943), 269–83.

18. See Charles Feidelson's discussion of Whitman in *Symbolism in American Literature* (Chicago, 1953), pp. 16–27, for a different approach to Whitman's emphasis on process.

19. Roger Caillois in *Man, Play, and Games,* trans. Meyer Barash (Glencoe, Ill., 1961) divides play into four broad kinds: competition, chance, mimicry, and vertigo. He then notes that by basic polarities these tend to appear in pairs—competition vs. chance, and mimicry vs. vertigo. He sees modern Western culture with its patterns of competition as favoring the games of competition and chance. Yet Whitman's example especially suggests that the paired elements of mimicry and vertigo could go some way toward defining the game pleasures of a confidence culture and the basic *separation* of these from a predatory business world.

20. The merging in William James's work of physiology, psychology, popular religion, and self-help practicalism was not unique. At the same time he was working out his ideas Mary Baker Eddy was organizing a church, a college, and a science of healing. Like James she drew on the how-to-do-it tradition and the promissory one to create confidence in individuals—especially women—and show them that they could master many of their own problems. See the significantly entitled chapter "Confidence Builders" in Caroline Bird's *Enterprising Women* (New York, 1976), pp. 90–95.

Chapter 6

1. Ironically, the light, carefree flexibility of the jack-of-all-trades made him a *better* model than the self-made man for long-range success in the economic world, for the increasing rate of change in industrial and post-industrial organizations put a premium on constant adaptability, and one of the modern *conditions* for promotion is willingness to relocate. See Alvin Toffler's *Future Shock* (New York, 1970).

2. I am not trying in this chapter to indicate the full range of metamorphic American heroes in literature and folklore. Daniel Hoffman has done that in his admirable study, *Form and Fable in American Fiction* (New York, 1961). And I have given less space to Holgrave and Ishmael than they might deserve, for Hoffman treats both of them as shape-shifters in Chapters 10 and 12, respectively. My entire book owes some of its inspiration to his Chapter 3, "The American Hero: His Masquerade."

3. In his memoirs, the confidence man "Yellow Kid" Weil repeatedly notes how in his wanderings he would spot a foreclosed bank, a stock

office going out of business, a pile of unloaded stock shares, and would then put them together in a complex con game. The con man has a sharp eye for the phenomena of transition. See Brannon, *"Yellow Kid" Weil,* passim.

4. Two instances will illustrate my point. Near the end of *Magnalia Christi Americana,* Cotton Mather devotes a chapter, "Wolves in Sheep's Clothing," to a cluster of confidence men as preachers coming to Boston who capitalize on the transition from early seventeenth-century piety and saintliness to later seventeenth-century doubts and confusions. For a fuller commentary, see David Levin, "Forms of Uncertainty: Representation of Doubt in American Histories," *New Literary History,* 7 (1976), 61–68, esp. p. 65. Sacvan Bercovitch points out in *The American Puritan Imagination* (Cambridge, 1974), pp. 9–10, how the confusions and setbacks of the 1660s led to the creation of the legend of the founding fathers, the saga of a golden age in the early seventeenth century, from which the present was a marked falling away. Something of the same pattern can be seen in Edward Eggleston's *The Circuit Rider: A Tale of The Heroic Age* (New York, 1878). Eggleston equates Methodism in the early West with Puritanism in early New England, and he repeatedly indicates how difficult it will be for skeptical readers in the late nineteenth century to enter into the spirit, the belief, the sincere feelings of the early nineteenth-century circuit riders and their enthusiastic converts. Clearly by Eggleston's time "circuit rider" had become one more of the many names for confidence man.

5. See Chapter 1 above for a full discussion of the implications of this split.

6. This idea is widely recognized in relation to symbolic reading in the novel. Ahab's error is to limit himself to a fixed allegory, whereas Ishmael preserves the constant potentiality for symbolic perception. See especially Charles Feidelson, Jr., *Symbolism and American Literature* (Chicago, 1953), pp. 28–35, 240–46, and William Ellery Sedgwick, *The Tragedy of Mind* (Cambridge, Mass., 1944), pp. 84–88, 119–26.

7. Compare the famous image at the end of "Brit": "For as this appalling ocean surrounds the verdant land, so in the soul of man there lies one insular Tahiti, full of peace and joy, but encompassed by all the horrors of the half known life." Here it is not the turbulence of the outer world or the external roles of the self that surround a central calm, but rather the complications of the psyche itself ("half known life" is analogous to what post-Freudian commentators would call the unconscious or the preconscious). Whereas Hawthorne simply presents two different views of the "deeper self," Melville suggests that there is a calm center within the psyche as well as within the shape-shifter. In *Pierre* he goes a step further and suggests that the center is calm because it is empty: "We lift the lid—and no body is there!—appallingly vacant as vast is the soul of a man!" (Book XXI, Chapter I).

8. *The Complete Works of Ralph Waldo Emerson,* ed. E. W. Emerson (Boston, 1903–4), II, 75–76.

9. See Henry Nash Smith, "Emerson's Problem of Vocation—A Note on 'The American Scholar,' " *New England Quarterly,* 12 (1939), 52–67.

10. *Works,* IV, 89.

11. John G. Cawelti, *Apostles of the Self-Made Man,* Chapter 3, makes a forceful case for Emerson's shrewdness and realism about worldly success and shows how much his theories were in harmony with the popular philosophy of success in the mid-nineteenth century. Like so many other proponents of success, Emerson saw the need for a higher form of success than wealth and power. Cawelti sees Emerson relating outward to inward success through the notion that a lower law of things disciplines one to a higher law of character.

12. *The Journals and Miscellaneous Notebooks of Ralph Waldo Emerson,* ed. W. H. Gilman, A. R. Ferguson, et al. (Cambridge, Mass. 1960–), VII, 117.

13. *Works,* I. 82–83.

14. See Stephen Whicher, *Freedom and Fate: An Inner Life of Ralph Waldo Emerson* (Philadelphia, 1953), esp. pp. 94–99, 111–19, 144–48, for a fuller study of the increasing importance of flux in Emerson's thinking.

15. "Montaigne," *Works,* IV, 176.

16. Ibid., p. 160.

17. *The Journals of Ralph Waldo Emerson,* ed. E. W. Emerson and W. E. Forbes (Boston, 1909–14), VII, 130.

18. *Journals and Misc. Notebooks,* VIII, 329.

19. "Experience," *Works,* III, 55.

20. For an excellent study of metamorphosis in Emerson's work from a different perspective, see Daniel B. Shea, "Emerson and the American Metamorphosis," in *Emerson: Prophecy, Metamorphosis, and Influence,* ed. David Levin (New York, 1975), pp. 29–56. Shea notes how vitally important change was to Emerson, who belonged to a tradition in American literature celebrating and testing the proposition that "men are convertible." But Shea sees Emerson's emphasis on becoming, regeneration, progressive development, whereas I want to indicate Emerson's delight in change itself and endless transformation.

21. *Journals,* VII, 117.

22. "Circles," *Works,* II, 306.

23. Ibid., p. 309.

24. *Journals and Misc. Notebooks,* V, 337.

25. See Quentin Anderson, *The Imperial Self: An Essay in American Literary and Cultural History* (New York, 1971), esp. pp. 3–58.

26. *Works,* I, 50–51.

27. "The Transcendentalist," *Works,* I, 354.

Chapter 7

1. "Town and Rural Humbugs," *Knickerbocker,* 45 (1855), 236.

2. The most influential single study is F. O. Matthiessen's in *American Renaissance* (New York, 1941), pp. 76–99, 113–19, 153–75, which focuses on Thoreau's artistry, his ability to think in images, his organic vision, his incorporation of mythic patterns. Also important in this approach to Thoreau as visionary artist are Stanley Edgar Hyman's emphasis on rebirth rituals in "Henry Thoreau in Our Time," *Atlantic Monthly,* 178 (1946), 137–

46, and Sherman Paul's study of *Walden* as an act of personal regeneration in "Resolution at Walden," *Accent*, 12 (1953), 101–13. The extreme statement of Thoreau's spiritual concern is in Daniel Shea's *Spiritual Autobiography in Early America* (Princeton, 1968), esp. pp. 256–62. Shea rejects the Mather-Franklin model of doing good through imitable methods and stresses instead the similarity of *Walden* to the tradition of Quaker autobiography with its concern for sharing illumination rather than recounting experience. In Shea's view Thoreau draws on a materialistic-commercial vocabulary only to demolish it in order that readers might find themselves in losing themselves.

These fine readings are examples of the basic approach to Thoreau in mid-twentieth-century criticism. Different as it sounds, my own reading here is not intended as a denial of Thoreau's spirituality or his inward focus. I simply wish to bring out another aspect of the self in *Walden* and to see how it complicates the image of the visionary hermit.

3. The most vilified of Thoreau's early critics has been James Russell Lowell, who accused Thoreau, in *A Fable for Critics*, of hooking neighbor Emerson's apples, and who went on in a fuller review of Thoreau's posthumous publications to show the extensive connections of Thoreau and the transcendentalist movement. See "Thoreau," *North American Review*, 101 (1865), 597–608. He is now remembered solely as the person who saw Thoreau only as a minor imitator of Emerson, a recollection that does as little justice to his fuller analysis of Thoreau as he himself did to the unique powers of Thoreau's work. When people put as much emphasis on their own originality as Poe and Thoreau did, they invite suspicion about their debts, and Lowell noted these well. Furthermore, he made passing observations about Thoreau's habits that are still wonderfully suggestive: "He turns commonplaces end for end, and fancies it makes something new of them" (p. 603). "We cannot help feeling as if he sometimes invited our attention to a particular sophism or paradox as the biggest yet maintained by any single writer" (p. 603). "He wishes always to trump your suit and to *ruff* when you least expect it" (p. 604).

4. Constance Rourke notes that being "obstinate and headstrong and full of notions," Thoreau was closely related to the Yankee peddler: "he made the same calculations, many of them close and shrewd, often in the air of bargaining. He had that air of turning the table on listeners or observers which had long since belonged to the Yankee of the comic mythologies." *American Humor* (Garden City, N.Y., 1953), p. 136 (originally published in 1931).

5. For a fuller account of this issue, see Leo Stoller, "Thoreau's Doctrine of Simplicity," *The New England Quarterly*, 29 (1956), 443–61, and John G. Cawelti, *Apostles of the Self-Made Man*, Ch. 3.

6. *The Writings of Henry David Thoreau*, 20 vols. (Boston and New York, 1906), XX, 281–82. Cited by Stoller.

7. Sherman Paul relates this doubleness to the imagery of the self, suggesting that the pond symbolizes the essential self, the center of renewal and regeneration, while the activities around the edge of the pond are the gestures of the outward self. The eternal self at the passive center, in this

reading, acquires consciousness by observing the empirical self at work on the circumference. See "Resolution at Walden," *Accent*, 12 (1953), 101–13.

8. Again I am drawing on Paul Radin's fascinating account in *The Trickster*.

9. James Russell Lowell, "Thoreau" (1865), p. 605.

10. This sometimes mechanical inversion has repeatedly opened Thoreau to the charge of being a stylistic trickster, a possibility that has been noted from the time of Emerson's and Lowell's contemporary comments to Theodore Baird's "Corn Grows in the Night," *The Massachusetts Review*, 4 (1962), 92–103. Baird sees Thoreau as talking in paradoxes to get himself set up as a sage; surface obscurity pretends to be profundity.

11. My emphasis here, as elsewhere in the book, is on the development and variations of cultural stereotypes. I do not try to address the particular personal needs that these popular images may have satisfied for the individual writer. Readers who wish to consider that issue could look into Richard Lebeaux, *Young Man Thoreau* (Amherst, 1977). Lebeaux uses Erik Erikson's model of male identity crises to interpret Thoreau's pre-Walden experience, and he sees the identity toward which Thoreau was moving as that of artist-naturalist. In this sense, like most modern commentators, he disregards the gaming, shape-shifting, role-playing side of Thoreau. But Lebeaux's assessment of Thoreau's psychological experience is that he desperately needed to put off adult commitments, to avoid wrong choices within a too-narrow field of options. "Given the long-standing and deeply-embedded *fear* of commitment to any one course of identity, it is not surprising that he was often tempted to make the moratorium an *end in itself*" (p. 162). Perhaps the gambits I have analyzed were Thoreau's means of sustaining the fluidity of that moratorium, in which case the stereotype of the confidence man could be taken to express a cultural yearning for prolonged adolescence.

Chapter 8

1. My discussion of the con game in Southwestern Humor is brief. For a fuller treatment of the importance of the confidence man in that world, see Kenneth S. Lynn, *Mark Twain and Southwestern Humor* (Boston, 1959), esp. Ch. 4.

2. The notorious wreckings of competitors, waterings of stock, and discontinuings of public services through which Cornelius Vanderbilt consolidated the New York Central system and battled Drew, Fisk, and Gould for control of the Erie railroad are described by the commissioned historian of the Vanderbilts, William A. Croffut, as Vanderbilt's rescue of the railroads from a band of speculators and plunderers. See *The Vanderbilts and the Story of Their Fortune* (Chicago, 1886), esp. pp. 272–76.

3. See Lynn, *Mark Twain*, pp. 182–97, for a quite different approach to the yearning for an earlier innocence in the Happy Valley.

4. For a different and fuller approach to these descriptive patterns and their bearing on *Huckleberry Finn*, see Leo Marx, "The Pilot and the Passen-

ger: Landscape Conventions and the Style of *Huckleberry Finn*," *American Literature*, 28 (1956), 129–46.

5. In this sense Huck is similar to the *pícaro* of European tradition, and he has often been seen as an heir to the *pícaro*. See, for example, Robert Alter's fine discussion of him in *Rogue's Progress: Studies in the Picaresque Novel* (Cambridge, Mass., 1964), pp. 117–21. C. Guillén, however, provides a perspective on the *pícaro* that allows us to see what is special about Huck and his situation. He sees the *pícaro* as first the victim of his social experience with no family to bend him to convention and no preparation for the shocks he receives. As everything conspires to make him an enemy and outsider, he comes upon the solution of roguish behavior to try to keep society at some distance. "Toward a Definition of the Picaresque," pp. 257–58. Whereas the traditional *pícaro* shapes his roguish behavior as an *alternative* to social convention, Huck Finn, as I have been arguing, simply heightens self-consciously the social habits themselves.

6. Surely Henry Nash Smith is right in arguing that the experience and the image of floating down the river replace any sense of determinate journey. See his Introduction to *The Adventures of Huckleberry Finn* (Boston, 1958), pp. x–xi.

7. Compare James Cox's reading of the novel in *Mark Twain: The Fate of Humor* (Princeton, 1966), esp. pp. 173–84. Cox also emphasizes that Huck's mode of being is escape and evasion, that his decision to go to hell emerges from his effort to find a way out of practical difficulties, that it involves a commitment to principle that is basically alien to Huck's nature. But Cox argues that Huck represents the pleasure principle resisting conscience of any kind. The joke at the end of the novel, in Cox's reading, is that Tom's bit of safe play in setting a free slave free duplicates the post-Civil War reader's complacent enjoyment of a moral issue already settled historically. As my analysis suggests, Mark Twain was making a more sardonic comment on social capacities to fictionalize and conceal personal experience. These capacities were not diminished by the Civil War.

Chapter 9

1. See Matthew Josephson, *The Robber Barons* (New York, 1934), pp. 196–201, for a description of Jay Gould's buying up a nearly worthless competitive railroad and using it to threaten *his own company* into purchasing the shares at an inflated value. See also "Yellow Kid" Weil's autobiography, which is filled with examples of complex transactions in which the victim's participation in one deal is entangled by a "switch" of interest, so that his fever of speculation makes him forget the original and more honest-sounding offer. In the history of American confidence games, the period from 1900 to 1930 was the gala time of highly elaborate cons—the magic wallet, the big store, and the wire game. The first and third of these were celebrated in the film *The Sting*. For a fuller study of these games, see David W. Maurer, *The American Confidence Man* (Springfield, Ill., 1974) and Jay Robert Nash, *Hustlers and Con Men* (New York, 1976).

2. Compare this full title of T. S. Denison's novel of 1885: *An Iron Crown: or, The Modern Mammon. A Graphic and Thrilling History of Great Money-Makers and How They Got Millions. Both Sides of the Picture—Railway Kings, Coal Barons, Bonanza Miners and Their Victims. Life and Adventure from Wall Street to the Rocky Mountains. Board of Trade Frauds, Bucket-Shop Frauds, Newspaper Frauds, All Sorts of Frauds, Big and Little.*

3. The span of Barnum's career suggests that the transition from Yankee Peddler to Robber Baron was not merely a development of American folklore. Collis P. Huntington began as a Connecticut peddler, and Jim Fisk, in a colorful career, was a Vermont peddler, then managed an itinerant circus, sold shoddy uniforms to the government during the Civil War, and finally graduated to massive stock swindling with Jay Gould.

4. The change in Faulkner's own mode of narration and sense of comedy can be seen at a glance by comparing the psychologically claustrophobic narrative in *The Sound and The Fury* (1929) with the more inclusive perspective established in the Appendix to the same book (1945), written after Faulkner had mastered the Snopes mode. See especially the rich, comic changes in the account of Quentin's robbery from her uncle Jason's savings and expropriations.

5. The art of bluffing has, of course, a broader cultural base. Poe's invention of an American hero—C. Auguste Dupin—depended in part on a contrast between two kinds of games, chess with its complexity of strategy and moves as against checkers with its simplicity of moves and its dependence on the reading and mimicking of the opponent's personality. Dupin would also have been good at poker, which, if not exactly an American invention, received its essential developments in the Louisiana Territory and in the Civil War, so that by the 1870s it had been sufficiently identified with the United States that the U.S. Minister to Great Britain could describe it as "our national game." Faulkner's own comment on psychology is suggestive in this context: "What little of psychology I know the characters I have invented and playing poker taught me." *Faulkner in the University,* ed. Frederick L. Gwynn and Joseph L. Blotner (New York, 1959), p. 268.

6. Compare this description by a mid-nineteenth-century wildcat banker: "Well, I didn't have much else to do so I rented an empty store building and printed 'bank' on the window. The first day I was open for business a man came in and deposited one hundred dollars. The second day another deposited two hundred fifty dollars, and so along about the third day I got confidence enough in the bank to put in a hundred myself." Quoted in Nathan Miller, *The Founding Finaglers* (New York, 1976), pp. 164–65.

7. See Norman O. Brown, *Hermes the Thief* (Madison, Wis., 1947), especially Chapters 1 and 2.

8. It takes Cleanth Brooks and Hervey C. Lewis five pages of notes to sort out the trade between Flem and Ratliff, and even at that they disregard the non-economic stakes. See Cleanth Brooks, *William Faulkner: The Yoknapatawpha Country* (New Haven, 1966), pp. 402–6.

9. There is a similar pattern at the end of *The Great Gatsby*. The successful confidence man as manipulator of promise and personality is murdered

by a maskless self, desperately incapable of raising himself, spurned for simply working hard according ·to the rules, and frustrated by the very promise that one can improve one's lot by such effort. Although George Wilson and Mink Snopes murder for immediately distinct personal reasons (Wilson even mistaking the victim), on a symbolic level they converge as the con man's nemesis.

Chapter 10

1. Tony Tanner's *City of Words: American Fiction 1950–1970* (New York, 1971) has been immensely helpful to me in finding my way through some contemporary American fiction. His thesis is that the contemporary American novel issues in flight from rigidity, over-organization, fixed plots that would trap the self. He sees the heroes of this fiction as overturning or fleeing such rigid formulations. Their risk is moving to the other pole—a fluidity so extreme as to be formless.

2. Published originally in *Partisan Review* (1958). Reprinted in *Shadow and Act* (New York, 1964), pp. 61–73.

3. Although I basically find the essay persuasive, I think Ellison strategically ignores here the heritage of black American fiction dealing with racial masquerade and passing as complex games of survival. Charles Chesnutt's stories and James Weldon Johnson's *Autobiography of an Ex-Colored Man* are merely two early examples of black fictional characters learning to become strategically invisible by holding up the mirror to white preconceptions. And even *Up from Slavery* takes on a new cast if read with the Invisible Man's grandfather's advice in mind as a hypothetical vantage point.

4. Tony Tanner in *City of Words* argues that this novel, like much contemporary American fiction, exhibits distrust of plotting—the protagonist needs to keep his own space by escaping others' formulations of his experience and not being fixed in their pictures of reality. I read Augie as more curious than fearful, more detached than resistant. He is ungrudgingly interested in people's plots but cannot give any one of them primacy.

5. Aside from their apparently heartless detachment, another strong resemblance between Augie March and Charles Brockden Brown's Arthur Mervyn is that both characters, with innocent desires to please and to be of help, produce highly dubious impressions in a murky, appearance-oriented world. But the consequences of such wrong impressions barely touch Augie, for he has invested even less than Arthur Mervyn in the plots that produced the entanglements.

Chapter 11

1. The literature that Neal Cassady haunts is extensive. He is Dean Moriarty in Jack Kerouac's *On the Road* and Cody in Kerouac's *Visions of Cody*. He is Houlihan in Ken Kesey's *Over the Border* (included in *Kesey's Garage Sale* [New York, 1973]). He appears often as himself in Tom Wolfe's *Electric Kool-Aid Acid Test* (New York, 1968). Biographical material is available in

Ann Charters, *Kerouac: A Biography* (San Francisco, 1973); John Tytell, *Naked Angels: The Lives and Literature of the Beat Generation* (New York, 1976); Carolyn Cassady, *Heart Beat: My Life with Jack and Neal* (Berkeley, 1976); and Barry Gifford and Lawrence Lee, *Jack's Book: An Oral Biography of Jack Kerouac* (New York, 1978). "Appreciations" include an interview with Carolyn Cassady in *Rolling Stone* (October 12, 1972) and two pieces by Ken Kessey, "An Impolite Interview with Ken Kesey" (1971) and "Neal Cassady" (1971), both included in *Kesey's Garage Sale*. Finally, there is Cassady's own incomplete, posthumously published autobiography, *The First Third: A Partial Autobiography and Other Writings* (San Francisco, 1971), which develops extensively his experience in Denver and on the road from ages six to nine, an alternation between half-years on Larimer Street with his wino father and half-years with his mother and half-brothers; it also contains some fragments on teenage and adult experiences and several letters to Kerouac and to Kesey.

Chapter 12

1. These are gathered by Claude Steiner and Carmen Kerr in the posthumous *Beyond Games and Scripts* (New York, 1976).

2. Robert Jay Lifton, "Protean Man," *Partisan Review*, 35 (1968), 13–27, postulates a personality type rather like Burlingame's as the common psychological product of modern experience. He notes that in virtually all economically developed countries of the modern world, connections with nourishing cultural symbols and attitudes have been broken and that people are exposed ceaselessly to superficial and undigested cultural fragments. The historical dislocation and the flooding of imagery have, he argues, produced a new style of self-process—the self engages with an interminable series of experiments and explorations, each readily abandoned in favor of a new psychological quest. The fluctuation of emotions and beliefs breaks down the relationship of outer and inner worlds, producing a tone of mockery and a sense of absurdity. From Lifton's perspective Henry Burlingame would not be a modern extension of American habits and styles but a representative of contemporary psychohistory on a global scale. Ultimately, for Lifton, "protean man" is on a "never-ceasing quest for imagery of rebirth" and thus remains young in spirit and ready for survival in a complex world. Burlingame himself expresses the feeling exactly: " 'Tis a wondrous tonic for defeat, to murther an old self and beget a new!' "

3. George Santayana's essay on "Emerson" in *Interpretations of Poetry and Religion* (1900) and his famous lecture "The Genteel Tradition in American Philosophy" (1911) present full philosophical critiques of transcendentalism motivated by virtually the same question as Burlingame raises.

INDEX